INTRODUCTION

I've spent the best part of my life working as a brand and marketing strategist, creating stories to help businesses sell more products and services. Over the years, I've crafted brand and marketing narratives for lots of organisations, both large and small, helping sell everything from banking services to beer, sporting events to sardines and winning quite a few awards along the way.

One reason for my success as a brand and marketing strategist is the strong training I received in economics at school, Business Studies at university, marketing and brand management at an FTSE 100 company, and entrepreneurism at business school. I applied all this knowledge in co-owning and operating a profitable, award-winning brand and marketing agency for over a decade. With such an impressive CV and a wealth of relevant case studies to draw upon, I thought I had the perfect ingredients to write a book about brand and marketing strategy - a guide to help businesses craft compelling stories to boost sales, authored by an accomplished, award-winning expert in the field.

A few years ago, I began writing that very book, focusing on purpose-driven businesses and entrepreneurs with a strong sense of their place in the world. While money and profit are undoubtedly important, this sense of purpose truly allowed their businesses to thrive. I titled it Purpose-Fuelled: How Entrepreneurs with Soul Can Turn Purpose into Profit. It seemed like a solid concept for a book, so I started putting pen to paper.

However, that book was never finished, as my life took an unexpected turn, and I underwent a profound change. In her famous TED Talk, Brené Brown reveals on the big screen that she had a "~~breakdown~~ spiritual awakening." I assume she presents it this way because she's much more comfortable telling the world about her spiritual awakening than admitting to a breakdown. Well, something similar happened to me, although I would refer to my experience as a "breakdown ~~spiritual awakening~~." Unlike Brené, I am much more comfortable disclosing my breakdown than claiming a spiritual awakening, though I'm not particularly thrilled about sharing either. I find the whole topic of spirituality quite uncomfortable. That's because I see myself as a businessperson. And we just don't talk about spirituality in business circles.

So it feels slightly surreal to be sitting at my kitchen table, doing something that makes me incredibly uneasy: writing a book about spirituality that I hope will not only have a positive impact on people but may eventually have a positive impact on the businesses those people work at. And maybe even the economy itself.

A big part of me would feel much more at ease if this book were about helping businesses increase revenue, grow market share, improve brand equity, or even how entrepreneurs with souls can turn purpose into profit. In short, anything related to the logic of making money. Anything that neatly fitted into our economic way of thinking. Anything that supported growth. Well, anything that wasn't, just a bit out there and woo woo.

But I know that the part of me saying these things isn't the part I should listen to. I've done that in the past, and it's got me into trouble.

THE HABITS OF HAPPINESS

THE HABITS OF HAPPINESS

SW FARRELL

To James, Lorna, Amy, and Daniel.

You always bring me happiness.

CONTENTS

So, I'm listening to the other part of me, the part that says, "You should get this story of spirituality written. It might not feel comfortable - in fact, it will feel decidedly uncomfortable - but it might mean something to somebody. It might help people. And even if it never gets published, it's more important that you do what feels right than protect your delicate little ego."

So here goes...

The truth is, I honestly believe that spirituality has the power to help us in countless ways as individuals, communities, businesses, and even as a society. It's a bold claim, and I wouldn't make it if I hadn't experienced the transformational nature of spirituality firsthand and seen so many others benefit from it.

Seven years ago, I had a breakdown that resulted in and exacerbated my drinking problem, leading to a dependence on and addiction to alcohol. This problem was resolved through a spiritual solution that I found by adopting a number of soul-nurturing habits. A solution that not only put an end to my drinking but opened a whole new world to me. As a result of living my life along more spiritual lines, I was able to find freedom, wholeness, peace, joy, and fulfilment. As well as getting a real sense of my calling in life and finding the power to make it a reality.

This book is my attempt to make sense of the bad habits that led to a downward spiral of addiction, the good habits that led to an upward spiral towards spiritual happiness and ultimately the pathway to purpose and power. It's been such a profound journey that is hard to put into words. But I want to try as I am convinced that others can benefit from following the same spiritual disciplines that transformed my life - disciplines that I had no faith in nor liked at the time.

Those in recovery from addiction may find this book interesting and useful. They will recognise aspects of the 12-Step Recovery Programme that I reference. But that's not my primary audience. My intention is not to re-create the 12-Steps in another form. My intention is to translate the incredible transformation that the 12-Step spiritual solution had on my life and make it relevant to people who don't see themselves as addicts.

That's because I believe many, many people would benefit from having a spiritual solution in their lives. People who may be struggling with the anxieties and stresses of modern life. People who are numbing or distracting themselves with unhealthy habits. People who feel stuck in meaningless jobs or have recently been made redundant. People who have suffered bereavement and feel lost. Or people who simply want to find more purpose and meaning in their lives but don't know how to find it or don't have the courage to live it out.

All these people could benefit from the spiritual solution. All these people could bring spiritual happiness into their lives. All these people could live with more purpose and power.

I am convinced that there is suffering and confusion in the world, both big and small, that is currently being ignored, suppressed, numbed away, or treated with chemicals, which could be much more effectively addressed by embarking on a spiritual journey.

It's a journey I never thought I'd take, as I never imagined I would embrace spirituality in my life. But then again, I never thought I'd be the sort of person to fall prey to addiction. Yet this spiritual adventure has completely turned my life around and bestowed countless gifts along the way. I now see that my preconceived and mistaken ideas about spirituality almost prevented me from receiving the help that undoubtedly saved my life.

What's more, I recognise that these preconceived and mistaken notions are pervasive in our society, particularly in the business world and the way we view work. I held these misguided beliefs because I was immersed in a culture laden with them. I believe our money-obsessed way of living and the way we are encouraged to numb ourselves to deal with discomfort is creating a gaping hole in our collective souls and restricting our ability to feel life's true vibrancy. It is also stopping us from receiving the help many of us desperately need - help we are crying out for as individuals, as businesses, and as a society, but help we may not even realise we need.

This book is for anyone experiencing some sort of pain, suffering, or confusion in their life. It's for people who are yearning for more peace and purpose, people who believe in their hearts that there must be another way to live but don't fully understand where that direction lies, people who don't feel they have the power or confidence to follow the path of their soul's desire, people who intuitively sense there's more to life, and people who want to bring spiritual happiness into their lives.

However, I am particularly keen for people in business to read this book - those who run businesses, those responsible for the well-being of people in business, and those who believe business has a greater and more meaningful role to play in society than simply generating more and more money. I see a direct connection between our current growth-obsessed business culture and the ever-increasing stress it places on people, communities, and the planet. Stress that is causing immense pain and suffering, much of which is being endured, going unnoticed, and simply not acknowledged or discussed.

The economic culture in which I was raised, educated, and worked is consumer-driven, financially motivated, technologically focused, information-rich, logically minded, fiercely competitive, and individualistic. There are winners and losers, and it celebrates one particular type of success above all else: financial growth—growth of profits for businesses, growth of GDP for the economy, and growth of salaries for individuals.

The mantra of this culture is, "Growth is good." And the mantra of our business culture is, "Growth is everything." If you don't grow, you die.

That's the message I heard, even if growth causes undue stress. Even if growth means promoting unhealthy products and services. Failing to grow sounded like a failing to succeed to me, and I couldn't bear the thought of that. As the Managing Director and Co-Owner of a small business, I acutely felt the expectations to grow and the fears of failing to do so. Those expectations justified my willingness to work with clients promoting unhealthy products with dubious morals.

I had trouble dealing with the fears of failure and the stress I experienced. But I did find something that helped. It was a coping solution that I had seen many people using. It was a solution that was widely promoted in our culture. It was a solution that was readily available. That solution was alcohol. I drank because I saw everyone else drink, and it helped numb all the anxiety and stress away. But eventually, it led to my addiction and breakdown.

That pressure to grow is suffocating us and damaging the very things that make life worth living: loving relationships, natural beauty, supportive communities, and our own personal sense of joy, freedom, and fulfilment. Without these, we suffer as human beings, and the worst part is that we don't even recognise the extent of our suffering. We're learning to live without that sense of joy, freedom, and fulfilment, focusing so intensely on growing the financial bottom line for ourselves, our businesses, and our economy that we're allowing the loving relationships, natural beauty, and supportive communities we rely on to wither away - and we're growing accustomed to the pain.

I lived with that pain for years, and I sense that many others do as well. They will be feeling the pain I felt - anxious, overwhelmed, stuck, depressed, discontented, restless, unhappy, unfulfilled, lost. They will be trying to numb those feelings or distract themselves by drinking, overeating, overworking, shopping, self-medicating, bingeing on social media, video games, box sets, porn, gambling, and on and on. None of these things will relieve the pain for long; all of them will lead to addiction. The feelings of discontentment will grow deeper, and people will feel increasingly anxious, unhappy, lost and helpless.

This book is for those people, for you, for anyone feeling anxious, unhappy, lost, and helpless. I'm not suggesting that the spiritual solution replace medication, treatment, or therapy. I am suggesting that there may be another way of thinking about the problem and, consequently, another way of solving it. This "other way" is a spiritual way, a way you may well turn your nose up at right now, but a way that has worked for hundreds of thousands, if not millions, of people who were suffering exactly as I was and exactly as you are if any of the descriptions of suffering above ring true for you.

Yet this way, this spiritual solution to our cultural problem of living our everyday modern lives isn't talked about much in our modern, Western, secular society. It isn't discussed in our GP surgeries, where solutions are sought. When I told my GP about my impending breakdown and heavy drinking, I was prescribed antidepressants. They didn't work for me, but no other solution was offered. And it isn't talked about in our workplaces, where many of the problems arise. Businesses are waking up to the harm they cause and the benefits of promoting physical and mental well-being in the workplace. But spiritual well-being doesn't get much attention.

My observation is that if the spiritual solution and the supporting habits were talked about more openly and more often, there might be an opportunity to solve some of the problems of modern-day stress and unhappiness and offer healing to those in need. Moreover, because the spiritual solution includes the concept of service and helping others, the ripple effects could reverse the damage we're doing with our narrow-minded goal of solely pursuing financial growth. With a more selfless outlook on life, we could promote more soul-nurturing ideals to live by. We could promote healthier products, services and ways to spend our time. We could put more effort into rebuilding those withering relationships, communities, and natural environments and arguably heal the crumbling foundations of our sick economy.

This book is my attempt to capture these observations and provide a practical guide for anyone interested in trying out some of these spiritual principles and habits to address their own situation. The spiritual solution restores us to the natural human state of loving life rather than enduring the daily grind of coping with its pain. That's why the first half of the subtitle of the book is A solution to the Struggles of Modern Life.

However, I recognise the challenge ahead. The idea of introducing spirituality into a world obsessed with financial growth, material accumulation, and mind-numbing distractions is a bit of a long shot, and that's being optimistic. I'm not sure how many people will be open to a discussion about spirituality, let alone embark on a programme of spiritual practice. Hence my discomfort in even mentioning the idea. However, there is one aspect of the spiritual journey that is very relevant to everyone. And that is purpose.

From my work as a brand and marketing strategist, I know how compelling and effective purpose can be for any organisation of any size and how motivating it can be for individuals working there. I also know how much more people who find meaning in their work bring to their work; it becomes so much more than a 9-to-5 job.

However, I now also understand that the way most organisations think about purpose and how they communicate it to their workforce is flawed. Cultivating a sense of purpose for employees is not about crafting a purpose statement; it's not a corporate activity at all. It's an individual endeavour. Finding and living our purpose is about discovering who we really are, what gifts we have to offer the world, who truly needs our help, and having the courage to follow that path with all our heart. That's why the second half of the subtitle of the book is A Pathway to Purpose and Power. Finding our purpose and having the power to carry it out is part of the spiritual journey, and it's one that I find myself on right now. It's a pathway that has brought me to this kitchen table, writing this book, a book I thought I'd never write.

I sense that my purpose is to try and help other people find meaning, direction and courage in their lives by introducing them to the extraordinary gifts a more spiritual life has to offer. The spiritual journey I've been on led me out of misery, anxiety, fear, depression, and an addiction to alcohol. It led me towards a more meaningful and purposeful way of living. And I now know what it means to feel freedom, joy, peace, and fulfilment when I honestly thought those feelings were beyond me.

You might think that spirituality is nonsense. Many people do. I did.

You might hate the idea of doing spiritual things. Many people do. I did.

You might cringe at the thought of becoming a spiritual person. Many people do. I did.

But if you're feeling the stresses and unhappiness of daily life brought about by a growth-obsessed economic culture, if you feel anxious, overwhelmed, disconnected, and unfulfilled, if you find yourself in the grip of unhealthy habits to help you take the edge off, if you don't want to put up with the pain anymore, if you feel stuck or lost with no sense of direction or purpose and are craving another way of dealing with life but just can't find that other way - why not read on and give spirituality a shot? This stuff really works. It really does.

How To Read This Book

I've structured the book into two parts. In Part 1, I describe the problem. In our quest to be wealthy, we've forgotten how to be naturally happy. Through the lens of my own experience, I explore the stories we use to live our lives and how this leads to a modern way of living that is doomed to result in unhappiness. I then go on to suggest a solution to the problem, that being a spiritual solution. A solution that many will reject and turn their noses up at, just as I did. But a solution that can help everyone find natural happiness, even if they don't believe in spirituality, just as I did.

In the first chapter, The Stories We Live By, I introduce the key themes of the book through a series of stories. By presenting these themes up front, I aim to give you a flavour of what's to come and a sense of how they interrelate.

In the second chapter, I delve into the problems we face as individuals and as a society. The main argument is that our pain and suffering stem from the economic culture we inhabit, the norms of success that have evolved, and how we have unwittingly become accustomed to the ill-feted habit of trying to meet internal human needs with external material solutions. A habit that, over time, leaves us feeling empty, lost, anxious, stuck and confused. A habit that is forcing us down the path of numbing and distracting ourselves from these uncomfortable feelings. A habit that is addictive and self-destructive.

If this is the problem we're facing, a problem of trying to meet our inner human needs with material solutions, then a different solution may be needed. A non-material solution, maybe. A spiritual solution even. And that's what I introduce in chapter three. For many people, this will be their first introduction to spirituality, so I use this chapter to describe what spirituality is and what it means to me and provide an overview of some of the big spiritual concepts we'll go on to explore.

If you relate to the argument I put forward in Part 1, if you recognise the problem in yourself and are open-minded enough to give the spiritual solution a go, press on and read Part 2. This is where you'll find the practical tools to change your thinking, to change your outlook on life, and through the practice of five spiritual habits, find the happiness you yearn and deserve. I spend most of Part 2 going into the five habits in quite some detail. Then, at the end of Part 2, I present a framework for cultivating the five habits into a programme of action by evolving structured morning and evening routines. This is a method that can guide us away from self-destructive habits and towards healthier, soul-nurturing ones every single day. And as we do so, we find ourselves further and further down the path towards spiritual happiness.

These are the practices that can, over time, help fill the inner human need we experience as an empty void in our heart and soul. The more we embed these practices into our daily lives, the less we experience the void and the more we experience the five different aspects of spiritual happiness (freedom, wholeness, peace, joy and fulfilment). The goal is to embed these practices seamlessly into our lives so they become second nature to us. That's why I talk about them becoming habits. Good, soul-nurturing habits that replace the life-sapping bad habits we've relied on in the past.

While it may appear to be a super-organised and logical five-step process for having a spiritual awakening, I hope you'll grasp the nuanced and paradoxical nature of the spiritual path. It's not as straightforward as starting at Point A and reaching Point B. Rather, it's about experimenting with these ideas and seeing what resonates. The five pillars represent spiritual wisdom that requires understanding. There's reading to be done and knowledge to be gleaned. However, each pillar also has to be experienced for the benefit to be realised. Knowledge alone is not enough. That's why the habits are expressed as practices and routines. Embedding these habits into all aspects of daily life, alongside a deep understanding, is where the magic happens. This is how spiritual happiness arises.

I am not presenting this framework as a definitive solution, as the one and only true way. My aim is to present what is a non-logical process in a relatively logical way. It is bound to be flawed. But it's my way of trying to make sense of the work I was encouraged to do and the results I got. It's my way of explaining how and why I experienced a spiritual awakening. My goal is to try and marry up my knowledge with my experience to guide your knowledge and your experience.

And do so in a way that introduces spirituality by breaking down barriers and misconceptions and setting you on the initial stages of the journey. From there, it's up to you to forge your own path.

Finally, in the Epilogue, I explain how I believe that continued exploration and practice of the five pillars of habits leads to discerning your Pathway to Purpose and Power. This pathway allows you to hear your calling and gives you the courage to act on it. This mirrors my own experience, and I sincerely hope you find clues to your own path using the approach outlined here.

What I Hope You Gain From This Book

By sharing my story, experiences, and observations, I aim to spark inspiring and intriguing thoughts and feelings that spur you into action, action that will help you navigate your own way from pain to spiritual happiness and forge your own Pathway to Purpose and Power.

If you feel the stress, confusion, and unhappiness that our current economic culture is causing you, I hope you come to recognise and acknowledge your pain, seeing it for what it is and where it might originate.

If you recognise and acknowledge the pain, I hope you find the courage to accept that a spiritual solution could help relieve that pain.

If you accept that a spiritual solution may resolve your problem, I hope you embark on your own spiritual journey by implementing some of the practices suggested in Part 2. I hope you have the strength and wisdom to break the bad habits holding you back and develop a new set of soul-nurturing habits to take you forward.

If you start your spiritual journey, I hope you experience elements of spiritual happiness and have a breakthrough spiritual awakening that gives you sufficient motivation to persevere.

If you stick with the spiritual journey and begin experiencing the benefits, I hope you hear your calling and start living your purpose by using your unique gifts and talents to help others, finding fulfilment and flow in all you do.

And if you start living your purpose and find fulfilment in life, I hope you share your experiences with others and support each other on your spiritual journeys.

Together, we can have the broader societal impact that is so desperately needed.

Why Should You Believe Me That Spirituality Will Work?

That's the question I asked when someone presented the spiritual solution to me. "Why should I believe you? Where's the proof that this stuff works?" I was the hardened cynic, unwilling to do anything without evidence. So, if you're thinking, "Why should I believe this SW Farrell character?" I'm afraid I won't attempt to build a watertight rationale with proof, facts, or figures. When it comes to spirituality, it's all about faith! That may not satisfy those accustomed to detailed business cases and cost-benefit analyses for every new initiative. But that's the truth.

Actually, that's part of the truth. It's not just about faith. It's about faith, work, and experience.

You can trust me because my truth stems from my experience. I know the spiritual solution works because I did the work. I applied it to my life, and my life changed. Even though I had very little faith initially, I had enough to get started. And that's all it takes - enough faith to do some work, enough work to have an experience, enough experiences to build more faith.

My truth also comes from witnessing others benefit from the spiritual solution. I've introduced people to it and guided them through a spiritual process. They were in pain and suffering like I was, sceptical like I was. And it worked for them as it worked for me.

I've heard hundreds of people share how the spiritual solution has positively impacted their lives. I believe them. I can see it in their eyes and hear it in their voices. I don't have scientific proof to offer, only honest testimony.

However, if you still can't hear the truth in my words, look for the truth within yourself. There are clues you can search for to reassure yourself that spirituality will work for you, helping to build faith and spur further investigation. These clues are the seeds of truth you'll feel growing inside when nurtured with divine truth. It may be a phrase, a story, or an insight that arises after putting this book down - something that occurs to you in a moment of reflection. You'll experience the seeds growing as "aha" moments really hitting home and resonating deep within. When you feel that you've found truth--truth you can believe in and have faith in. Search for those clues and follow them as they signal the start of the spiritual journey and point the way along the path.

If you remain unconvinced, I'll leave you with a story from the Buddha as told by Vietnamese Zen Master Thich Nhat Hanh:

> One day, a group of young people asked the Buddha, "Of all the teachers, whom shall we believe?"
>
> "Don't believe anything, not even what I tell you." Replied the Buddha. "Even if it's an ancient teaching, even if it's taught by a highly revered teacher. Use your intelligence and critical mind to carefully examine everything you see or hear. Then, put the teaching into practice to see if it helps liberate you from your suffering and difficulties. If it does, you can believe in it."

Why should you believe me that spirituality works? You shouldn't. Do what the Buddha says --put some of these teachings into practice and see if they help—simple and wise words from someone a bit more enlightened than I am.

PART 1

WHY ARE WE SO UNHAPPY?

ONE

THE STORIES WE LIVE BY

ONE

THE STORIES WE LIVE BY

THE POWER OF STORY

As a brand and marketing strategist, I fancy myself as a bit of a storyteller. I gather information from various sources—data about a business's products, research on customers to understand what drives them, and analyses of competitors in the market. I then weave the most compelling elements together to create a brand or marketing story—a story crafted to serve the client well by helping them sell more products, generate more revenue, and ultimately achieve success for their business.

The story I am writing now is about spirituality, happiness, and the habits that can take you there. That story is called The Habits of Happiness. I have collected data from a vast array of sources, conducted research with people who have experienced the sort of happiness as I have, and woven the most interesting bits together to create this narrative. My hope is that this story serves you well by helping you view your life and the way you live it through a slightly different lens.

This is the first story I have written in the form of a book. My brand and marketing stories are usually much shorter, often just a few pages long. Some of my best work has been in the form of a strap-line - something pithy that captures the essence of a brand and conveys it in a catchy way. Think "Just Do It" for Nike. While I didn't write that particular line, it exemplifies a three-word story that makes the brand more compelling, its trainers more appealing to a certain demographic, and ultimately helps sell more products.

Stories, in any form, are crucial to us as humans. We are meaning-making beings who make sense of the world by creating stories about it. These stories influence the choices we make and the actions we take, from the type of trainers we buy to the jobs we pursue, how we spend our free time, which football team we support, and even the clothes we wear when we go and watch our team play. They are all stories. Some are more significant than others, but stories are the way we navigate life. The stories we hold in our heads and hearts shape our relationship with the world around us, often without us even realising the power they have over us.

When you start becoming more aware of these stories, you experience an "aha" moment - a moment of truth akin to seeing the matrix. You realise that they are just stories picked up over the course of your life from parents, school, friends, work, media, and our culture in general. They are not the truth or reality itself, but rather your, my, their, our interpretation of truth and reality. They are hugely subjective stories, but we trust them to guide us through life.

Some stories may appear truer than others because they are backed by scientific evidence and data. However, even the most evidence-backed story is simply an interpretation of facts, some facts, not all of them. Newton's story of our universe, built on the foundations of atoms acting like billiard balls, is based on his interpretation of certain facts known to be true at the time. These facts make the story seem unquestionably true until you get down to the sub-atomic, quantum level, where something altogether different is happening. The interpretation of quantum facts creates a different story about the foundations of our universe.

Similarly, business books can be presented in a way that appears to reflect reality based on factual evidence. During my university and business school training, I read many such books, lapping up classics like Built to Last and Good to Great by Jim Collins. They are based on seemingly robust research and data - factual, evidence-based truth. However, a closer look at the data reveals that the "facts" are actually people's interpretations of reality, with the stories in these books based on other people's stories. (Source: The Halo Effect) The stories are not reality; this is true for most business books, even the so-called well-researched classics.

This book, my book, is also a story. The bibliography lists all the books I have read to inform The Habits of Happiness. While I would like to think it is a well-researched story, there is no escaping the fact that my interpretation of this research is influenced by my experiences. But it is still a story, not reality. No story is reality.

The point here is not to undermine Sir Isaac Newton, Jim Collins, or myself. Newton and Collins created incredibly useful stories that led to scientific breakthroughs, better businesses, and more secure jobs and helped millions of people navigate the world more successfully. The stories they wrote were very effective, but they are stories, nonetheless.

The huge benefit of realising that these are stories and that we live our lives via stories is that we can question them. We can be curious about them, interrogate them, and choose not to blindly follow the stories we believe to be reality. We can discover different stories to believe in and create a whole new raft of stories to help us navigate our lives differently.

We are meaning-making beings who make meaning by making stories, and we can choose which stories to make. A large part of this book and the spiritual process, in my opinion, is the realisation of this point. If we can see through the stories we are living by and identify which ones may be causing us pain and suffering, we can choose to change those stories or leave them behind and adopt new stories to live by instead. Change the story, your story, and you can change the future, your future. It sounds quite simple, and it is, but as we will discover, it is not so easy. Stories are very powerful.

In his book Lost Connections, Johann Hari explores the troubling problem of anxiety and depression that has a hold on our society today. These were the mental health issues that led to my drinking, so like Johann, I went to my GP for a solution and was prescribed antidepressants. I remember feeling quite pleased at the time, relieved that I had something that would sort everything out - simply swallow a pill with water once a day, and all will be cured. But it wasn't. Not for me, anyway. And not for Johann, either.

Throughout his book, he investigates the history of antidepressants and the influence big pharmaceutical companies have had in making the "antidepressant pill" the go-to solution for many of the stress-related problems in GP surgeries around the world. He goes on to make a series of recommendations that he believes would be better solutions to tackling our huge anxiety and depression problem. Spoiler alert - the recommendations are about making better connections in our daily lives. (We will cover some of these later in Part 2 of this book under The Habit of Connection.) However, one fact that stood out for me related to the efficacy of antidepressant pills and the power of story.

From a pharmaceutical perspective, anxiety and depression are meant to be caused by a chemical imbalance in the brain, which antidepressants allegedly redress. However, from studies carried out by the pharmaceutical companies themselves, Johann discovered that of those people who benefited from taking antidepressant pills, 25% of the effect was due to the natural recovery of the individuals in the test,

25% was due to the actual chemical (so it did have some effect), but 50% of the effect, the biggest effect of all, came from the story of taking the pill - the placebo effect. If you have anxiety and depression and take this wonderful pill, 50% of the effect comes from your belief in the story that it will help you. That is how powerful stories are for us meaning-making human beings.

So, if stories are so powerful, how do we get underneath the skin of these things that have such an impact on us? My suggestion is to start with the big stories of our lives and see how they fit together and influence us. These are the stories that are so big, so invasive, that most of us just take them for granted. I did. I didn't even think of these as stories, and yet they have the biggest influence on our experience of life and how we feel on a daily basis.

To help bring this to life, I am going to introduce the concept of nested stories, a mental model I picked up from Brian Greene in his book Until the End of Time. He used it to convey the idea that the richest understanding of the world around us comes from creating a series of stories at different levels that fit together to create the most meaning for us. He used the story of a batter hitting a baseball.

There is the subatomic particle story of what is happening within all the atoms that make up life, including the baseball and the batter. There is the chemical story of the specific atoms that come together to form the baseball itself. There is the Newtonian story of the ball being hit, the impact, and its trajectory. There is the human emotional story of what the baseball player felt as he hit the ball for a home run and the social and philosophical story of what that meant to the thousands of people watching -- different stories, different perspectives.

As Brian Greene puts it, "Deep mysteries call for clarity delivered through a collection of nested stories. Whether reductionist or emergent. Whether mathematical or figurative. Whether scientific or poetic. We piece together the richest understanding by approaching questions from a range of different perspectives."

If we apply the nested story approach to our own lives, I would suggest there are four big stories worth piecing together and looking at from a range of different perspectives. These four stories, if we manage to understand them and align with them more effectively, would not only help us build a much richer understanding of the deep mystery of our own life but also help us experience it in a much better way. They would help us feel better about life.

The first story we all have is the story of "me." The story we hold in our heads about my life, my identity, my purpose, and how I go about living the life I have. Our second story is the story of the people around "me"- - my family, friends, relationships, and the living and working communities I belong to. The third story in our minds is the story of work, including the story of the organisations we work for, the economic culture we find ourselves in, and what we believe success looks like in this culture. Our final story is the big story of life itself - the story of nature, the environment, the living world, death, the universe, God, and the creative forces that drive everything.

For most of my life, I had built a story of "me" based predominantly on the story of our economy and the way we work. My purpose and identity were built to succeed in business and do well, as defined by our current economic culture. Doing well meant earning more money so I could buy and consume more stuff. That's what success was for me. I rarely thought about my relationships or the connections I had (or did not have) with anyone else outside my family and work. Even then, I took those relationships for granted and thought financial success was the key to keeping them strong. I never gave a second thought to the bigger story of life, the universe, and the creative force that drives everything. It never occurred to me that such a myopic view of life could have such a detrimental impact on me and the way I felt. As a result of the stories, I had built up over the years, I had created an experience of life for myself that, at my core, felt miserable and was getting worse.

The path out of that misery was a spiritual path, one I did not want to take, but I had no other viable option. The journey I was guided along took me from a place of pain to a life of purpose. Along the path, I was encouraged to reimagine and realign myself in a different way with the stories I had built my life upon. I was encouraged to align myself more with the story of life and less with the story of our economic culture. And specifically, to value success in life over success in our economic culture. Quite a big shift in perspective. And quite a radical shift in quality of life.

Before I delve into the substance of the book, where we will explore the problems we suffer from and the spiritual solution on offer, I would like to share a handful of stories to set the scene. These are the stories that mark key learnings and experiences in my own journey, represent the key themes of the book and how I believe they relate to each other. So, if you are sitting comfortably, let us begin.

THE STORY OF MY STRUGGLES

Finding My Way

I'm lucky. I know I am. For the most part, I've enjoyed a happy and healthy life. Compared to many, many people I should have very little to complain about. So, I feel quite self-conscious writing about my struggles; they feel so petty in many ways. And yet, even though everything may have seemed perfect on the outside, I often had difficulty coping with what was going on in my inside. That, in a nutshell, is the story of my struggles.

I was blessed with a great start in life. Loving parents. Caring sister. Nice home. Good primary schools. Lots of friends. There were a few family dramas. Some seemed quite big at the time, but we pulled through and got on with it. All was good.

The first struggle I faced came when I started secondary school. I went to the local grammar school that had just turned into a private, fee-paying school the year I started. It was an all-boys school. Well regarded in the area. Traditional in its approach. And strict. That's the thing I remember most. How strict it was. Back then, it was "okay" to hit children with rulers, canes, slippers, or chalk dusters if they were out of line. In my first week at the school, I asked the boy next to me what time it was during class. Apparently, that was "out of line," and I received the appropriate physical punishment. (Obviously, it was totally inappropriate, but that's an altogether different story).

Stories ran rife in the playground in that first week of boys acting "out of line" and getting the odd smack, belt, slipper, ruler, etc. I didn't act out of line again. Very few boys did. In fact, there were very few instances of people getting hit at all after that first week. The message had obviously sunk in. Behave like we want you to behave; don't act out of line, and you'll do alright here. And so, the seed was sown. The die was cast. The pattern was set for how I thought you got on in life: follow the rules, do as "we" say, and you'll be alright

And to be fair, it seemed to work. After a couple of years of getting used to the strict regime, my grades started going up, I found a good group of friends, I was on the rugby team, and I felt accepted in the establishment. I wouldn't say I was thriving, but at least I was able to get on with it.

Things shifted considerably when I reached the age of fifteen. That's when I discovered a deep passion for music. I found myself with an unquenchable urge to become a musician. It was such a strong, creative internal force that it took over most of my free time and mind space. In a year, I taught myself to play keyboards and guitar and joined a band. I felt I had discovered my purpose in life. To be a musician. To be a musician in a goth band, to be precise. I was incredibly proud of my newfound status as a band member, so most people knew about it - my friends, my family, and a lot of the teachers at school. However, the teachers at school were much less impressed than everyone else.

It wasn't long before I thought we were heading to stardom. We were writing songs and organising our own gigs, booking halls, hiring sound systems and selling two hundred tickets for each – quite entrepreneurial for a bunch of sixteen-year-olds! But as the band was rising, it felt like the school was pulling me down. They told me to cut my hair when I grew it long. They told me I had to play rugby instead of going to band practice. They wouldn't let me take time off to set up for the gigs we had organised. They wanted me back in line. Their line. Not mine.

When I think back on this time, the interesting thing is that I didn't put up much of a fight. I fell back into line quickly. I acquiesced at every stage without much fuss. I cut my hair. I played rugby. I gave up band practice. I didn't bunk school (well, I did once but got caught and didn't do it again). Even though my parents were supportive of the whole music thing, I fell back into line very quickly. And the reason I didn't put up more resistance was that I sensed that music wasn't a "proper" career. The path to success, as far as I could see, was much more likely to be along the lines of continuing to do well at school, building a good CV, getting good grades, going to university and getting a good degree. That way I could get a job that pays well, better than a musician anyway, and that means I could afford to buy a nice house, get a good car, and be successful. That's the story of success I heard. That's the story of success I believed in. That's the story I followed.

I don't remember anyone telling me that this was the story of success to believe in. I just thought it was. It's what everybody else did. My Mum and Dad were successful because they had their own business, a nice house, and could afford to send their son to private school. All my friends' parents were the same. The only stories of success I heard about involved good jobs that paid good money, so that's the path I took.

. . .

The Path to "Success"

I left the band. I put my head down, and I worked hard. I got good grades at A Level. I got a first-class honours degree at university. I got a decent first job with a small entrepreneurial business. I got a great second job at a medium-sized advertising agency. Then, I got a fantastic marketing job at a large PLC business. I got promoted regularly. I got pay raises regularly. I got a company car. Then a bigger company car. I was given the opportunity to study at a top business school to get an MBA. I could afford my first house. And before too long, I could afford a bigger second house. I was a success.

It was during this golden period of success that I first met my wife. We fell in love pretty much from the first time we met in a bar in London. Within a year of meeting, we were living together in Manchester. And then, within six years, we were married. We had our first child within a year of marriage and three more over the next seven years.

By the time our fourth child came along, we had moved the family to Scotland. I got the opportunity to buy out the founder of a business up there and grasped the opportunity with both hands. And so, by the age of forty-two, I was a proud husband, father of four children, and Co-Owner and Managing Director of a design and branding agency. Now, I was an even bigger success.

The Pressure of Success

The only problem was I didn't feel that successful. I felt pressurised. I felt tired. I was struggling.

My world was centred to a large degree on my work. I did spend time with the family. We had fun as a family. I coached the boys' football teams. We went on nice holidays together. And nights out with friends. But my focus was on work. I wanted to be a success. And being a success meant being a success at work. If I were successful at work, I could pay myself more money and treat the family. I could give the staff bigger bonuses and be seen as a good boss. I could get the reputation of being a successful businessperson and who wouldn't want that?

I worked hard to be a success at work. I worked hard at growing the business, and it grew. I worked hard at winning awards, and we won awards. I worked hard, and I paid myself more. I treated the family. I gave staff bonuses. My reputation grew. I worked hard, and I became more successful. But I still didn't feel successful. The pressure felt more like stress. The tiredness felt more like overwhelm. It was all beginning to feel a bit too much to cope with. But fortunately, I had discovered a solution to the stress and overwhelm-- alcohol, beer and wine, to be exact. And they became my coping superpower.

At the end of the working day, I liked nothing better than to go for a couple of pints after work. It was the ideal time to recalibrate—time to take my mind off the busy working day and reset myself for being with the family. Two pints seemed the perfect way to take the edge off everything and become a much nicer person at home. It worked perfectly.

When I got home, I felt less stressed and less overwhelmed, much more myself and more able to have fun with the kids. I'd then have a couple of glasses of wine with my wife as we got the kids ready for bed and had dinner and downtime together. It was a daily routine that meant I could cope with the pressure I felt at work. And be present and helpful at home. A routine that worked well for a good few years. A routine that I cherished because it made me happy. Or I thought it did. That's because one day, I noticed my daily drinking routine didn't make me happy anymore. It had stopped working.

The first time I thought I might have a problem with drink was when I tried to do dry January one year. This is a commitment to have one month without alcohol. I had done it once a few years before and knew I'd feel healthier afterwards. The first couple of days were okay (I had

had a rather excessive Christmas period, so I didn't feel too much like drinking anyway). But after day four, I remember having quite intense cravings. I wanted those couple of pints after work to take the edge off. I noticed becoming much edgier at night. More irritable and not at all happy. This went on for about a week and a half when I thought, "F*** it. Who cares if I don't drink for a month or not?" So, I secretly went for my couple of pints after work, on my own, and no one was the wiser. At home, I would sneak out to the shops to top up with two large glasses of wine as they were stronger and easier to drink quickly.

After January was over, I went back to my daily drinking routine. But the seed had been sown. The diecast. The pattern set. I had established a secretive, rushed pattern of drinking, which seemed ideal when I needed to overcome those edgy, irritable, and not-at-all-happy feelings. The problem was those feelings were happening more and more often. The more I worked hard at being a success, the more stressed and overwhelmed I felt. The more stressed and overwhelmed I felt, the more edgy, irritable and not-at-all-happy I became. I drank more. More alcohol. Stronger drinks. In secret. Quickly.

The spiral continued downward. More stress. More drink. More overwhelm. More drink. Anxiety. Drink. Depression. Drink. Drink. Drink. Drink. I was officially in trouble.

Seeking Help

It was at this stage I went to see my GP. I knew I was on the verge of a breakdown. I knew I needed help, so I admitted to the doctor that I was struggling with stress and anxiety and I was drinking too much. She listened patiently, advised that I cut down my drinking and prescribed me anti-depressants. I remember feeling delighted that, at last, I had the medication that would sort it all out. Only it didn't.

The downward spiral continued. The anti-depressants didn't solve anything. Mainly because I didn't cut down on my drinking. Within a few months, I had reached a place where I was physically dependent on alcohol. That meant having a drink in the morning to stop my hands shaking and then topping up every couple of hours just to function. Or what felt like functioning.

I'm not exactly sure when it happened, but at some point, somewhere between having a couple of pints in the evening to becoming physically dependent on alcohol, I had become addicted. There was a point where I couldn't stop drinking even if I wanted to. And it was well before the dependent stage. Well before me going to see the GP. Well before my dry January attempt. I was an addict, and I didn't even know it.

The Addiction Takes Hold

I may not have known that I was an addict, but I did know that my drinking was harming me. I knew it was not doing my family and my relationships any good. I knew it was harming my work and reputation. But despite all this knowledge, I didn't do anything to stop it. I didn't want to stop it. I couldn't stop it. I tried a handful of times, but it was beyond me. As the addiction grew stronger, the only thing I could do was to try and hide it. To try and hide the evidence I was drinking excessively and try and hide the worsening consequences. This involved a lot of secrecy, a lot of lying, and a lot of pretending. And huge amounts of guilt and shame. I hated the fact that I couldn't control my drinking. I hated the fact that I was causing all this damage. And that made the feelings inside even worse. A constant cycle of fear, anxiety, guilt and shame. It's a horrible affliction of pain and suffering to be in.

My family knew I was drinking a lot. So did the people at work. But nobody knew how bad the problem was until the signs and consequences became so obvious and public that an intervention was required. Only then, when confronted with the problem head-on, did I admit the problem openly. Up until then, I would deny everything to protect my ability to drink. Even though the pain and suffering were so deep and the drinking problem so glaringly obvious, admitting it was hard. Once I'd overcome the shame and guilt, I checked into rehab for a four-week stay to try and get myself sorted.

Rehab and Relapse

The first few days of rehab are horrific, and dealing with the withdrawal symptoms is a very unpleasant experience. But once that was done, my dependency on alcohol was over. My body no longer needed it physically. After that, it was all about the mental obsession. And that was a huge challenge. How on earth was I to deal with life, stress, anxiety, and overwhelm without having a drink? I couldn't see how that would be possible. I knew I couldn't carry on living with a drink in my hand. But I also couldn't see how I could live without one. Alcohol had been a constant companion of mine for over thirty years. It was the thing I relied on to make me happy. And the thing I relied on to make me feel less anxious, sad, angry or any sort of uncomfortable feeling. How on earth do you live without alcohol?

Fortunately, I was introduced to several people who had figured out how to do this. They had suffered the way I had suffered and drank the way I drank. But they had learned how to live without drink. And what surprised me most was they seemed pretty happy about it. I mean, really happy. They told me that the solution was The 12-Step Programme of Recovery; a process that addicts of all types can go through to find a life "beyond their wildest dream." That's what they told me anyway. I mean. How ridiculous?! A life beyond my wildest dreams would be a life of untold riches, all-day partying and excess. How could a spiritual programme deliver that? That's right. This 12-Step Programme of Recovery turned out to be a spiritual programme. It's got God written all over it. It seemed more like a religious cult than a pathway to freedom. It wasn't for me at all. So, whilst I could see it worked for some people, I just knew anything spiritual wasn't for me. That's why I chose to ignore it.

What did seem to work for me was not drinking. After my four-week rehab experience, I left the hospital as a healthier and thinner person. I felt pretty good and looked much better than I had for years. I had broken the drink cycle. I was learning to live without a drink in my hand. I had beaten my addiction. I was a success.

But I still didn't feel like a success. It was tough. I hated being sober. All I could think about was how much I wanted to drink but couldn't. How much I missed my couple of pints in the evening. How great it would be to go out occasionally and get absolutely smashed and then get on the wagon again. But I knew I couldn't. I'd tried that before, and I knew if I had one drink, I would go straight back to daily drinking, all day, every day. So, I gritted my teeth and knuckled down. And there was a lot of gritting and knuckling required.

Tragedy Strikes

Over two years after coming out of rehab, a lot happened. First, my best friend died. He was the best man at my wedding, and I was his. We were drinking buddies and had such a laugh together. We suffered from the same addiction to drink, but he lost his life before he could get the help I did. He was only fifty-one years old and had two teenage kids. It was a tragedy, and it hit me hard.

What hit me harder, I'm ashamed to admit, was that I lost my job and the business I co-owned. As a direct consequence of my drinking, my co-owners had had enough. I had become unreliable and a liability to the business. So, they asked me to leave and bought my share of the business from me. As I look back now, I can see that this was absolutely the right thing to do; not only for the ongoing health of the business but also for their own sanity and my own well-being. But I didn't see it that way at the time. In my mind, I had beaten addiction. I was sober. I was back and deserved a second chance. However, I had been given dozens of second chances. Plus, I was in no fit mental state to go back and run a business. But at the time, in my mind, I was left high and dry. I was being treated badly. It wasn't fair. And I built up a tremendous amount of resentment about the situation.

Then, my mother-in-law passed away. She had been battling cancer for several years, and in some ways, we knew this day would come. But it hit my wife and her sisters hard. They were a tight-knit family, and she provided considerable support and help to us as a family. And indeed, all the family. It was a real blow.

And then, just a few months after her mum passed away, my wife was diagnosed with cancer. She passed away within seven months. It was that sudden. It was devastating for everyone. For me, my kids, her sisters, her dad, my family, her friends, the local community. It was such a shock. Our worlds were broken. It was so unfair. It was horrible.

There's a lot I could write about my wife, how important she was, how she impacted everyone's life for the better, and how much she was and is missed. But that's a different story to be told at a different time.

This story, the story of my struggles with addiction, and the story of two years without a drink, continues in a sad but almost predictable manner.

On the day my wife passed away, I drank again.

Falling Back into Addiction

Drinking was the only thing I knew that could take away the pain, overwhelm, and stress. It was the only thing I knew that could work. And it did. After that first drink, I didn't feel in quite as much pain. I didn't feel quite as anxious as I had. I didn't feel as sad, lonely, or lost. That first drink made me feel better for about twenty minutes. After that, it went on to make me feel a lot, a lot worse.

Within days, I was drinking daily, from 10 am (and sometimes earlier) to 10 pm (or when I passed out on the sofa). I was in the grips of addiction again. I was completely lost, but this time, I was without a job, without a supportive wife to guide me into sobriety, and wholly responsible for my four kids. I hated the fact that I had fallen back into this way of being, and that made the feelings inside even worse - an even deeper cycle of fear, anxiety, guilt, and shame. It's worth repeating addiction is a truly horrible affliction of pain and suffering.

It took me seven months of drinking and seven months of trying to stop and failing every time to finally admit that I couldn't do this on my own. I finally listened to what everyone was saying: "You need to get back to rehab and sort yourself out - again." And so, I did.

This was the rock bottom that I had heard people talk of. I had to come to terms with the fact that I was the person who chose to drink again, knowing where it would lead. I was the person who, instead of looking after his four children, who had recently lost their mother, ended up in rehab, leaving them stranded. I was a complete failure, and I felt it.

Embracing The Spiritual Solution

I was back at the same rehab place I had been to two and a half years previously. I recognised several of the same therapists - familiar people, familiar surroundings, and a familiar message. They told me, once again, that if I wanted to recover from this horrible addiction, I should embrace The 12-Step Programme, the spiritual path that had worked for so many others - the spiritual solution that I had rejected because I thought I was different.

I was broken and couldn't bear the idea of going back to drinking again. I'd do anything to stay sober and give myself half a chance of bringing up the kids as a sober dad, even if that meant becoming a spiritual person - a prospect that sounded just awful, so boring. But anything had to be better than being a lifelong drunk. So, I caved in. I gave in to the idea that I'd have to give this spiritual solution a go, even though I didn't fancy it. I chose the spiritual path.

That decision, a reluctant one made in desperation, was the best decision I ever made. I didn't want to go down that path. I hated the idea of spirituality being my only saviour, but I had run out of alternatives, and so I took it. And because the stakes were high, I would do anything not to drink again. I embraced it with everything I had.

I found someone who could guide me through The 12-Step Programme, a sponsor, and I did everything he suggested I do, even though I didn't like any of his suggestions.

To begin with, we met once a week at his house for an hour to go through a blue book that described The 12-Step Programme of Recovery as applied to people with drinking problems. We would read it together and discuss the most relevant bits. As we worked through each of the 12 Steps, there would be some sort of workbook or ritual for me to complete. I quite liked those sessions as I was learning more about myself, my drinking problem, and how to solve it. And I thought that this newfound knowledge would be sufficient to cure me. But he knew different. He knew that I needed to 'work' at this spiritual solution.

Day in, day out, week in, week out, I did all these things to the best of my ability - not liking them, not seeing the point of them, and not enjoying life all that much. But I was learning more about myself and the "disease" of addiction. I would go to meetings where I met people that were like me. I quite liked these people; it felt like we were in this "recovery" thing together. I was starting to feel useful at these meetings, and they weren't as bad as I thought they might have been. And miraculously, I wasn't drinking. In fact, before I knew it, four months had passed, and I hadn't had a drink at all. Then, six months passed, and I noticed that I had stopped thinking about drinking.

Then something miraculous happened. After about seven months, I woke up one morning, and I felt great. I felt amazing. I felt free. I felt like a huge weight had been lifted from me. And most amazingly, I didn't feel anxious or worried. For years, I'd been waking up most mornings in the grips of some fear - either mild worry, heavy concern, or deep, paralysing anxiety. Sometimes, there would be a focus and a reason for the fear. Sometimes, it was simply hidden impending doom.

But not that day. That day, I felt free of all that fear. I felt whole. I felt spacious. I felt naturally happy. Happy without a specific reason for being happy. I felt unconditionally happy. As I lay in my bed, feeling all these amazing feelings, I remember thinking two things. Firstly, ordinary people must wake up feeling this way every day. How lucky are they? Secondly, I thought surely this was a fluke, and I'd go back to feeling my usual anxious way in a day or two. And as predicted, I returned to feeling my usual sad, fearful way after a day or two. But then those free and happy feelings came back again, and they stayed for longer. Just like the downward addictive spiral in reverse, the more I complied with the suggestions that were made to me, the more those free and joyous feelings stayed - deeper and longer the positive upward cycle went.

The day I first woke up feeling that positive way was the day I realised I'd had a spiritual awakening. That's the day I believed all that work had had a magical effect on me. I feel uncomfortable saying, "Oh, I've had a spiritual awakening, don't you know?" It sounds so pretentious, like I'm claiming to be an enlightened one - the next Buddha or something. But it's the only way I can convey in words the "thing" that happened to me and its lasting effect on me. It's the only way I can describe the turning point that influenced my life from that point on, the only way of explaining the complete shift in thoughts and feelings that have arisen in me as a result of doing what was suggested and completing The 12-Step Programme.

A New Way of Living

Much to my surprise and against my better judgment, the spiritual solution did for me what I could not do for myself. I was shown a way of living without alcohol that is literally unbelievable. I have experienced things sober that I never thought possible - feelings of joy, freedom, and meaning that I thought were lost to me. I have found a new purpose in my life, and my life is unfolding in a way that is definitely beyond my wildest dreams. It's not a life of riches, partying, or excess. In fact, it's the complete opposite. I earn a lot less money than I did a few years ago. I don't go out partying very much. And my life is better defined by frugality than excess. It sounds dull, doesn't it? And yet, I haven't been happier.

What spirituality has awakened in me is the realisation that health, happiness, and well-being have much more to do with what's happening inside my head and heart than what I can afford to buy. You may well think that's obvious, and I'd have probably paid lip service to the notion in the past. But I now know that realisation to be 100% true, and I know it deep down inside.

The spiritual solution didn't give me super-strong willpower to resist the temptation to drink. It filled me with a sense of happiness that meant I didn't need alcohol to find relief from the stresses of everyday existence. I didn't have to rely on anything to make me happy. It welled up naturally, unconditionally from within. I started enjoying life rather than simply bearing it, which brings all sorts of other knock-on effects.

The Fruits of Spirituality

In the five years since I embarked on the spiritual path, several positive changes have come about in my life. These are the natural consequences that spirituality has brought:

- I haven't felt the need to drink, and I haven't used any other substances or drugs, legal or otherwise, to make me feel better in more than five years.
- I look after myself better. I don't crave so many unhealthy foods. I wake up earlier. I now enjoy praying and meditating every day. I've started running in the mornings and doing mini workouts. I've lost two stones in weight.
- I'm nicer to people, especially my family. I've started taking more of an interest in their lives and meaning it rather than thinking purely about me and what I'd get out of any given situation.
- I'm more responsible and honest. I want to help in my local community a bit more and have taken up a number of volunteer roles. I've started picking litter up off the pavement and telling the cashier when she had given me too much change by mistake (maybe not world-changing activities, but these are things I'd never dreamed of doing previously).
- I'm doing something different with my work. I wanted a change from the purely commercially driven world of brand and marketing to do something that felt more meaningful and purposeful, with sustainability at its heart. I re-trained as a B Leader and started working with businesses to help them become B-Corporations, as well as joining the Well-being Economy Alliance.
- And finally, I made a decision to take time off work to write this book. I have no idea where this book will go. I don't know if it will ever get published or if anyone will read it. But I know I need to write it. I sense this is my purpose in life, and I've found the power to write it. This is part of my purpose for today.

And that's the story of my struggles.

A lot has changed in the past five years. I'm not a saint. I've got a lot more to learn and improve on. I know I'm in the early stages of this spiritual journey. I have tasted the benefits of spirituality, and they are massive. I remember well the pain and suffering I endured not so long ago. I know how much I resisted the solution to my pain when it was handed to me on a plate - a solution I now believe in with all my heart and soul and a solution I want to share with others to help relieve them of their pain and suffering.

The Big Themes

Why tell my story in so much detail? I'll be referring to this story as we go through this book. For me, it highlights some big themes that have been staring me in the face for years, but it's only now I'm on the other side of it all, that I can call out those themes for what they are.

The big things I want to get across are this:

1. I was raised, educated, and worked in a culture that defined success in a certain way. We could describe that way as extrinsic, material success. The symbols of this type of success being academic grades, qualifications, job status, earnings, possessions, and reputation.
2. Although I worked hard and accumulated a number of these external symbols of success, inside I was suffering. I didn't feel successful. I felt anxious and unhappy.
3. I numbed away those anxious and unhappy feelings with alcohol. It worked for a while but ultimately led to my addiction, which took me to a desperate place because I didn't want to admit to it.
4. Although I managed to stop drinking for a couple of years, and I could just about bear life without alcohol, I wasn't happy. When the circumstances of my life got hard, as life tends to do, I couldn't cope. I returned to the one solution I knew would

relieve the pain in the very short term. It did relieve it for a moment, but it inevitably resulted in all the longer-term, disastrous consequences that followed.

5. Only when I had reached the depths of humiliation was I prepared to listen to people who had experienced what I experienced and embark on a spiritual solution - a solution I didn't think would work and didn't like doing but did anyway. I was prepared to do anything to stop my obsession with alcohol.

6. I was guided through The 12-Step Programme and experienced a spiritual awakening. That experience didn't give me the strength to resist the temptation to drink. It changed me from the inside out and helped forge a connection with a higher power and life. It provided me with feelings of joy, peace, wholeness, and fulfilment that meant I didn't need or want to drink to make me feel better. I discovered a path to inner, natural happiness.

7. Finding the spiritual solution also led to many other natural, positive consequences. I've become a nicer and more responsible human being. The more I focus on the spiritual solution, the more the feelings of freedom, peace, joy, wholeness, and fulfilment grow deeper and last longer.

Spiritual Abundance and Material Sufficiency

Over the past few years, I've been investing more and more time in my spiritual well-being and tasting the fruits that come with it, experiencing what we might call spiritual happiness or spiritual abundance. At the same time, I've discovered I'm not chasing conditional happiness quite as much. I'm much more content to live with fewer symbols of external material success, experiencing what we might call extrinsic material sufficiency. This theme, the theme of spiritual abundance and material sufficiency, is at the core of what I believe could be an antidote to the cultural and economic situation we find ourselves in today.

My observation is that we are a society of overworked and overstressed individuals. We are suffering as a direct result of a 21st-century economic culture that requires us to run faster and faster on the unrelenting treadmill of ever-growing levels of mindless production and ever-growing levels of mindless consumption. The net result is the deteriorating well-being of people, communities, and nature. I believe there is a way to slow down, and maybe even reverse, that mindless treadmill of production and consumption. And that way is a spiritual way.

If people who are in pain and suffering are able to realise the benefits of a spiritual solution, they are better equipped to get off the treadmill that is causing them pain in the first place. That's my experience. And then, the more people that are able to get off the treadmill, the less power that treadmill will have. That's my hope.

So, what's the problem with this treadmill anyway?

That's the focus of my next story.

THE STORY OF THE ECONOMY, SUCCESS AND THE WAY WORK WORKS

From secondary school onwards, it was clear that I based much of my identity and purpose on the story of our economy and the way work functions in today's society. I wanted to succeed in life, and that meant succeeding within the framework of our economic system. To most people, our economy and our culture of work will feel more like the natural order of things - simply "the way life is" rather than a constructed narrative. But if we take a step back and look objectively at "the way things are," we can see that the status quo is far from ideal. By reframing our perspective, we have an opportunity to make meaningful positive changes.

So, let's take that step back.

The Growth Imperative

The story of the economy and the nature of work that I find most illuminating is the one told by Kate Raworth in her book Doughnut Economics. It offers an excellent overview of how the economic culture we live in has evolved. The critical problem, as Raworth brilliantly exposes, is that our economy is singularly focused on one overarching goal: perpetual growth. The central tenet of our economic worldview is that as long as the economy keeps growing, everything else will fall into place.

The metric we use to gauge whether the economy is growing or not is Gross Domestic Product (GDP) - the total market value of all goods and services produced within a country in a given year, measured in pounds.

Historically, governments of all political stripes have viewed rising GDP as inherently positive. Growing GDP is seen as a sign that businesses are thriving, which means more job opportunities for workers, giving people more money to spend as consumers, which in turn means more tax revenue to fund public services.

Consumerism: The Engine of Growth

For GDP to keep growing, businesses must keep growing. And in our economic narrative, the primary fuel for business growth is consumerism. We are a society trained and conditioned to constantly buy things. And we excel at it - to the point that we routinely spend more than we earn. The average UK household carried £65,434 of debt in 2023, amounting to 131% of household disposable income (source: Finder.com/UK/loans). We may not always have the funds, but that doesn't stop us from spending with abandon. Buying things has become one of our favourite pastimes.

This tendency is no accident; we are heavily influenced to behave this way. We are a nation inundated with advertisements. Businesses of every kind bombard us with messages encouraging us to buy their products and services. In 2021, it was estimated that the average consumer was exposed to up to 10,000 ads per day (Source: Lunio.ai Blog). That means each of us is being sold up to 10,000 times a day. The very fact that we, the British public, are more often referred to as "consumers" than as "citizens," "subjects," or "residents" speaks volumes about the nature of our culture.

At the heart of consumerism is the promise that you'll be happier if you buy more stuff. You'll be happier if you have a bigger house, or a nicer car, or more clothes, or a holiday abroad, or eat out more often, or drink more alcohol. This promise is presented to us 10,000 times a day. This promise is so deeply embedded in our culture that we hardly question it. And at the heart of that promise is an assumption that happiness is conditional. It is outside us. Over there. Tantalisingly close. If only you splash the cash and bring that thing into your life.

The Commercialisation of All Aspects of Life

This economic ethos is so pervasive that it permeates virtually every facet of our lives. In my lifetime, the drive to commercialise and monetise daily life has impacted everything from education (my former grammar school transitioned to a private institution) to higher learning (university students now face tuition fees of up to £9,000 per year, a burden I never had to bear) to sports (the astronomical salaries commanded by today's Premier League footballers) to healthcare (despite the UK's free National Health Service, the percentage of adults with private medical insurance has nearly doubled since 2019 to 22%, according to Statista's Consumer Insights) to childcare (a Guardian article noted that British households with two children under five in full-time nursery care spend 22% of their disposable income on it, twice the proportion in most European countries) and even to the way we care for our animal companions (in 1980, who would have imagined dog-walking as a viable business venture? Today, 1.75m people in the UK pay to have their dogs walked each week).

It was against this cultural backdrop of unfettered economic growth, increasing commercialisation, and rampant consumerism that I built my career as a brand and marketing strategist. At the time, it all made perfect sense. More is better than less, and growth is preferable to contraction. So, let's encourage people to buy more things. They'll be happier if they do, and it will help businesses expand, too. What's the downside?

Like countless others, I never questioned the underlying assumption that economic growth is anything but inherently good. The more money you have, the better off you'll be and the higher your quality of life. It seems intuitive that as a nation's economy grows, so too should its collective health, well-being, and happiness.

The problem is that the data tells a different story.

The Decline of Well-Being Amid Rapid Growth

The evidence suggests that our myopic focus on economic growth and the relentless pressure to produce and consume more is ultimately leading to declining health, well-being and happiness across our society. In Britain, aggregate happiness has been steadily falling since the 1950s, even as average household income has tripled (Source: Less is More). The UK's mental health is suffering, with 35% of the population distressed or struggling with their mental health. That's the highest percentage of all 71 countries included in the Mental State of the World Report 2023. We are witnessing an alarming deterioration of community life, with rising loneliness, eroding trust and waning civic participation among young people becoming the norm (Source: New Statesman 2021 / An Age of Alienation). At the same time, we are consuming far more than our fair share of the world's natural resources - resources that our planet is increasingly struggling to replenish (Source: Earth Overshoot Day).

In our drive for endless growth and escalating levels of consumption, we're quite literally harming ourselves, eroding our social fabric, and damaging the planet. When you step back and examine it, it's utter madness. Our dogged pursuit of growth, the non-stop pressure to produce and consume more, is not making us happier and healthier. On the contrary, it's subjecting all of us - and the Earth itself - to rising and unhealthy levels of stress.

This is precisely the point Gabor Maté makes in his book The Myth of Normal. Maté writes "It is my contention that by its very nature, our social and economic culture generates chronic stressors that undermine well-being in the most serious of ways, as they have done with increasing force over the past several decades....amid spectacular economic, technological and medical resources (our economic culture) induces countless humans to suffer illnesses born of stress, ignorance, inequality, environmental degradation, climate change, poverty and social isolation. It allows millions to die prematurely of diseases we know how to prevent or of deprivation we have more than enough resources to eliminate."

That's a damning indictment, but one that resonates with my own lived experience. I've found that the more I chased growth and economic success, the more stressed and anxious I felt and the sicker I became. And I'm far from alone. In his book The Stress Solution, Dr Rangan Chatterjee notes that the World Health Organisation has deemed stress the "health epidemic of the twenty-first century," with up to 80% of all GP visits thought to be stress-related in some way. Stress is a critical factor in a wide range of ailments, from anxiety, depression and other mental health disorders to obesity, type 2 diabetes, hypertension, cardiovascular disease, strokes and Alzheimer's. These conditions are exacerbated by the chronic stress generated by our modern fixation on economic expansion - in our overall economy, within the businesses we work for, and even in our personal finances.

Disengagement: When Work Isn't Working

If we at least derived genuine enjoyment and fulfilment from the work we do in pursuit of growth, perhaps it wouldn't be quite so problematic. But for the vast majority of us, that simply isn't the case. A Gallup poll conducted from 2019-2022 found that a mere 10% of UK employees feel engaged in their work, while the remaining 90% reported being either not engaged or actively disengaged. Engaged employees tend to have higher well-being, better job retention, lower absenteeism, and greater productivity. Conversely, the 90% of British workers who aren't engaged exhibit diminished well-being, shorter job tenures, more missed workdays, and lower output.

Clearly, the prevailing narrative around the economy and the nature of work isn't serving us well on any level. So why do we cling to it? Why do we remain so single-mindedly focused on money and financial growth? Why do we keep returning to the treadmill, even as it grinds down our health, our happiness, our relationships, and the planet we depend on?

The Personal Price of Success

In a word, it's because we're desperate to succeed and terrified of failure. We've been conditioned to believe that working relentlessly is the only path to success.

The story of work that underpins our economic growth narrative is that if you put in the effort and apply yourself, you can achieve great things and become whatever you want to be. It's a seductive tale of meritocracy, where success rests squarely in our own hands. What often goes unsaid, however, is how individualistic, comparative, and competitive this mindset makes us.

While success in our economic paradigm may appear self-determined, the system is inherently set up to create winners and losers. And only a select few get to be winners. Some may earn their victory through genuine hard work and talent, but many do not. Likewise, some may find themselves on the losing end because they didn't put in sufficient effort, but many others fail for reasons beyond their control. When we see others around us succeeding while we lag behind, we feel like losers. And we blame ourselves; we just aren't working hard enough or simply lack what it takes.

Our culture makes it obvious who the winners and losers are. In school, the winners get high marks and academic accolades. In the workplace, the winners are the supervisors, managers, and those who keep moving up the ladder. In the broader world, the winners live in lavish houses and drive high-end cars. Outward material abundance becomes the most visible signifier of success.

So, the pattern is established from a young age, and the die is cast. We grow fixated on our individual performance, effort and material rewards. In the process, we become disconnected from everything else. We lose touch with our own inner state, ignoring the toll on our physical, mental and spiritual health as we strive to please others and appease our teachers or bosses. We grow disconnected from those closest to us, devoting more of our scarce time and attention to work and our omnipresent digital devices than our loved ones. We disengage from our communities, focusing on our own advancement and asking, "What's in it for me?" rather than considering the greater collective good. We see nature merely as a cache of resources to exploit and convert into the material trappings of success, even if it impoverishes future generations.

The deeper you dig into the story of economic growth, the more you see how destructive it can be. Not only does the drive for relentless expansion cause immense stress, but the individualistic, hyper-competitive view of success cuts us off from our environment and our fellow human beings.

From Disconnection to Entitlement

Chronic stress and profound disconnection are destructive enough on their own, but they also breed selfishness and entitlement - and an abdication of responsibility. Why should I go out of my way? What's in it for me? I don't have time for all this nonsense.

This may sound harsh, but it's the unfortunate reality. No one sets out to be selfish and entitled. No one wants to feel perpetually stressed out and alienated from the world around them. But these are the inevitable by-products of striving for success in a system predicated on eternal economic growth. I see it all around me. I see it in businesses that desire to do good but stop short if it might impact their bottom line. I see it in neighbourhoods where people are too caught up in the rat race to invest time in helping their neighbours. I see it in myself when I work for an organisation that only cares about pushing more product because the money is good.

The story of economic growth permeates every aspect of modern life, and its influence is immense. It is so immense that it can leave us feeling ensnared and powerless. Trapped on the hamster wheel of working ourselves to the bone to claim the material trappings of success. Trapped by the stress and disconnection from constantly pushing ourselves past our limits. And at a loss as to how to break free. We may wish to act more responsibly and do the right thing, but the prospect of living differently can feel daunting, if not impossible. That's just "the way things are."

Trapped and helpless. That's precisely how I've felt at times and still do on occasion. The net result is that we've had to learn to live with the physical, emotional, and existential pain. We've grown accustomed to our toxic culture. Or, as Gabor Maté puts it, we've become "acculturated to what plagues us."

The Story of Our Economy in a Nutshell

In the narrative of our economic culture and the structure of work, we find ourselves entangled in a web of assumptions and practices that have far-reaching consequences. At the heart of this narrative lies the belief that growth is an inherent good, a necessary catalyst for creating opportunities and ensuring livelihoods. To ensure our economy continues to grow, we are encouraged to buy and consume more stuff because that's where happiness can be found. And that means we have to work harder, to earn more money, to have a fighting chance of being happier.

However, as we delve deeper, we uncover the stark reality that this exponential pursuit of growth has become a source of immense stress, eroding our physical, emotional, and societal well-being. The very people, communities, and environment we seek to uplift are buckling under the weight of this relentless drive.

In a culture obsessed with growth, success is measured by the abundance of material possessions, creating a system that inevitably produces a small number of winners and a multitude of strugglers. We are fed the narrative that our personal efforts are the key to success, compelling us to return to the economic treadmill time and again, driven by the fear of failure and the allure of extrinsic status symbols. This desperation to succeed breeds individualism, comparison, and ruthless competition, disconnecting us from our inner lives, relationships, communities, and the natural world.

The chronic stress and disconnection that result from this system give rise to selfishness and a sense of entitlement, making it increasingly difficult to make responsible choices. Despite the widespread desire to break free from this cycle, the story of economic growth and the current world of work holds such a powerful grip that it can feel inescapable, leaving us trapped and resigned to the way things are. Over time, we grow accustomed to the pain, accepting our toxic culture as normal, even as it continues to take a heavy toll on our lives and the world around us.

Surely, there must be another way!

THE STORY OF LIFE, THE UNIVERSE AND EVERYTHING

The story of our economy and the way work functions isn't necessarily an evil tale. It's simply the narrative we've chosen to adopt as a society. And probably with the best of intentions. However, as we've embraced it, some dire consequences have emerged—and they're only getting worse.

I once wholeheartedly believed in the story of economic growth. I spent years chasing symbols of success and material abundance. From that perspective, I guess I did okay. But in the end, it left me feeling stressed, anxious, and unhappy. I turned to alcohol to numb this underlying unhappiness. An unhappiness and a type of pain I had grown accustomed to.

I clung to this story and its definition of success even though it caused me so much anguish. I identified with it. I wanted to succeed in it. I aligned my own story, identity, and purpose directly with it. I didn't realise there was a different story, an even bigger one, that I could align myself with instead.

I didn't realise there was another way to be successful.

Accepting the Problem

The first step to discovering this new story was accepting that I had a problem with the old one. I had to acknowledge that the way I was leading my life was leaving me feeling trapped, helpless, in pain, and suffering. I wasn't sure why it was causing me to feel this way. But as the pain became unbearable, I came to the stark conclusion that something was wrong.

Over time, it became clear to me that my definition of success was causing me problems. I could see that my drive to earn more, possess more, and consume more was making me more and more unwell. Ever so slowly, it dawned on me that maybe what I earned didn't matter quite as much as I thought it did. Nor did the kind of car I drove. Or my job title.

In his book *The Myth of Normal*, Gabor Maté writes, "Our physical and mental health is intricately interwoven with how we feel, what we perceive or believe about ourselves and the world, and the ways that life does or does not satisfy our non-negotiable needs." This was a revelation to me. He was saying that when it comes to our health and well-being, our feelings, beliefs, and needs truly matter. Feelings, beliefs, and needs? Really? Could it be that what's happening on the inside is the thing that counts? Not what extrinsic wealth we have. According to Maté, it is.

It turns out that success is an inside job, not an outside one. There's one huge implication that comes from this insight. If success means cultivating beliefs and satisfying needs in order to feel happy, then we need to spend more time cultivating those beliefs and satisfying those needs. Conversely, we need to spend less time on the things that cause us stress and make us ill.

That seems so obvious now. How did I miss something *so* obvious?

The Buzz of Being Alive: Re-Defining Success

I missed this point because our culture misses this point. As a society, as the culture of economic growth has tightened its grip, we've become increasingly "life blind." Philosopher Mary Midgley coined this term to describe what she observed happening in the sciences, specifically biology. As biology claims to study life, scientifically minded biologists delve deeper into the minutiae of cells, genes and the like. In doing so, they're losing the ability to account for the fundamental nature of existence—not least of which is "the buzz of being alive."

It strikes me that we're all becoming increasingly life blind, losing the ability to account for and tap into our fundamental nature of existence. We're losing touch with the very buzz of being alive. Businesses are losing it. Communities are losing it. Society is losing it. I lost it. We're so caught up in working for a living that we're forgetting how to truly live.

Enter the story of life, the universe, and everything—the story of what it means to be alive and what matters to us about life. It's a story where it's more important to discover what brings us joy, peace and fulfilment than to figure out how to make more money. Interestingly, this story is almost the opposite of the story of economic growth.

The story of life, the universe, and everything else does not focus on us as individuals and what we need to do to get ahead of others. It is a bigger story, focusing on us as part of the whole fabric of life. It highlights how we are interconnected with everybody and everything else and how reliant we are on each other and all of existence to succeed.

This story does not result in comparison and competition but in cooperation and co-creation. It creates situations where I win if you win—and ideally, they win, too. That's because this story is one of abundance, not scarcity. In the story of our economy and the way work works, we all end up fighting each other for limited amounts of money, possessions and status—the extrinsic material symbols that define success. In the story of life, success means flourishing. Success means happiness. It means feeling joy, peace, fulfilment and freedom. There's no limit to those feelings; they're available to everyone in unlimited supply because they come from within. They are not contingent on me getting something from somebody. The more I help others achieve these things, the more I receive in return. It's a gift that keeps on giving.

In this story, life is imbued with goodness. It is all around us. Our challenge is to find that goodness, even if the specific circumstances of our lives feel quite difficult at any given moment. Yes, there are disappointments, hardships, sickness, and death. But there is always goodness surrounding those circumstances. There is always peace, meaning, and hope to be found. We just need to seek them out.

The key to success in this story is finding richer ways to relate to the world around us. Rather than becoming more stressed, disconnected, selfish and entitled—the side effects of success in the economic growth story—in this story, success yields better, deeper, more meaningful connections with ourselves, with other people, with our communities and with Mother Nature. As we flourish, so do they.

A Different Kind of Economy

Although this story might sound at odds with the world of business and work, it needn't be. This is not a story of anti-business or anti-work but of anti-growth-at-any-cost. It's a story where businesses make money and profits to survive, but it's not why they exist. They exist to increase the well-being of as many of their stakeholders as possible: customers, employees, communities, suppliers, the environment, and shareholders. They don't exist to make more profit than last year exclusively for shareholders' benefit while everybody else loses out.

And this is a story where people engage in good work—work where they find meaning and purpose and a level of financial security that affords a reasonable living. Mahatma Gandhi said, "The truth is that man needs work even more than he needs a wage." In the story of life, the universe and everything, people are afforded the freedom to apply their unique skills towards achieving goals that are meaningful to them. They do not feel trapped in a job that drives them crazy because they need to pay the bills.

The story of life may feel like a pipe dream, a New Age fantasy that doesn't reflect the commercial reality of the world we inhabit. That may be true. Or, more precisely, it may be my truth or your truth. That's because we may believe in the story of our economy and the way work works more than we believe in the story of life, the universe and everything.

When I strongly believe in the story of life, I align my own story, identity and purpose with it. In doing so, I choose to act in certain ways. I choose to work on projects that give me the most meaning rather than the ones that pay the most. I choose to help people even if there is no immediate payback rather than manipulate situations to my advantage. I choose to gauge my success by how I feel—by my well-being and happiness—rather than by how much money is in the bank. And I tend to feel joyful, fulfilled, free and at peace.

Unfortunately, I don't always choose to align my actions to the story of life. Sometimes, I worry about money and choose the projects that pay the most, trying to manipulate situations to my advantage. Sooner or later, I pay the price. Anxiety, stress, overwhelm, and feelings of being trapped return. These are my danger signals, signs that I need to examine what story I believe and want to live by.

I know that the story of life is very real when I believe in it. I can affirm that it creates the experience of life as described above. I can attest to its truth because I believe it to be true—sometimes. When I believe the story with all my heart and align my life, identity, and purpose with it, everything falls into place. The only problem is that I'm prone to fall back into the story of economic growth that I've been educated in for fifty years. That's hard to forget. That's when feelings of inadequacy, fear and being overwhelmed return. That's when I can start feeling trapped and hopeless once more.

Aligning Our Lives to The Stories That Matter Most

The key point here is that both these stories are just that—stories. They exist in our minds, not out there somewhere. They are not reality but interpretations of reality. Yet both these stories have a considerable impact on how we live our lives, the decisions we make, the actions we take, and ultimately, the way we feel about life.

Who would have thought that the stories we believe in would have such a profound effect on the way we feel? Not me, for one. It doesn't sound very rational or scientific, does it? But maybe that's because you and I are not quite as rational or scientific as we'd like to think we are.

THE STORY OF THE SPLIT SELF

The more I've become aware of these two stories—the story of economic growth and the story of life—and how we can align our own story, our own identity and purpose with one or the other, the more I realise how quickly I can change allegiance between the two.

In one moment, I believe in the story of life, feeling that we rely on each other for our mutual well-being. During these times, I feel connected to the world and sense I'm part of the greater network of life. I'm compelled to do good things and help others, knowing they want to help me, too. I remember the unconditional love from my parents and the support of colleagues when working on new initiatives. I feel the abundance and energy of being connected to life itself. Gratitude fills me for what I have—true, deep gratitude. I'm at peace, content, fulfilled, happy.

But then something changes. An unexpectedly high utility bill arrives, transporting me into the story of economic growth. The bill irks me, reminding me of the greed of businesses and the impossibility of reaching them by phone. Customer service seems a relic of the past.

I'm lucky. I'm relatively wealthy and know I have sufficient funds to get by. And yet worries about money creep in. Why does it always feel that I never have quite enough? How can maintaining a home and keeping the kids happy be so costly? Retirement feels distant and unfair, with single parents deserving better tax breaks: anxiety, frustration, deflation, and a sense of being trapped and helpless set in.

Fortunately, when those feelings arise, I recognise I'm aligning my story with the depressing narrative of economic growth—and I can choose to think differently. By shifting my focus to the story of life, I realign myself. But for years, I was unaware of this unconscious alignment or the existence of an alternative, better story. And this made me wonder: Why did I, and likely millions of others, live within this destructive story of economic growth for so long? Why do we do this to ourselves? Why hasn't society figured this out yet?

The Concept of the Split Self

The answer, I believe, lies in another story: the story of the split self. I'll delve deeper into this concept in the chapter The Habit of Awareness, but I want to introduce the idea here as one of the key themes of this book.

For millennia, humans have experienced what's been described as a battleground of "two deadly hostile selves; one actual, the other ideal" (Source: William James, Varieties of Religious Experiences). We sense the influence or control of a little angel on our right shoulder and a little devil on our left. This divided aspect of human nature has been articulated in various ways: true self vs false self, soul vs ego, authentic vs inauthentic, observer vs personality, and intuitive heart vs thinking mind. However, I'd like to introduce you to another version. A version that is told in the story of The Master and His Emissary by Iain McGilchrist.

I present this story upfront for two reasons. First, it's based on extensive research—a 650-page book with a vast number of references and a bibliography of around 1,500 books. For those new to spirituality and potentially quite cynical (as I was), this story serves as a relatively rational gateway to what might be construed as the more spiritual (and therefore woolly) concept of true self versus false self. Second, McGilchrist not only brilliantly articulates the split nature of our individual experience but also explains the impact our divided nature has on our culture, especially in the last couple of centuries. For me, it provides a sound explanation of why we've been so seduced by the story of economic growth and why we might be stuck in it.

The Hemispheres of the Brain

McGilchrist's story is based on the fact that our brains have evolved with two connected hemispheres: a right hemisphere and a left hemisphere. They perform many similar functions but process information differently. Broadly speaking, our right hemisphere has evolved to allow us to take in the context of our surroundings. It enables us to be aware of what's happening in our world and remains open to whatever may present itself, be it opportunities (a new mate or food source) or threats (an angry neighbour or wild bear). The background awareness afforded by our right hemisphere allows our left hemisphere to focus and concentrate on specific tasks (making tools or picking berries from a tree). This specialisation of tasks leads to two quite different ways of processing information. The right side is more attuned to observing the whole, taking in the general, accepting uncertainty, appreciating the real, and seeking out connections.

In contrast, the left side is more attuned to dissecting the whole into parts, analysing the particular, seeking out certainty and control, translating the real into the abstract, closing out distractions, and helping to focus on tasks in isolation.

It's not difficult to see how both these aspects of processing the world complement each other and how they have helped humans thrive as a species. It's also not difficult to see how we have become much more accustomed to processing the world from a predominantly left-hemisphere mode of thinking. The modern Western world thinks and acts in a very logical and analytical way, is very task orientated and is constantly searching for certainty and control. We are not very good at seeing the bigger picture and acting from a perspective of connection. This is where McGilchrist's story of the master and his emissary becomes a very telling tale.

In his story, the master is the right hemisphere—a wise and benevolent ruler who sought to bring peace and prosperity to everyone under his rule. He has several talented emissaries or "viziers" who carry out important tasks on his behalf. One particularly gifted emissary grew tired of taking directions from the master, thinking he could do a much better job on his own. After all, he did all the cleverest thinking and hardest work anyway. So, the emissary (our left hemisphere mode of thinking) took control, deciding what tasks should be undertaken, where to focus the kingdom's resources, and the missions to complete. But the emissary lacked the wisdom of the master and couldn't see the destructive consequences of his actions. As a result, the kingdom suffered and lost its prosperity. As McGilchrist puts it, "The master's cleverest and most ambitious vizier (the left hemisphere), the one most trusted to do his work, began to see himself as the master. The domain became a tyranny, and eventually, it collapsed in ruins."

• • •

The Destructive Impact on Us and the Destructive Impact on the World

This parable helps us understand what is happening inside ourselves. We can sense that our intellectual, left hemispheres are in charge. We are driven by "what makes rational sense" and less so by "what we sense or feel." We tend to do so because our culture is very left hemisphere driven. That's what we value. The dominance of valuing left hemisphere thinking has impacted the cultural history of the West, particularly in the last 300 years and the rise of the Industrial Revolution.

"The hemispheres should cooperate but have, for some time, been in conflict. This is played out in the history of our Western culture, which is in the hands of a vizier, who, however gifted, is effectively an ambitious regional bureaucrat with his own personal interest at heart. Meanwhile, the master, the one whose wisdom gave the people peace and security, is led away in chains. The master is betrayed by his emissary."

The Dominance of Language and Logic

Why have we allowed our rebellious left hemispheres to take over? Essentially, we have come to rely more and more on the certainty of language and logic to convey ideas. Language and logic are the domain of our left hemisphere. We've come to trust and believe in them more than the intuitive, metaphorical, nonverbal, internally experienced ways of communicating used by the right hemisphere.

As language and logic have become more sophisticated and widespread throughout recent human history, we've tended to veer to the left side. In the past, we've known when things have gone too far to the left because of a feeling of inauthenticity—a sense that we're living too much in our heads, that life is too abstract, cold, and regimented. We don't feel grounded in reality or in awe of it. At times like this, as in certain periods of history, we overcome this tendency by embracing a more intuitive, creative, and expressive way of life. The Renaissance was a time when we allowed our right hemispheres to come to the fore.

The danger is that access to a more intuitive life is being closed off to us. The story of economic growth influences virtually every decision we make, from the jobs we choose to the way we spend our spare time and the advice we give our children. We are so attuned to listening to the logic and language of our left hemisphere that anything our right hemisphere may add is pretty much ignored or even belittled. Being in a goth band isn't perceived as a logical thing to do when you're sixteen; going to university is. It's easy to list all the reasons why attending university makes sense, but hard to articulate why being in a goth band makes you feel the buzz of being alive.

Logic and language will always win in our current society, and that's the biggest danger we face. Unless we can reverse the left hemisphere's domination, we're likely to let the story of economic growth rule everything. We're likely to continue on the treadmill, causing ourselves even more stress because we can't see past the logic of the story of economic growth and how to succeed in it. We believe happiness can only be found by spending money and consuming more. And when we don't feel happiness, we'll be compelled to find unhealthy ways to cope. Alcohol, gambling, sex, overworking, overeating, shopping. Anything to distract us from our internal unhappiness. We won't even know we're making this huge mistake, as we won't be aware of other ways of knowing, or other stories to live by, or other means of finding happiness, or different ways of being.

Unless we can learn to value what our right hemisphere is telling us, we will continue to live in a story valued by our tyrannical left hemisphere. Unless we listen to the feeling that something's not right, that there's an inauthentic, lifeless quality to our lives, that we don't feel whole or free or alive, we will continue to align our lives with the story of economic growth, stressed and disconnected from everything else, feeling trapped and helpless as we do so.

Reinstating the Master

How do we learn to value and listen to our right hemisphere and reinstate the master? That is the story of nurturing the true self—the right hemisphere, soulful, authentic, intuitive observer and heart—and taming the false self—the left hemisphere, egotistic, inauthentic, personality-driven thinking mind. This is a spiritual task and a spiritual process.

Welcome to the story of the spiritual solution.

THE STORY OF THE SPIRITUAL SOLUTION

The title of this book may suggest that what you're reading is a book about happiness. And to some degree it is. However, the book you are reading is actually about spirituality. But, as I've alluded to before, I envisage a problem. That problem is the word spirituality. And that's why I've crossed it out. Why would I do that?

Mainly because of my own insecurities. Remember my "breakdown spiritual awakening"? I feel decidedly uncomfortable "coming out" as a spiritual person. I was deeply sceptical about spirituality a few years ago. I know how I felt about it then, so I know how many others feel about it now. My insecurities are around being judged and ridiculed (so more inner work for me to do on that front.)

I also crossed the word out because I don't want to turn off other sceptical readers too soon. I know that spirituality can be a controversial, or maybe that's better expressed as a misunderstood topic. If you haven't had a spiritual experience or you don't believe in spirituality, chances are your left hemisphere calls the shots. You believe in a world that can be clearly articulated through language and logic. However, there are very few words that can be strung together rationally to convey what is essentially a deeply subjective experience in a way that would make sense to you. When it comes to spirituality, feeling is definitely believing.

But I'm not going to let that put me off. The time has come to reverse the crossing out and talk openly about spirituality and why I believe it is so vitally important to us as individuals and potentially to society as a whole.

Misconceptions About Spirituality

Let's start by acknowledging and tackling two big misconceptions about spirituality that usually stop the conversation dead in its tracks.

The first misconception is that spirituality is religious. In our extremely secular society, religion is often perceived as divisive, irrelevant, and a topic to be avoided at all costs in polite company. The good news is that spirituality is not inherently religious. I consider myself a spiritual person, but not a religious one. I don't adhere to a particular faith, attend a house of worship, believe in religious doctrine, worship a specific God, or follow a strict set of rules.

Having said all that, I have found great wisdom, insight, and inspiration in some of the religious texts I've read. There are elements of Christianity, Buddhism, Hinduism, ancient Chinese wisdom, and indigenous cultures that I've found extremely helpful. As I continue to explore other religions, I'm sure I will find them equally inspiring and useful in my spiritual journey.

The second misconception is that spirituality is fluffy, fanciful, or "woo-woo." I'm glad to say it isn't, at least not in my world. I see spirituality as a very practical solution to very real problems. For thousands of addicts like me, spirituality is the way we broke our active addictions.

It was the solution that saved our lives. That's why it is called a spiritual solution.

The 12-Step Spiritual Solution

The non-religious, practical solution to my own problems came in the form of the 12-Step Recovery Programme developed in 1935 by Bill Wilson and Dr. Bob Smith. This programme is used to help people overcome addictions to alcohol, drugs, gambling, sex, overeating, pornography, and more. When I first heard this, I couldn't comprehend how a programme to help me overcome alcohol dependency could also help someone with a gambling or video game compulsion. Aren't they completely different problems? Not really. The addiction is only a symptom that something deeper is not quite right.

C.G. Jung indirectly inspired Wilson and Smith to develop a spiritual solution to their own drinking problems. Jung had treated hopeless alcoholics but had never seen a single case recover, with one exception. Once in a while, alcoholics could recover if they had what Jung called a "vital spiritual experience."

Vital. Spiritual. Experience. I think these three words get to the heart of what the spiritual solution is all about:

1. It's vital - not just important or transformational, but also inextricably linked to life. It's life-affirming, full of vitality and the buzz of being alive.
2. It's spiritual - there's a certain mystery that cannot be measured or quantified by rational, scientific methods. It doesn't involve chemicals but rather an internal investigation into the thoughts, beliefs, and emotions causing suffering and tapping into different ones to restore health.
3. It's an experience - it isn't something you can simply read

about and learn. The spiritual solution must be felt and
experienced to be known; words alone are not enough.

A vital spiritual experience emerges from the realm of our life-
affirming, mysterious, and grounded right hemisphere. It puts us on
the path to nurturing the true self - the soulful, authentic, intuitive
observer and heart. As our rightful master is restored, it naturally
rebalances and tames the false self - the egotistic, inauthentic,
personality-driven thinking mind.

The Root of Addiction

What's interesting about the solution Jung, Wilson, and Smith evolved
is that it gets down to the root cause of addiction rather than just
treating the symptom. Problem drinkers don't have a problem with
drink; they have a problem with life. Drink is the solution they've
found to deal with life. The same applies to gamblers, overeaters, sex
addicts, and others. They don't have a problem with specific
behaviours but coping with everyday life.

Through The 12-Step Programme, I learned that my alcohol addiction
results from a physical allergy alcoholics suffer from. Once we put
alcohol into our system, an allergic reaction takes place that makes us
crave more and more. That's the physical problem, and the solution to
that physical problem is simple: don't put alcohol into your system. If
you have a peanut allergy, you go to great lengths to avoid peanuts.

It's not so simple for alcoholics because we also have a mental
obsession. That obsession arises when we find life too difficult to bear
without help, without the ability to take the edge off. For most of our
lives, we've needed a drink when stressed to feel more peaceful, when
angry to calm down, when socialising to feel more social, and when
celebrating to....... well, how are you supposed to celebrate without a
drink?

We've needed a drink by our side to help us deal with just about every situation life presents us with. That's what makes stopping virtually impossible for those addicted. Weaning off the physical dependency is excruciating, but that's nothing compared to the challenge of dealing with the anxieties, anger, shame, elation, excitement, boredom, and confusion of everyday life without a drink.

It's fair to say that I was a chronic alcoholic, and I suffered greatly from this mental obsession. But the reason why I believe the spiritual solution could apply to lots of people, and the reason why I've written this book, is that I believe many people don't consider themselves addicts but have a similar mental obsession. Think about yourself. What do you do when you feel life is too difficult to bear? Do you reach out for something to ease the pain? Do you drink, eat, shop, watch TV, or scan social media to distract yourself from everyday life's anxieties, anger, shame, excitement, boredom, and confusion? I suspect you do. Not because you're a bad person or weak-willed. I say that because our culture of economic growth has guided us down a path to becoming a nation of people unable to deal with difficulties or find natural happiness without some external stimulus.

We're all addicted to numbing uncomfortable feelings. We're all addicted to keeping ourselves entertained rather than sitting still and being quiet. Take away the external stimulus, and we're anything but happy.

The Spiritual Malady

This inability to deal with life without external help is what Jung, Wilson, and Smith called the spiritual malady - a toxic mix of thoughts, beliefs, and emotions that cause pain and suffering when we're confronted with life without a crutch. In 12-Step circles, they describe the malady's symptoms as the "bedevilments" - feeling useless, full of fear, unhappy, prey to misery and depression, restless, irritable, and discontent.

That was *me*. That's why I needed a drink. I felt like that all the time.

When I first stopped drinking, I spent two years feeling this spiritual malady and in the grips of the bedevilments every day. It was horrible. I felt physically better because I wasn't pouring alcohol into my body, but mentally, emotionally, and spiritually, I felt just as tortured as before, possibly even more so without alcohol's brief relief. Only after hitting rock bottom following my wife's passing did I agree to give the spiritual solution a try. Only then did the bedevilments start to lift. Only then did I start to truly heal.

Bill Wilson claimed that only "when the spiritual malady is overcome do we straighten out physically and mentally." That has been my experience. Sort out the spiritual side first—the thoughts, beliefs, and emotions—and then everything else falls into place. Physical, mental, and emotional well-being all rest upon the foundation of spiritual wellness.

Based on my personal experience, I think the spiritual solution may be relevant to millions of others who are suffering but might not consider themselves addicts.

A Universal Problem and Solution

Wilson and Smith developed a solution based on having a "vital spiritual experience" to solve a "dealing with life" problem that becomes very evident for addicts. But I believe the spiritual malady is much more widespread in our society and isn't restricted solely to addicts.

You may not be a chronic alcoholic, heroin addict, or problem gambler. (If you are, I suggest seeking professional help and finding the nearest 12-Step group.) However, there's a good chance you feel unhappy, fearful, restless, irritable, and discontented. If so, you may be using external stimuli to distract yourself and ease these feelings - regularly drinking to take the edge off, spending too much time on social media to ease boredom, working excessively to avoid going home, and so on.

In that case, like millions of others, you're probably suffering from the same sort of "dealing with life" problem we addicts suffered from - a problem I believe is caused and exacerbated by the stress and disconnection of our economic growth-focused and left hemisphere-dominated way of life.

My observation is that the bedevilments suffered by alcoholics are the same symptoms presented to doctors every year in their millions; approximately 20% of the UK population suffered from anxiety in 2022. The bedevilments could be the reason why the UK ranks at the bottom of the Mental State of the World Report. It's also my observation that the vital spiritual experience could be a solution, or part of a solution, to reverse this ranking. It's an antidote to our logical, mechanical, material culture of economic growth. It reconnects us to a story of life, the universe, and everything. It nurtures our true self - the soulful, authentic, intuitive hearts we all have - and tames our false self - the egotistic, inauthentic, personality-driven thinking minds we've come to rely on.

That's why I suggest the spiritual solution isn't just for addicts suffering from the bedevilments and some sort of spiritual malady. It's for everyone. Everyone who feels the struggles of modern living, who feels restless, discontented, and unhappy, relies on external stimuli to cope or feel happy, and feels disconnected, stuck, lost, and confused.

I also believe the spiritual solution has the potential to help our broader societal and cultural issues - one that can redress the balance towards a more life-affirming culture, less hell-bent on self-destructive habits and more aligned with the natural way we heal.

So, there we have the stories that make up the backbone of this book: the story of my struggles, the story of our economy, the story of life, the story of the split self, and the story of the spiritual solution. These are the central themes that run throughout this book. These are the central themes that I hope you can identify with and take with you as you leave this book behind. These are the central themes of why I believe a spiritual solution could help us on so many different levels.

But before we delve into the details of the solution and The Habits of Happiness that form the foundations, I think it's worth spending a bit more time really getting to grips with the problem we're trying to solve.

TWO

THE PROBLEM WE'RE TRYING TO SOLVE

TWO

THE PROBLEM WE'RE
TRYING TO SOLVE

CHASING FALSE IDOLS

What We Value & Worship

If you search online, "What do people want most in life?" you'll find a variety of suggestions and a load of "top 10" lists. Despite the differing opinions, a consensus emerges: the key to a successful life involves achieving some combination of health, wealth, and happiness. This makes sense to me. If you ask me about my aspirations for my children, I'd wish them nothing more than a life filled with health, wealth, and happiness.

I'm lucky. I had ample opportunities to enjoy health, wealth, and happiness, and a family who wanted that for me. I wasn't born with disabilities or serious illnesses, nor into poverty. I had access to a good education and climbed the career ladder. I recognise these privileges aren't afforded to everyone. Yet, despite my good fortune, modest wealth, and health, I still found happiness elusive. Why would that be?

A recent survey asked young people, "If you were going to invest your time and energy in becoming your future best self, where would you invest your resources?" 80% said a major life goal was to get rich, and 50% said it was to become famous. Many of us work hard to achieve these goals, believing it's the best path to a good, successful life. We place faith in jobs, self-image, status, and, above all, money to make us happy, successful, and fulfilled.

It's hardly surprising. Our money system converts virtually anything of value into currency. Everything has a price tag. As we witness the monetisation of the world around us—education, health, even dog walking becoming commercialised—it's easy to see why we would believe money was the key to fulfilling any need or desire. What started as a means to facilitate transactions has become an end in itself. Money is now the be-all and end-all, a God with an insatiable demand for sacrifice.

Worship in a Secular Society

Comparing money to a God is interesting because it's the one thing we've all come to worship in our modern, secular society. David Foster Wallace observes, "In the day-to-day trenches of adult life, there is no such thing as...not worshipping. Everybody worships. The only choice we get is what to worship."

Consider your own life. Ask yourself:

1. What do you value most? What's important to you?
2. What do you spend most of your time doing?
3. What are your aspirations for the future?

If you're like me, you probably value your health and happiness, as well as the health and happiness of those around you. But you likely spend most of your waking hours working. I do. And I tend to associate work with earning money. I'm not working to make myself happier or healthier. And I'm not working to improve the health and happiness of other people either. As for my aspirations for the future, the brutal honesty is that any vision I have for the future can't help but be framed by the desire to earn more money so I can spend it on a nicer house, more nice clothes, and more holidays abroad. These are the things we have come to see as important for improving the quality of our lives. These are the tangible signs that we're succeeding in life. We work hard to pay for these things because we value these external, material symbols of success.

And therein lies the basic problem: We value health and happiness but worship wealth.

The Goals of Conventional Success

This is nothing to be ashamed of. You and I aren't bad people; we've simply grown up in a cultural story with specific goals that define conventional success. We go to school for good grades, which help us get into college or university. We invest in education and training to get a better job. And when we get on the career ladder, the path to success is laid before us. Success is usually attained and measured by aiming for these conventional goals:

1. Earn more money to buy more possessions. The more you earn, the greater your financial security and ability to enjoy life.
2. Gain greater power and influence. The higher your standing, the more control you have over your future and ability to influence others.
3. Improve the prestige of your role and reputation. The more you are seen as "one of us" and a "good guy," the more approval and likability you receive.

Money. Power. Status. These are the big three goals, the conventional signs of success we celebrate in our culture of economic growth. It's a compelling list. I can't help but think, "Yep, if I achieved all that, life would be good." That's what we've come to believe.

The observation from David Foster Wallace about worship that I quoted earlier has an interesting ending. He warns, "An outstanding reason for choosing some form of god or spirituality to worship...is that pretty much anything else will eat you alive."

Why would becoming richer, more powerful, or even more popular "eat us alive"? Why does our preference and drive for a wealthy, famous future put us at risk?

Let's look deeper.

The Toxicity of Materialistic Junk Values

In the 1960s, an MIT management professor, Douglas McGregor, put forward a theory about leadership and the assumptions leaders have about employee motivation. The traditional assumption was that most people disliked work and would shirk at every opportunity. Leaders of such people would assume that "most people must be coerced, controlled, directed, and threatened with punishment to get them to put forth adequate effort toward the achievement of organisational goals"—an approach McGregor called Theory X.

However, McGregor identified another approach: Theory Y. In this approach, leaders assume employees are more rounded individuals who take a natural interest in their work, willingly applying creativity and ingenuity. Under the right conditions, people will accept and even seek out responsibility.

McGregor's work inspired Daniel Pink's insights into human motivation in his book Drive, which identifies two types of behaviour:

Type X behaviour is fuelled more by extrinsic desires than intrinsic ones, concerning itself predominantly with the external rewards of an activity. The conventional goals of success—money, power, popularity—are extrinsic goals. Type X behaviour and type X people are motivated by the prospect of earning these rewards.

Type I behaviour is fuelled more by intrinsic desires, concerning itself with the inherent satisfaction of an activity. The main motivations are freedom, challenge, and purpose. Type I behaviour and Type I people are more likely to be motivated by doing something meaningful to them.

While it's wrong to say Type X people are never motivated by inherent satisfaction or that Type I people wouldn't be motivated by money, Pink suggests that Type X are mostly motivated by external rewards (with internal satisfaction being secondary), while Type I are mostly motivated by purpose and meaning (with external rewards being a bonus). Based on these classifications, Pink highlights two very interesting findings:

1. Type I behaviour promotes greater physical and mental well-being. When we align ourselves with meaningful, purposeful work, research shows that our self-esteem, relationships, and general health and well-being improve. In contrast, Type X behaviour leads to poorer psychological health.

2. Type I behaviour is made, not born. These patterns of behaviour and motivation are learned, not fixed, because Type I behaviour comes from a universal human need to apply ourselves to something meaningful. Science has shown that any Type X can become a Type I in the right supportive settings, causing motivation and performance to soar. Without that support, it's clear to envision the frustration and demoralisation Type I face in a predominantly Type X world.

The Dangers of Materialism

Tim Kasser, Professor Emeritus of Psychology at Knox College, agrees with Pink: "Research consistently shows that the more people value materialistic aspirations as goals, the lower their happiness and life satisfaction and the fewer pleasant emotions they experience day-to-day. Depression, anxiety, and substance abuse also tend to be higher among people who value the aims encouraged by our consumer society." Furthermore, research has shown that the more materialistic we are, the less empathetic, generous, and cooperative we become.

Kasser identifies four characteristics of our materialistic culture and the behaviours it encourages:

1. Being extrinsically motivated (Type X) pushes us towards prioritising self-interest, which poisons relationships as we tend to manipulate situations with an eye on "what's in it for me?"

2. Being extrinsically motivated prioritises financial reward as the measure of success, restricting our ability to relax into the flow of an activity, reducing both enjoyment and performance. Think about being paid to play the piano versus doing it for pleasure.

3. Being extrinsically motivated makes you more concerned about what others think of you—what bosses think about your work (so they pay you more) or what friends think about your car or clothes (so you're perceived as being successful). This comparison can lead to manipulation or unnecessary consumption to put yourself in the best possible light.

4. Being extrinsically motivated divorces us from what really matters in life, forcing us to do what brings external rewards rather than internal satisfaction. This keeps us separated from our inner human needs, away from doing what we value so we can worship what we worship.

This is why chasing materialistic goals will "eat us alive." This is why our culture of economic growth puts our health and happiness at risk.

A Shift Towards Purpose

You'd think we'd have figured this out by now. You'd think that there would be enough pain and misery going around to wake us up to the fact that chasing after these conventional material goals is severely affecting our health and well-being. But the sad truth is that we're not. I didn't. I continued to cling to the material goals as the symbols of my success despite the pain I was in. I didn't appreciate that it was the chasing of the wrong goals that was causing me pain. And I didn't know there were alternative goals to chase that might reverse the pain and misery.

To be fair, both employees and businesses are starting to acknowledge the value of intrinsic goals in the workplace. More people are trying to pursue purpose in their lives and find more meaningful jobs. More workplaces are trying to create supportive settings and promote Type I behaviours.

But there's still work to be done. In the report Putting Purpose to Work, PwC highlighted the disconnect between the role leaders see purpose playing for their business and the role employees want it to play in their working lives. "While business leaders prioritise the commercial value of purpose, employees see purpose as a way to bring meaning to their work and understand their contributions to the company and society. Employees need to find this meaning in their daily work to be fully engaged. However, few business leaders guide supervisors to have conversations with their teams about why their work matters. Leaders readily appreciate the myriad benefits that greater engagement can bring—both culturally and commercially—but don't prioritise purpose as a means to amplifying this."

The challenge for business leaders, as for all of us, is that our economic growth culture is riddled with "junk values," a term coined by Johann Hari to describe how we've lost the connection to meaningful values. "Just as we have shifted en masse from eating food to eating junk food...we have shifted from having meaningful values to junk values. These materialistic values, telling us to spend our way to happiness, look like real values; they appeal to the part of us that has evolved to need some basic principles to guide us through life, yet they don't give us what we need from values—a path to a satisfactory life. Instead, they fill us with psychological toxins. Junk food is distorting our bodies. Junk values are distorting our minds. Materialism is KFC for the soul."

MEETING INNER HUMAN NEEDS WITH MEANINGFUL, SPIRITUAL VALUES

In his classic book Man's Search for Meaning, Viktor Frankl noted, "People have enough to live by but nothing to live for; they have the means but not the meaning." Frankl highlights the simple fact that meaningful values are the opposite of junk values. While junk values promote the pursuit of extrinsic material goals, meaningful values encourage the cultivation of intrinsic spiritual goals. But what exactly are those goals?

In seeking an answer, I found a passage from Charles Eisenstein's book The More Beautiful World Our Hearts Know is Possible particularly insightful. He writes, "A multiplicity of basic human needs go chronically, tragically unmet in modern society. These include the need to express one's gifts and do meaningful work, the need to love and be loved, the need to be seen and heard and to see and hear other people, the need for connection to nature, the need to play, explore and have adventures, the need for emotional intimacy, the need to serve something bigger than oneself, and the need to stop doing and simply be." This list of deeply authentic, inner human needs resonates deeply with me. Eisenstein goes on to describe how an unmet inner need can cause us pain while fulfilling that inner need brings forth inner joy.

In our quest for health, wealth, and happiness, we have done a poor job of striking the right balance. Inundated with junk values, we have been led astray, chasing wealth at the expense of health and happiness. As Timothy Keller noted, "If we stand back to ask what we have learned about happiness over the centuries, it is striking to see our lack of progress. Think of how we have surpassed our ancestors in our ability to travel and communicate and in our accomplishments in medicine and science. Think of how much less brutal and unjust to minorities many societies are today compared to even one hundred years ago. And yet, even though we are unimaginably wealthier and more comfortable than our ancestors, no one is arguing that we are significantly happier."

The Emptiness of Material Pursuits

We are not happier. In fact, we are unhappier. We attempt to satisfy our inner human needs with external material stimuli, but it isn't working, and we suffer as a result. Material goods, sensual gratification, holidays, cars, food, drink, drugs, sex, success, and status all provide fleeting moments of pleasure—short-lived highs of synthetic happiness. However, they quickly fade away, leaving us feeling empty as if something is missing. We're missing "IT" but don't know what "IT" is. We believe "IT" must be out there somewhere, so we spend more time trying to grasp "IT" by consuming more products, seeking more thrills, and buying new, exciting experiences. Yet, nothing fills that "IT" shaped hole inside.

"IT" cannot be found in an extrinsic, material thing. It can only be found intrinsically as a quality of the inner life. This concept can be confusing for anyone raised in our culture of economic growth and junk values, and it often goes unnoticed.

For years, I chased those extrinsic material goals, unaware of how miserable I was becoming. In my youth, I was happy, joyful, and free. However, over time, I began to feel less so. It was a gradual process that went undetected. I thought it might be a symptom of growing older, part of the responsibility of being an adult, or the psychological cost of working and achieving financial success. I wondered if feeling a bit cheesed-off with life was just the way things had to be in one's mid-forties.

But the mild unhappiness grew into deeper feelings of sadness and despair. I couldn't pinpoint the exact date this happened, but most days of my life could be described as feeling:

- Trapped, stuck in a rut, with no way out and nothing to look forward to.
- Inauthentic, not being myself, out of sync, desperately trying to please others.
- Fearful, anxious, worried about the future.
- Unhappy, disconnected, alone, resentful.
- Unfulfilled, lacklustre, unenthusiastic.

In 12-Step circles, these feelings and attitudes towards life are sometimes called the "bedevilments." They are symptoms of a spiritual malady, signs of spiritual poverty that have nothing to do with material poverty and everything to do with a life spent focusing on trying to satisfy a need for "IT" materially—a life spent trying to meet intrinsic needs by chasing extrinsic goals.

The Central Cause of Pain: Unmet Authentic Human Needs

It's worth reflecting on the central cause of this pain, these bedevilments, in more detail. It boils down to our inability to meet our inner authentic human needs. In our drive to be successful extrinsically, we are unsuccessful intrinsically. In our drive to be successful materially, we are unsuccessful spiritually. As a result of this mismatch, a gap appears, and a disconnection wells up within us. We forget who we are deep inside. We become separated from our authentic selves. We lose touch with the ability to meet those inner authentic human needs. The disconnection appears, and the gap widens.

If only we knew that the craving we felt inside could never be satisfied by chasing extrinsic material goals. If only we realised that there were other ways to meet our unmet inner human needs. Ways which involved prioritising spiritual goals rather than material ones. But what are these intrinsic spiritual goals?

Core Human States of Being

In my search for a definitive answer, I realised that if the bedevilments result from chasing extrinsic material goals, a good starting point would be to look at the opposite side of the equation. What do you get if you set your mind and priority on achieving intrinsic spiritual goals? The answer I've come up with is a set of five core human states of being. These are the states of being and the way we feel when we meet our inner human needs. A culture driven by meaningful values would promote the cultivation of these states of being as the primary path to success and the natural way to real happiness: spiritual happiness.

I define our core human states of being when our inner human needs are met as follows:

1. Freedom: Feeling free, hopeful, optimistic, excited about future opportunities. (NOT trapped, stuck in a rut, with no way out and nothing to look forward to.)
2. Wholeness: Feeling whole, aligned, at one, comfortable with myself and my world. (NOT inauthentic, not being myself, out of sync, always trying to please others.)

3. Peace: Feeling peaceful, contented, serene. (NOT fearful, anxious, or worried about the future.)
4. Joy: Feeling joyful, happy, grateful, and connected. (NOT unhappy, disconnected, alone.)
5. Fulfilment: Feeling fulfilled, life has meaning, inspired, and creative. (NOT unfulfilled, lacklustre, unenthusiastic.)

Life definitely has its ups and downs, and it can never be 100% trouble-free. We are bound to experience pain and suffering at various points in our lives. We are human, after all. However, when life is going well, and we think of making the most of it, I'd suggest these core human states of being are what we aspire to feel. They're possibly the best articulation of "IT" I can come up with. That's what I was trying to find back in my drinking days. I'm glad to say I now experience these states, to some degree or another, on most days of my life.

Imagine if our culture encouraged us to meet our inner human needs in order to experience these core human states of being. Imagine if experiencing these states is what success looked like, rather than how much money we earn, what car we drive, or what job we have. What a different world we would inhabit.

The key point to take out here is that to be successful in life, we have to have the balance right. If we want to achieve health, wealth, and happiness, we have to worship health, wealth, and happiness in the right proportions. My observation is that we've fallen foul of focusing far too much on the wealth side of the equation, and our health and happiness have suffered as a result. If we want to reverse this trend, we need to worship health and happiness and not just wealth. To do that, we need to consciously look at our purpose in life.

CHANGE THE PURPOSE, CHANGE THE STORY, CHANGE THE FUTURE

In her book Thinking in Systems, Donella Meadows introduces key concepts behind systems thinking. She defines a system as having three kinds of things: elements, interconnections, and a purpose. And she makes a very interesting point about the purpose of a system: "A system's purpose is not necessarily spoken, written, or expressed explicitly, except through the operation of the system. The best way to deduce the system's purpose is to watch for a while to see how the system behaves." The key point is that "purposes are deduced from behaviour, not from rhetoric or stated goals....The least obvious part of the system, its purpose, is often the most crucial determinant of the system's behaviour."

Viewed in this way, it could be argued that the purpose of most Western economies is to process the world's limited natural resources into products that can be consumed and/or thrown away as quickly as possible while making a minority of the population incredibly wealthy. I would suggest this is the purpose of our economy because this is how our economic system behaves. We have clear evidence of this behaviour and know we're successfully carrying out this purpose because we measure it as a growing GDP. We're good at it.

Now, let's apply this philosophy to ourselves. We are a system, after all —a living system - made up of many interconnecting elements, dynamic forces, and an overarching purpose. We may not have considered our purpose in much detail, but it's worth doing so now. As Donella suggested, don't think about the rhetoric or purpose statement you may have written for yourself in a workshop or the stated goals you may have jotted down as part of your New Year's resolutions. Look at your behaviours. What are you doing day in and day out? What are your defining behaviours? What are you currently doing very well, whether you're proud of it or not? And what are the net results?

In my days of active addiction, my purpose was clear: to struggle through the day as best I could and drink as much alcohol as necessary to keep me "topped up" while pretending to be sober and happy. That's what I spent my days doing. That was my purpose in life.

I didn't fully appreciate it at the time, but the start of my spiritual journey involved changing my life's purpose. At the beginning of every 12-Step meeting, a paragraph called the Preamble is read aloud to remind everyone why they are there. The same words are read at every meeting around the world. The last line of the Preamble reads, "Our primary purpose is to stay sober and help other alcoholics to achieve sobriety." I didn't consciously say, "Okay, this is now my primary purpose," but it was clear from my actions that this was indeed my primary purpose. I did everything that was suggested. I wanted to stay sober, and after a while, I wanted to help other alcoholics achieve sobriety. Once you redefine your primary purpose, consciously or not, things change. Your behaviours change. Your outlook changes. Your identity changes. You change. I changed my primary purpose, I changed my identity, and I changed as a result.

Initially, "sobriety" to me meant not drinking. My primary purpose was to stop the habit of putting alcohol into my system. As the years have passed and I've started to experience the fruits of a spiritual awakening, "sobriety" has come to mean "emotional sobriety," which I equate with spiritual well-being. Emotional sobriety is the opposite of the bedevilments, the opposite of spiritual poverty. Part of my drive to write this book is to open up the benefits of spirituality to a much broader group of people. I know the spiritual solution can help relieve the pain of addiction, but as we discussed in previous sections, many people may be experiencing the same pain and suffering as I was. They may be numbing away that pain with some form of destructive habit without realising or appreciating that they are addicted. Those are the people I think I can help.

So now, I see my primary purpose, my inner purpose (we'll come back to the issue of inner and outer purpose in the Epilogue of this book, The Pathway to Purpose and Power), as "staying emotionally sober and spiritually well and helping other people achieve emotional sobriety and spiritual well-being." I know that's my purpose, as that's what I spend many hours of my day doing. It is visible from my actions. Not from what I may have written down as some aspirational purpose statement.

As we've seen, our culture of economic growth and the way work works has forced us down a path where our purpose and identity are very much focused on becoming wealthier. We may not be very conscious of this, but our behaviours betray the fact that we spend most of our waking hours and efforts earning money. Such a focus on extrinsic, material goals is likely to be at odds with our health and happiness if we're not careful. That's because we are probably not meeting some or all of our inner human needs. Health and happiness can easily be relegated to distant sub-purposes if we get caught up in the busyness of earning a living. Again, look at your own behaviours to see how your health and happiness purposes are surviving in your efforts to earn money.

I'm going to suggest that if you're not satisfied with the way your life is going, if you feel that you, as a living system, aren't functioning successfully, then you might want to review and change your primary inner purpose. Review and change your identity. Review and change the daily behaviours that demonstrate your inner purpose and identity in action. Rather than focus on the extrinsic goal of accumulating material possessions, focus on the intrinsic goal of feeling good about life. Rather than trying to be a successful person in the story of economic growth, try to be a successful person in the story of life. Rather than spending most of your day chasing material wealth, spend most of your day chasing spiritual well-being. That's what this shift means.

It may not seem like a big change, but the implications are massive, and the results, from my experience, are miraculous. Shifting our inner purpose and identity to someone who wants to be spiritually happy rather than someone who wants to be materially rich shifts the emphasis of our daily habits and actions. When we change our identity, we change our goals. When we change our goals, we change our behaviours to reach those goals. What we're talking about here is a shift from setting ourselves extrinsic, material goals to setting ourselves intrinsic, spiritual goals. It means focusing our efforts on how we feel inside and working towards achieving the core human states of being. It means we recalibrate our inner purpose, our identity and our daily commitment to become the type of person who wants to experience:

- Freedom: Feeling free, hopeful, optimistic, excited about future opportunities. (NOT trapped, stuck in a rut, with no way out and nothing to look forward.)
- Wholeness: Feeling whole, aligned, at one, comfortable with myself and my world. (NOT inauthentic, not myself, out of sync, always pleasing others.)
- Peace: Feeling peaceful, contented, serene. (NOT fearful, anxious, or worried about the future.)
- Joy: Feeling joyful, happy, grateful, connected. (NOT unhappy, disconnected, alone.)
- Fulfilment: Feeling fulfilled, life has meaning, inspired, creative. (NOT unfulfilled, lacklustre, unenthusiastic.)

If you change your identity and the inner purpose of your life, you change the story of your life. If you change your story, you change your future.

The Problem We're Trying to Solve

In this chapter, we've gone into quite some detail to better understand the exact nature of the problem we're facing. We've discovered that much of the pain and suffering we experience in today's world is caused by our misplaced belief that we can meet inner human needs by chasing extrinsic, material goals. We can't. It creates a gap, a disconnection. We feel there is something missing, and we can't seem to find the solution. We can't find "IT."

The start of the process to close the gap and find that elusive "IT" is to realise that we have been grounding our inner purpose, our identity, and our idea of success in the wrong story. We realise that we can't find lasting inner happiness by chasing success as defined in the story of economic growth. And that means we can't find happiness by chasing money, status and consumption.

Once we realise this and appreciate that lasting, natural happiness can only come when we meet our inner, authentic human needs, we can then make the decision to change the focus of our life. We can then decide to ground our inner purpose, our identity, and our idea of success in the story of life, the universe and everything. We can then decide to spend more of our time meeting our inner human needs. We can then decide to start pursuing different, more spiritual goals. We can then decide if we're ready to embark on the solution to the problem. That's when we're ready for the solution.

The only problem is the solution is spiritual.

PART 2

HOW TO BE HAPPY

THREE

THE SPIRITUAL SOLUTION

THREE

THE SPIRITUAL SOLUTION

THE SPIRITUAL JOURNEY OF TRANSFORMATION

The Transformation Begins

The stories we believe in and align our lives to have a profound effect on what we do and how we feel. We've talked about the story of economic growth, the way work works and how our culture's junk values have influenced us towards measuring success using extrinsic material symbols. When we align ourselves with this story, it seems to narrow our purpose down to that of wealth accumulation. And it does so at the expense of our health and happiness. But what if we didn't align ourselves to this story? What if we set our sights on a different purpose? What if we want to be a different type of person? What if we shaped our purpose and identity to put happiness first? Not that we'll completely forget about wealth and health, but let's, for the time being, decide that success for us now means achieving lasting natural happiness by meeting our inner human needs.

It doesn't sound like a big deal, does it? But if we take our primary purpose and our renewed identity seriously, it's a massive deal. It's not something that we can do with the click of our fingers. It requires a transformation in mind, body and soul. There are years of habitual thinking, believing and behaving to be undone. That's why we need a thorough process to help us prioritise happiness.

There's a phrase that often gets said in 12-Step meetings, which really confused me in my early days of recovery. I'd often hear people say, "Hello. My name is XYZ, and I'm a grateful alcoholic." Grateful? What's there to be grateful about being an alcoholic? I'm an alcoholic. I know what it means to be addicted to alcohol. I've just had the most painful, most miserable and demeaning period of my life. I'm sat here, on a Friday night, in a cold church hall. I feel full of shame and guilt about the damage I've caused by my out-of-control drinking. All I can think about is having a drink. I'm looking around at a group of people who must be thinking and feeling the same thing as I do. And all we've got to look forward to is the prospect of never having another drink in our entire lives. Ever. Why, in God's name, would you be grateful for being an alcoholic?

I now know what they're grateful for. They were presented with a solution that not only helped them stop drinking but also transformed their purpose, their identity, their behaviours and, ultimately, the way they feel about life. That solution unlocked a new life filled with happiness, joy, peace, and fulfilment. That solution was spiritual in nature. And it would have been rejected, just as I rejected it, if they were not as desperate as most addicts are. As I had to be to give spirituality a chance.

Nobody wants to be an addict. Nobody wants to feel the pain and misery, the guilt and shame, the demoralising and demeaning places that our addictions took us. For many of us, especially me, that is the only way to find the spiritual solution. If I wasn't in so much pain, if I wasn't so utterly lost in the problem, I would never have found spirituality. I rejected the notion outright to start with. I had to be in the pit of desperation to take it on board.

That's why you'll hear 12-Step people talk about hitting "rock bottom." For many people, it's only when their addiction gets so bad that they find there is nowhere else to go, nothing else to try, that they become willing to accept the spiritual solution and start the process of change. And not just change but transformation. There's a difference. Change can be incremental; it can improve things slightly by tweaking the odd thing here or there. Transformation, on the other hand, is, well, transformational. It's regenerative.

The spiritual solution is available to anyone. You don't have to be a hopeless alcohol or drug addict to benefit from it. You can be an everyday, low-level addict. An addict who is unaware of their addiction to the story of economic growth and extrinsic material symbols. Or an addict who is unaware of the unhealthy way they think about life and their everyday unhealthy behaviours. From this perspective, I think it's useful to view the spiritual solution not as the answer to a life-threatening addiction but as a way to shift our primary purpose and identity away from pursuing wealth and towards pursuing happiness, away from chasing after extrinsic, material goals towards pursuing intrinsic, spiritual goals.

The 12-Step Programme of Recovery is the spiritual solution that not only frees us from our addictions (no matter how big or small) it also helps us prioritise happiness. It has the power to transform our lives for the better. A transformation in what we believe, how we act and how we feel. A transformation of body, mind and soul.

In my story, I talked about the two years of my life after rehab when I didn't drink. I was introduced to The 12-Step Programme, the spiritual solution, but I chose to ignore it. Those two years were painful. I had changed certain behaviours. I had stopped drinking. That meant I wasn't putting alcohol into my system, so I wasn't setting off the physical allergy I have to alcohol. But I hadn't addressed the mental obsession and the underlying spiritual malady. I was, what they call in 12-Step circles, a dry drunk. I showed all the discontentment, restlessness, and irritability of a drunk but without a drink.

I had changed, but I wasn't transformed. My primary purpose was still wealth accumulation and chasing extrinsic symbols of success. I was trying to do that without the soothing effect of alcohol. I succeeded in not drinking, but I didn't feel like a success because I felt all the same old feelings.

I see this confusion of change versus transformation in the business community as part of my work as a B-Corp Leader. Some companies are transforming how they do business by becoming purpose driven. In doing so, they shift their primary purpose away from making money and towards helping a specific group of people or a specific cause. For these types of businesses, sticking to that primary purpose becomes transformational. Their priority is making an impact rather than making money. Growing their impact is crucial. Making a profit is important as it enables them to deliver more impact. Growing profit is not the end. It's the means to an end. Profit is not the purpose. It's incidental.

Other businesses are changing how they do business by saying they have a purpose but using that purpose as a cover for continuing to prioritise money. Their primary purpose is to make a profit. Making an impact may be desirable. Growing profit for the sake of growing profit is still the internal motivation that drives decision-making.

That's the difference between transformation and change. That's the difference between embracing a whole new set of beliefs and internal attitudes and clinging to the old ones. Transformation is a shift in consciousness. As I experienced with my two-year stint as a dry drunk, if you simply change behaviours with no transformational shift in beliefs, attitudes and consciousness, eventually, old habits break in. Plus, you never get to experience the joy, freedom, peace and fulfilment that the spiritual solution delivers. It's then, and only then, once you've experienced the fruits of the spiritual solution and had a shift in consciousness, that you can say, with hand on heart, "I'm a grateful alcoholic." I now know what that means, and I'm pleased that I get to say, "I'm a grateful alcoholic."

That transformation wasn't easy. Not for me, at least. I had to hit that rock bottom before I would even contemplate the idea of adopting new beliefs and internal attitudes. My options boiled down to making one stark decision: adopt this spiritual solution or face a life of misery and certain alcoholic death. That was it. There were no other options. Even then, I took the decision begrudgingly. Many people do. Sadly, some choose misery and death. Thankfully, I made the decision and adopted the spiritual solution wholeheartedly. I chose to prioritise intrinsic success over extrinsic success. I chose to prioritise happiness over wealth. And so the transformation began.

Not everyone has to be confronted by such a stark ultimatum. There are such things as high rock bottoms. Lots of people are drawn to spirituality without experiencing the pain and misery of addiction and its resulting humiliations. We are all spiritual seekers deep down. We are all drawn to some form of spirituality at some point in our lives. Throughout history, human beings have displayed unwavering commitment to their search for the ultimate truth. Or the search for higher levels of consciousness. Or the search for God. We're naturally drawn to some sort of allusive power that we can sense beyond ourselves. We have an in-built need for a soulful story that acts as an antidote to the cold reality of our short-lived material existence followed by an abrupt death. A story that makes sense of our God-given values and virtues.

These quests to unearth a deeper truth are expressions of the spiritual drive within us, which wakes up at some point and creates a yearning to discover what it means to be a human being. I love what Viktor Frankl wrote in the preface of the 1992 edition of his classic book Man's Search for Meaning. The book was first published in German in 1946 and has been published in fifty-two other languages. It has sold more than sixteen million copies since then. Commenting on why he thought the book had become a bestselling success, he wrote, "I do not see the best-seller status of my book an achievement and accomplishment on my part. If (millions) of people reach out for a book whose very title promises to deal with the question of meaning to life, it must be a question that burns under the fingernails." Is the meaning of life a question that burns under your fingernails? Is it possible not to think about it?

As a young adult, I was interested enough in the question of meaning to read a few books. I thought I knew about the meaning of my life, but it didn't burn under my fingernails enough for me to do anything about it. I read the words on the pages and left them as words in my intellect. I didn't translate the words into actions or beliefs. It took a rock bottom for me to feel the burning under my fingernails.

That's when my interest in meaning and spirituality turned into an interest in healing and the spiritual solution. I was interested because I was now in desperate need of something to relieve the pain, not something to read at night.

Whether we're pulled by natural curiosity to find the meaning of life or pushed by pain and misery to heal the soul, what we're seeking are answers. Answers to questions like "Why do I feel so miserable? What is this pain I feel? How did I get it so wrong? What is missing in my life? What is this hole I feel inside? How can I fill it? What will make me whole? How can I live my life more successfully?"

The spiritual solution answers these questions. It is the path to recovery and a return to wholeness—a return to the feeling that we belong. We belong in our own skin, and we belong in the world around us. The process of healing – a word that means "return to wholeness" – begins when we accept that the story we've been living our lives by hasn't been working. We admit that our primary purpose has taken us down a wrong path. We become willing to explore a new story to live by a new identity to embrace: a story and an identity we can build faith in. Once we've reached this point of acceptance and willingness, we're ready to embark on the process of transformation.

The journey of transformation and return to wholeness is a Hero's Journey. The myth of the Hero's Journey stands in contrast to the myth of the tyrant. It's an adventure that embraces life and all its wonderful mysteries and requires a certain amount of bravery to meet the challenges along the way. It's not a comfortable journey, but it does give rise to levels of peace, joy, fulfilment, and freedom that the tyrant never thought possible.

A Heroic New Identity Emerges

The journey starts by aligning ourselves with a big new story and re-imaging a new identity for ourselves. A heroic new identity ready to take on a new journey and live life in a bold new way in an exciting new story. The emergence of this new identity is a process with two parts:

1. The breakdown and dismantling of the old story and old identity, which is experienced as a crisis, full of pain and confusion.
2. The emergence of a new story and a new identity, better than you ever imagined, which is experienced as a miracle, full of joy and wonderment.

I use the word crisis deliberately. That's what the breakdown feels like. It is a state of confusion where we want to desperately cling to the old story of us and achieving success based on the conventions of our culture of economic growth and its junk values. Not because we like them so much. But because it's what we're used to. It's what the whole world is used to. It's familiar. It surrounds us. This old story has been our comfort blanket. It might have been suffocating us to death, but at least we felt comfortable while it did so.

The pain we feel is our ego, our left hemisphere, shallow, rational way of thinking, struggling to retain control of its old identity. It resists the loss of security. It resists the loss of certainty. We need to work through this pain while we wait for our belief in the new story to emerge. This is where faith is required. Faith that a miracle will occur.

And I use the word miracle deliberately. Not to mean an act of an angel or the intercession of an all-powerful, omnipresent God but to mean something that would not seem possible in the old story. In my experience, a miracle is not usually a sudden change in external circumstances but a dramatic internal shift in perception and consciousness. Situations that appeared hopeless, desperate, and permanent suddenly and miraculously appear to be anything but hopeless, desperate and permanent. That's the miracle of the spiritual solution. The miracle I hope you experience as you follow your own spiritual journey is a shift in perception that makes you realise that the big new story and your role and identity within it make so much more sense. And how destructive the old story has been.

We have to find some faith to get us there. We have to believe in something bigger and better. So, as we come to terms with our old story based on economic growth crumbling away, realising the damage it has been causing, our mind, our heart, and our soul start opening up to the possibility of a new story. Something enticing and powerful enough to put our faith in. Brené Brown talks about faith as "a place of mystery, where we find the courage to believe in what we cannot see and the strength to let go of our fear and certainty.'" Without faith, we cling to that fear. But what is the basis of the big new story we can build our faith upon?

Believing in a Friendly Universe

The new story is the biggest story of all. It's the story of life, the universe and everything. Finding your identity in this story isn't like finding your identity in the story of economic growth. It's more of a mystery than a prescription of how to live. It can never be fully understood. It unfolds over time the deeper you fall into it. Our Hero's Journey is a journey of discovery, a quest to find out what this story means to us. A quest to fulfil our inner human needs. Needs which may be elusive and hard to pin down. These are needs that require exploration and experimentation to be fully understood. And in the searching, we find the meaning of our lives and work our way back to wholeness.

If you're new to spirituality, I know that may all sound a bit vague—more of a cryptic clue than a story. But my experience of spirituality has been very much like that. Seemingly unfathomable paradoxes that make no sense one minute but become deeply meaningful the next. However, rather than leave the big new story as an inaccessible paradox, let's ease ourselves into the mystery with something a little more concrete: a foundational belief.

It's claimed that Albert Einstein once said, "The most important decision we make is whether we believe we live in a friendly or hostile universe." There appears to be some doubt about whether he said those exact words. There is no doubt, however, that he did say, "Subtle is the Lord, but malicious he is not." Regardless of whether he said the first quote, it's clear the greatest scientific mind of our times made that most important decision for himself. He decided to believe in a friendly universe. And that's the decision we need to make. It could be said that the spiritual solution cannot work, and the spiritual path cannot be embraced until we firmly make this decision. We are not just agreeing to it, but deeply knowing it. It seems that if we can make this decision, then prioritising spiritual happiness becomes a real possibility. Are you able to believe that we live in a friendly universe?

As you ponder this question, here's a little food for thought. Richard Rohr in Jesus's Alternative Plan suggests there are three world-views we can adopt:

1. The universe is against us.
2. The universe is indifferent or neutral.
3. The universe is for us.

If we decide the universe is against us, we are left as the hopeless victim. A downtrodden individual, powerless against an all-powerful universe. Moaning. Complaining. "The world is out to get me." There are many people who adopt this belief. You'll know who they are. They tend to be a miserable bunch.

If we believe the universe is indifferent or neutral, we join the vast majority of people who live in our secular society. The universe is inert —science proves it is—and it is neither good nor bad, just as an atom is neither good nor bad.

The problem with adopting this belief is that we can quickly fall into the victim belief when things don't go our way. If the universe is neutral, we're left with the daunting task of trying to fix everything ourselves. We have to arrange the world around us in order to manipulate circumstances in our favour. This is hard, stressful work. We end up with the weight of the world on our shoulders. This is the belief underpinning the old story of economic growth and the way work works. You'll know the people who adopt this belief as you'll see them all around you, struggling to control every aspect of their lives in order to succeed. They tend to be a stressed-out bunch.

That leaves us with the belief that the universe is for us. This is the belief that, despite the difficulties and challenges we face, at its core, life is good, life is trustworthy, and life is benevolent. This may be a hard belief for many of us cynical, rational types to adopt. How can you prove this to be the case?

It's hard to prove scientifically, but there's strong evidence that the story of life, the universe and everything has goodness at its heart. Carl Jung called it synchronicity. Christian thinkers called it provenance. Hindus called it karma. These, and many other spiritual traditions, suggest that at the core of the universe, in the foundation and fabric of everything, there is a powerful, positive force that some call unconditional love. You'll know the people who adopt this belief as they exhibit a calmness and a sense of joy as they go about their daily business. They are not submissive to fate but have enough faith that "all will be well." Enough faith that they are able to give generously and happily from a place of abundance. They tend to be a contented bunch.

Is the belief that the universe is good something you can build faith in? Are you willing to build this faith and make spiritual happiness a possibility? It might feel like a big ask just now. It may feel like you would like to believe the universe is good, but at this very moment, at the very start of your spiritual journey, it's just a bit too much of a tall order to give it your all. That's okay. I didn't buy it to start with, either. It didn't feel at all comfortable for me a few years ago. But as I mentioned in the introduction, you shouldn't take my word for it, or Carl Jung's, or the Christian thinkers', or Hindus. Find out for yourself. Work with what little faith you have and see how it grows.

Building Faith Through Experience

Step 2 of The 12-Step Programme of Recovery states, "We came to believe that a Power greater than ourselves could restore us to sanity." When I was guided through the 12-Step Process, it was suggested to me that all I needed at the very early stages of the spiritual journey, as a cynical, rational, non-spiritual person, was to have the merest belief that maybe, just maybe, there is a Power that is greater than me, that I do not yet believe in, know or understand. And maybe, just maybe, it is a friendly and benevolent power. And maybe, just maybe, this Power was for me, not against me or neutral, but for me, and it could help me recover. If I had just the tiniest sliver of the merest of beliefs, then that was enough to work with. What I was aiming to achieve through The 12-Step Programme was to build on that tiniest sliver of the merest of beliefs and transform it into deep knowing. And I was to do that through experience.

Building faith and belief in the spiritual solution is all about experience. It doesn't matter what you read or what you are told. It's only when it happens to you that you really start believing. When you experience even the smallest of examples of this power working in your favour, when you see for yourself the universe as a friendly place, and you directly benefit from it conspiring to help you out, that's when you experience something that never leaves you. As Emmet Fox says, "You have the witness of Truth within yourself. You are no longer dependent upon the word of someone else; you know for yourself, and this is the only authority worth having."

This is the spiritual solution in action. This is the Hero's Journey. Discovering for yourself that the universe is for you. And you'll know it because, as Emmet goes on to say, "You feel yourself to be free and useful and joyous and unconscious of either fear or doubt." You'll experience "greater freedom, greater self-expression, wider and newer and brighter experiences, better health, greater prosperity, wider opportunities of service to others – life more abundant." Yes, Emmet, life more abundant. You'll feel the buzz of being alive.

This is the big new story we're trying to build faith in. It's a story that's always been right in front of us, but we've never really seen it. Getting to know this story and understanding what it means to us and the way we live life successfully is the Hero's Journey of transformation. It is an inner journey. A spiritual journey of self-discovery. A journey that will uncover past hurts, stop destructive habits and unearth healthy new ones. It's the challenging and rewarding journey to discover the story of the true you and your true purpose. It can take heroic efforts to stick with the journey. But it starts with a beginner's mindset. The requirements being honesty, humility, open-mindedness and willingness (H.H.O.W.). With these simple traits, anyone can prioritise happiness and experience the miracle that spirituality can deliver. Are you ready to experience spirituality?

WHAT IS SPIRITUALITY?

The Non-Material Aspects of Reality

I had, and still have, many misgivings in writing a book about spirituality. It feels uncomfortable because it's so at odds with our modern way of living and working. I have this notion that I'd like to get spirituality higher up the agenda in businesses and even in our economy, but the word evokes so many contentious connotations. Religious connotations. Mystical connotations. And associations that aren't business-like, ethereal, superstitious, or magical. And of course, the word spirituality evokes the word God. And if you ever want to make a group of businesspeople feel uncomfortable, try bringing the "G" word into the conversation.

Undaunted by my misgivings, I do want to bring the idea of spirituality into our modern way of living and even into the business world. And I'm not going to shy away from the contentious nature of the word. So, let's get into it and explore what spirituality means to me and what it could mean to you.

The first point is that not all things exist in the material realm. Not all things can be observed and measured using scientific equipment. Things such as consciousness, thoughts, emotions, and beliefs are every bit as real as atoms and cells, but because they can't be measured, they tend to fall outside of scientific scrutiny. And because our culture of economic growth worships science and technology above all, these non-material aspects of reality tend to be thought of as "less than." Less important. Less tangible. Less valuable. And therefore, they get left out. In the reality of our day-to-day existence, I would argue they are equally, if not more, important. I'm not sure I can fully believe any story, no matter how scientific, that tries to capture the full nature of my reality and excludes things like feelings. That's because I know 100% that my feelings are real. I can 100% feel my feelings. I'm inclined to trust my feelings. This is important if our primary purpose is to prioritise happiness. Therefore, if we are to try to answer the big questions of life, of our lives, it would make complete sense to consider all aspects of reality, not just the material ones we can measure.

Integral Theory: Valuing Both Interior & Exterior Aspects of Reality

This is the idea at the heart of Ken Wilber's Integral Theory. It is a philosophical framework that seeks to integrate all forms of human knowledge, experience, and wisdom into one integrated "theory of everything." From hard sciences such as chemistry and physics to softer sciences such as psychology and psychotherapy. From modern academic philosophy to ancient practical wisdom. From theories on the development of individual consciousness to theories on the development of collective business culture.

The idea is to provide a framework by which each specific theory or area of knowledge can be viewed, valued and understood in relation to all others. It gives us a way to value non-material knowledge alongside material knowledge. And in this way, it makes space for and gives a role for spirituality to sit alongside the more "acceptable" forms of science valued by today's society.

I won't attempt to explain Wilber's theory in detail here. But I would recommend you read his book Theory of Everything. What I do want to highlight, however, is his basic four-quadrant matrix. What this does brilliantly is acknowledge that there is an "interior" aspect to our reality, which is every bit as valid as the "exterior" aspect. This "interior" aspect can be experienced individually (as thoughts, emotions, perceptions, and feelings) or collectively (as shared values, relationships, and culture). Similarly, the "exterior" aspect of reality can be observed individually (as our body, our brain, our behaviours and so on) as well as collectively (as economic systems, government processes, and the natural environment).

The big point here is that whilst science, technology, and accountancy may be incredibly useful tools for making sense of the exterior reality of our world (including our economy and our businesses), spirituality is an incredibly useful tool for helping us make sense of the interior reality of these worlds. Spirituality has an immensely important role to play. Spirituality is incredibly valuable and valid.

Spirituality Defies Definition

The next point to make, however, is that, unlike the hard sciences, spirituality defies definition. There are so many spiritual pathways that no one description could possibly capture them all

William James makes this point well. He says that because there are so many different definitions of spirituality, it proves that the word "cannot stand for one thing or any single idea or principle but rather a collection of ideas and principles. The analysing mind likes to categorise things as one absolute thing or another. It is either this or it is that, but it cannot be both. But let us from the start acknowledge that we will not, and cannot, find one neat definition and essence but explore and highlight a number of equally important characteristics that together form a rich tapestry of what spirituality is and what it brings."

From that point of view, it's good to know that no one has the answer. No one has the definition. No one can tell you with absolute certainty what spirituality means to you. No spiritual leader, no scientist, no philosopher. That's because no one can answer the most basic spiritual questions of what life means to you and how you should live it for yourself. Only you can answer those questions.

. . .

Spirituality vs Religion

And that brings us to another key point to raise. Spirituality, as far as this book is concerned, is not religion. Or to be more precise, it is not an organised, institutionalised religion. When I talk of spirituality, I'm referring to the feelings, beliefs, practices and experiences of individual people who are trying to better understand themselves and how they relate to other people, the world around them and whatever they may consider the "Divine."

Defining spirituality, therefore, is more like a personal quest than an exercise in wordsmithing. It is experienced rather than understood intellectually. And it requires a certain frame of mind to get there. As Elizabeth Lesser wrote, "Spirituality is an attitude of fearlessness, a sense of adventure. It is a way of looking boldly at the life we have been given here, now, on earth, as human beings. And asking ourselves Who am I? And how should I live?... Spirituality is nothing more than a brave search for the truth about existence. Your existence. Nothing more. But equally nothing less."

They sound relatively simple questions, don't they? Who am I? How should I live? And with so many people trying to figure these things out over so many millennia, you'd think we'd have an idea of how to answer them. But we don't. The answers and the best way to find those answers remain frustratingly elusive, largely because of the layers of stubborn misconceptions about ourselves and the nature of life that we've built up over the years. The story of economic growth is so embedded in our cultural psyche that much of the spiritual journey is about unlearning engrained junk values as it is about learning new spiritual ones. We need to re-train ourselves to see the simple truth of life that lives in plain view of all of us.

So, spirituality is your personal examination of life. And, to be a bit more emotive, your personal adventure of being alive. It's a process that should result in you learning to fall head over heels in love with life. In love with the flow of life. In love with your life. In love with the flow of your life.

The Paradoxical Nature of the Spiritual Journey

As you embark on this adventure, it's worth bearing in mind the paradoxical nature of it. There's an ancient Chinese proverb that says, "No one catches the wild ass by running after him. Yet only those who run after the wild ass ever catch him." What on earth does that mean? I don't know. And by that, I mean I don't have a definitive answer. But I do have a sense of what it's getting at. I get some sort of inner knowing by contemplating the paradox held within the proverb. I can live with the tension of both these opposite ideas being true at the same time. That inner knowing is an integral part of the spiritual journey. It comes to us from the contextualising right hemisphere of our brains rather than the logical left hemisphere. And that's a big part of the retraining that we need to undergo.

By deciphering the clues hidden in paradoxes, we begin to answer the questions of who we are and how we should live. We get to see why life includes death, eternity includes now, and freedom includes responsibility. Why meaning includes tragedy. Why unity includes diversity, why we are connected to everything yet feel separate and isolated, we begin to "know" the answers even if we can't articulate them very well. Just as you "know" how to ride a bike but would find it hard to write down the instructions, just as you "know" how music makes you feel but don't know why.

The Role of Science in Understanding Spirituality

One aspect of our unlearning has to do with the fact that religion, science, and art are taught as individual, unconnected disciplines. Today, only "science" is viewed as being able to deliver the truth. That wasn't always the case. In times gone by, our way of understanding the world around us was as likely to be informed by a poem as by an algorithm. Possibly more so. But once science was divorced from the other two, it became the go-to expert of the material world and a trusted source of information for the logical mind. A combination that has held power over our culture, our way of thinking, our way of learning and ultimately our way of being. We became experts in seeking out and valuing theoretical knowledge. We lost interest and became sceptical of "gnosis," which is experienced knowledge.

Scientific knowledge about the physical world of matter is objective and impersonal in nature, which is thought to be its strength. But our spirituality is a personal quest. We need personal and subjective answers to metaphysical questions of the mind—answers that relate to the way we think and feel, take account of our personal histories and destinies, and guide us towards our personal purpose in life.

That's not to say that scientific thinking has no role in helping us understand spirituality. We just need to be mindful of its limitations. Limitations that the scientific world itself recognises. At the turn of the twentieth century, scientists such as Einstein, Bohr, Park, Nernst, Schrodinger, and Bohm made discoveries that moved science away from the mechanistic, Newtonian view of life towards a more mysterious, quantum view of reality. There also seems to be a shift away from science being purely reductionist (getting further and further into the detail of what components make up the living universe) and becoming more systemic (exploring the emergent nature of complex living systems and what makes those component parts come alive). My understanding of this subject area is limited. However, from the small amount I do understand, it appears that some people think there is a connection between the quantum field, consciousness, and our personal view and experience of reality. And who am I to say there isn't?

Regardless of the detail, my observation is that some of this thinking is bringing spirituality and science back together again. And that can only be a good thing if it helps some of us with our own personal examination of life.

For example, this quote from Albert Einstein helped me:

> *"A human being is a part of the whole, called by us, "Universe"; a part limited in time and space. He experiences himself, his thoughts and feelings as something separated from the rest − a kind of optical delusion of his consciousness. This delusion is a kind of prison for us, restricting us to our personal desires and to affection for a few persons nearest to us. Our task must be to free ourselves from this prison by widening our circle of compassion to embrace all living creatures and the whole of nature in its beauty. Nobody is able to achieve this completely, but the striving for such achievement is in itself part of the liberation and a foundation for inner security."*

Source: *New York Times*, 1950

It helped me because it seemed to say, in a more logical, rational way, what Thich Nhat Hanh wrote in his poem about interbeing:

> "You are me, and I am you.
> Isn't it obvious that we "inter-are"?
> You cultivate the flower in yourself,
> so that I will be beautiful.
> I transform the garbage in myself,
> so that you will not have to suffer.
> I support you;
> you support me.
> I am in this world to offer you peace;
> you are in this world to bring me joy."

Einstein's words spoke to my logical, rational brain and validated Hanh's words that spoke to my heart. I believe Hanh's words are more powerful. They move me more. But because of Einstein's words, I now have more faith in them.

This has been an important part of my own spiritual journey. Trying to find the cross-over between the spiritual and the scientific and intuitively warming to right hemisphere words of beauty and validating them with left hemisphere words of logic. This is consilience. Where complementary stories from different fields of knowledge support each other. This is the intersection I tend to gravitate towards and what tends to influence the things I believe in. This is why Ken Wilber's Integral Theory appeals so much to me. I don't always need intellectual grounding to put theory into action. Sometimes, I just do what I see other spiritual people doing. However, to keep the action going and fully commit to prolonged periods of practice, intellectual validation gives my logical brain enough evidence to keep going when progress feels a bit slow and cumbersome.

The Power of Reconnection

I said that spirituality, in this book, is not about institutionalised religion. And that's true. It's not. But that's not to say I'm anti-religious, far from it. I've read many religious books and been introduced to many religious ideas as part of my journey. Excerpts from The Bible, passages from the Bhagavad Gita, Buddhist meditation techniques, verses from the Tao Te Ching. All have played a part in helping me explore the nature of life and my role in it.

The word religion comes from the Latin word re-ligio, which means to re-connect or re-bond with reverence. That's the positive power religion has to offer the world. A solution for the human race that, for the most part, seems disenchanted, isolated and at odds with each other. If there's one word that sums up the effect the story of economic growth has had on us with all the resulting comparison and competition, it would be disconnection, disconnection from ourselves, from each other, from the planet.

Unfortunately, too many people on all sides of all religions seem to get hung up on the rituals, the dogma and the doctrine. These are the aspects of religion that can be so off-putting and even incendiary. But if we could focus on the reconnection aspect at the heart of all religion, well, what a different world we would have. We would have a vast array of knowledge, tools, and processes to help us reconnect everything, reconnect separated worlds. To re-bond with reverence the divided self, our inner and outer lives, the logical and the mystical, the material and the spiritual, man and nature, east and west, life and death. It's been suggested that the opposite of addiction isn't sobriety. It's reconnection. Religion could be the answer to our modern, addicted society.

Isn't it interesting to think that religion has been around all these years as a technology (if that's the right word to use), freely available to virtually everyone on the planet, which is there to bring us into harmony with ourselves, each other and the unseen order of the universe? But we messed religion up. We let pride, stubbornness, comparison, competition, and other junk values poison what was good and pure. As Francis Spufford comments in his book Unapologetic, "We applied our 'HTtFTH' to religion. This stands for the "Human Tendency to F*** Things Up." As we have seen with our economy and the way work works, we have applied the 'HTtFTU' to many aspects of life.

But all is not lost. Spufford also recognised that we have a "HPtLWG." This stands for the "Human Propensity to Love What's Good." I believe we instinctively know what's good. We know what's right and what's wrong. What's good for us. What's good for others. What's good for the planet. We might not do it all the time. We might let our "HTtFTU" overrule our "HPtLWG." But, deep down, somewhere in our hearts, we know. And we know because we are all, as Einstein said, as Thich said, interconnected parts of the whole. We feel alive when we are fully connected to the whole. We feel the pain when we're disconnected from the whole. And this theme of reconnection is a big part of spirituality. One of the key "jobs to be done" as we embark on the spiritual journey and our exploration of life and our role in it is for us to reconnect to it, to reconnect to all aspects of it. And feel that connection.

For the scientifically minded, left hemisphere seekers, the basic principles of this "interconnectedness" may look like this:

1. At a sub-atomic level, everything is made of energy and information. (Some may call this quantum foam. Some may call this Spirit.)
2. This energy and information is life-affirming and conscious. (The universe is for us. It wants to promote life and evolve in a positive way.)
3. Everything is part of a living interconnected web of energy, including human beings.
4. By opening ourselves up and feeling connected to this web of energy, we gain a deeper empathy and reverence for every other living thing that is also part of the web.
5. Empathy and reverence help us live in harmony and have the right relationship with everything and encourage us to take responsibility and take the next right action.
6. Humans have the unique ability to disconnect ourselves from the web ("HTtFTU")
7. When we disconnect, we remove ourselves from a right relationship and right action.
8. Feeling disconnected, out of a relationship and taking the wrong actions makes us ill and causes suffering. As individuals, as organisations, as communities, as a society, we become physically, mentally, emotionally and spiritually unwell. More selfish and more prone to addiction.

9. Reconnecting ourselves to the web of energy and all other living parts of the web restores our health. It brings physical, mental, emotional and spiritual well-being for individuals, communities and society. We are regenerated. We are happier.

This nine-point list could be one way to define spirituality if it works for you.

The "Biggies" and the "Dailies"

But as I mentioned earlier, spirituality defies definitive definition. Yes, it is about reconnection. It's about felt-connection. But it's also about many other things too. Elizabeth Lesser points to the "biggies" and the "dailies" of spirituality. The "biggies" of concern are life, purpose, love, human suffering, higher consciousness, death and beyond. The "dailies" of concern are physical and mental health, feelings, relationships, work and family. It seems nothing is really out of bounds when it comes to spirituality.

There are also less tangible, mysterious things to consider as part of the spiritual journey. We mentioned earlier about the pull of curiosity to find a deeper meaning in life. For many, there is an inexplicable longing that pulls hard on the heart. There's an unknown force, a presence, that draws them forward, wanting them to discover it. Some call this force their destiny, their purpose in life.

Some call this force and presence God. Some call it peace. Some call it love. Some heed the calling and follow the Presence. Some choose to blot the Presence out with TV, drink or drugs. I sense this Presence and feel the longing. Some days, the longing is palpable.

Some days, I couldn't care less.

And that's another aspect of spirituality in my experience. The hunger for it changes from day to day.

The Soul and the Inner Compass

There's also the issue of the soul. The soul is said to be that part of us that yearns to be in contact with the Divine. Maybe it is the soul that draws us forward towards our purpose, towards God, towards peace. Or maybe the soul is that part of us that has access to the innate, creative intelligence of the universe and can draw on divine wisdom. It knows what is good. It may be the source of our deep knowing and the wellspring of our "HTtLWG." Maybe it can guide our logical, egotistical selves towards right action if we nurture it enough and listen to its soft silent advice. Maybe it knows what's best for us, despite ourselves and our "HTtFTU."

I can't say for sure what the soul is or isn't. For me, it is an integral part of the intuitive, right hemisphere, true self idea. That's why I describe it as soulful. I believe our soulful, true self is the part of us that is attuned to the story of life, the universe and everything. It is the means by which we access the essence of life itself and the subtle energies that connect it all together. And it does that in a way that our egoic, logical, false self can never do.

I also believe our soulful, true self acts like an inner compass. It lets us know when our actions are "on track" by making us feel free, whole, fulfilled and joyous. And it lets us know when we're not in right relation by making us feel anxious, unsettled and closed down. That could be our soul, but I need to do more exploring within my own soul to be sure. And that's all part of the spiritual journey. Exploring. Questioning. Seeking. Is there part of you that you would call your soul? Is it calling out to you? What is it telling you? What direction does it want you to take? Can you trust it's still, small voice?

The Full Rapture of Being Alive

As we come to the end of this section on spirituality, what it means to me, and what it could mean to you, I thought I'd finish with a couple of quotes that have helped me on my journey. I'm still exploring. I'm still seeking. I still need to remember why I'm on this journey and what I'm trying to achieve. As a recovering addict, I need to remember that, first and foremost, spirituality is a solution. It is a solution to my spiritual malady. It is a tool to help me prioritise my new inner purpose of seeking spiritual happiness rather than my old outer purpose of accumulating wealth. And therefore, it has great healing qualities. It is restorative. It is regenerative.

The first quote I want to share is from Thich Nhat Hanh and alludes to this beautifully and succinctly. And I love the way he describes spirituality as "discovering" and as "a field of research and study."

> *"Spirituality is not religion...It is discovering ways to handle life's difficulties and generate peace, joy and happiness right where we are on this beautiful planet. Spirituality is a field of research and study. We want to understand ourselves, the world around us and what it means to be alive on Earth."*

I love this. This could be another definition of spirituality if it works for you. The second quote comes from Joseph Campbell. We talked about spirituality being an investigation into our lives and trying to understand "Who am I?" and "How should I live?" Yes, these are important questions, as the answers will give us a sense of purpose and meaning to our lives. But Campbell goes beyond these questions. He gets to the heart of the spiritual journey and captures what I'm really seeking and why it's important to continue the spiritual journey.

> *"People say that what we're seeking is a meaning for life. I don't think that's what we're really seeking. I think what we're really seeking is an experience of being alive, so that we actually feel the rapture of being alive."*

What an amazing insight. And what an amazing phrase to remind me why I'm doing what I'm doing. I know when spirituality is working for me, not when I read a certain book, not when I do a certain meditation, not when I understand a new spiritual concept, not when I know my purpose in life, not when I take the next right and responsible action, but when I feel the full rapture of being alive. That's what spirituality is for me. That's why I do the work. That's when I know I need to do more work.

Feeling the full rapture of being alive is what spirituality is all about for me. Feeling the full rapture of being alive is a sign of restoration. It's a sign of healing. It's a sign of transformation. It's a sign of prioritising spiritual happiness. This is what the spiritual solution has to offer anyone who feels the pain and suffering of being alive. And the doorway to feeling the full rapture of being alive is what we'll talk about next, the spiritual awakening.

AWAKENING THE SPIRIT WITHIN: A TRANSFORMATIONAL JOURNEY

I may be uncomfortable admitting it, but the truth is that a spiritual awakening changed my life—it saved me. Awakening the spirit within was the transformative turning point—the liminal space that made all the difference. The spiritual solution is a regenerative, restorative healing process, and the spiritual awakening marks the moment when that spiritual medicine kicks in.

The entire purpose of the 12-Step Process is to guide people towards this magical point of awakening. Step 12 begins with the definitive words: "Having had a spiritual awakening." Not "if you have" or "there's a high possibility" – the language is clear. Follow the steps, carry out the suggestions, and put in the work, and by Step 12, you will have experienced an awakening. But what exactly is this mysterious event? What does it look and feel like?

The Nature of Spiritual Awakenings

There's no straightforward answer, as one would expect when dealing with matters of spirituality. From my research and discussions, it seems spiritual awakenings come in a spectrum of shapes, sizes, and timeframes. My own awakening occurred about seven months after fully immersing myself in The 12-Step Programme. Seven months of following suggestions, doing the spiritual work, and persevering.

I woke up one November morning, a morning like any other, except on this day, I had no fear. I was struck by my newfound freedom from worry. For years, I had lived with an undercurrent of anxiety and a background noise of discontentment. But not that morning. I felt a huge weight had been lifted, leaving me freer than I could ever recall. I felt great. I felt happy.

I remember thinking, "This must be how normal people feel when they wake up." I was deeply grateful to be unburdened by anxiousness. But then the thought crept in: "This won't last. I'll return to my old worried, anxious self soon enough."

And indeed, I was.

I continued following suggestions, putting in the spiritual work, and persevering. Sure enough, the feelings of freedom, joy, wholeness, peace and contentment returned. The more I did the work, the longer these periods of freedom lasted. The more I persevered, the stronger and deeper those feelings grew. That pattern continues to this day. I've heard from people who have been on this spiritual path for decades, and they constantly tell me it just keeps getting better. I'm inclined to believe them.

This awakening moment is most commonly described as a turnaround in worldview, a change of heart and mind, and a shift in perspective. It's like being given new glasses that make the whole world look so much better when, in fact, the world hasn't changed at all – only the way you see it has. Your eyes are now open to a truth that you couldn't see before.

As William James put it, *"A new heaven seems to shine on a new earth."* And because the world looks better, we feel better about it. I experienced this as a beguiling mix of peace, joy, and contentment. James likens it to *"reaching the smooth waters of inner unity and peace."* Wholeness. Serenity. *"The humdrum ecstasy of everyday serenity."* That's what the spiritual awakening felt like to me.

In his classic work, The Varieties of Religious Experience, William James delves into the nature of spiritual experiences. He describes the spiritual awakening as follows:

> *"The time for tension in our soul is over, and that of happy relaxation, of calm deep breathing, of an eternal present, with no discordant future to be anxious about has arrived. Fear is positively expunged and washed away. It adds to life an enchantment which is not rationally or logically deducible from anything else. This enchantment, coming as a gift when it does come – a gift of our organism, the psychologist will tell you; a gift of God's grace, the theologians say - is either there or not there for us, and there are persons who can no more come possessed by it than they can fall in love with a given woman by mere word of command."*

This resonates with my own experience and that of others I've spoken within 12-Step groups. However, James is not quite as definite about the inevitability of the awakening as the 12th Step might suggest. He says it's "either there or not there", and maybe there are persons who can't "come possessed."

These caveats warrant further examination.

The Spectrum of Awakening

On one hand, I understand James' point. You either have had a spiritual awakening, or you haven't. There don't seem to be half-measures. I distinctly remember the November morning I saw the world through a different lens. I knew it. I could feel it.

On the other hand, some people don't always recognise the change right away. Often, friends and family notice a difference in their eyes, their attitude, and their behaviours before they do. The recognition dawns on them slowly. But then, one day, it hits them – they look back and realise that somewhere along the way, something shifted. They can't pinpoint the exact day; there was no blinding shaft of light, but they know they've changed. The magic has happened. That's when they feel the gratitude of having experienced an awakening.

Five years into my spiritual journey, I know I still have much to learn, explore, and experience. If the last few years are any indication, I will encounter deeper levels of spiritual freedom, peace, and joy, as well as confusion, resentment, and pain. It's all part of the process. Given this depth, it would make sense that there are levels or a spectrum to the journey.

Some forms of Buddhism suggest different stages on the spiritual path:

1. Preparation: Building an adequate foundation of intellectual knowledge, virtuous behaviour, and good manners.
2. Commitment: Beginning to clearly see the spiritual goal, intensifying interest and effort.
3. Awareness: Obtaining a clearer view, tasting the fruits, fears and doubts subsiding, recognising the Four Noble Truths, intensifying practice as faith increases.
4. Concentrated Practice: Staying within meditative awareness, overcoming obstacles, and progress occurring on its own momentum.
5. Enlightenment: Fulfilment in Buddhahood.

Using this spectrum, the spiritual awakening I'm referring to, and that James refers to, would be Stage 3 – becoming aware, tasting the fruits, fear beginning to subside. It's about having the first experiences of freedom and realising the work is beginning to yield results. There is a realisation that the spiritual solution actually works, leading to real faith in it. The moment of realisation may be fleeting, but it leaves an indelible trace of deep knowing. That moment is priceless.

The Timing of Spiritual Awakenings

Spirituality arrives in its own time, as James suggests, like a gift. Emmet Fox describes it this way: "The spiritual (awakening) cannot be hurried or forced, but must appear in its own good time, when the consciousness is ready, exactly as the flowering of a bulb can only be the result of natural growth."

It can't be forced or chased, like the paradoxical wild ass we talked about earlier. For me, it happened after seven months of work; as I went through Step 9 of The 12-Step Programme, I know it happened sooner for some during earlier steps. Others experienced a fleeting moment of knowing even before starting The 12-Step Programme. And yet others are still waiting over a year into the journey. This can be frustrating – if you're putting in the work without feeling results, it's easy to conclude you're one of those who cannot "come possessed" and give up. But we should never give up. The fruits are there for all to experience.

Can Anyone Experience a Spiritual Awakening?

The 12-Step Programme is clear that anyone can experience an awakening. But there is a condition – as long as we embrace the programme, follow suggestions, and do so with honesty, humility, open-mindedness, and willingness (H.H.O.W.). I suspect this applies to any spiritual path. H.H.O.W. are everything when it comes to embracing change, so much so that I have given them their very own acronym. In my experience, those who approach the spiritual journey with these qualities are the ones who experience awakening. The more H.H.O.W., the quicker they get there. No H.H.O.W., no awakening.

Herein lies the challenge for most of us coming to spirituality after decades in the culture of economic growth. We find it very hard to be H.H.O.W. I did. As someone who had enjoyed material success and revelled in past achievements, my ego found humility difficult. I had spent years pretending to be whatever others needed me to be to get what I wanted, not to mention the lies I told to cover up my drinking. Honesty was a struggle. I thought of myself as intelligent, with a first-class honour's degree and my own company, so I wasn't very open-minded to ideas that challenged my acquired knowledge. And because of all that, I was only willing to do something if it made sense to me, not because someone suggested I do so.

This attitude of non-H.H.O.W.ness kept me from the spiritual journey during my two-year "dry drunk" period. It prevented me from experiencing a spiritual awakening, taking the spiritual solution away from me. It's an attitude I see regularly in people who want a solution for their addiction but aren't willing to approach the journey with H.H.O.W. It's heartbreaking to witness.

Bill Wilson gave addicts an ultimatum: *"To be doomed to an alcoholic death or to live on a spiritual basis."* Those are the options. Interestingly, it goes on to say these "are not always easy alternatives to face." I've seen people choose not to live spiritually and succumb to an alcoholic death as a direct result of lacking H.H.O.W. And there's one particular aspect of The 12-Step Programme, one word, that seems to reduce H.H.O.W. to zero for many: God.

The G-Word: A Stumbling Block

The short-form version of the 12-Steps contains 200 words, with "God" appearing four times. But that one word has the power to stop people in their tracks, blocking access to spirituality and potentially leading to their alcoholic deaths. To be clear, it's not the word itself but people's interpretation of it. Our culture of economic growth has all but eliminated the word God from our daily lives. It's slowly being taken out of schools. It doesn't appear as an integral part of higher education. It is vehemently rejected by the world of business. It's being eradicated from our daily lives. This is weird in some ways, as it wasn't that long ago that God was a much bigger part of the way we lived.

There are eight churches of various denominations within five hundred meters of where I'm sitting writing this book. If you're reading this in the UK, I wouldn't be surprised if you were within five hundred meters of a church yourself. There are some 38,500 churches, chapels, and religious meeting houses in the UK. There are 1,300 McDonald's outlets. Which has a bigger impact on the nature of our culture and the hearts and minds of our children?

The big problem that I've witnessed fellow addicts facing when confronted with the dilemma of a spiritual life or certain alcoholic death is that God is such an alien concept for them that they've not been able to choose a spiritual life. It's just too far removed from any experience they've ever had. It's so invisible in the cultural story we've bought into. The spiritual life seemed just too difficult to choose, so they feel there is no realistic option other than the road that leads to an alcoholic death.

It's a dramatic statement to make, but it's true. Our cultural beliefs and lack of H.H.O.W. to explore new beliefs will send some addicts to their death. Imagine, then, how many millions of others who may not face a life-or-death addiction but could free themselves from suffering exclude themselves from a spiritual awakening due to a lack of H.H.O.W. when it comes to the word God.

My own lack of H.H.O.W. almost stopped me from accessing the spiritual solution and experiencing an awakening. Fortunately, the second time around, I had a different version of God. I had the "Gift Of Desperation (G.O.D)." I was so desperate to stop drinking that I was willing to explore anything with H.H.O.W. That was the G.O.D. I initially had access to. That gave me enough motivation to make me contemplate the more conventional concept of God, as well as my personal relationship with that God in a H.H.O.W. manner. This is how my understanding of God was established.

A GOD OF YOUR UNDERSTANDING

As I've said before, I'm a spiritual person, not a religious one. While I admire those who have faith in a particular religion, and I recognise the benefits it brings them, I struggle to fully commit to any one belief system. I'm not very good at being told what to believe, and therein lies the problem: I lack faith in anything but myself, my own thinking, and my experiences. And that means I lack faith, full stop.

One of The Habits of Happiness and a core spiritual principle is The Habit of Surrender. Surrender is about turning our ego-based self-will and desire to control things over to a power greater than ourselves. To successfully surrender control, we must have faith that this "something else" will do a better job than our own self-will could. That's a tough one. Especially for people like me, who believed their achievements were solely due to their own clever thinking and hard work. Why would I need God now when I didn't before? How can I turn anything over to something I don't believe exists?

The Freedom to Choose a Personal God

Fortunately, being spiritual doesn't necessarily mean believing in any one religion or any particular concept of God. The 12-Step Programme brilliantly references a "God of your understanding," not anyone else's understanding, but your understanding and yours alone. You don't even have to call it God if you don't want to. This was a pivotal moment in my own spiritual journey because it immediately lowered my barriers, keeping my inner cynic at bay and allowing me to explore those first tentative steps without feeling hoodwinked into a religious cult.

I was told that "my God" could be anything. It could be any form of God referenced by any religion, one I make up, or any "Higher Power" that wasn't me or another living person. Some people searching for a God of their understanding choose a Christian God. Some choose Mother Nature. Others choose a deceased loved one. Yet others choose pure universal consciousness, the quantum field of possibility, a Group Of Drunks (the people at 12-Step meetings there to help) or even a general sense of moving in a Good, Orderly, Direction. All these notions of God work as a starting point. It doesn't matter what notion we land on. What matters is that we start to have faith in the notion we choose, and we open ourselves up to the possibility that this notion has access to knowledge and power that we don't, that it is on our side, and that we can start building a relationship with it.

As we build this relationship, we build faith. Even the smallest sliver of faith allows us to surrender small parts of our decision-making process to something beyond ourselves. We can take suggestions from a Group Of Drunks rather than follow our own path. We can act in a Good, Orderly, Direction instead of our usual bad habits. We can find solace in a loved one watching over us instead of worrying incessantly. We can trust that nature's forces will heal us from within rather than by self-medicating. This gentle introduction to faith in a Higher Power (or combination of Higher Powers) has allowed me to bring a God of my understanding into my life. As I contemplate that God and build my relationship with it, my faith in its ability to look after me and my affairs grows. And with those small surrenders come increasing levels of immense peace.

What exactly am I surrendering to and turning parts of my life over to? What exactly is God? Isn't this Higher Power or God just a mystical fantasy? On one level, perhaps it is. You can't prove God exists under a microscope, just as you can't prove consciousness or non-physical, non-local aspects of reality. Yet science has identified emergent properties of living systems and entanglement of sub-atomic particles, suggesting there may be a field, a power, an intelligence, or a creative force connecting everything in the universe together and driving life forward. Maybe that's God. Maybe that could be a God of your understanding. After all, you can't prove that this type of God doesn't exist.

For me, my God lies in this metaphysical territory, the mysterious, hidden world beyond space and time that keeps life moving forward. My faith is in a life-affirming, all-pervasive, regenerative power that connects every part of the universe through consciousness. I can't explain it in detail; I just have faith that it exists, that its nature is towards goodness and wholeness, and that it is knowable through experience. This needn't be your understanding of God, and that's fine. Nobody can tell you you're wrong. What matters is you invest time connecting with your individual God and building faith in Him, Her or It.

William James suggests three characteristics to look for when determining if you can trust your version of God. First, your God must create a universe that makes rational sense to you, with the various strands of life, the universe, and everything aligning in your mind. Second, your God must provide emotional solace, giving you hope and making you feel loved and cared for. Third, your God must make a practical difference; when you turn over control to your understanding of God, you should feel relief and faith that everything will be fine, noticing that things are working out for the best, even if not how you envisioned.

A Scientific Route to Nature and God

For those struggling with the word "God," especially the more rational and scientifically minded, the world of quantum mechanics offers an interesting avenue to explore. The "living systems field" draws on the idea that subatomic particles are more like waves or strings of energy than hard, physical particles of matter, suggesting that, at our core, we are all part of this continuous sea of energy. This is the living systems field. We can choose to view ourselves as a separate entity, disconnected from the field. Or we could choose to believe we are part of the interconnected whole, drawing power from the field just as a wave gets its power from the sea. This field of potentiality, or quantum vacuum as some call it, could be the power greater than you that you build faith in. This could be your God of understanding or part of it. It's a matter of perspective and being open to the possibility that there may be some truth in this.

While the scientific route to God can satisfy the left hemisphere's need for logical, rational proof and help the ego relinquish control, it can feel cold and impersonal, lacking the magic, poetry, beauty, metaphors, stories, and imagery that penetrate the right hemisphere. The intuitive, soulful, true self has direct access to life and yearns to experience it rather than analyse or describe it. When the science of the intellectual brain reconciles with the beauty of the intuitive soul, knowledge turns into knowing, and facts and feeling combine to create a deep understanding that catalyses and supports transformation. Even if you are sceptical of religion and mysticism, be open to investigating parts of the Bible, exploring Buddhism, or reading Sufi poetry. This is how your conception of God will evolve, how you'll build a relationship with it, and how you'll build faith and surrender more.

My Higher Power is hard to describe. It's more like a God of my non-understanding from that perspective. However, a phrase that comes to mind with increasing clarity as I consider my relationship to it is "learning to love the flow of life." The flow of life is the simplest expression of my Higher Power. It is both rational and emotional. It is something I cannot control. It is something I can completely surrender to. This notion of my God keeps me anchored to the present moment when life is actually happening.

Accepting the flow of life is good. Loving it is my goal. While I'm not always happy about the way things go, if I can learn to love the uncertainty and possibilities that open up with every passing moment, that's where I find the most freedom, peace, and fulfilment. And that's what faith in a God of your understanding can bring.

Believing Words and Acting "As If"

Words like "spirituality," "God," "soul," and "Higher Power" can be divisive and, in some ways, meaningless. You can't point to a soul, God, or higher power and define it or dissect it under a microscope. Yet these words have the power to transform lives if we are willing to act as if they exist. We can act as if a God of our understanding is guiding our lives, as if a benevolent Higher Power is looking after us, as if Mother Nature is filled with special designs for life, as if we are immortal souls, and as if spirituality holds the key. Through these acts of faith, we discover the truth: these words have the power to transform our lives and heal us. We come to believe in a God of our understanding, not because someone told us but because we have seen the real impact that believing has on us.

I didn't believe in spirituality or God, but I acted as if I did. I saw the impact and transformation. I felt differently. And now I know differently. I have no choice but to believe. Spirituality can work this way. Acting "as if" can lead to a positive change in feelings, which in turn can lead to a new set of beliefs. You don't need to believe from the start; you can act your way to feeling and thinking differently from the slimmest of notions. The pathway to transformation is often thought to be think, feel, act, but in my experience, it's often act, feel, think.

Using God for a Richer Life

In closing, I want to share a passage from William James' The Varieties of Religious Experience, quoting Professor Leuba, *"GOD IS NOT KNOWN, HE IS NOT UNDERSTOOD; HE IS USED"*, sometimes as a meat-purveyor, sometimes as moral support, sometimes as a friend, sometimes as an object of love. If he proves himself useful, the religious consciousness asks for no more than that. Does God really exist? How does he exist? What is he? There are so many irrelevant questions. Not God, but life, more life, a larger, richer, more satisfying life, is in the last analysis, the end of religion. The love of life, at any and every level of development, is the religious impulse."

These amazing words capture how I found my Higher Power. I used God, and it worked. I found life to be a larger, richer, more satisfying life. I followed a path that led to spiritual happiness, a happiness full of wholeness, freedom, joy, peace and fulfilment. And that's what we'll look at next: the nature of the fruits that spirituality bears and the gifts that make all the effort worthwhile.

SPIRITUAL HAPPINESS

I've mentioned a few times that the spiritual journey isn't necessarily an easy one. It's more of a challenging adventure than a stroll in the park. When confronted with this fact, my self-obsessed and lazy mind springs into action and asks, "What's the point of doing all this spiritual stuff then if it's so much effort?" It's a good question, and it's one I have asked myself many times. Why bother?

Before exploring what "doing spirituality" entails and delving into the pillars and the habits that make up the programme of action, it's worth examining what we're trying to achieve when we commit (and it is a commitment) to undertaking the spiritual solution. So, let's answer the "What's in it for me?" question.

The Spiritual Solution: Spiritual Happiness and a Path to Higher Consciousness

What was initially in it for me was a way to stop drinking. I committed to the solution because I wanted to break the addiction that was causing me so much pain. That was the big goal I was buying into, and I was desperate to achieve it. Years later, having experienced a spiritual awakening, I now see that what I was buying into was a way of living that made me feel good enough about life that I didn't need to drink. I didn't need to numb out the feelings of fear, guilt, and shame because I no longer had those feelings. I felt good. I felt happy. That's why we've been talking about focusing on happiness rather than wealth. But there's more depth to the benefits that the spiritual solution brings, which isn't quite captured in the word "happiness."

The spiritual solution isn't really a happiness solution. It's more of a consciousness solution. It's a way of opening up to higher levels of awareness that allow a whole array of positive states of being and emotions to reveal themselves. These states of being are our core human states of being: wholeness, freedom, peace, joy, and fulfilment. They arise because we are more aware of the inner human needs our soulful, intuitive, true selves yearn for. We are better equipped to meet those needs because we understand and are practicing The Five Habits of Happiness (which we'll explore in detail in Part 2 of the book). When we do so, we achieve those human states of being, and we experience what I call "spiritual happiness."

I use this term to allude to deeper, more subtle, and longer-lasting forms of happiness that arise when higher levels of consciousness are achieved. This is what the spiritual solution delivers. This is "what's in it for you." This is why you should bother.

Conditional vs. Spiritual Happiness

The happiness we typically think about usually comes from external sources. Getting a pay raise, buying new clothes, starting a new romantic relationship, consuming food, drink, and drugs, or receiving a compliment all make us happier. This is the sort of happiness we've come to understand and value as part of our culture of economic growth. This is the sort of happiness we've been trained to chase because most of these external sources of happiness cost us money to some degree or other and, therefore, help drive material economic growth.

This type of happiness is "conditional happiness" because it is related to and conditional upon external factors. We rely on people, places, situations, or things to make us happy.

The hallmarks of conditional happiness are:

1. External: It relies on something other than ourselves to generate happiness and is therefore out of our control. People, places, situations, or things can make us happy or unhappy.
2. Short-lived: It soon fades. It doesn't take long for the impact of a pay raise, new clothes, a new lover, food, drink, drugs, and compliments to wear off.
3. Craving: Conditional happiness never fully satisfies; you are left wanting more. Seeking this type of happiness can never satisfy the yearning for more that it generates. In this way, seeking conditional happiness can be addictive.

Five words associated with "conditional happiness" are pleasure, excitement, indulgence, pride, and sensuality.

On the other hand, "spiritual happiness" is associated with a different set of five words. They are associated with the five words we've defined as our core states of being: freedom, wholeness, peace, joy, and fulfilment. If those seem a bit boring to you, then you probably aren't ready for and don't need the spiritual solution. And that's a good thing to know. There's no point investing time and effort in a process that won't achieve anything but frustration.

In my twenties, I was more than happy chasing any and every type of conditional happiness I could. At that time, I didn't feel any form of pain and suffering as a result. I revelled in chasing down the pleasures, thrills, and excitement that the ego craves.

As I grew into my late thirties, I began to feel the discontent, emptiness, and futility that chasing this type of happiness brings. I came to a point in my life where freedom felt much more appealing than pleasure, and fulfilment felt much more important than excitement. That was the time when I wished I had known that a spiritual journey could help me. But it took another ten years of numbing and pain to get me to the point where a spiritual solution became a credible enough alternative for me to commit.

As I approached rock bottom, I remembered all I wanted in my life was peace. That was my driving motivation. How do I find peace when all I seem to experience is worry and anxiety? The spiritual solution helped me find peace. It also helped me find freedom, wholeness, joy, and fulfilment. All these other aspects of spiritual happiness have emerged and blossomed in my life as my journey has unfolded, and my awareness has increased.

The hallmarks of spiritual happiness are:

1. Internal: Spiritual happiness is unconditional; it doesn't rely on external factors. We can choose to be happy whether external factors are the way we would like them or not.
2. Enduring: There's a permanence to this sort of happiness. It may not have the peaks of pleasure, thrills, and excitement, but it does have a much more enduring quality.

3. Satisfaction: Spiritual happiness is content with what is and doesn't yearn for more. It's the sort of happiness that generates gratitude for what we have rather than dissatisfaction with what we don't.

So, if you want to know what the point of spirituality is and what's in it for you, I suggest it is the path to spiritual happiness. It is the path to the core states of being human that exist at higher levels of consciousness. It is the path to freedom, wholeness, peace, joy, and fulfilment.

If those sound like things you want more of in your life, then the time might be right for you to commit to the tricky process of spiritual transformation.

THE TRICKY PROCESS OF SPIRITUAL TRANSFORMATION

Discovering the Hero's Journey

I first came across Joseph Campbell's conception of the Hero's Journey as a teenager. An article suggested that most great film scripts follow a short list of storytelling archetypes, including the Hero's Journey, providing budding screenwriters with templates to increase their chances of writing a blockbuster.

Campbell summarised the journey as follows: "A hero ventures forth from the world of common day into a region of supernatural wonder: fabulous forces are there encountered, and a decisive victory is won: the hero comes back from this mysterious adventure with the power to bestow boons on his fellow man." Think of Star Wars and you'll be on the right lines. Luke Skywalker's adventure in the original movie perfectly exemplifies this archetype.

Campbell conceived this story structure to capture the notion that all ancient myths of awakening, initiation, and conversion follow a common overarching narrative, the monomyth. It immediately resonated with me, not as a storytelling device, but as an analogy for the journey of spiritual growth and awakening.

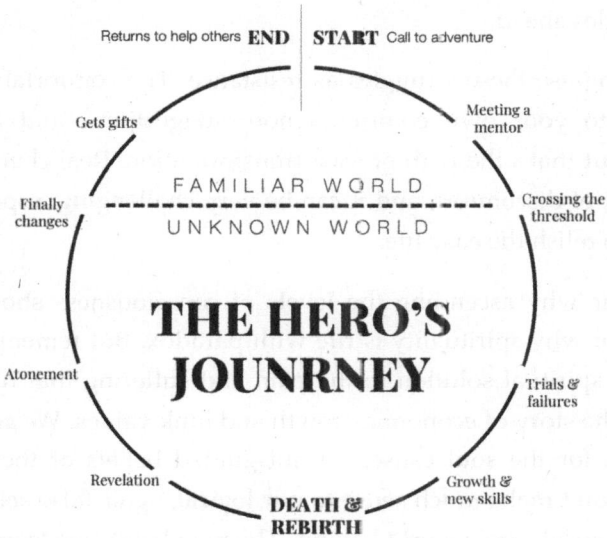

As you begin putting theory into practice, think of yourself as the mythical hero leaving the comfort of your known world to discover uncharted territories. Challenges lie ahead, but guides, mentors, and helpers will accompany you. Overcoming these challenges and learning pivotal lessons will transform you. You'll return to your known world as a changed person, with a deeper level of consciousness, able to share your newly gained wisdom with others. It's an exciting prospect.

The Death and Rebirth of the Self

However, a crucial point in the Hero's Journey is the bottom - the process of death and rebirth. Transformation isn't always easy. The hero must, metaphorically, die to be reborn, and this process can be uncomfortable, even painful. It requires hard work.

As you deepen your self-understanding and bring your true self to the fore, you'll need to let your false self die. This means casting off deeply held beliefs and beloved habits to see beyond them. Be prepared for the struggles ahead.

You'll recognise these struggles as resistance. The comfortable path is to listen to your own counsel, ignore suggestions, and avoid the "work." But that's the path of least transformation. Real change comes at the cost of discomfort, and it can be very challenging, especially for those who relish the easy life.

It's unclear why ascending the levels of consciousness should be so difficult, or why spirituality is rife with paradox. But remember, we're seeking a spiritual solution to the pain and suffering that result from living in the story of economic growth and junk values. We are seeking a solution for the soul caused by misguided beliefs of the ego. The process won't make much sense to our logical, egoic false selves as we leave its logical, egoic world behind. The new habits we learn will feel counter-intuitive to our normal way of thinking, but our soul will love them. As we journey forward, we will be hit by paradox after paradox after paradox.

- Spiritual happiness lives by the paradox that you need to know suffering to know joy.
- The Habit of Surrender lives by the paradox that you need to let go to win.
- The Habit of Awareness lives by the paradox that you need to unlearn to understand.
- The Habit of Discipline lives by the paradox that you need to die to live.
- The Habit of Connection lives by the paradox that you need to love to be loved.
- The Habit of Service lives by the paradox that you need to give it away to keep it.

None of this makes much sense to our rational, logical minds. But that's the point. We're not dealing with our rational, logical minds anymore. We're trying to get behind and beyond our rational, logical-thinking minds.

Richard Rohr points out in Jesus' Alternative Plan that the spiritual path of transformation isn't one of ascent or superiority. Quite the opposite, it's a descent, a humble search for who we are beneath the layers of ego-centric, culturally cultivated, and learned personality traits. It can be a demeaning process, as I discovered. I'm not as important, clever, attractive, or special as I thought I was. I wasn't thrilled to discover these facts. But it proved incredibly freeing once I accepted them.

The discomfort, struggle, and humiliation of transformation may not sound appealing, and that's perhaps the problem with many self-help books. Transformation is rarely a simple 30-day programme of easy steps. There is a necessary pain everyone must endure to benefit from the revelations on the other side. All recovered alcoholics, me included, have been through that pain. But I had the Gift of Desperation on my side. I had reached a painful rock bottom and felt I had no choice but to face the discomfort, struggle and humiliation head-on.

Ready for the Hero's Journey?

If you're serious about embarking on the transformational journey towards spiritual happiness, I would suggest you buckle yourself in and ready yourself for the ride. And by "ready yourself"; I mean, be prepared to acknowledge your current pain and allow yourself to feel the full range of emotions as part of the process.

If you're suffering now, I'm delighted for you. If you feel the full pain of living a discontented life, that's fantastic news. It means you'll not only benefit from the spiritual solution we're about to explore in detail, but you'll also have the Gift of Desperation to see you through the full hero's journey.

If you're ready to free yourself from pain and unhappiness and are willing to embrace the habits of spiritual happiness, let the adventure begin. It's time to surrender.

FOUR

THE HABIT OF SURRENDER
LETTING GO AND LETTING GOD

**Desired state of being and inner human need =
A sense of FREEDOM. Not feeling trapped
and confused.**

FOUR

THE HABIT OF SURRENDER

Necessary Pain

Surrendering seems like a negative place to start any journey. It conjures up images of losing, giving up, and failing. It is more like a disappointing conclusion to an unsuccessful attempt to achieve something rather than an inspiring start to a new adventure. We don't much like thinking about failing and surrendering, especially in business. It's not a strategy embraced by winners.

And that's exactly the problem. We're not very good at dealing with the uncomfortable feelings associated with failure, loss, and disappointment. We don't like acknowledging the pain and suffering that most of us feel as we deal with everyday life's failures, losses and disappointments. It's much easier to ignore these feelings and brush them under the carpet than it is to face them and deal with them. Much of the numbing behaviour we talked about in previous chapters is one way our culture has excelled in teaching us how to distract ourselves from these difficult feelings.

But the spiritual path demands that we do not distract ourselves or ignore or suppress or blot out these feelings. It demands that we embrace them. It seems that sitting with pain and suffering are the foundations of spiritual growth and that without pain and suffering, we don't really have the necessary raw materials to work with.

I've grappled with this unsettling truth as I've walked alongside people in various states of brokenness. Do "normal," well-adjusted folks need to endure a crisis to evolve spiritually? Is anguish an absolute requirement for enlightenment? While I believe everyone benefits from inner work, I can't deny that those dragged into the depths of despair often experience the most profound breakthroughs. Pain cracks us open in ways surface-level contentment simply cannot. The soul, it seems, loves to learn through adversity.

Thankfully, if it's suffering, we require this world dishes it up in spades. Beyond obvious "rock bottom" moments like addiction or grief, each day brings an array of opportunities to feel anxious, stressed, angry, lonely, and inadequate. Anything can trigger a free-fall into pain and confusion: divorce, death of a loved one, losing a job, retirement, serious injury, moving home, kids leaving home, becoming a parent, menopause and the famous midlife crisis. These are moments when we're primed for numbing. When free-flowing wine and never-ending takeaways seem like a good solution, but these are also the moments when we're primed for the spiritual solution. These are the moments when we have the raw material of suffering to work with. We have something the soul can grab hold of and transform into something beautiful.

It's interesting to note that the Chinese phrase for "crisis" is a compound of the symbols for "danger" and "opportunity." Maybe we all need a crisis of some sort to jolt us out of the hypnotic state we fall into when we let one day slip into the next in unconscious, habitual ignorance. I needed a crisis to stop me in my tracks and get me to examine myself and my life. As Brené Brown explains, "The

~~breakdown~~ spiritual awakening was tough, but I'm hard-headed. I guess the universe needed a way to get my attention."

However, the opportunity for pain and suffering exists even below major life events and crises. It's there in our everyday existence if we're willing to stop and notice it. As long as we don't run away from it and blot it out. Many spiritual traditions start with the premise that life is hard for the average human being. I've talked about the pressure our culture of economic growth has put on us and the pain and suffering that it's caused. But every culture in every period of history has had some sort of pressure that makes life difficult to bear. All the way back to the Garden of Eden, people have struggled with life. Those struggles express themselves as anxiety, stress, grief, anger, confusion, loneliness, depression and so on. We may think it's the pressure of modern life. It's actually the stress of all life. The stress of living. That's what the Buddha identified in the very first of his Four Noble Truths: life is suffering. Life is tough.

Surrendering starts by acknowledging this fact. It starts by admitting that we are suffering. That we are in pain. We are human. We would rather not be experiencing these difficult emotions but guess what? We are. And this is not a sign of weakness. We're not surrendering by giving in to the pain. We're not losing in the game of life. We're not giving up and letting it beat us. We're surrendering to the resistance and the denial that it even exists. We're letting go of the feeling that "I shouldn't be having these negative feelings." We're giving up the idea that we can ignore these feelings and numb them away, and everything will sort itself out. We're recognising and accepting these feelings and saying "okay" feelings. I know you're there. I know you want me to blot you out. But let's have an honest look at that. Maybe not this time.

We shouldn't be afraid of the suffering. We should only be afraid of not knowing how to deal with the suffering. And the first step is to acknowledge it's there. We need our suffering. It's a message. It's a message that something's not quite right with the way we're dealing with life. Surrendering allows us to listen to that message to better understand how we can move forward in the right way.

Acknowledging that pain and suffering exist in everyday life not only gives us the opportunity of transforming it, but also gives us the opportunity to recognise that life is so much richer because of it. It moves us out of the make-believe world of Barbie and into the glorious world of reality. William James makes this point by referencing a famous painting of Archangel Michael by Guido Reni. In the painting, the archangel is wielding his sword, and his foot is on Satan's neck. He is about to slay the Devil. However, James makes the point about how much richer the painting is for having the Devil in it. It brings forth Michael's energy, passion, courage, commitment, and strength. Qualities that wouldn't emerge if the Devil weren't there. The same is true for human existence. The Devil exists. He's in our painting, bringing us loss, grief, disappointments, failures, upsets, trials and tribulations to deal with. And life is so much richer with him there.

THE IMPORTANCE OF SURRENDER

As the adventure of the spiritual solution unfolds, we'll see that it is a journey of healing. I've used the disease of addiction as the focus of that healing because that's the specific type of healing I'm most familiar with. But in many ways, it is the disease of the split self at the heart of our addictions that we're trying to heal.

But we cannot heal what we do not acknowledge as a problem.

Acknowledging pain and suffering may be the first step in the surrendering process, but we then need to recognise that it's a problem we want to solve. Herein lies the first signs of the battle between our intuitive, soul-centred, deep, true selves and our thinking, ego-centred, surface false selves.

The Pain-Shame-Fear Cycle of Denial

In the midst of any addiction, no matter how big or small, we intuitively know we are suffering because of it. We know it is causing us pain. Our soul is pleading with us to transform this suffering. It is yearning for us to be healed. It wants to find peace. And deep down, we know that change is required. And yet, our ego resists.

First, it floods us with shame. The shame that we've got ourselves into this situation. That we're defective in some way because of this addiction and these destructive feelings. Shame is that "intensely painful feeling or experience of believing that we are flawed and therefore not worthy of love and belonging" (Source: Brené Brown, The Gifts of Imperfection). We are not worthy of being helped or healed. It's our own flaw and our own fault.

And after the shame comes the fear. Fear of change and what that would mean. Fear of a life without our much loved and addictive form of numbing. Fear of losing our comfort blanket. And that is scary. There's also the fear of what people would say if we did admit our suffering. What would they say if they knew the truth? Would they still like me? Would they think I was weak if I asked for help? What would they say if I changed my lifestyle?

This is the ego-centred cycle of thinking that keeps us in addiction. Pain. Shame. Fear. Pain. Shame. Fear. It's the root cause of our denial. The ego wants to deny the problem because that means it can keep hold of the addiction. If we deny we have a problem, we keep the problem. If we keep the problem, we keep the pain. Wanting to break the cycle and solve the problem is the second point of surrender. This is the point where we give up the responsibility of trying to work it all out for ourselves; we let go of our hold of the problem, and we resign the care of our destiny to something other than our whirring, intellectual brain.

Surrendering to our soul-centred, deep, true self is the start of the healing process. And this surrender comes in the form of opening up and being vulnerable. Firstly, to ourselves. To our true selves. We become H.H.O.W. Humble. Honest. Open-minded. Willing. Becoming H.H.O.W. with ourselves opens up a crack in the cycle of ego-centred thinking. It's the crack through which the light of our true self enters our mind in the form of courage, faith and hope. The courage, faith, and hope to concede that the problem can only be solved by someone or something other than our own logical thinking. The courage, faith, and hope to open up and be vulnerable to ask other people for help. The courage, faith, and hope to allow our higher power to pull us forward.

This type of surrendering is the single most important step in opening the door to the spiritual solution. Surrendering is at the heart of Steps 1, 2, and 3 in The 12-Step Programme. Surrendering opens up the opportunity to be healed. It allows us to recognise that maybe, just maybe, it's our thinking, false self-mind that is keeping us in pain. And maybe, just maybe, our soul-centred, true self can access the power to break free.

THE MANY FACES OF SURRENDER

We've talked about surrender as the very first step in the spiritual journey, acknowledging our pain and opening up to a solution. But surrendering isn't a one-time event that simply marks the start of the journey. It's an integral part of the entire journey, a skill and a habit that helps keep us humble, teachable and on the spiritual path.

Step 3 in The 12-Step Programme states, "We made a decision to turn our will and our lives over to the care of God as we understood Him." That's one almighty surrender—relinquishing our entire lives and all our will to a Higher Power we've only just been introduced to and hardly know.

I remember feeling very uncomfortable about even considering this idea. The good news is that we get a lifetime to practice this big, almighty surrender. And we're helped by the fact that just as there are different ways of talking about surrendering (letting go of something, turning something over, relinquishing power, etc.), there are also varying types and degrees of surrender.

I've found that practicing these different forms of surrender in different areas of life at different points of the journey gradually increases the overall level of surrender I'm willing to concede to. Small surrenders, every now and then, lead to bigger surrenders on a more regular basis. That's when surrender becomes a habit.

Let's look at some concrete examples of these different types of surrender in action.

1. Acceptance: Surrendering to the Flow of Life

At the most basic level, surrender is the simple but profound act of yielding rather than opposing the natural flow of life. Life unfolds as it will, and there is very little we can do to stop, slow down or speed up the passage of time or alter the fundamental nature of life. It is what it is.

The word most commonly associated with this form of surrender is acceptance. In the opening line of the Serenity Prayer, we ask for "the serenity to accept the things we cannot change." Understanding and appreciating that there is very little we can change means we have to accept much of what life throws our way. If we are able to surrender to all those undeniably unchangeable things, we will feel more serene, peaceful and free as a result.

In essence, this type of surrender is, as all types of surrender are, giving up the habit of struggling and fighting. It is the practice of accepting everything that comes our way, whether it fits our ideas and preferences or not. This is the path to freedom.

2. Releasing the Illusion of Control

I have an undeniable urge to control things. I like to have a plan, and I like everybody and everything to stick to it. It's how I try to control what's going to happen in the future. I sense that this desire for control is at the heart of the perfectionism that I, and many others, hold onto as a virtue.

Unfortunately, life doesn't care much for my perfectionism or my plans. It isn't bothered if things turn out exactly how I want them to. Life thrives on uncertainty, change, diversity, mystery, and imperfection. Learning to let go of these plans, this desire to control and cling to certainty is learning that we can never truly control or hold onto anything forever. This is a fact of life, a reality we must accept.

I'm especially prone to trying to control people, to get them to do things exactly the way I think they should be done. My natural instinct (or maybe my lifelong training) tells me that things will work out better for me and them if I get involved and tell them exactly what to do and how to do it. I think I know better than they do.

The trouble is, I don't. I can't know what's going on in other people's minds, hearts and lives. They need to work things out for themselves. I can give helpful advice if they find it useful, but trying to control people's behaviour only creates frustration and resentment for everyone involved.

By practicing this form of surrender, letting people get on with their own lives, I have found that situations and relationships are much better without my insistence on them being done my way. It's interesting to feel the resistance to letting go of control. What we're really holding onto is fear. We have so much fear of not being in control, of not being able to hold on to the things we love.

Surrendering is letting go of this fear.

The truth is, we are never really in control anyway - life is. And we never truly own anything outright, either. When life is over, we can't take anything with us.

Contemplate these two facts, surrender to the illusion of control and certainty, and feel a sense of freedom and peace slowly arise. In fact, consider this additional truth: embracing uncertainty is the same as embracing freedom and opportunity. Isn't that a great way to think about an uncertain future? How exciting!

3. Releasing Attachment: The Root of Suffering

The Buddha suggested in the first noble truth that life is suffering. In the second noble truth, he proposed that this suffering is caused by our craving and attachment to worldly desires. And the third noble truth is that we can reduce our suffering by reducing our attachments.

As a recovered addict, I know first-hand how debilitating attachment and craving can be. I have experienced no suffering quite as acute as that unquenchable need to drink alcohol during those times of drying out. It's horrible.

It's the same suffering we face every day when we crave things we don't have. It may not be on the same scale as withdrawal symptoms, but that clinging to desire has its own price. Think about a time when you desperately wanted a pay raise because you felt you deserved it. Or when you wanted a new car because your brother-in-law got one. Or you wanted a new dress because you saw a particularly nice one in an ad. These cravings and desires cause us suffering.

They may not seem like particularly painful events in isolation, but they should be considered in totality. Consider why you work so hard, why you live where you live, why you own the car you have, why you spend so much on clothes, why you go out to the places you do, why you watch so much TV, why you eat as much as you do.

All this activity and consumption are driven by an underlying "unsatisfactoriness" with life. We experience suffering as a general discontentment with the way things are, an uneasiness with just being ourselves, doing nothing, and accepting life as it is.

In our culture of economic growth and junk values, we've become attached to the idea of not just having enough money to get by but also having enough money to satisfy virtually all our worldly desires. If you want to feel the suffering of attachment, consider moving to a job that pays 25% of what you currently earn. In fact, don't just consider it - do it. My advice is to take the hit of a drastic pay cut, feel the pain of moving to a smaller home, switching to a smaller car, not going on holiday, spending less on clothes, not going out as much, watching less TV, eating less. Now, that's a way to taste true freedom.

Okay, I'm not advising that you stop work and risk homelessness. I want you to recognise the feeling you had if you took that thought seriously. Think how painful it would be to sell the family home. Move to a much smaller house in a less desirable part of the world. Get rid of your car. Not be able to go out. Think about all the consequences of not having the amount of money you're used to. That uncomfortable feeling is the suffering caused by your attachment to the lifestyle you've grown accustomed to.

Similarly, the attachment of wanting an even better lifestyle than the one we currently have is driven by a craving for more than we have. It's a craving at the heart of our culture of economic growth. It keeps the economy growing but also keeps the nation in misery, in a constant state of unsatisfactoriness. It's an underlying suffering that plagues the modern world.

This isn't to say that working is bad or that money, houses, cars, holidays, clothes, going out, or food are bad. They are neutral. They don't cause suffering. We cause suffering by being attached to them, wanting more of them, clinging to them, and not wanting to lose them. Learning to let go of these cravings and learning the art of detachment is another key type of surrendering.

4. Letting Go of Outcomes

Although letting go of outcomes is probably just another form of surrendering control or attachment, I think it's worth highlighting as a distinct form of surrender, as it will crop up later as we discuss service and purpose.

This type of surrender relates to doing something in order to achieve a specific outcome. The attachment is to the desired result of an activity. This leads to expectations and, if they aren't met, suffering.

For example, if I invest money in a property, knowing full well that property prices go up and down, but I'm attached to the expectation that it will deliver a certain return on my investment, I will be bitterly disappointed if the property market flops.

Or if I help a neighbour and expect him to return the favour, and he doesn't, again, I'll be disappointed. It's often said that expectations are resentments waiting to happen. Learning to let go of desired outcomes helps free us from future resentments.

5. Surrendering to the Present Moment

For me, this is the most useful and important Habit of Surrender to remember and practice. Surrendering to the moment, appreciating that life can only happen and be experienced in this very moment, not in the past or the future, is a surefire way to find freedom.

Eckhart Tolle's classic book The Power of Now is one of the bestselling spiritual titles on Amazon and is frequently recommended as a must-read. The idea is simple: be as present as possible and live in this moment because "the Now" is all we have.

This principle is at the heart of the 12-Step movement's famous clarion call of "one day at a time." Surrendering to the moment, being fully aware of and connected to what is happening right now, sounds easy, but it's a habit that takes time to master.

That's because we, or rather our ego-centred thinking minds, are addicted to dwelling on the past and worrying about the future—two time periods that don't exist and that we certainly can't access. The problem with constantly thinking about the past and future is that it causes us, you guessed it, suffering.

When we dwell on the past, we tend to do so with feelings of regret, resentment, grief, sadness, bitterness and lack of forgiveness. When we ruminate on the future, we tend to do so with worry, fear, anxiety, stress, and anticipation. All these feelings move us away from peace and serenity and towards those feelings of unsatisfactoriness.

Letting the stories of the past and future go, knowing that they aren't real, they don't exist, allows us to live in the present moment, which is usually, if not always, far more pleasant than our imaginings of the past or future. As Mark Twain wisely observed, "I've lived through some terrible things in my life, some of which actually happened."

6. Befriending Our Emotions

As with attachments, emotions are neither good nor bad. They just are. However, as a result of our culture of economic growth and junk values, we haven't been very good at learning how to deal with emotions in a healthy way. I certainly wasn't. My go-to response to most uncomfortable emotions was to suppress them, block them out or numb them. I suspect most people do the same.

In general, when we're not doing that, we tend to hold onto negative feelings more than we need to while attempting to cling to our positive feelings much more than we can. The key lesson here is to learn how to feel our feelings, to learn how to let the emotions be in the moments they arise, to learn that it's okay to feel bad, to surrender to those feelings and let them flow through our body.

Emotions are simply our body's way of dealing with thoughts and external stimuli. Being aware of these feelings and getting comfortable with them simply being there allows them to run their natural course without us getting wrapped up in worry about them. We avoid a short-lived physical emotion turning into a longer-term mental obsession.

I have found the practice of surrendering to my emotions to be the most practical way to surrender overall. When I don't seem to be able to surrender to life, or I can't let go of control or attachments, or I can't surrender to the now, surrendering to the resulting negative emotions seems to be my faithful backup plan.

When I look inside to try to discern what's going on and why I'm finding it hard to let go, there's usually an uncomfortable emotion lurking in there that's keeping me clinging to my view of life, my control, my attachment, my desired outcome, or my past or future. And in my case, that uncomfortable emotion is usually fear.

Learning to feel fear and let it pass has been a Godsend—literally. Surrendering to our emotions, befriending and accepting them, is a powerful way to practice the overarching spiritual Habit of Surrender. It gradually frees us from the suffering and struggle of fighting against the reality of the present moment.

WHY IS SURRENDERING SO DIFFICULT?

The honest answer is that very few people like change. And nobody wants to be transformed. As W.H. Auden wryly observed, "We would rather be ruined than changed. We would rather die in our dread than climb the cross of the present and let our illusions die." That's because to be transformed is to die--or at least, to let our ego and self-image die. To let go of the carefully constructed story we tell ourselves about who we are and how we succeed in life.

The process of surrender means admitting that the intellectual, self-reliant approach to life we hold in such reverence has utterly failed us. It means opening ourselves up to the notion that our old ideas are dead and that we can't figure it out on our own. In today's society, which is obsessed with success and achievement, that hardly sounds like a recipe for happiness.

Yet the path to true spiritual contentment is all about surrendering. It's about letting go of our preconceived notions and allowing a Higher Power--a God of our own understanding--to take the lead. It's about becoming "like metal poured into a mould, or a canvas waiting for the brush, or marble under the sculptor's hand," as the spiritual writer Jean-Pierre de Caussade puts it.

Once we find the willingness to release our white-knuckled grip on all the carefully laid plans and schemes we've concocted to guide our daily lives, we open ourselves to a whole new way of being guided. Our rigid agendas are gradually replaced by a growing trust in moment-by-moment inner guidance from our intuition, our deeper knowing, our Higher Power.

This guidance arises and strengthens as we progress on our spiritual adventure and diligently work on all five of the spiritual habits. Clinging to our illusion of control and mapping out detailed plans may feel comfortingly natural, but it's a false sense of security. Relinquishing those delusional plans is sure to trigger some short-term anxiety. But the long-term rewards are immense - a newfound freedom to embrace and a chance to savour the inherent uncertainty of reality.

THE PROCESS OF SURRENDER

So, how do we take that first monumental leap into surrender? What do we need to do to make that foundational surrender that underpins transformation? I believe it's a fourfold process:

1. Acknowledge your pain.
2. Commit to the change you want to see.
3. Adopt a Humble, Honest, Open-minded, and Willing (H.H.O.W.) attitude.
4. Submit to the Hero's Journey and plunge into the spiritual solution.

This requires an enormous leap of faith onto a path you don't yet understand, probably don't like, and possibly don't even want to walk. If you truly desire to heal and reap the benefits of spiritual happiness, it's a journey you simply have to embark on.

Later in the book, in the Cultivating the Habits: A Spiritual Programme of Action section, I suggest re-imagining your identity as someone who prioritises spiritual happiness and writing a description down on an index card. If you're the type of person who is committed to bringing spiritual happiness into their life, then you're the type of person who is willing to surrender.

My advice? Suck it up and get over yourself. It took me three long years of stubborn resistance before I finally caved in and submitted to the journey. I hope you're a quicker learner than I was.

Take a deep breath, close your eyes, and surrender.

You won't regret it.

Micro-Moments of Surrender

Once you've taken that first courageous plunge, you'll quickly find that the journey presents daily, even hourly, opportunities for surrender. Start tuning into your inner state of being. Notice how you're feeling at any given moment. Tense? Anxious? Simply out of sorts?

These are all openings to practice letting go. Can you surrender to the natural flow of life? Can you release your white-knuckled need for control? Can you dial down your craving for certainty and instead embrace the exciting possibilities that uncertainty brings? Can you bring yourself into this very moment? Stop thinking about the future. Stop thinking about the past. Surrender to the now and focus on what's happening this minute.

Watch out for the sneaky tendency towards perfectionism. See if you can detach from obsessive material cravings and instead practice gratitude for what you already have. Can you fully immerse yourself in the present activity without fretting about the outcome?

If you're still feeling tense, anxious or unsettled, try simply letting go of those uncomfortable feelings themselves. I've found David R. Hawkins' "letting go" technique incredibly helpful. He explains:

"Letting go involves being aware of a feeling, letting it come up, staying with it, and letting it run its course without wanting to make it different or do anything about it. It means simply to let the feeling be there and to focus on letting out the energy behind it. The first step is allowing yourself to have the feeling without resisting it, venting it, fearing it, condemning it, or moralising it. It means to drop judgment and to see that it is just a feeling. The technique is to be with the feeling and surrender all efforts to modify it in any way. Let go of wanting to resist the feeling. It is resistance that keeps the feeling going. When you give up resisting or trying to modify the feeling, it will shift to the next feeling and be accompanied by a lighter sensation. A feeling that is not resisted will disappear as the energy behind it dissipates."

In my experience, uncomfortable emotions dealt with in this gentle way can often be released and transformed in mere minutes. The key is to anchor yourself in the present moment - resist the temptation to replay the past or catastrophize about the future. Then, the negative feeling will dissipate.

Feel Your Feelings and Let Them Pass

Remember, feelings are just feelings. In early recovery, I would often get overwhelmed by crushing waves of guilt and shame about my drinking or consumed by extreme anxiety about an uncertain future. At times, these emotions felt suffocating, but I had to keep reminding myself that no one ever died from a feeling.

A wise mentor advised me to simply sit with the discomfort and trust that "this too shall pass." And while riding out the emotional storm, it never hurts to keep the Serenity Prayer on repeat, a potent reminder to surrender and radically accept life on life's terms:

> *"God, grant me the serenity to accept the things I cannot change, the courage to change the things I can, and the wisdom to know the difference."*

Sure enough, the acute feelings always passed. They still do. Over and over, I'm practicing The Habit of Surrender, relinquishing my illusion of control and trusting in a power greater than myself. It's not always comfortable, and I certainly don't have it mastered. But when I manage to let go, miraculous things tend to happen. Surrender, as it turns out, is the gateway to true serenity and freedom.

FIVE

THE HABIT OF AWARENESS
RE-EDUCATING AND TAMING THE EGO

**Desired state of being and inner human need =
A sense of WHOLENESS. Not feeling out
of sync and misaligned.**

FIVE

THE HABIT OF AWARENESS

WAKING UP TO REALITY

In his book The Myth of Normal, Gabor Maté concludes, "It all starts with waking up: waking up to what is real and authentic in and around us." It is such a simple yet insightful observation, brimming with profound implications.

It all starts with waking up.

To what is real and authentic.

In and around us.

I suspect I wouldn't have fully appreciated the richness of this beguilingly simple insight a few years ago precisely because I hadn't yet woken up. I was living in a trance, completely unaware that the world I inhabited was essentially an illusion. With misguided confidence, I thought I knew everything and understood precisely what was real and what wasn't. Armed with this distorted version of reality, I set out to "succeed" in it. How wrong I was! As Bill Wilson so aptly put it, I had become a "victim of the delusion that he can wrest satisfaction and happiness out of this world if he only manages well." Well, I couldn't. I didn't manage well at all. I failed. Miserably.

It's very likely that you are failing miserably too.

That might be inaccurate. Maybe you are shining success. But take note of the reaction you had when I suggested you might be failing miserably. How did you immediately feel when you read that sentence? Did you feel attacked? Did you get defensive? "How dare he assume that I'm failing miserably!" Bear that feeling in mind for a moment. You might not like the fact that I suggest you're failing miserably. Or to be more accurate, your ego might not like the fact that I suggest you're failing miserably. But I say that because the sad truth is that many people living on this planet today are failing miserably. And I suspect you might be one of them. And I say that because of the reality of the way we, as a human race, are going about living our lives. I believe that the way we are building communities, cities, nations, and economies using social norms, values, educational systems, businesses, and sometimes even religions is based on a version of life that isn't real or authentic.

The "Normal" Myth

This leads us to the "myth" Gabor Maté alludes to in his book. It's the myth that the way the typical modern person lives their life - going to work in their typical 9 to 5 job, earning money to spend in typical ways, sending their kids down the typical educational path - is based on reality. It isn't. We only think it is because it's all we see. We only see the way things are done around us and presume it is the "normal" way of doing things. If "normal" seems to be working for us, why would we question it?

We wouldn't.

But then there comes a time when "normal" breaks us. Life breaks down enough to stop us in our tracks and forces us to confront the danger of what normal is doing to us while offering the opportunity to look into it. Crisis opens up a chance to wake up and become more aware of what's really going on for us, to fully discover what is real and authentic, inside and around us. Crisis gives us the opportunity to become more aware.

The Cornerstone of Spirituality: Awareness

Awareness lies at the heart of all spiritual traditions. It is the lifelong practice of seeking truth, the foundation of our natural human tendency to grow to ever higher levels of consciousness. It is the cornerstone of the spiritual solution and a key habit to finding spiritual happiness.

For most people experiencing a crisis, and certainly for me as a confused addict in the early stages of recovery, the first inklings of awareness kick in once there's been that initial big surrender. Once we've acknowledged the pain, once we've adopted an H.H.O.W. attitude (Honesty, Humility, Open-mindedness, Willingness) and fallen into the spiritual solution, we experience awareness arising in the form of a natural yet powerful curiosity to find answers to some big, seemingly unfathomable questions.

What is going on in my life? Why did this happen to me? Why did I act that way? What was I trying to achieve? How am I going to cope now? What am I going to do? Who am I? How do I make sense of all this? Will I ever be happy again?

If you're going through or have been through a crisis, you'll have your own set of perplexing questions piquing your curiosity.

Our curiosity about life and these arising questions mark the start of a lifelong journey into seeking truth. We begin investigating and interrogating the stories that are in and around us - the story of me, my purpose and feelings, my relationships and communities, the economy and the way work works, life, the universe, and everything, along with the many other stories that make up our lives.

The truth of these stories becomes clearer and more profound the more we investigate with an H.H.O.W. attitude. The clouds and haziness fall away the further our vision is aimed towards timelessness, the wider our perspective is set without boundaries, and the deeper within we are prepared to go. Further vision, wider perspective, deeper within - that's how awareness is nurtured as part of the personal journey to seek your truth. That's how awareness becomes a habit.

The Truth We Seek

Awareness isn't just about understanding facts with our thinking minds. More importantly, it's about recognising the truth deep within our intuitive hearts. In the spiritual realm, truth has to be experienced in the body rather than simply rationalised in the mind. That's why it's incredibly hard to communicate. Even if I could find the words to accurately describe the reality of life as I see it, there's a strong probability that you wouldn't believe me. Firstly, because it's my interpretation of the truth I feel within me. I can't interpret what you may feel within you. Secondly, it is because you didn't discover it for yourself. When it comes to truth-seeking, it's very much like eating - no one can eat your food for you, and only you know when you feel nourished. In that sense, feeling is believing.

So, what is this reality we're on the lookout for? What truth are we trying to "feel"? It all sounds a bit confusing and cryptic, doesn't it?

We're searching for the truth about "us"—the truth about who we are as individual human beings living on this spinning rock called planet Earth, floating around in space. And that truth can be found by each and every one of us. It's lodged deep inside the confines of our soul, usually hidden by our busy, distracted minds. But it's there to be unearthed. It's trapped deep inside our bodies, hidden in our closed hearts, waiting to be released.

The Four Pillars of Perennial Wisdom

This truth is sometimes called perennial wisdom—a profound set of insights into the nature of life and love, health and happiness, suffering and salvation. It's called perennial because it has been developed over thousands of years, based on direct insights from some of the world's most exceptional spiritual leaders, and has endured for centuries. It is the common essence of all the great religions and represents a treasure trove of accumulated wisdom.

In his book Essential Spirituality, Roger Welsh suggests that this truth, this perennial wisdom, can be captured in four central observations:

1. The Dual Nature of Reality

According to perennial wisdom that has echoed through the ages, reality is composed of two distinct realms. The first is the material realm—the world of physical objects and phenomena that we perceive through our senses and investigate through the lens of science. This is the realm of the tangible, the measurable, and the observable.

But beneath this surface layer lies a deeper, more subtle realm: the spiritual realm. This is the domain of consciousness, the mind, and the spirit—the intangible essence that underlies and animates the physical world. Perennial wisdom suggests that this spiritual realm is not merely a passive backdrop but rather the very source and foundation of all that exists in the material realm. It is the timeless, infinite, and eternal ground of being from which all else arises.

2.   *The Human Experience: Bridging Two Realms*

As human beings, we find ourselves in a unique position, straddling these two realms of existence. On one hand, we are undeniably physical creatures, possessing bodies that allow us to interact with and navigate the material world. We are equipped with sensory faculties and thinking minds that endeavour to comprehend and make sense of our surroundings.

Yet, at the core of our being, there is said to be something more – a centre of pure consciousness, a transcendent awareness that connects us to the very fabric of the spiritual realm. This is our true self, the Divine spark within us that is intimately linked to the sacred ground of existence.

The challenge we face is that our thinking minds, our "false selves," are often too preoccupied with the demands and desires of our physical existence to recognise this deeper spiritual reality. The false self, driven by the survival instincts of the body, constantly seeks pleasure and avoids pain, all the while reinforcing the illusion of a separate, isolated identity. It is this sense of separation that keeps us from fully embracing and experiencing the spiritual realm, leading to unnecessary suffering and discontent.

3.   *Discovering the Truth Within*

For many of us, the idea that the person we "know" and love is "false" and we've been living in some sort of an illusion comes as a radical shock. We don't buy into that idea at all. Fortunately, the perennial wisdom offers a compelling invitation: we need not merely accept these ideas as a matter of faith or belief. Rather, we have the capacity to directly experience and validate the truth for ourselves. By turning inward and exploring the depths of our own consciousness, we can begin to uncover and connect with our true spiritual nature.

This process of self-discovery and realisation is one of quiet introspection and soul-nurturing. It involves creating space in our lives for contemplation, meditation, and inner exploration. As we learn to observe and disengage from the incessant chatter of the false self, we open ourselves to the possibility of encountering the divine spark within.

4.   The Highest Aspiration

The perennial wisdom goes on to assert that the realisation of our true spiritual nature is the ultimate goal and highest aspiration of human existence. It suggests that all other pursuits and achievements in the material realm pale in comparison to the profound fulfilment and ecstatic joy that comes from aligning ourselves with the spiritual realm.

This sentiment is echoed by the great sages and mystics from diverse spiritual and religious traditions throughout history. They consistently point to the realisation of our inherent spiritual nature as the key to unlocking genuine happiness, peace, and freedom. It is a goal that transcends the confines of the individual self, offering benefits not only to the seeker but to all of humanity.

By engaging with these ideas and embarking on the path of self-discovery, we open ourselves to the potential for profound personal transformation and a greater sense of connection to the sacred ground of existence. Ultimately, the perennial wisdom encourages us to embark on a journey of inner exploration, to question our assumptions, and to seek direct experience of the spiritual realm that is said to be the very essence of our being.

I suppose it could be said that the whole spiritual journey is a quest to confirm these four pillars of perennial wisdom for ourselves and experience the benefits detailed in point four. That's the task at hand - at least, that's how I see it. It's not a task that can be completed in a matter of days or weeks. It's a lifelong endeavour. I've been at it for over five years and have hardly scratched the surface. However, I've experienced enough truth to satisfy myself that the claims of perennial wisdom are absolutely true. That's why I'm committed to the journey.

The habit we're currently exploring as part of the journey is awareness. This is the habit that will allow us to see, intellectually, intuitively and experientially, who we actually are and the fact that we are both physical and spiritual beings. We come to understand that we have physical bodies that can sense the material world around us, guided by our thinking minds. At the same time, we have a centre of pure consciousness and transcendent awareness that recognises our own Divine spark and senses the sacred ground to which it is connected. I've called these two parts of our human existence the false self and the true self. The Habit of Awareness allows us to recognise these two aspects of "self" and appreciate how our true self is more closely aligned with reality. That process takes time to sink in. It doesn't happen overnight. So, where do we begin? How do we start nurturing the habit of awareness?

LET'S START WITH OUR STORY

In rehab, one of the first exercises I was asked to complete was to write my life story—a "warts and all" assessment of my life to date, including both apparent successes and all too obvious blunders. It was an exercise in brutal honesty. For the first time in my life, at the age of forty-nine, in a surrendered and vulnerable state, I wrote down in vivid detail the most significant phases of my life and how I felt about them. I delved into the pain I felt, the mistakes I made, the regret and shame I harboured, and the fears and secrets I kept. Although difficult to write at times, it felt like a necessary part of the healing process—a crucial step in recognising the problems I had created for myself and others, based on a story of who I thought I should be to succeed in our culture of economic growth.

The Realisation: An Identity Built on External Factors

Although this truth didn't dawn on me immediately, I now see it clearly: all the pain and suffering I experienced stemmed from creating an identity for myself that wasn't truly me. I was trying to be somebody—somebody successful, liked, and respected. I gauged my progress based on feedback from other somebodies—teachers, parents, friends, and bosses, all influenced by our culture.

The somebody I created was moulded almost exclusively by external factors. While I had some innate drives and personality traits, I often suppressed my own intuitions in favour of suggestions made by others. Remember that seventeen-year-old would-be goth band member? The life story I wrote exposed a reality I hadn't previously been aware of, years of suppression led to unsatisfactoriness, which eventually led to numbing uncomfortable feelings, pain, and addiction.

I now see that the urge and drive to create a successful somebody is a primary function of the false self. This false self-part of our existence is desperate to create a personality and ego that will thrive in the material world—a world constructed entirely by external influences, with little regard for what's going on internally.

This is one of the biggest challenges and most damaging aspects of modern culture. We pride ourselves on our meritocracy, telling our children they can be anyone they want to be if they put their minds to it, stay dedicated, and work hard. They could make a real success of life. They could be somebody. But this success is defined almost exclusively by external factors—being somebody as defined by our culture of economic growth. We've created an education system and way of working that trains and rewards us to succeed at being somebody, even if it's not ourselves. The pressure we put on ourselves to be somebody is crushing. It creates pain. It causes the sort of breakdown I suffered.

We live in a world dominated by the false self's drive for material success—a world dominated by self-centred personalities and egos. It would be easy to blame the false self for all my ills to conclude that the false self is bad and the true self is good. But that would undermine the subtlety and nuance of the spiritual journey. Remember Guido Reni's painting of Archangel Michael and the Devil—the painting is all the richer for Satan's presence. It's part of the story. The same is true for our false self. We can't deny its existence, and our life is richer for it. We just need to recognise its presence and know its limitations.

A Searching and Fearless Moral Inventory

In The 12-Step Programme, Step 4 urges addicts to make a searching and fearless moral inventory of themselves. This process helps people objectively examine their behaviour and conduct over the years, building awareness of false self-drives and the tendency to act in self-centred ways that benefit us even if those ways hurt others. Step 5 makes these behaviours and character defects all too obvious when confessed aloud.

Digging into our story, identifying our pain and the harm we've caused others in the name of building a successful somebody, is a humbling experience. It's part of the process of deflating the ego. But this process isn't just about airing dirty laundry to make us feel bad. It's about learning who we are, going inward, and building deep self-awareness as objectively as possible without the barriers and facades we normally create to protect our fragile ego. This gives us three great assets.

1.   Owning Our Story: The Path to Shame Resilience

Firstly, compiling our warts-and-all life story allows us to take ownership of our story. Brené Brown, a self-declared shame researcher, talks about owning our story as part of dealing with the shame we may feel. It's a way of building shame resilience. "Admitting our perceived weaknesses and admitting them is owning our own story and not trying to fit in or pretend to be someone we're not. Owning our story is being able to bring our true self out of the closet for ourselves and others to meet and love." No more pretending. No more trying to be somebody. What a relief that is!

Owning our story also allows us to share it and empathise with and help others who are suffering as we suffered. This act of sharing our painful pasts is at the heart of the 12-Step Recovery Process. No one can reach an addict lost in the madness of their addiction like another addict who has been there and come out the other side. Owning and sharing the stories our false self might want to conceal to help others is the cornerstone of the recovery movement. It's the magic that heals everyone. It helped me get sober. It helps me stay sober. It helps me get other people sober. It's helping me write this book. Owning and sharing our painful past is healing. It makes us whole.

2.   Building Self-Awareness: A Daily Practice

Secondly, creating a detailed, thorough, honest review of our life story helps build the skill of objective self-awareness. With this skill, we're better equipped to review our behaviour and actions on a regular basis. Step 10 of The 12-Step Programme, one of the "maintenance steps," suggests completing an objective review daily or even several times during the day. Being able to look at our everyday behaviours not only allows us to rectify them, to make amends or apologise but also makes us more comfortable with the fact that we're not perfect. We're not saints, as Bill Wilson said of recovering addicts. The spiritual journey is one of progression, getting incrementally better. It's not one of perfection.

With self-awareness comes self-acceptance—a trait many people struggle with. Being comfortable in our own skin, when it usually feels more comfortable trying to fit into the skin of the somebody we'd rather be, is a skill we need to nurture. The more self-accepting we are, the more we see that everything within us, no matter how negative or disappointing it might be from a perfectionist point of view, is there for a reason. It's there because it s part of us. It's there for us to observe and learn from rather than deny, hide from, or pretend it doesn't exist. And if we can share that negative and disappointing observation of ourselves with someone we trust, we move out of shame and into healing.

Learning about my warts-and-all self and allowing myself to own my story and share it openly and proudly has created a priceless sense of authenticity and wholeness. I hope you can learn to do this, too.

3.   *Recognising Our Unique Gifts and Talents*

But self-awareness isn't just about the negative, disappointing, warts-and-all side of our story. We may not be saints, but we're also not complete psychopathic sinners. As we review our life story and conduct our daily review, we should be on the lookout for our unique gifts and talents—the things we do well, the things people compliment us on, the things that are helpful and useful and seem to come quite naturally to us.

Brené Brown makes this point beautifully, "You may not think your gifts are that unique or that valuable. But they are. They can only be delivered by you and they can only be received by the people you serve. This is how your unique purpose in life becomes reality, meaning is created in that moment and that's God will."

Embracing Authenticity in a Culture of Conformity

We started this chapter with Gabor Maté's quote about waking up to what is real and authentic in and around us. I would like to end this section with another quote from Brené Brown and her book The Gifts of Imperfection, an amazing guide on how to deal with the often-debilitating shame that our society is riddled with. She repeats Maté's call for us to wake up to our authenticity, to wake up to our real story and own it, to wake up to our true selves.

"Being authentic in a culture that wants you to fit in and people-please is difficult. It needs practice... Authenticity is the daily practice of letting go of who we think we're supposed to be and embracing who we are. Choosing authenticity means:

- Cultivating courage to be imperfect, to set boundaries and allow ourselves to be vulnerable.
- Exercising the compassion that comes from knowing that we are all made of strength and struggle.
- Nurturing the connection and sense of belonging that can only happen when we believe we are enough.

Mindfully practicing authenticity during our most soul-searching struggles is how we invite grace, joy and gratitude into our lives."

Courage. Compassion. Connection. These are the gifts we get to practice every day when we own the story of our own imperfections. These are the gifts we are given precisely because we're human. Precisely because we aren't perfect.

KNOWING THE WAY RIGHT WAY FORWARD

A New Guiding Principle: RESPONSE-ABILITY

It's one thing to have a clear understanding of our own story of the past and the problems we've created for ourselves and others in trying to be somebody. It's an altogether different task to know where to go from there. In our previous attempts at life, we may well have got it wrong, but at least we had a guiding principle behind our actions: please people. Our mantra might well have been, "Do what will make other people think well of us and, therefore, more likely to give us what we want." I sense that was the unconscious guiding principle behind many of my actions. But if we're to drop that principle because of all the troubles it's caused, what should our new guiding principle be? How do we know what the right way forward is?

I suggest that our new guiding principle should be RESPONSE-ABILITY, our ability to be of maximum use by responding to any given situation for the benefit of all.

This might sound like a relatively simple principle to follow, albeit slightly worthy, but it's one that doesn't come naturally to many of us, myself included. I think this is mainly for two reasons:

1. Response-ability has to be sensed by ourselves. We have to discern the right course of action using our own judgment. We can't defer the decision to the sources we've previously relied on - what other people think and say, what our culture dictates, or the conventional wisdom of our times. We have to discern it for ourselves, to know it from within. This is a skill we haven't necessarily had many opportunities to hone.

2. The main benefactor of our actions has changed. We're no longer being of maximum use to us. We're no longer seeking to benefit just ourselves. We're trying to benefit everyone. That includes ourselves, but not at the cost of others. This is a whole new mindset. The idea of doing anything that doesn't in some way lead to a direct benefit to me was and is counter-initiative. I suspect it's countercultural. At the heart of this notion of "benefitting all" is the concept of interdependence, something we'll consider in The Habit of Connection. For now, let's focus on the "knowing" aspect of our response-ability. How do we "know" what the right way forward should be? How do we "know" what to do? How do we "know" anything for that

matter? This is the next phase of building the habit of awareness.

How Do We "Know"?

If you're anything like me and want to "know" anything, your first instinct will probably be to Google it. How do you know if you have food poisoning? Google it. How do you fix a washing machine? Google it. How to write a book? Yes – I Googled that too.

We live in the Information Age, an era where access to information is so freely and easily available that we hardly need to refer to anything other than a search engine on our mobile phones if we want to find the answer to virtually any question. The human race has experienced a number of seismic shifts that have massively impacted the social, economic, and cultural elements of people's daily lives across the globe. First came the Neolithic Age, then the Scientific Age, followed by the Industrial Age. Traditionally, these epochs spanned hundreds or even thousands of years. Now, we find ourselves in the Information Age, which has swept through the world in just a few years. It's mind-blowing to step back and realise just how profoundly different the world has become during the information age.

I was twenty-seven when I got my first phone, which worked without being connected to a landline. I was in my forties when I finally had a device with internet access that allowed me to send and receive emails away from my desk. It's hard to imagine a world without that sort of connectivity now. My kids can hardly believe I travelled the world in my twenties without a phone, keeping in touch via pay phones and postcards and booking hotels by snail mail.

Our world is now so full of instantly accessible information that it's easy to overlook the fact that we may rely on this type of information too much. Data transmitted from various sources relies on us processing information in a specific way through our minds and cognitive faculties. The information age, for all its amazing benefits, has led us to a place where there's a huge emphasis on our "thinking" to figure stuff out. We "think," therefore, we think we "know."

The Think-Feel-Do Framework

In my advertising days, we used a "think-feel-do" framework to build campaigns. The philosophy was that if you want to influence people's buying behaviour, you start by providing compelling information. This new information leads to them "knowing" something new, which changes their thinking. Changed thinking makes people feel differently. For example, knowing that a particular company has a phone with internet connectivity, helpful apps, a great camera, and stores a thousand songs is likely to make you feel that you want it in your life. You feel drawn to the possibilities it could bring. You may even feel jealous of others who already have it. If those feelings are strong enough, you'll go ahead and buy it. Think – Feel – Do.

Since then, the field of behavioural change has become much more sophisticated, but the think-feel-do logic still plays out in everyday life. We tend to over-rely on information to inform our choices, believing we can "think" our way forward. We gather research, find information, "think" about it, and come up with a rational plan of action. In the Information Age, we've come to rely on "thinking" with our rational mind as the primary, if not the only, way to "know" things. But thinking is not the only way to know.

Sensation-Perspective-Agency

Dan Seigel offers a slightly different take on the "think-feel-do" idea with his notion of "sensation-perspective-agency":

- Sensations give us information about the world around us through our ability to see, hear, touch, taste, and smell the physical world. We also have internal sensations that provide information.

- Perspectives are formed as we use that information to create a picture of what's going on. Our perspectives include thoughts, beliefs, ideas, judgments, decisions, and story-making. This is how we make sense of all the information our senses have gathered.

- Agency is what we do in the world - our behaviours, habits and actions.

What appeals to me about this model is the primacy it gives to sensations as the foundation of our actions. The think-feel-do model has lost credibility because it's now widely known that much of our behaviour is dictated by our emotional response to situations. We rarely make decisions and act based purely on rational evidence. Instead, we tend to decide based on our emotional response and how we feel about something. We then gather rational evidence and data to support that decision after the fact.

Think about buying a house or a car. The decision to buy is usually made once you walk through the house or test-drive the car. It's then rationalised afterwards by revisiting brochures and spec sheets to pick out appealing details. You then have a story to explain to people why you're making that particular investment. Rationale ratifies the emotion to buy. The story ratifies the urge to act. Perspective ratifies the sensation for agency.

I introduce the sensation-perspective-agency framework because it provides a useful tool for learning how to move forward. It's a tool for mastering self-knowledge, not just fact-based knowledge.

That's why it's the ideal tool for discerning and building our response-ability.

The Dynamic Relationship between Sensation, Perspectives and Agency

Response-ability is our ability to sense the world around us, gather as much relevant information from a wide variety of sources, feel the richness and detail of what's happening around us, and sense reality. We can then use those sensations to inform and calibrate the perspectives we build or hold onto. Do our perspectives make sense? Is there a credible story that creates meaning from all those sensations? If so, we can view our actions in relation to those sensations and perspectives. We learn to respond to the reality of what we sense. We also learn the impact our response has on the sensations and perspectives that arise as a result.

From that point of view, the model is more of a triangle than a straight line. Agency can influence perspectives and sensations, just as perspectives can influence sensations and agency. Analysing this dynamic relationship becomes our compass for navigating the spiritual journey.

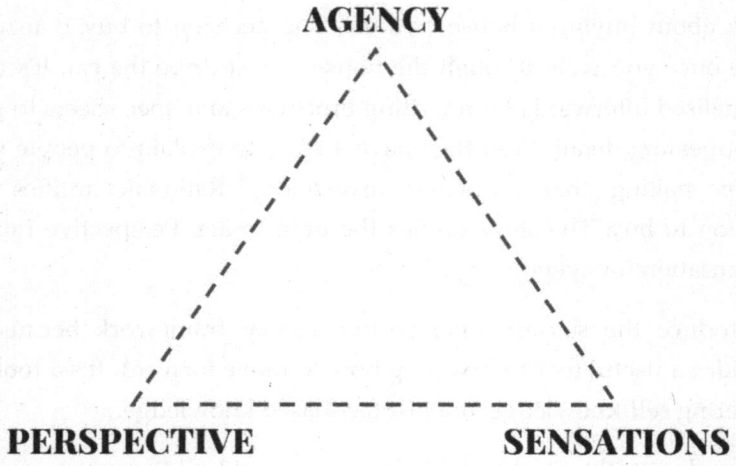

Reliance on Sight and Sound

Using this model to examine how we make decisions and act in the Information Age, it's not difficult to see how reliant we've become on our senses of sight and hearing to inform the majority of our perspectives. Social media, newspapers, magazines, TV, books, radio, videos, gossip, word of mouth, and personal advice. These are the tangible sources of information that dominate our world. We consider these sources credible and trust them, as we should if we have a reasonable BS detector!

The Information Age has given us easy access to unlimited amounts of this type of information. But that's both a blessing and a curse. As we've grown accustomed to sensing our world using bite-sized, social media-friendly chunks of information, our attention spans have dropped. We are less likely to sense our world using more nuanced, in-depth sources of information that require prolonged attention, like storylines unfolding over hundreds of pages rather than in a two-minute YouTube video. Even so, these sight and sound sources tend to provoke a certain perspective based on a certain type of knowing - rational, logical, thinking knowledge. However, different sources of information can provoke a different type of perspective based on a different type of knowing.

Four Ways of Knowing

C.S. Jung suggested that there are actually four ways of knowing:

1. Thinking / Rational intelligence (IQ) – The rational, logical way of knowing we traditionally associate with information processing and analysis, usually linked with reason and intelligence.
2. Feeling / Emotional intelligence (EQ) – The sensations that

arise from within, the ebb and flow of our emotional world and the feelings that wash through us.

3. Sensing / Physical intelligence (PQ) – Taking in information from our environment using our body and the resulting internal sensations (hairs on the back of your neck, gut feeling, heavy heart).

4. Intuition / Spiritual intelligence (SQ) – Knowledge that comes from inner insight, deep knowing, or intuition. This knowledge makes us feel whole, coherent, and aligned. It just feels right.

Our culture has a large bias towards thinking rationally. Because of that, we are failing to draw on large chunks of the reality we live in. Research has found that our bodies as a whole offer a more reliable assessment of reality than our logical mind's reasoning (Source: John Coates, Radical Wholeness). The rational, logical left hemisphere thinks in abstraction, using concepts and ideas to make sense of the world. Our largely subconscious right hemisphere, on the other hand, takes in the context of our world using sources of energy flow that don't bother our intellect.

Have you ever entered a meeting room at work and sensed "an atmosphere"? Or met someone new that you felt you'd known for years? Or been out in town at night and sensed danger? Our bodies pick up energy that our thinking mind can't process and articulate. The problem is that we've come to ignore these types of information. We don't trust them. In fact, we've forgotten how to use them. We've become desensitised.

Expanding Our Senses

This point was brought home to me when I read about the Anlo-Ewe tribe of West Africa in Philip Shepherd's book Radical Wholeness. In their culture, they recognise nine senses, not just the five we've chosen in our Western culture. For them, the primary sense that drives their response-ability is their sense of balance - not just in the way they move, but in the way they live. Just consider that: having a sense of balance so well-developed and attuned to the environment that you trust it to inform every perspective and every action. They also recognise "speech" as a sense. They have a felt relationship with the spoken word that goes beyond simply hearing.

I've come to appreciate this wider conception of how we sense the world through my relationship with music. As a would-be goth band member, music means a lot to me. I have a felt relationship with it, especially certain types of music. I sense something in the sound patterns that is meaningful to me in a way that's hard to articulate. The information isn't just aural; I feel it. I suspect some people have the same felt relationship with style and design. They just know when something looks right in a way that goes beyond just seeing lines, colours, and textures.

Maybe we all have these sensibilities. Maybe some people are more sensitive to certain aspects of life than others. But maybe we don't appreciate them because our society, unlike the Anlo-Ewe, doesn't value the wider world of sense. Consequently, we're just not used to using them.

Bottom-Up Conduction and Top-Down Construction

Dan Seigel suggests that humans are equipped to experience what he calls "bottom-up conduction." We sense energy flowing around us, through us, and in us. From a quantum physics point of view, that makes sense to me. After all, we are just balls of undulating energy. As is everything else. And maybe this is the role of our right hemisphere: to make sense of the different energy and information sources that flow around us.

My intuition is that we can use this information to inform our perspectives and agency. The problem is that our right hemisphere can't use language; that's the domain of the left hemisphere. So, the right-hand side passes the information to its left-hand logical neighbour to create a top-down construction of the energy flow, using abstract words, descriptions, or stories to help us articulate the experience of that particular energy flow. This is consistent with Iain McGilchrist's Master and Emissary view of how our brain works.

In this way, we can re-visit our model and say that:

- Sensation = The felt texture of experience, the feel of energy in flow.
- Perspective = The perceptual dimension and the point of view of that flow.
- Agency = The actions that arise from processing the flow.

I realise that all this may sound just a bit too "out there" and ethereal at the moment. It would have sounded that way to me a few years ago. But I want to plant a seed in your mind because I want you to use the sensation–perspective–agency tool to find out for yourself. To feel for yourself. To sense for yourself. To reach out with your wide variety of senses and feel your way forward.

As you progress through the spiritual journey and start using some of the practices we discuss in the next chapter, The Habit of Discipline, I want you to contemplate the fact that we may have more than our five chosen senses to inform our perspectives and agency. I want you to consider that we may not be able to fully experience and navigate reality because we are under-utilising the following senses:

- Our inner sense of self (the inner sensations of the body – we'll talk more about this in the section called Embodied Knowledge as part of The Habit of Discipline).
- Our sense of the Divine (the connected sensations to what is universally good – which we'll talk about in the sections called

Embracing Silence and Asking for Guidance & Power, also part
of The Habit of Discipline).

- Our sense of intra-connection (feeling an individual part of the
  whole – which we'll discuss in The Habit of Connection).
- Our sense of purpose (the motivational sensations to do the
  right thing – which is fully covered in the Epilogue of this book
  A Pathway to Purpose and Power).

These sensations are hard to rationalise and articulate in words, but
they undoubtedly exist. Using the sensation—perspective—agency
model, we can put these sensations, and possibly many more, to good
use and start the process of beginning to trust them as much as our
chosen five senses.

The point to emphasise here is that in order for us to "know" the way
forward and to "know" how to be response-able, we have to appreciate
all the ways of "knowing." Our culture of economic growth has
narrowed our focus to one way of knowing. We rely too heavily on our
rational, thinking brain. And it is costing us. By appreciating and
practising all ways of knowing, we open ourselves up to new
sensations, new perspectives and new agency. In fact, some go as far as
saying that if we successfully integrate all four ways of knowing, we
open up an inspirational fifth way. In their book Regenerative
Leadership, Giles Hutchins and Laura Storm suggest that integrating
all forms of knowledge allows us to access wisdom from outside
ourselves. We can draw on the wisdom of nature, on the wisdom of the
universal mind, on the wisdom of the living systems field, and on the
wisdom of God. Now, that's an awareness worth having on your side.

WHO ARE WE REALLY? DISCOVERING OUR SPIRITUAL NATURE

In our exploration of "waking up to what is real and authentic in and
around us," we've delved into the story of "us," our past, the trouble
we may have caused ourselves, and the authentic true self that lies

beneath the layers of the persona we've created. We've also explored new ways of perceiving reality as we embark on our journey of honing our response-ability by carefully observing our sensations, perspectives, and agency. Now I want to circle back to a more specific aspect of our real and our authentic selves: our spiritual nature.

The Neglected Realm: Spirituality in the Modern Era

Perennial wisdom tells us that human beings are both physical and spiritual beings, inhabiting and experiencing both realms. However, the experience of being human in the modern era has been dominated by the physical realm. The prioritisation of the sciences and the bias towards rational thinking have left the spiritual realm behind, out of reach for most people in modern Western society. It's almost considered a relic. This imbalance comes at a cost. Without access to our spiritual nature, we feel out of sync, misaligned, and separate. We feel our "unsatisfactoriness." We feel the "hole in the soul" that many people in addiction recovery talk about.

Emmet Fox noted, "Man is essentially spiritual and eternal, and this world, and the life we know intellectually, is but a cross-section of the full truth...To accept the truth is the first great step, but not until we have proved it in doing is it ours." This highlights the importance of sensations, perspectives, and actions. Perspectives from rational thinking alone are not enough; we also need to learn from our actions. We need to prove it in our doing.

The Illusion of Separation

The big intellectual idea that we need to "know" and feel deep inside is that we are not separate beings living unconnected lives. We are deeply and irrefutably interconnected with all other human beings, all other living things, consciousness, and life itself. This can be a challenging concept to grasp, especially when we don't always "feel" very connected to the rest of humanity or the living world. But that's the illusion we need to work on. And it is an illusion.

Our spiritual, interconnected nature can be articulated in a very physical way. If you were to count all the cells that make up your physical body, you'd find that there are more cells that aren't "you" than are "you." Less than half of the cells in the body are human; the rest belong to microorganisms, bacteria, parasites, and viruses. According to Rob Knight, Director of the University of California San Diego Centre for Microbiome Innovation, we are in fact only 43% human. This fact alone makes it very hard to claim that any human being, or indeed any creature, can be self-sufficient. We simply can't exist without the 57% of cells that aren't us. We are irrefutably interconnected with them.

Another interesting observation is that you can't mark out where one creature ends, and another begins. This is made even more perplexing when you consider that the vast majority of our cells are replaced over a seven to ten-year period. If there aren't many cells in our bodies that were there seven years ago, can we really say we're the same physical being? Now, that's something to contemplate.

The Art of Contemplating Being Human

For anyone embarking on the spiritual exploration of human nature, I suggest reading The Art of Living by Thích Nhat Hanh. Thich was a Vietnamese Buddhist monk, peace activist, prolific author, poet, and teacher. He was recognised as the main inspiration behind the idea of "engaged Buddhism" and known as the "father of mindfulness." This book, although short and easy to read, is by far the most compelling thing I read in the early part of my spiritual journey. It really got me thinking about the issue of separation and interconnection (or inter-being as he calls it) and vividly opened my eyes to the illusion of us being individual entities.

Thích Nhat Hanh identifies three wrong views we often hold that keep us in unsatisfactoriness:

1. We are a separate self, cut off from the rest of the world, born one minute and dead the next.
2. We are only this body, and when we die, we cease to exist. This blinds us to all the ways we are interconnected and continue to exist after death.
3. Whatever we are looking for – happiness, peace, love, etc. – can only be found outside us and in a distant future.

If you're anything like me, you'll be looking at this list and thinking, "I pretty much think those three views are right. How are they wrong?" Or even if you don't think that completely, there'll be part of you that thinks there's at least some truth in there. If you do, then that's a very good reason why you should read the rest of his book.

He goes on to say that there are three fundamental practices that can help us liberate ourselves from these three wrong views. He calls these practices:

1. Concentrations on emptiness: Contemplating emptiness helps us shift the illusion of separation so we can marvel at the wonder of interbeing. Emptiness can be thought of in terms of interbeing across space – our relationship and connection to everything and everyone around us. It can also be thought of in terms of impermanence across time – like the cells in our body or the water in a river, nothing lasts forever.
2. Concentrations on signlessness: We classify things and give them names as if they are concrete entities, there one day and gone the next. But a cloud, for example, never goes away or dies; it re-manifests itself as rain, then as a stream, water in a

kettle, tea in a cup, and a drink in our stomachs. An acorn is part of the tree, a wave is part of the ocean, and the child is part of the adult. We are much more fluid than we realise, more like a dynamic process than a fixed entity.

3. Concentrations on aimlessness: Our culture of economic growth is very goal-oriented. We know where we want to go and are very intent on getting there. While this may be useful, we often forget to enjoy ourselves along the way. Aimlessness is the idea that you do not put something in front of you and run after it because everything is already here, within yourself. This is the heart of mindfulness – being aware of what is here in this very moment, fully engaged in it, and enjoying it without being caught up in what it might lead to.

Contemplating these concentrations over time (a practice we'll discuss in the next chapter, The Habit of Discipline) was ground-breaking for me. It helped create a new awareness, a new way of thinking, and a new perspective around the death of my wife, my drinking, and the loss of my business. It transformed sensations of grief, guilt, and resentment into acceptance, hope, and gratitude, allowing me to act differently as a result. It was an amazing and transformational experience that still fills me with awe.

Manas and the Struggle to Remain Interconnected

Reading and contemplating these concentrations helps make a shift in perspective, but all too often, the shift isn't permanent. Before long, we find ourselves back in the "real world" struggling to see the interconnected nature of life. For me, that's usually associated with somebody doing something to me, like a driver pulling out in front of me, causing me to brake suddenly, spilling my coffee over the car seat, and then blaming me for the incident with a loud honk of his horn and a few choice words and hand gestures. In moments like this, and many other moments throughout the day, I feel very much like a separate self. I feel completely like an individual fighting my way through the struggles of everyday life, trying to survive in this dog-eat-dog world. If all these feelings of a separate self are an illusion, why does it feel so very, very real?

Thích Nhất Hạnh would say that these feelings arise because of what is known in Buddhist psychology as "manas"—our survival instinct, our inbuilt drive to avoid pain and seek out pleasure. Manas cannot see that we are interconnected; it is the thinking mind, the false self, and cannot see this spiritual part of our reality, at least not without training.

We cannot and do not want to get rid of manas, as it is a natural part of human existence. We have a strong instinctual will to live, to avoid pain, and to seek out pleasure. Manas gives us our strong desire to cling to and protect our life and defend ourselves from danger. That's not a bad thing in and of itself. But unchecked, without training, manas can make us self-centred and selfish, urging us to do things that are damaging to ourselves, others, and the environment around us.

Our culture of economic growth has let manas take control of life, with our false selves in charge. It's time to start breaking the illusion and allowing our true selves to come to the fore. By engaging in practices that help us connect with our spiritual nature and see the interconnectedness of all things, we can begin to transform our perspective and live more authentic, fulfilling lives.

THE SPLIT SELF: RECONCILING OUR DUAL NATURE

We mentioned the story of the split self at the very beginning of the book. This is the tale of the left hemisphere (the logical, intellectual, superficial, thinking, false self) working alongside the right hemisphere (the soulful, intuitive, deep, sensing, true self). As our discussions have progressed, we've alluded to this narrative as I believe it gets to the heart of the matter. The split nature of human experience is, I believe, the cause of the spiritual malady and why we feel unsatisfactoriness in the first place.

This split has become increasingly evident in the last couple of centuries as our culture of economic growth has enthusiastically embraced and worshipped the value of the left hemisphere, rational thinking. This has created an ever-widening divide as our soulful, intuitive, true selves have been neglected and under-utilised. The spiritual solution is all about resolving this split by recognising the value of our true selves and nurturing that aspect of ourselves back to health and prominence, thus relieving us of the spiritual malady and allowing spiritual happiness to arise.

Exploring the Complexities of the Human Mind

This is the crux of the matter, which is why I think it's important to consider the split self in more detail. Unfortunately, it's not an easy topic to articulate. The more I read, the more I realise I don't understand the complexities of the human mind and how it impacts the way we act and feel. However, what I do see are stories emerging from the fields of neuroscience, psychology, human behaviour, and spiritual wisdom that intersect. This appears to be where the action is. This is where I believe truth resides.

What follows is my best attempt at drawing on these fields of knowledge to try and bring to life my experiences of spirituality, the spiritual awakening, and what's going on inside us in a more rational way. I do this because I think it helps demystify the spiritual process for those who may be struggling with the more magical and mystical aspects of spiritual practice. My analysis may not provide a watertight and scientifically accurate account of any one of these specific fields, but it does reflect my experience in a way that makes sense to me—in a way that I can recount to others. And that's the important part.

As I've learned throughout my 12-Step journey, facts alone won't get you sober, even if they are scientifically watertight. When it comes to spirituality, you need to do the work and commit to practises that don't make any sense. And you only do this because someone who has experienced the benefits talks you through the process. They share their experience and strength and hope that things will work out just fine if you just keep on doing the work. Yes, they tell you stories. And yes, they give you books to read. But you believe them because you see the results in their eyes. You see it in their demeanour, in their actions, in the tone of their voice, in their very being. Words and facts are not enough because language and logic don't take precedence in the realm of spiritual experience.

The Objective and Subjective Parts of Existence

Let's take a step back and first consider the very nature of our existence. The world, as we experience it, is always constructed of two parts. There is the objective part, the things that exist and happen out there. These things include people, cars, work, music, nature, space, and so on. Then there is the subjective part: the things that exist and happen in here. These things are our thoughts, our feelings, our beliefs, our moods, and so on. The objective part is what we might call reality. It consists of everything, whether we are able to sense it consciously or not.

If we meet someone in the street, the objective reality of the person we see in front of us is just a dynamic energy field consisting of trillions of interconnected cells that are related to and interacting with countless other atoms whizzing around the universe. We can't sense and perceive all that reality. We see a "person." "Person" is the name we've come up with for the specific dynamic energy field and community of whizzing cells that look like that. "Person" is a category of reality we've created to make life easier for ourselves. It helps us make sense of the world. If we can make sense of the world, we can exist more successfully in that world. But the category "person" is not reality. It is an abstraction—a word we've created to describe a certain part of reality we can sense.

On the day in question, we don't see any old "person" in the street. We see "Dave." "Dave" is the abstract name we've created for the specific dynamic energy field and community of whizzing cells that we've learned to distinguish from the broader category we call "person." Dave is a "friend" who we "like" because he is "funny." Dave is not reality. Liking is not reality. Funny is not reality. These are all subjective parts of our experience. They all happen on the inside. These are all aspects and feelings that have been generated internally as a result of the stories we've created out of the objective reality we've been able to sense.

I hope you get the picture I'm trying to paint here. There are two important points that come out of this interrogation of reality and our experience of it. Firstly, we only capture the tiniest glimpses of reality. Some of the reality is captured consciously, and more is captured unconsciously, but most of what is going on outside of us doesn't make it in.

The second point is that the names, the words, and the stories we create are abstractions. They are simplified concepts we play within the thinking mind to make sense of the very limited amount of objective reality that makes it in. They are not real. But they feel very real. The experience of seeing "Dave," "liking" him, and finding him "funny" is real. That's why the wise Hebrew scholars in the Talmud tell us, "We don't see things as they are. We see them as we are."

We don't see reality.

We experience reality through the stories we create. But those stories feel very real.

And we live our lives based on those stories.

. . .

The Role of the Right and Left Hemispheres

What I find fascinating is how we take in information and process it to create abstract stories that we then use to influence our actions—a process that informs the whole sensation-perspective-agency approach we discussed earlier. It is a process that uses two different parts of our brain: the right hemisphere and the left hemisphere. I've mentioned Iain McGilchrist's book The Master and his Emissary a number of times. Here are a few passages from the book that explain this process brilliantly:

> *"Like a radio tuned into a particular station, the right hemisphere picks up certain wavelengths of reality outside us and delivers it to us. It doesn't pick up everything, just those wavelengths we're attuned to. The left hemisphere, in turn, grasps, sees, and receives only some of what the right hemisphere has received. Its method is selection, abstraction—in a word, negation."*

> *"Our apprehension of the world begins in the right hemisphere in awareness, passes into the left hemisphere for analysis, and then returns back to the right hemisphere as a state of being."*

The Right Hemisphere: Empathy and Wholeness

"The right hemisphere's understanding of the world includes empathy and intersubjectivity as the ground of consciousness. It values intuition, the overriding of all humanly contrived boundaries, a sense of oneness or wholeness, physical pleasure and pain, and the celebration of nature beyond human control, as she really is."

I also see the right hemisphere as the observer of our thoughts and feelings. There is a part of our brain that can almost take a step back and see ourselves in the process of thinking. We can catch ourselves being angry from a detached perspective. We know that we know things, for example. We can sense that we're feeling sad, but we're not sure why that is. We can look down on ourselves and see that we are worried about something but know that the worry is unfounded.

The Left Hemisphere: Order and Rationality

McGilchrist continues, "The left hemisphere cannot deliver anything new "direct from the outside," but it can unfold, unpack, what it is given. It's very strength—and it contains enormous strength, as the history of civilisation demonstrates—lies in the fact that it can render explicit what the right hemisphere has to leave implicit."

> *"The left hemisphere values order, rationality, clarity, a sort of beauty that comes with perfection, human control of nature, and the celebration of masks, representations, or appearances."*

I also see the left hemisphere as the source of the internal chatter that goes on incessantly in our minds. Try to sit still in silence and think of nothing. Before too long, you'll be thinking of something. You'll be having a conversation with yourself in your mind. You'll find yourself in a train of thought and suddenly realise you're no longer sitting in silence, trying to think of nothing. Instead, you'll be talking to yourself about a task that needs doing, what you'll eat tonight, or what your boss will say when she finds out you're handing in your notice. The constant chatter is your left hemisphere working out its next move. The sudden realisation that you're NOT sitting still thinking about nothing is your right hemisphere interjecting to point out you've been lost in thought for these last few minutes.

The Need for Reintegration

McGilchrist goes on to explain that, despite its undeniable ability to analyse the world, the left hemisphere cannot appreciate it. "Yet that is also its weakness. The clarifying explicitness needs to be reintegrated with the sense of the whole, the now unpacked or unfolded whatever it may be being handed back to the domain of the right hemisphere where it once more lives."

This final paragraph highlights the problem. The right hemisphere is the one in contact with life. It is the one that delivers the lived experience of being part of the world using its deep inner wisdom and intuition. It integrates what the left hemisphere has analysed and allows us to live peacefully with what's going on around us. It allows us to abide calmly and simply be with the reality of what is. It doesn't require a rationale or logical reason to achieve this, but it does require our left hemisphere to stop its incessant chatter and rationalising and hand the story back. It needs the left hemisphere to let go of its desire to control, to loosen its tight clench of certainty. It requires the left hemisphere to surrender—a skill and a habit that we've become increasingly out of practice.

What's more, our left hemisphere is the home of our "point of view" and our self-aware intelligence. It also benefits from the skill of clever argument through its ownership of language and logic. It likes to keep its self-conceived story of "itself" safe. It likes certainty and security. And if it doesn't make logical, rational, safe sense to hand the created story back to the right hemisphere to enact, it will keep control. It will dictate action from its own perspective. And so, begins the hole in the soul: the feeling of being out of sync, the sense of unease and unsatisfactoriness.

When we start living our lives predominantly from our left hemisphere logic, when we don't integrate our conceived stories back into the realm of life and reality as sensed by our right hemisphere, we create a disconnect. We create a split. The split is between the story of life we believe we should live as designed by our logical left hemisphere (our false self) and the life our right hemisphere is yearning for us to live to be in tune with reality (our true self).

I sense this when part of me wants to go to the gym because "I know" (and I know at a deep level) that it is good for me. But I decide not to go because "I prefer" to stay in bed and keep cosy, warm, and comfortable. I'm the one who wants to go to the gym, but I'm also the one who prefers to stay home. My "deep knowing" that the gym will be good for me comes from my soulful right hemisphere—my true self. It doesn't matter whether I find it pleasurable or comfortable. It knows what's good for the whole of me, given all the information it has access to and its perception of reality.

On the other hand, my left hemisphere cares only about keeping me away from danger and drawing me ever closer to comfort. It doesn't care about the reality of the situation. Even if it could create a very rational and logical reason why I should go to the gym, if the story it contrives to keep me in bed sounds more appealing, that's exactly what I'll do. This is the dance we do between the right hemisphere, true self, and the left hemisphere, false self, all the time—every day, in virtually all aspects of our lives. We can sense this same disconnection arising between "deeply knowing" a course of action and "preferring a more comfortable" approach. It shows up in what we eat, how we treat other people, what we do for work, what we do in our spare time, and how we act in every living moment.

Building Awareness and Discernment

Building our Habit of Awareness is the process by which we become more familiar with these modes of thinking, knowing and processing information going on inside us. We become more aware that there is tension and that different sources of motivation are arising. We become more skilled in discerning whether these motivations are coming from the true self or the false self. Am I drawn to take action because it's the right thing to do, given the reality I'm facing? Or am I drawn to take action because I simply want a more comfortable life?

The more we follow the path of the false self, the more self-centred we become, the more we look out only for ourselves, the more isolated we become, and the more disconnected we are from the flow of life that is passing by us and through us. The more we follow the path of the true self, the more aligned and whole we feel, the more at ease we are with life as it is, and the more chance we have of feeling the full rapture of being alive.

This is why The Habit of Awareness is so important. This is how we start using it to build our response-ability—a response-ability that draws more from the knowing we glean from our right hemispheres, which are connected to life and the world around us, and less from the knowing we generate from the left hemisphere, which lives in self-absorbed abstraction.

The Dominance of Left Hemisphere Thinking

As we've discussed previously, it's not hard to see how our society has been totally dominated by logical left hemisphere thinking. We're highly sceptical of anything that doesn't have a rational "What's in it for me?" argument. We need a structured, well-thought-through business case for everything. We've lost the ability to let go of control and certainty. We've lost faith in our intuition to do the right thing. We've lost faith in the inner wisdom that allows our left hemisphere to surrender. We've forgotten how to live with the unqualified assertion that all will be well. And we're poorer for it.

The spiritual solution is all about reversing this trend. It's about nurturing the true self so we can have confidence in our intuition. It's about learning to let go of the left hemisphere stories that keep us separated from life. It's about building faith in actions that don't seem to make logical sense to us just now but will lead to a much richer and more fulfilling life in the fullness of time. Our right hemisphere, intuition-guided actions can make unsatisfactoriness disappear if only we unlearn the habits that have caused the split in the first place.

I hope this makes some sense to you. I hope I've done justice to the work of people like McGilchrist, from whom much of this thinking comes. As part of his conclusion in the book The Master and The Emissary, he states, "The left hemisphere's raison d'etre is to narrow things down to a certainty, the right hemisphere's is to open them up to possibility. In life, we need both." That's so true. The problem is, however, that we have let the left hemisphere take prominence in our culture of economic growth. We've lost touch with the story of life, the universe, and everything with which the right hemisphere has direct contact. The story of reality we've engineered in our left hemisphere lacks texture, nuance, context, and depth. In short, it lacks life. That's why many of us don't feel the full rapture of being alive. It may appear that the problem is that we've let the left hemisphere take control. But the real danger is that we're so taken with our left hemisphere, which is a logical way of thinking, that we don't realise its limitations. Our logic doesn't know what it doesn't know. And it doesn't appreciate what it can't know. Consequently, we don't appreciate what we're missing out on. However, there are ways to overcome this dilemma of limited knowing.

McGilchrist suggests that there always has been and always will be a natural tendency for humans to take the authenticity of the right hemisphere's "presence" and convert it into the inauthenticity of "representation" in the left hemisphere. This reminds me of HTtFTU (the Human Tendency to F*** Things Up). Over time and history, however, this tendency has been counteracted by a swing back to authenticity when life begins to feel too inauthentic. When life becomes just too lifeless, this reminds me of HPtLWG (the Human Propensity to Love What's Good). The Renaissance is a period of time when there was a natural swing back to the vibrancy of the right hemisphere. It was a period of time that celebrated the fullness and beauty of life following the fall of the logical, left hemisphere-dominated years of rule under the regime of the Roman Empire and the stagnant middle or dark ages that followed the Romans' domination, a period of time when we were naturally drawn to love and celebrate all that is good.

Maybe we'll experience a similar shift. Maybe our culture of economic growth will wake up to the inauthentic, lifeless way we are currently living. Maybe we'll all wake up to the unsatisfactoriness we're feeling because of our disconnected and unintegrated existence. Maybe this will happen naturally, as it has in other periods of history.

There is a catch, though. A warning even. The clever ways of our left hemisphere-dominated culture have all but taken over and drained the power of sources that can break through clever, logical arguments. McGilchrist highlights three potential sources that can strike a blow for a return to authenticity because they can send a message directly to the right-hand side, by-passing clever, logical argument directly. Those three sources are our bodies, art and spirituality.

A RETURN TO AUTHENTICITY

In the next section, The Habit of Discipline, we'll cover a spectrum of practices that improve our ability to use our bodies, art, and spirituality to communicate directly with our right hemisphere without relying on logic or language. These practices rejuvenate our souls, empowering and regenerating our neglected true selves and allowing us to feel the authenticity of being connected to life. They create a pathway to experiencing a spiritual awakening and the transformation required to break free from our addicted, left-hemisphere-dominated way of being.

But first, let's finish this section by examining the vital role awareness plays in this transformation.

The Power of Awareness and Understanding

A breakthrough in awareness is the catalyst for transformation—the starting point of the process. It opens a door of perception, suggesting that another way of being is possible. It allows us to entertain the idea that perhaps spiritual practises are worth trying and that they could serve us well if we give them a chance. This shift in awareness may come as an inspired intuition, a thought naturally bubbling up from the subconscious right hemisphere, drawing us forward into action. Alternatively, it may be a breakthrough in thinking resulting from a breakdown of being, where we are pushed into action by a logical, left-hemisphere train of thought that says, "I'm done. I'm all out of ideas. I'll try anything to escape this pain." This is the surrender of the left hemisphere that comes with hitting rock bottom. In either mode, awareness is the key to initiating change.

Once we embark on the spiritual path, continued nurturing of The Habit of Awareness fuels the transformation process, keeping us going. As we begin experiencing the benefits of spiritual practice, awareness manifests as curiosity—a longing to understand why these practices work and to discover more about the strange phenomenon called spirituality. We wonder what else could help us continue our journey.

This has been my experience. Growing my awareness through in-depth understanding has been crucially important, and I see growing awareness as a two-sided task. There's the task of building awareness through our right hemisphere, our true selves, which involves developing a stronger sense of detachment from our logical thinking and emotional feelings. We achieve this through spiritual practices like meditation and prayer, which take time to bear fruit. In our world of instant gratification, where our addictions can provide a fix in seconds, we struggle with patience without compelling reasons.

That's why we also need to focus on building a logical story for our left hemisphere, our false selves. This is especially important in the early stages of the spiritual journey because it keeps the left hemisphere content. Having logical reasons why this spiritual journey makes rational sense appeases the false self and allows the journey to continue with much less resistance. It provides a sufficiently clever argument to pacify our false self, giving us rational hope and patience to persevere until we start feeling the effects.

Maintaining this logical argument has been a significant part of my process. I know the spiritual solution works, as I have experienced its manifold benefits. My life has been transformed by it. However, the experience alone has not been enough for me. I also need to understand why this spiritual solution is working and what is happening to me for it to fully sink in and become a permanent shift in my consciousness. I need to convert experience into belief and belief into faith.

The Bible says that faith without works is dead, which is absolutely true. There's no point in believing in something if you don't carry that belief into the real world and act on it. But I also believe that works without understanding can be hollow—doing something for the sake of doing it without understanding why can lead to misguided efforts and manipulation by others, almost like doing something by rote. I'm human. Part of my make-up is that of a rational, logical thinker; therefore, that part of me needs a compelling reason to maintain the works.

Over the years, I credit this dual approach to awareness building as the source of delivering certain truths to me. As I have patiently practiced the spiritual disciplines that nurture the right hemisphere and have helped build true self-intuition and a deep sense of knowing, I have also learned about a logical, left hemisphere story supported by rational facts that support my true self-experience. When these two forms of awareness building and understanding collide, I get a deep sense of knowing that hits me hard. I viscerally feel the truth of being deep inside. The world around me, and myself as an integral part of it, makes complete and utter sense. That's when I feel aligned and whole

—when I feel the full rapture of being alive. That's when I feel I have returned to authenticity.

The Walking and Listening Practice

I experience this deep sense of knowing and aliveness on my morning walks while listening to inspiring books and podcasts. Every morning for the past four years, I have practiced walking and listening.

I started this practice during the COVID-19 pandemic lockdown. As part of my 12-Step journey, I had been praying and meditating most mornings for about a year. I felt spiritually good, but with gyms closed, I was starting to feel physically unhealthy. That's when I decided to start jogging in the morning straight after my meditation and prayer session. My fitness wasn't great, but I always felt better after a twenty-minute run. The problem was that lockdown rules only allowed us to go outside once a day. You could stay out as long as you wanted but couldn't go out again later that day. After only twenty minutes of freedom, I wasn't ready to consign myself to a full day inside the house, so I would simply walk for a while, aimlessly at first. I then came across a well-being app that supported a few online spiritual courses, comprising ten or so short videos, each no more than fifteen or twenty minutes long. At the time, I had embraced The 12-Step Programme and read a handful of books about addiction and other 12-Step "approved" literature, but I hadn't been exposed to other spiritual books or heard about people like Marianne Williamson, Deepak Chopra, or Ram Dass, who appeared on this app. I thought I'd pass the time listening to a few of these courses since the weather was nice, and I had nothing better to listen to.

The information I gleaned from these people in this form was transformational. There was something about listening to people out in nature after praying, meditating, and engaging in vigorous exercise that made a huge difference. It was like a new channel opened for me, allowing me to absorb and appreciate the information in a way I had never experienced through pure reading. I experienced many moments of truth during that summer of 2020—moments when the world made complete sense despite the madness of the pandemic.

I still get those moments of truth when walking and listening. I've listened to over 170 books using this method (the booklist is available at the back of the book in the bibliography). It's a source of awareness that has cemented the experience of spiritual awakening and built complete faith in the spiritual solution. I experienced the awakening because of the practises that nurtured my true self (more on this in the next section, The Habit of Discipline). I also built an understanding of how that solution was working by satisfying my false self's curiosity. That's why many religions insist on scripture study alongside prayer and meditation.

Intellectual learning helps support the soul's journey of rediscovery and our return to authenticity. It certainly did for me. Walking and listening built the bedrock of my understanding and, consequently, my faith in the spiritual approach. It formed the bedrock of knowledge and the many sources of information I used to write this book. It allowed me to create a story in my mind (my left hemisphere thinking mind) that supported me on my spiritual journey in a relatively rational and logical way. It supported the nurturing of my true self in a way that made sense to my false self.

Creating Spiritual Stories that Make Sense

I have to admit that the story I've just told you, the story of awareness that I fully believe in, may be flawed. I appreciate that what I have written about the true self and the false self represented by the right and left hemispheres may be wrong. I may have misinterpreted the facts. Someone may be able to drive a bus through the holes in my logic. That doesn't matter. I'm fully aware of the fallibility of my intellect when it comes to articulating these things because I know that language and logic aren't the domain of my true self. Trying to articulate the spiritual experience using logic and language is like trying to describe a great painting using words—it's impossible. My faith doesn't rest on the completeness and watertightness of my logic; it rests on the deep knowing that exists in my intuitive right hemisphere.

The point is that the story of awareness that I am conveying here is a story that keeps my left hemisphere happy. It may help keep your left hemisphere happy, too, or it may not. In some ways, I hope it doesn't because my main hope is that the story I've just told about awareness gives you enough curiosity to create your own Habit of Awareness. I hope you start walking, listening, and working through the books listed in the appendix. I hope you build a different story—a story that keeps your left hemisphere content.

My story is my story; your story will be yours. We don't have to agree on a single story that excludes the possibility of other stories. All that matters is that our individual stories satisfy our individual intellects, much like a God of our own understanding. It's my God, based on my understanding. And it's your God based on your understanding.

What matters is that we develop a story of why the spiritual solution is working for us that satisfies the dance between our true selves and our false selves. It builds a bridge between these two modes of being and the different modes of knowing that can support us on our spiritual journey. It allows us to explore and build an ever-deepening and profound awareness of life by reassuring our false selves that it's not blind faith that there is some method behind the madness and that we've not completely lost the plot. It supports the nurturing of our true spiritual nature by letting our logical left brains think they're still in control while our intuitive right brain knows we're on the way to full enlightenment. And in that way, it helps create a sense of alignment and wholeness in our lives.

The Desired Outcome: Wholeness

Ultimately, the desired outcome from this pillar of awareness is a sense of wholeness. By nurturing our true selves and re-educating our false selves by engaging in spiritual practices that directly communicate with our right hemisphere while building a logical story that satisfies our left hemisphere, we create a harmonious dance between these two aspects of our being. We begin the process of reintegrating the two and establishing a healthy balance.

This alignment allows us to experience the fullness and authenticity of life, to feel connected to something greater than ourselves, and to find peace and purpose in our existence. It is through the habit of awareness, this constant balancing act between the intuitive and the rational, that we gradually return to our true, whole selves and rediscover the joy and meaning that lies at the core of our being.

SIX

THE HABIT OF DISCIPLINE
RE-DISCOVERING & NURTURING THE SOUL

**Desired state of being and inner human need =
A sense of PEACE. Not feeling anxious
and worried.**

SIX

THE HABIT OF DISCIPLINE

Re-Discovering and Nurturing the Soul

Throughout the section on The Habit of Awareness, we focused our attention on helping our rational, logical, left hemisphere, egoic, false self understand that there is another side to our human experience that it isn't aware of. It was a process of re-education and quite a rational and logical re-education at that.

Now, we're turning our attention to our intuitive, experiential, right hemisphere, soulful, true self. We want to rediscover and nurture this neglected and often forgotten side of our human experience – a side that has been under-utilised and undervalued by our culture for many decades. This is no easy task. It's going to take time and effort to nurture our souls and re-ignite and reinstate the rightful master. And it's a task that is likely to cause some discomfort, just like going to the gym and working a muscle you've not used in years.

There will be resistance, not so much physical resistance, but intellectual resistance. That's because we will need to undertake actions that bypass our dominant, logical left hemisphere to go directly to the soul. As we discussed at the end of the last section, we will need to adopt the body, art, and spirit as the main vehicles of communication and sources of inspiration. These will become the key tools of our trade - sources and tools that don't make much rational or logical sense to our rational and logical minds.

A Reluctant Start

The 12-Step Programme is a phased programme of action that features, unsurprisingly, 12 consecutive steps. They are designed to be taken one by one sequentially. You start at 1 and finish at 12. However, from the very first day I embarked on the programme, I was encouraged to start work on establishing a daily routine, a morning routine and an evening routine built around Steps 10, 11, and 12. These steps are commonly known as the maintenance steps. They come after the more processional Steps of 1 to 9, which feel very much like they build on each other.

The maintenance steps, however, feel like they could be done at any time, regardless of where you are in the process. Steps 10, 11, and 12 are designed to keep us in good spiritual health for the rest of our days. They emphasise the importance of prayer, meditation, reviewing our behaviours, trying to do the right thing in all aspects of our lives, being helpful to others and making amends when we've been less than perfect. As a valued friend once told me, that means trying not to be a dick and saying sorry when we inevitably do something dickish.

As a raw recruit into The 12-Step Programme, I had never prayed or, meditated or reviewed my behaviours in any form. I was sore from my latest drinking binge and fresh out of rehab. I felt embarrassed and vulnerable. I wanted help rebuilding my life and getting my family and career back on track. I'm not sure what type of help and advice I was expecting to get, but it wasn't the type I was given. From day one, it was suggested that prayer and meditation would be a critical part of rebuilding my life and getting my career back on track. I was told that if I didn't practise these things every day as part of my 12-Step programme, there was a very good chance I'd drink again. And if that happened, any grand ideas I had about my future would be down the drain. They had a point. I didn't want to risk that. So, I took their advice. Much against my better judgment, I learned, rather awkwardly, the daily practice of prayer and meditation.

The Struggle and Rewards of Consistent Practice

I want to say that I took to both prayer and meditation like a duck to water, but I didn't. I hated both. I was told to pray and meditate every day. I tried but found it hard. Meditation felt a bit less excruciating than praying. That's because I started with ten-minute guided meditations, and I could just about cope with that. After a while, I progressed to silent meditation. I watched a couple of YouTube videos about meditating and read a couple of books on Buddhism and the role that meditation plays on the path to enlightenment. That gave me a better understanding of what meditation could do. I learned some breathing techniques and built them into my meditation time. I extended the time to twenty minutes. Sometimes I'd do it twice a day. After about five or six months, I actually enjoyed meditating. I could feel the benefits, a sense of peace, clarity, and deep well-being that I associated directly with meditation. I knew the meditation was working because these feelings would disappear as soon as I stopped doing it. Within a matter of months, what felt like a right royal pain in the ass became a valued morning ritual I couldn't live without.

It was a similar story with praying. I remember getting down on my knees to pray for the first time and thinking what a stupid thing to do. It felt so unnatural, and I thought I looked so stupid doing it. I certainly felt stupid. But I stuck with it. I learned a few prayers by heart that I could always fall back on. I read a book about praying and started to create my own prayers. I made a structure to guide my daily prayers. The amount of time I spent praying increased. I would do it at different times of the day. And, just as with meditation, within a matter of months, prayer became a daily ritual and a habit that I couldn't live without.

We'll discuss both prayer and meditation in more detail shortly, but the point I want to make here is the importance of discipline—The Habit of Discipline and practice. Trying something, experimenting with it, noticing the effects, changing it if it doesn't work, sticking with it, persistence, patience, and disciplined practice—that's what makes the difference.

The tools I've been taught as part of the spiritual solution work miracles. They really do. They deliver the sorts of miracles that result in you seeing the world differently - the miracle of changed perceptions and seeing life through a new pair of glasses. It takes time for the miracle to happen - time dedicated to disciplined, patient practice.

Miracles don't happen overnight. Well, not all of them do. They require us to put in the work. They require us to take action, action that we don't want to do and action that we don't understand or believe in. And that's a challenge that is becoming all the harder in our world of instant gratification. We're used to getting the "good stuff" quickly. We like the instant thrill and buzz we get from a shot of tequila, a line of cocaine, a passionate encounter, a flutter on the races, or a triple chocolate brownie. We're used to getting the benefits now. We're yearn for the quick, easy, convenient impact. That's what we like. That's what we're used to. Unfortunately, the spiritual solution doesn't work like that. There's not a pill you can take that will transform your pain into joy and peace and freedom and fulfilment twenty minutes after taking it. You need to work for it.

. . .

The Gift of Desperation and the Miracle of Spiritual Awakening

As I've said before, I had the gift of desperation to keep me going on the spiritual adventure. I desperately wanted to be rid of the pain and affliction that my addiction had caused. That gift pushed me through the embarrassment I felt when I first got down on my knees to pray. That gift gave me the persistence to meditate every day. That gift gave me the tenacity to get up early every morning to do my full routine before the kids got up. Eventually, that gift transformed into the gift of a spiritual awakening, a wondrous miracle that I can still hardly believe.

For me, this area of disciplined practice is the sensation—perspective—agency model in a different order. It demonstrates to me the power of using our bodies as a source and a tool—physically doing the work and physically feeling the benefits without necessarily understanding why.

When it comes to starting out with spiritual practice, if you've not done any of it before, my advice is not to think too much about it. Just get your body to do the action. Don't think. Do. Don't try to work out your perspective about why you're doing it or focus too much on the sensation that it feels uncomfortable to start with.

Persist with the discipline of practice, and eventually, you will experience a shift in sensation. You will begin to feel the benefits inside. And because you feel differently, you will think differently. You'll know there's been a positive impact because of the sensations in your body, and therefore, you have no choice but to re-evaluate your perspective. What once seemed unnatural, uncomfortable, and pointless practices now become indispensable parts of a much-loved and invaluable daily routine. You'll come to experience and believe in miracles. In fact, you'll come to rely on them. But before that belief kicks in, we need the discipline to kick-start the miraculous process.

RE-DISCOVERING AND NURTURING THE SOUL

Opening up Inner Spaces, Emptying the Mind and Filling the Heart

Before we get on to specific practices, it's worth spending a bit of time contemplating what it is these practices are trying to achieve. As with all things spiritual, there's no one definitive answer. As always, words fall woefully short in trying to articulate what is impossible to articulate using language. But here goes anyway.

One of the best and shortest descriptions of what these practices are trying to achieve comes from Richard Rohr. His book Breathing Under Water describes authentic spirituality as "opening up inner spaces." These are the inner spaces we find within our bodies, within our hearts, and within our souls. There is no scientific proof that these spaces exist. We can't measure the impact of spiritual practice to assess how much "opening up" has gone on. But we can sense it. We sense the opening up as an expansion within our bodies. We sense a freedom. A feeling of wholeness. A weight being lifted off our shoulders. And peacefulness descending. These senses are felt in the body. They are felt in our very being. They are not of the material realm but are very, very tangible.

Rohr then goes on to explain that the way we open up our inner spaces is by "emptying the mind and filling the heart." This is a much more elegant way of describing the process I talked about earlier. I see emptying the mind as re-educating the left hemisphere's false self (emptying the rational mind of what it currently thinks of as true) and filling the heart as re-discovering the right hemisphere's true self (filling our hearts and nurturing our souls).

As an aside, it's worth noting that, in the language of the spirit, "heart" is another synonym for true self. Or even another word for soul. The heart is where we tend to sense truth. It's where we feel deep knowing in our bodies. It's often said that we follow our hearts when we follow our intuition. What's more, it has been discovered that both the heart and the gut have clusters of neurons that can process, store, and transmit information, just like the brain. And as our brains, hearts and guts are all connected by the body's longest nerve, the Vagus Nerve, there's increasing evidence that we don't (and shouldn't) just think with our brains. We should think with our whole bodies. With our brain, with our heart and with our gut. Or maybe a better way of saying that is that we should sense our way forward with our whole bodies. This is much more aligned with our true self-nature and our true self-intelligence. More of this later.

As we open up our inner spaces, not only do we feel expanded and free, we create space for goodness to flow in. We create space that allows us to experience the Divine. And a channel appears. I experience that inflow of goodness as my Higher Power, or a God of my understanding, giving me the guidance and power to do the next right thing. I get a real internal sense of what I should be doing with my life. And also what I shouldn't be doing. Right now. Right here. I get a real sense of my response-ability.

To give you a very small but very real example, the more I've travelled down this spiritual path, the more I've noticed that I find it very difficult to walk past litter on the floor. It doesn't feel right to leave it there. I sense that the right thing to do is pick it up and put it in a bin. It's not my litter. I didn't drop it. But I sense that it is my responsibility to pick it up. On my early morning walks through the local park, listening to something spiritual, I often see the remnants of a party left abandoned by the park benches. Half-empty cider cans and bottles of vodka strewn across the grass. In the past, I would have walked on by, berating the unruly teenagers and thinking about how disgraceful they were in leaving such a mess. Now, I tend to pick it all up and put it in the bin. Not because I want to be seen doing good (there aren't many people around at 6 am in my park) but because I think that the park, my park, is much nicer without the mess all over the place. But to be truthful, it's not that I "think" that at all. I "feel" that. I feel that if I walk on by, I would feel worse. I would feel like I had left the litter myself.

It's an internal sensation driving my actions rather than a logical train of thought. I notice this same internal sensation when I've been given too much change by a cashier. In the past, receiving an extra £10 in my change was cause for a celebration. Now, it's cause for me to immediately highlight the mistake and give back the money to make sure the cashier doesn't get into trouble. Again, that's not what I'm thinking. I'm actually sensing that if I walk away with this unwarranted money, I will feel bad. Like I've stolen the money.

As we'll discuss later, this internal guidance system is a felt, experienced sensation that guides my actions. The more I've become familiar with this internal guidance, the more I entrust it with bigger, more consequential actions in my life. Actions that allow me to follow my purpose. But that's getting ahead of ourselves. We'll discuss purpose later in the book. Let's get back to nurturing the soul.

Conscious Contact with the Divine

Step 11 of The 12-Step Programme states, "Sought through prayer and meditation to improve our conscious contact with God as we understood Him, praying only for knowledge of His will for us and the power to carry that out." This idea of "conscious contact with God as we understood him" is at the heart of all the practices we'll discuss shortly. This idea of consciously contacting God is how we experience the divine. William James describes the logistics and experience of conscious contact with God well in his hypothesis of how we experience the Divine:

> "Let me propose as a hypothesis that whatever it may be on the farther side, the "more" with which in religious experience we feel ourselves connected is on its hither side the subconscious continuation of our conscious life. We might feel

that this power from a higher place is external, and we are connected to it, but
as it is part of our subconscious experience, we are indeed in union with it."

In spite of the slightly outdated language, I sense that his hypothesis is spot on. That's the way I experience the Divine. Through dedicated spiritual practice, I open up inner spaces and allow goodness to flow in. Goodness could be called God or a Higher Power. James calls it "the more." And we may conceive of this goodness, this God, this power, this "more," as being external to us that it is on the farther side of our souls. But because we're connected to it. Because we sense it's part of our true self, our hither side of the subconscious continuation of our conscious life, we feel it within our bodies. We feel it in the opened-up inner spaces.

However, the conscious part of the conscious contact is not necessarily the consciousness we associate with the thinking mind. It is the consciousness associated with the felt experience in the body. When we feel this connection, when we sense this power within, that's when we are indeed in union with it. That's what we're trying to achieve through spiritual practice and the habit of discipline.

Music and Art as a Channel to the Soul

This idea of being connected to and in union with an external power might seem a bit out there if you've never experienced it. A bit too ethereal for those new to spirituality. So, let me draw on my experience as a would-be goth band member and use music as a metaphor for experiencing the Divine.

Music is the most physically compelling of the arts. Music doesn't exist as a physical entity in the material realm. It cannot be touched and measured empirically. It's a connection between the composer, the artist, the sound system and the listener that evolves from moment to moment. The impact is in the moment. It's in the rhythm and the drum beat. It's in the silence between sounds. It's in the harmony of different notes being played at the same time.

C.S. Lewis said, "Music exists between worlds. The physical world of acoustics, the aesthetic world of harmony and the spiritual world of vitality. It transmits a great sense of reality."

When I think about pieces of music that move me, I feel a strong sense of connection between the sound and my body. I feel it inside. I sense a reality that is not picked up by my logical thinking mind. It is sensed through my body and my soul. Feeling connected to music is the best analogy I can think of when describing the felt-connection we're seeking when we're trying to make conscious contact to God. When I listen to music I love, I can sense an opening up of inner space that allows the soul of the music to flow in. The soul of the music fills my own soul. The music is in here. It's not out there. We become connected. I am in union with it. And it creates energy, vitality, and meaning that is impossible to articulate with words. That is a spiritual experience.

We mentioned earlier that McGilchrist suggested in The Master and his Emissary that the body, art and spirituality are gateways to the soul; they go directly to the right hemisphere and bypass the left. Music is an example of art doing just that. It could be poetry or a painting that does it. If we can find this connection with music or any art form, we can find it with the Spirit or the Divine.

Connecting to the Source

Finding this connection and union with the Divine is the spark that ignites the spiritual awakening. Nurturing that spark into a flame deepens faith. Faith that the goodness that is growing within our souls is a much better guide to living than our rational and logical left hemispheres could ever be. Some see the connection as the source of unconditional love. Some as the source of truth. Some see it as the source of creation and intelligence. Yet others see it as the source of consciousness and life itself. I sense it could be all these things. But what's important is that you find this connection for yourself. You discover what is revealed as you open up your inner spaces and allow the goodness in. Only then will you be able to discern whether the unconditional love, the truth, the creative intelligence, the consciousness and life you are becoming increasingly aware of is from your experience of the Divine or not. I suspect you find it is.

FIVE AREAS OF SPIRITUAL PRACTICE TO NURTURE THE SOUL

We've previously explored the idea of perennial wisdom. We noted the four central observations Roger Walsh made in his book Essential Spirituality about the common threads of wisdom that are found across the main spiritual traditions. Threads of wisdom that have endured for centuries and are still valid today. Later in the book, Walsh goes on to discuss what he calls perennial practices. Here is how he introduces them:

> "How to achieve this discovery of our true self is the central question of life, and it is here that the great religions offer their greatest gift. Each of them contains a set of practices designed to help us reach this goal. Whether they be the commandments and contemplations of Judaism, Islam and Christianity, the yogis of Hinduism, or the disciplines of Taoism, each tradition offers spiritual practices that awaken."

He then goes on to identify a number of practices that are common to authentic religions, which he calls the perennial practices. I strongly urge you to read his book and discover these practices for yourself. He offers great insights and provides lots of specific practices and techniques to explore, techniques that I hope will act as a source of inspiration as you experiment with your own disciplined practice.

I've undertaken a similar process to Walsh and created my own version of the perennial practises. These are the techniques that I've found to be most useful in my own spiritual adventure. The tools that have been most effective at opening up my inner space and allowing the goodness to flow in. These are the tools that have been indispensable in emptying my mind and filling my heart. They are the tools that have helped build my habit of discipline.

I have found there are broadly five areas of spiritual practice to focus on. Five areas of activity that will nurture your soul. I'd love for you to investigate these practices for yourself and add to them. Or focus on one or two of them. Evolving these areas to meet the needs of your own soul is all part of discerning your own spiritual path. Doing the work for yourself. Eating your own food. But here's my take on the perennial practices as a starting guide to begin with:

1. Embodying Knowledge
2. Embracing Silence
3. Asking for Guidance and Power
4. Growing through Discomfort
5. Living Virtuously

These are the five areas that I've worked on that I believe led directly to my own spiritual awakening. In the final section of Part 2, Cultivating the Habits: A Spiritual Programme of Action, I provide a framework for building your own morning and evening routine. This is very much the starter pack or beginner's guide to get you going. But I believe it's a very effective way to turn all the good intentions you have into consistent action and, in time, into the enduring habits that lead to spiritual happiness. In the chapter, I suggest practises that you might try out as part of your routine. However, it's not important what I recommend. It's what you do that matters. It's what you experiment with that will make the difference. Find your own path. Nurture your own soul. Evolve your own routines.

1) EMBODYING KNOWLEDGE

The modern Western world has largely treated the body and mind as separate entities. In the UK, if you see a GP about a particular ailment, they will primarily focus on treating the physical symptoms with medication. The diagnosis is usually based on some biological malfunction - something has gone wrong in the flesh and bones of your body. The treatment usually involves physical intervention, in the form of pills, ointments, or surgery, to rectify the issue. The problem is perceived to exist solely in the physical realm, so naturally, the solution is sought there as well. Rarely is the spiritual realm considered as part of the healing process.

In his book The Biology of Belief, Bruce Lipton, a lecturer of medicine, research biologist, and forerunner in epigenetics, highlights the myopic view of medicine in narrowly focusing on the physical aspects of illness and treatment, and ignoring the spiritual traditions throughout history that have recognised the powerful mind-body connection and the phenomenon of mind over matter.

The Power of Placebo

Consider the placebo effect, for example, the power of the mind to heal the body without any physical intervention, which we discussed earlier in the book. The mind believes it is taking an effective pill with active ingredients. The body responds, and the ailment is cured. But in reality, the mind has been tricked - the patients are taking a sugar pill, not an active chemical. The cure originates 100% in the spiritual realm and 0% in the physical. The placebo effect is widely known and supported by extensive data. Like Johann Hari, Lipton suggests that most anti-depressants prescribed in the US, worth $5 billion, work largely due to the placebo effect rather than their active chemicals. Food for thought.

This becomes even more poignant when you realise, as Lipton points out, that dying from medication side effects is the third leading cause of death in the US. Yet more and more money is invested in developing new medications, while almost none is put towards advancing the science of placebos. Could it be because pharmaceutical companies profit greatly from medications and stand to lose if placebos take off? This is a prime example of the unhealthy nature of our culture of economic growth.

Despite the evidence, Western society still refuses to acknowledge the power our mind has over our body. It undervalues this vital connection. That's the crux of this first pillar of spiritual practice. Embodying Knowledge is all about recognising and appreciating the body-mind interconnection. It's about valuing the impact our spiritual well-being and thinking mind have on our physical body, as well as the reverse—the impact our physical body has on our thinking mind and spiritual well-being. It pays to appreciate both aspects equally.

Becoming Attuned to Our Inner Spaces

Building on the idea of opening up inner spaces, the practice of Embodying Knowledge involves becoming aware of those inner spaces, both physically and emotionally. Once we develop this awareness, we can become more attuned to them—noticing, feeling, and respecting them.

I liken this attunement process to viewing ourselves not as a single entity but as a cooperative community of 37 trillion cells. Each cell can sense its environment, detecting the slightest chemical traces and electric charges. It uses this information to make decisions, take actions, and respond to its surroundings to do its part in keeping the cooperative thriving. In this way, cells operate in a sensation-perspective-agency mode very similar to humans.

Now consider the vast amount of data your 37 trillion cells are sensing and acting upon every moment of every day to respond to their environment. Constantly making decisions and taking actions to keep the cooperative alive and well. Yet how much of that information are you consciously aware of? Very little. Obviously, we can never be fully cognizant of all the incredible complexity that sustains us. But we can become more attuned to the intelligence flowing throughout our bodies.

We can do this in two key ways:

1. Becoming more attuned to the intelligence and energy flowing within our bodies in the form of emotions.
2. Becoming more attuned to the intelligence and energy flowing around our bodies in the form of felt relationships.

The Intelligence of Emotion

Let's first address becoming more attuned to the intelligence and energy of emotion flowing through our bodies. Intelligence and energy are normally referred to as emotions. Emotion can be thought of as "e-motion" - energy in motion. It is a natural and vital aspect of human existence. The flow of different energies around our bodies is how the cooperative community of cells communicates. It signals that something in our internal or external environment warrants our attention.

The emotion may be positive, like joy from meeting a friend or admiring a beautiful sunset. The emotion signals the brain to pay attention to this moment. It's essentially saying, "We, the cooperative community of cells, really like this moment. It's worth remembering what we're doing right now so we can repeat this rewarding activity in the future." The positive emotion could stem from a shot of tequila, a line of cocaine, or feeling grateful to a neighbour for taking out your trash. We need to be mindful and aware of not only the positive emotions but also the negative emotions that might be associated with them and follow them as a consequence.

Conversely, the emotion may be negative, like fear of being attacked by an aggressive dog or the prospect of losing your job. The emotion draws your brain's attention, signalling, "We really don't like this moment. We need to take evasive action to escape this dangerous situation." Sometimes, we need to recognise that it's important to face up to these negative emotions rather than just run and hide or numb them out.

The issue is that we often struggle to deal with emotions effectively. Especially for men of a certain age, educated in the 1980s and indoctrinated into the 1990s corporate world, where emotions were not part of the school, university or business curriculum. The prevailing attitude was to deny these pesky emotions even existed; "We don't do emotions here." has often been the mantra.

In recent times, we've become more culturally attuned to the emotional side of life. We're more likely to consider how people "feel" about situations. We even regard Emotional Intelligence (EQ) as a core business and life skill. Yet the central issue of dealing with emotions, especially difficult ones, remains a hidden art. We are far more inclined to numb challenging emotions with external, artificial stimuli like alcohol, drugs, food, gambling, and so on than to deal with them internally and naturally. We are not taught to "feel our feelings" - the simple yet incredibly effective way to process uncomfortable emotions.

The Addiction of Numbing Emotions

As an active alcoholic, I used alcohol to numb every emotion, whether positive or negative. I drank to try to enhance positive emotions. I drank to try to make difficult ones go away. But you can't selectively numb emotions on demand. You end up numbing them all, all the time. When it came to difficult emotions, numbing only provided a temporary reprieve; fear always reared its head again as soon as I sobered up. For positive emotions, numbing did a great job of completely extinguishing them; I lost the natural ability to feel joy.

In recovery, slowly weaning myself off addiction, I was told to expect both good and bad news regarding my emotional life. The good news is that I'd regain my emotions and start feeling life's joy again. The bad news is that I'd also get back the fear, resentment and grief that life inevitably brings. Now, I couldn't numb them away with alcohol. I'd have to learn to deal with them by "feeling the feelings," allowing them to simply be.

Learning to cope with these difficult emotions has been, and continues to be, a challenge. But what a gift it is to be able to sit with my feelings without having to numb them. To use these challenging emotions as tools for growth. To recognise that something in my inner or outer world isn't quite aligned. To appreciate that the cooperative community is trying to tell me that our collective well-being requires some attention. To be able to use that information to respond in a positive way. To be response-able, rather than drink a bottle of wine or eat a pack of cookies.

The Practice of "Feeling the Feelings"

Eckhart Tolle describes the process of "feeling the feelings" well in The power of Now. This is how he describes the process:

> "Focus attention on the feeling inside you. Know that it is there. Accept that it is there. Don't THINK about it - don't let the feeling turn into thinking. Don't judge or analyse. Don't create an identity for yourself out of it. Instead of saying, "I am sad" or "I am anxious," say, "I feel sadness inside me" or "I feel anxiety arising in my body." Stay present and continue to be the observer of what is happening inside you. Be the objective observer, looking at your

body and experiencing the feeling. Make the feeling a thing to be looked at from a distance. Become aware not only of the emotional pain but also of the "one who observes," the silent watcher. This is the power of now, the power of your own conscious presence."

By using this technique, I've been able to handle difficult emotions that previously would have pushed me over the edge into a destructive bender. Instead of blotting the emotions out, I've found that they pass through the body naturally. By resisting the urge to turn feeling into thinking, the feeling dissipates much more quickly.

It's the difference between getting cut up in traffic and feeling annoyed for a few minutes versus holding onto the anger by engaging in an intricate mental dialogue about what you'd say to the driver if you saw them again or what you'd do differently if the incident could magically be replayed.

This simple yet powerful practice reconnected me with my feelings. It heightened my awareness of my inner experience. I developed a greater appreciation for the undulating patterns of emotional highs and lows. I became more accepting of difficult feelings, acknowledging them and allowing them to flow out naturally. I also became more aware of positive emotions, feeling grateful for them and savouring them while they lasted. Always remembering: this too shall pass. All emotions, positive and negative, are fleeting. Positive emotions fade. Negative emotions fade. This, too, shall pass. Always.

This technique makes us much more aware of our inner spaces and more attuned to the energy and intelligence within.

Unveiling the Hidden Currents: Attuning to Life's Subtle Energies

The second type of energy and intelligence we can become more attuned to is the kind that exists around us outside of our bodies. Most people are aware of certain forms of energy that the body consciously senses, such as sounds, temperature, vibrations, and pressure. We can imagine the energy of a sound wave hitting our eardrum and how we might process that sound energy to relay a message to our brain. The energy doesn't stop as it hits our skin; it passes right through us. Think of standing by the speakers at a concert and feeling the bass in your chest. Or consider another type of energy: gravity. This force field of energy passes through every cell in our bodies, keeping us firmly attached to the ground.

These may be the more obvious forms of energy we're conscious of, but what about more subtle forms? High-frequency sounds, non-visible light waves, radio waves, and electromagnetic currents are all examples. Even our thoughts and emotions are subtle forms of energy. Could they be transmitted beyond our physical brains? Could emotions be detected at a distance? What if love was a universal form of subtle energy that behaved like gravity? Perhaps we could detect the energy of love using our bodies and convert it into emotion.

Cells as Energy Receptors

From this energy-based perspective, we no longer have to rely solely on our five physical senses to experience reality. We can add our energy receptors into the mix, too. Each of our 37 trillion cells has the ability to detect and interact with subtle forms of energy. Our individual cells detect subtle forms of energy which guide their response to the ever-changing environment. This interaction with energy is how gene strands in our DNA are activated, the mechanism at the heart of epigenetics, which studies how our behaviours and environment can influence our genes.

By recognising our individual cells' capability to detect subtle forms of environmental energy to stimulate cellular change, we open ourselves up to the possibility that we, as a cooperative community of 37 trillion cells, could have the capability to detect subtle forms of energy to stimulate change. Our whole body could be one big receptor of such energy if only we knew how to decode the information to respond to our environment more effectively.

In his book Radical Wholeness, Philip Shepherd develops this idea further, articulating the body's capability to interact directly with the environment. He explains that the body feels the currents of reality in their yielding, rich, and changeable aliveness. By attuning to those currents, the body attunes to the relationships that guide the unfolding of the Present. This "felt relationship" of the body is in contrast to the "known relationship" of the head. When the body "knows the world" in a way that feels the sights and sounds, it is not relying on the abstraction of language. Its knowing is non-verbal, unmediated, and direct. Its thinking is sensorial.

When I contemplate the notion of us all being interconnected by subtle forms of energy, I know deep inside that we are all part of the whole. I feel part of the whole. But what if this doesn't make sense to you? Or even if it does, how can we train ourselves to be more attuned to these more subtle forms of energy? How do we turn known facts about living into felt knowledge of our relationship with life?

Meditation and contemplation are the top two practices. These two forms of embracing silence are almost ubiquitous spiritual techniques that support all five areas of spiritual practice. We'll discuss both in the next section. Beyond meditation and contemplation, there's one very important thing we can do to help us feel more attuned to what's going on in and around us. That is to fall in love with our bodies.

Falling in Love with Your Body

As Elizabeth Lesser puts it in her book The Seeker's Guide, "Falling in love with your body first means learning to like and respect it. Without a basic respect, or better yet, a reverence for your body, you won't instinctively be drawn to nurture it. We want to care for the things we love. So, the first thing to do to achieve health, strength, and beauty is to fall in love with your body. Get to know your body, listen to it, and treat it as the miracle of nature that it is."

Unfortunately, our culture doesn't make it easy for us to respect our bodies and treat them with reverence. The drive for economic growth puts far more value on working through stress to earn more money than ensuring we have enough rest to recuperate properly. Our need for excitement and thrills means we are more likely to look forward to a night on the town than a quiet night in. Our supermarkets make it much cheaper and easier for us to buy high-fat, high-sugar, and high-salt foods than healthier alternatives.

These are all the by-products of the junk values we take for granted as we drive for more economic growth. They surround us in every aspect of life. No wonder we feel the odds are stacked against us when it comes to looking after our bodies. But that's the task at hand: learn to love your body, learn what it takes to love your body, and let nature and your community of 37 trillion cells look after your body for you.

A common side effect I see in alcoholics who start reaping the benefits of the spiritual solution is the natural inclination to eat healthier and exercise more. My experience is exactly as Bill Wilson famously observed: "When the spiritual malady is overcome, we straighten out mentally and physically." Get the spirituality side right, and mental and physical health soon follow.

There's a corollary to learning to love our bodies. If we need to treat our bodies with respect and reverence to feel more attuned to life, then the opposite must be true; we will find it hard to feel attuned and connected if we continue to disrespect and abuse our bodies.

I know from my own experience and talking to others that alcohol acts as a barrier. It blocks our channel to perceiving subtle energy forms. I suspect other drugs and addictions do, too. Even if I didn't have a physical allergy to alcohol, even if I could have a blowout every now and then, I suspect drinking regularly would impair my ability to attune myself to life. I wouldn't be as effective in finding a conscious connection to my higher power. I would begin to feel more and more separated. Isolation is a classic symptom of addiction. We go further and further into ourselves, the further into our addiction we get. And I believe that the process of isolation sets in motion the moment you start treating your body as anything other than the miracle of nature that it is.

That's why, as part of the morning and evening routines featured in the Cultivating the Habits: A Spiritual Programme of Action section, I recommend abstaining from the one or two habits that undermine the reverence you might want to cultivate with your body. It could be smoking, drinking, drugs, sugar, or inactivity that negatively affects your physical health. Or some form of compulsive behaviour like gambling, shopping, gaming, or social media consumption that negatively affects your mental health. Addressing the bad habits in our life as we nurture the good ones is the way to spiritual happiness.

Nurturing Attunement Skills with Wonder, Awe, and Gratitude

Once we've started to love our bodies and are looking after ourselves as nature intended, there are three types of activities that can help nurture our attunement skills (thanks to Mark Vernon for these ideas, as suggested in his book Spiritual Intelligence in Seven Steps). These are ways we can enliven our soul and sense the subtle forms of energy in and around us.

1. Attuning ourselves with life in its physical form: These activities involve feeling out and connecting our internal spaces with the subtle energy forms of nature. This includes getting out in the countryside, walking in the wind and rain, gardening and feeling the soil in our fingers, swimming in the sea, and hugging the people you love.

2. Attuning ourselves with life in its less tangible forms: These activities involve feeling out and connecting our internal spaces with non-physical entities. This includes listening to your favourite song and feeling lost in the music, watching a baby smile and feeling instant joy, playing with a dog and laughing at its antics, appreciating the architecture of a building, and being grateful that someone gave you a gift.

3. Attuning ourselves with life in its abstract forms: These activities involve connecting our inner spaces to concepts or ideas. This includes appreciating the wisdom in a spiritual book (I get this when reading a verse from the Tao Te Ching), having an "aha" moment when an idea occurs to you, reading a particularly poignant poem, seeing an elegant solution to a problem, or the beauty in a fractal pattern in nature.

Anytime you get an opportunity to do any of these things, try to remember to do them with a sense of wonder, awe, and gratitude. Feel out for the hidden beauty in all of these activities. Reach out with your heart and try to connect your soul with the soul of the activity. You can even close your eyes and imagine doing these things in your mind's eye. But do so in a way that tries to fill your inner spaces with the subtle energy forms around you. If you practise this technique, you should start to feel that energy inside. It creates a tingling sensation, almost like goosebumps. Get familiar with feeling that feeling. That is the feeling of connection. That is the feeling of embodying knowledge from the world around you. That is the feeling of spiritual happiness.

2) EMBRACING SILENCE

If there is one thing that seems to be universally valued by all spiritual and religious traditions it would be meditation. The skill, the art, the practice of sitting still in silence is something that seems to be the perennial of all the perennial practices. As Elizabeth Lesser describes it, "Meditation is the centrepiece of a spiritual practice." And yet this same ability to sit still in silence is a skill, an art, a practice that has all but been forgotten in our Western, modern culture.

As I've mentioned previously, I initially hated the idea of meditating. It just seemed so pointless and hard to do. I didn't seem to be able to sit still for any length of time and empty my mind. As I stuck with it, as I learned more about it, and as I experimented with it, meditation became the backbone of my daily morning routine, and it has benefitted me hugely.

For such a seemingly simple practice, there are lots of different views about how it works, how to do it and what benefits you can receive from it. I don't claim to be a meditation expert, but I have experimented enough with different styles to know what works for me. I recommend you do your own research: experiment, read, review, experiment, read, review. I will talk about three forms of meditation that have been integral to my own practice of embracing silence: mindfulness meditation, contemplation and moving into the Now.

Mindfulness Meditation

When we think about meditation, the picture we usually conjure up in our mind is that of us sitting on a cushion, cross-legged, with our eyes closed, thinking of nothing. In essence, that form of meditation is known as mindfulness meditation. This is the form of mediation I practice. Chogyam Trunpa describes it as follows:

> "By meditation here, we mean something very basic and simple that is not tied to any one culture. We're talking about a very basic act: sitting on the ground, assuming a good posture, and developing a sense of our spot, our place on this earth. This is the means of rediscovering ourselves and our basic goodness, the means to tune ourselves to genuine reality without expectations or preconceptions....Through the practice of meditation, we can learn to be without deception, to be fully genuine and alive."

From this simple overview, you can see how meditation underlies some of the big themes we've covered in this book, rediscovering ourselves, our true selves. Allowing goodness, our basic goodness, the goodness of life, to flow in. Attuning ourselves to genuine reality. Learning to live without deception; learning to live honestly, humbly, open-mindedly, and with willingness (H.H.O.W.). How to be fully genuine and alive, feeling the full rapture of being alive. These are all aspects of mediation I can attest to.

Of all the books I've read about meditation, the most helpful description came in Elizabeth Lesser's The Seekers Guide. I highly recommend reading this book. It covers a lot of ground about the spiritual journey and what it can mean in our modern world. Meditation is just one area she covers, but she does so in a way that I found accessible, easy to understand and easy to implement. Here are a few tips from Elizabeth's book:

Daily Practice

She sets the scene by stressing the importance of establishing a daily meditation practice.

> "The practice of meditation is like the practice of anything we want to learn. Meditation is like piano scales, basketball drills, ballroom dance class. Practice requires discipline; it can be tedious; it is necessary. After you have practiced enough, you become more skilled in the art form itself. You do not practice to become a great scale player or drill champion. You practice to become a musician or athlete. Likewise, one does not practice meditation to become a great meditator. We meditate to wake up and live, to become skilled at the art of living. And like any art form, the need to practice continues at every level of achievement."

She then goes on to talk about five elements that are common to all forms of meditation: breath, posture, thoughts, time and place.

Breath

Most forms of meditation use the simple act of breathing as a focus for the meditation.

> *"I have heard many explanations as to why the breath is universally used in meditation. Some traditions say it's because breathing is the most basic act we do. It connects us to life in an immediate way...Awareness of breathing makes us aware of the precious nature of life; it sweeps away the clutter that gets in the way of a basic appreciation for being alive."*

In my own meditation practice, I start each session with a deep breathing exercise. Something along the lines of the 4-2-6 technique: breathe in through the nose for 4 seconds, hold for 2 seconds and breathe out through the nose for 6 seconds. But I try to do it for much longer on each part—more like 12-6-18. I make sure I breathe by pushing my stomach out to fill the bottom of the lungs first, gradually filling the lungs up from the bottom to the top. Also, breathing out all the air I naturally can on the out breath. After a few minutes of this, I then settle down and breathe naturally (which is usually deeper and longer as a result of the 4-2-6) and follow the breath going in and out of my nose, focusing on it lightly.

Posture

I used to think that I could meditate lying down. Honestly, that was me just being lazy and using meditation as an excuse for napping. A good, strong sitting posture is important for meditation. Chogyam Trunga stresses that good posture in sitting meditation is a way of demonstrating your basic human goodness. It tells the world that you take pride in being a human and you believe in yourself. He likened a good, strong posture to "sitting tall in the saddle" when riding a horse. It tells the horse you are in control. He then goes on to suggest a six-part posture checklist:

- Take your seat. Sit on a firm pillow on the floor or in a straight-backed, firm-seated chair. If you are on the floor, make sure the pillow is high enough, so your knees touch the floor. If you're in a chair, sit forward so your back doesn't touch the back of the chair.
- Place your legs: As above, if you're on the floor with the pillow, knees touching the floor. Or feet flat on the floor, knees a few inches apart if you're sitting on the chair.
- Torso: Keep your back comfortably straight, your chest high and open, and your shoulders back and relaxed.
- Hands: Some traditions suggest the hands be placed in a traditional Christian prayer position. Personally, I prefer to rest my hands on my knees, palm upwards, sometimes with fingers and thumbs spread naturally apart, and sometimes with the thumb and middle finger gently touching.
- Eyes: I always meditate with my eyes closed. I recommend starting this way. But if you find you get sleepy, try keeping them open but with a soft focus on something directly in front of you.
- Mouth: keep the mouth closed, the jaw relaxed, and the teeth apart, remembering to breathe in and out of your nose. Thich Nhat Hanh recommends having the slightest of smiles on your lips to keep the jaw soft. It also brings a gentle tone of joy and gratitude to the meditation.

Thoughts

This is tricky for many people. Sitting down, being quiet, and focusing on the breath all sound pretty straightforward—until you start realising the craziness that's going on in your head! This is how Elizabeth Lesser describes it.

"Breath, posture, placement of hands, eyes open or shut: all of these techniques form the container for meditation practice. But none of them eradicate the

absurd amount and the aggravating intensity of the thoughts that flood the landscape of the mind when we sit down to meditate. Please expect this. Good thoughts, bad thoughts, pleasurable ones, disturbing ones – they will come and go as we sit in meditation, watching our breath and maintaining our posture. They are the weather of the mind. Our goal in meditation is not to get rid of thoughts. Rather, the goal is to abandon identifying with each thought as it comes and goes; to watch the thoughts as we would watch the weather from an observation tower."

This, for me, has been one of the great benefits of mindfulness meditation; a daily practise that builds the ability to realise that I am not my thoughts. I can look at my thoughts, mood, and feelings and not get lost in them. Or at least appreciate that I don't have to get lost in them. I can choose to be the observer of those thoughts and moods and feelings and allow them to flow through me, just as we talked about in the previous section.

This strengthening of our observer capability is why I recommend this form of meditation over guided meditations (meditations where you listen to someone talk to you throughout the meditation). Guided meditations have a role, especially in the early stages of the spiritual journey. I used many guided meditations to get comfortable with the idea, and I still enjoy them. But in my opinion, the daily practice of sitting in silence is where the transformation takes place.

Time

As Lesser says, "People often ask how many times a day one should meditate and for how long. This is a difficult question to answer. If you want to jog to stay in shape, your daily exercise regime will be quite different from someone who is preparing for a marathon. If you are meditating to calm your daily stress and become more clear headed at work, then your practice will differ from someone who wants to know God's thoughts."

A daily twenty-minute meditation practice is the most frequently recommended time period for anyone who wants to benefit from meditation. Many traditions suggest forty-five. If lack of time is an issue, it is better to meditate for ten minutes – even five – than not to meditate at all. It is usually suggested that you meditate in the morning because you are fresh and alert. But you can meditate at any time of the day.'

The 12-Step Programme suggests that our thoughts of prayer and meditation, the cornerstones of Step 11, should happen "upon awakening." First thing in the morning before we get caught up in the daily distractions of the daily grind. So that's what I do and what I've done for the past five years. Every morning (well, almost every morning), I get up early (around 4:50 am) and devote 40-50 minutes to quiet time, reading something spiritual, saying some prayers and meditating for twenty minutes. Early mornings are ideal for me. The kids are still sleeping. Nobody is pinging messages to my phone. The world is silent. The quiet hours before dawn, before the world awakes, feel like a sacred time to me and the perfect time to devote to sacred stillness.

This early morning ritual is one that I find hard to do without. It felt like a bind to start with, but I now realise it played a significant part in catalysing my spiritual awakening. It keeps me in daily conscious contact with a God of my understanding.

Place

The next tip from Elizabeth Lesser comes in the form of establishing a special space in your house that you can call your meditation space. It certainly doesn't have to be a whole meditation room, but it is beneficial to have an area that you associate with sacred silence. A space you can adorn with pictures, symbols, candles, and mementoes. A place you could call your altar even. I meditate in my bedroom, and in front of where I sit, I have created a small altar consisting of a candle (that I sometimes light and sometimes don't), a small statue of Lakshmi (the Goddess of abundance – something I felt I was short of when I first started meditating), two wooden crosses (given to me by my Mum when I was in the throes of addiction), an engraved stone (given to me by my Dad at the same time) and a variety of healing crystals given to me by various people throughout the years.

It's not a particularly elaborate altar, but it is where I meditate every day. It's an integral part of the routine and ritual. It's a visual reminder to help me keep the discipline going.

Goals

The final bit of advice from Lesser is to establish some goals. Be clear with yourself about why you want to meditate. Without those goals, goals that come from your inner passions, you'll find it hard to keep the practice going. It doesn't matter if those goals are large or small. Achievable or pie in the sky. And those goals are likely to change over time.

The benefits of mediation are manifold and yet so hard to describe. Mark Epstein, MD, a psychiatrist and author of Thoughts Without a Thinker, describes this meditation conundrum as "There's a 2000-year tradition of finding it impossible to describe." The challenge of articulating the logical reasons why one might want to dedicate a good proportion of time to meditation is that the meditative experience takes us into deeper and deeper inner spaces where language and rational thought lose their potency. To me, this sounds like the realm of the right hemisphere. Meditation is a process that directly nurtures our soulful, intuitive, deep, true selves. The benefit is felt away from the seat of language. It's hard to describe in words. But what I can say is that regular, disciplined practice of mindful meditation helps our spiritual journey in four clear ways:

strange that I've just written that last sentence. But that is the truth. My understanding of the truth. I know that a God of my understanding exists. I don't believe it. I know it because I've felt it. Only through meditation and stillness have I been able to do that.

4. *An ability to hear our soul's true desires:* Only in silence can we hear the true self and the direction it wants to take us. In our culture of economic growth, we're all too easily led by junk values and our false self's drive for wealth and fame and the promises of comfort and security they promise. We're bombarded by the noise and messages of what the "good life" looks like. But that drive for the good life has led to nothing but pain, suffering, disappointment and addiction. Once we've learned to clear our mind and manage our cravings, once we've learned to cultivate freedom, peace, gratitude and abundance, once we've been able to connect to a Higher Power, we can then start to listen out for our soul's true desire. We can listen out for that "still small voice" mentioned in The Bible or the "soft murmuring sound" described in the Hebraic Tankah. In the nurtured silence of meditation, we can start to feel our soul's true desires and discern them from the selfish desires of our false self. We can allow our inner spaces to fill with goodness and trust the direction that goodness wants to take us. As we'll discuss later in the Epilogue, The Pathway to Purpose and Power, learning to trust this small, still voice takes time, but it is ultimately the source that guides us to our purpose in life. It is the source of the power that enables us to act on that guidance. And this is the path to feeling the full rapture of being alive. It's the key to being aligned with life and finding our role within it. It comes with stillness. It comes by sitting in silence. It comes with practice. Once it does, it becomes a source of inspiration and power that will support you for the rest of your spiritual adventure. A line in a poem by Rumi sums up beautifully what the ability to hear our soul's

true desires does for us. It allows us to "Let yourself be silently drawn by the stronger pull of what you really love."

When I first started meditating, my only goal was to get sober. I knew that it was one of the tools that would help me stop drinking. I soon realised it could also give me peace from my racing mind, so that then became my primary goal. As my spiritual adventure has unfolded, my goal for meditation is not only to continue deepening my sense of peace and joy but also to better understand my soul's true desire: to try and hear that still, small voice that I increasingly see as a source of insight and strength that can be trusted to guide and support my actions. Especially when it comes to the bigger decisions in life, sitting in silence to let the "next big fork in the road of life" sink into the inner space is a surefire way to quell any doubt about which side of the fork my true self is nudging me towards. This is how I increasingly discern my purpose in life. A topic we'll return to later in the book.

Contemplation

The next practice in our spiritual toolbox to help us in our quest to embrace silence is the art of contemplation. In our modern Western culture, we've come to think about contemplation as deep thinking. Something that sits predominantly with our logical, rational left hemisphere. However, true contemplation, as practiced in the spiritual context, is meditation with a thought in mind. It is the planting of a specific idea into the fertile soil of a still mind. It is the bringing together of a mediative state and a focused imagination.

Like meditation, contemplation starts with sitting in silence, quietening the mind. Once we have calmed the chatter, we introduce an idea—an inspiring idea or a challenging idea—something about the nature of life or our life that is worthy of contemplation.

Unlike the mindfulness meditation tips we discussed earlier, I'm not going to provide any guidance for contemplation. There are no right ways or suggested ways to contemplate. You don't need to sit upright, or close your eyes, or breath in a certain way. All you need to do is be aware of the still quality in your mind at any point in the day and allow an idea to sit there. An idea that intrigues you. An idea that feels important to you. An idea that you can place gently between your left hemisphere and your right hemisphere and let the contemplative stream take its course.

I find myself naturally contemplating life when I'm out in the morning, walking and listening to spiritual books. I'll come across an idea that stops me in my tracks. Sometimes, it's an idea that hits that truth button and blasts out a massive "aha" moment. Or sometimes it's an idea that turns my preconceived ideas of the workings of the world upside down with a great big "WTF is that all about?" Either way, that's a great time to pause the audiobook, appreciate the stillness of the moment, take in the fresh air and nature around me and let that idea sit there. I let the idea be contemplated. I let the notion sink in and gently encourage it to circulate around my mind, body and soul. I'm not looking for an answer to emerge. I'm looking for a feeling to arise. A sense that the idea, the insight, the paradox is being worked on by my intuitive soul. In fact, it's a feeling that it's being worked on by my whole body, safely embodied somewhere in my cells, waiting for the right time to re-emerge as a useful intuition.

Thich Nhat Hahn calls contemplation "concentration." In his book The Art of Living, he says, "As you sustain mindfulness, that is concentration. Wherever there is concentration, there is insight – a breakthrough – bringing more peace, understanding, love and joy into your life."

In the chapter The Habit of Awareness, we mentioned Thich Nhat Hahn's three concentrations, which we could call three contemplations. I would highly recommend getting a copy of Thich Nhat Hahn's audiobook The Art of Living; listen to it when you are out walking peacefully (i.e. not in a rush going somewhere) in chunks of thirty minutes and when you get to a key passage on emptiness, signlessness or aimlessness, pause the audio. Stand in silence. Let the idea sit there between your left and right hemispheres and contemplate. Think about the idea and what it might mean to you and your life. Don't look for an answer. Just ponder the thought. This is an amazing way to deepen the understanding of your inner spaces and fill them with goodness. This is the art of contemplation.

Moving into the Now

David Bohm, one of the pioneers of quantum physics and one of the most influential physicists of the 20th Century, was fascinated by the nature of time and the insights that arose when contemplating time. He asked his peers to consider the following: if the present moment is the point between the past, which no longer exists, and the future, which doesn't yet exist, then the implication is that the present is the joining point between two periods of time that don't exist. What does this lead us to believe about the nature of reality? He went on to develop a theory of the implicate order and the explicate order that culminated in him proclaiming, "Ultimately, all moments are really one, so now is an eternity." That's quite a proclamation. One that needs much more contemplation on my behalf before it fully sinks in.

However, a similar take on the nature of time that is much more accessible is that of Eckhart Tolle, as brought to life in his book The Power of Now. Like Bohm, Tolle could see that both the past and present are periods of time that don't exist. Tolle then went on to make the remarkably simple and yet piercingly insightful observation that human beings tend to spend a lot of time thinking about the past and the future (periods of time that don't exist and aren't real) and very little time focused on the present moment (the one period of time that does exist and is real). Not only that but when we think about the past and future, we tend to do so in a negative way. When we focus on the present moment (the Now), negativity tends to disappear. This is how Tolle explains it:

> "All negativity is caused by an accumulation of psychological time (holding on to ideas about the past and future which don't exist) and a denial of the present. Unease, anxiety, tension, stress, worry – all forms of fear – are caused by too much future and not enough present. Guilt, regret, resentment, grievances, sadness, bitterness and all forms of non-forgiveness are caused by too much past and not enough presence."

This simple insight hit me like thunder when I first heard it. I'd often thought of myself as a "worrier." I knew how my worrying had turned into anxiety and, ultimately, the breakdown in 2015. I was also aware of the background fear I experienced in the early days of getting sober. I think there's been an ever-present, low-lying sense of fear and dread that's been there lurking in the background for most of my adult life.

Tolle describes this sort of fear as psychological fear. As he sees it, it's natural to feel afraid of fire, or of a wild animal, or any form of violence. However, we need to be aware of the "psychological condition of fear that is divorced from any concrete and true immediate danger." This kind of fear is based purely on something that might happen, not on something that is happening. When I dig deeper into that ever-present, low-lying sense of fear and dread, I find a whole host of specific fears: fear of failure, fear of being hurt, fear of losing something or somebody, fear of being wrong, fear of being found out as an imposter. These are the fears that make me a "worrier." These are the fears that cause unease, anxiety, nervousness, tension, phobias and so on. In The 12-Step Programme of Recovery, these sorts of fears are classed as self-centred fears. They are fears of the ego. Fears that our false self, personality-driven image will be dented in some way. We will be less secure, less comfortable, or less popular. All of them are based in the future. They are not real. These are fears of things that may happen. They are not happening. And more specifically, they are not happening now. You are here Now. But your mind is not. It is in the non-existent future. And this gap between the reality of now and the future imagining of your mind creates anxiety. This is the anxiety gap.

I suspect many people experience this anxiety gap. That's because a lot of people worry. A 2023 report from the Mental Health Foundation found that almost three-quarters of the UK population (73%) had felt anxious at least some of the time in the previous two weeks. And the biggest cause of worry in our culture of economic growth is money. One in three people (32%) said worries about "being able to afford to pay my bills" made them anxious in the previous two weeks. 20% said "debt", and 15% cited job insecurity or unemployment. We may be one of the world's wealthiest nations, but we still worry a lot about money.

And yet here is Eckhart Tolle suggesting that all that worry, all that anxiety, all that fear is unnecessary. It is simply a result of our minds spending too much time in a non-existent place, the future. The cure to all our worries, whether they are financial or otherwise, Tolle suggests, is to put all our attention on the Now. Be present. Focus on this very moment. Be here. Now.

It seems almost too good and too simple to be true. Can it really be that easy to pack up our troubles in our old kit bag and smile, smile, smile? In the Now, Now, Now?

My experience is that it's not that easy at all. But it is possible. By focusing all our attention on this moment, whenever that moment might be, no matter how chaotic the surrounding circumstances might appear to feel, we reduce our fears by moving into the Now and sensing that everything is absolutely as it should be right Now. We reduce our worries, our anxieties, and our stress by focusing on the Now. This is a form of meditation that we can use anywhere. It doesn't require finding a twenty-minute slot in a silent, sacred space. You can move into the Now in a traffic jam, in a queue for the bus, in a meeting with your boss. This form of embracing silence quietens our racing mind and stops it from rampaging in a non-existent place.

Thich Nhat Hahn describes the process of moving into the Now as "arriving in the present moment to discover that the present moment is the only moment in which you can find everything you've been looking for and that you already are everything you want to become." You may find it hard to believe that you are enough and have enough in this present moment when you are in the midst of a worry storm about paying the bills. But it's true. The reality is that, right Now, in this very moment, not next week, not tomorrow, not this afternoon, not even in an hour's time, you have everything you need Now. You are enough; you have enough right here, right Now.

Trying to build this "enough Now" mentality is a form of instantaneous meditation we can practise any time and all the time. It's a mentality that Brené Brown talks about when she talks about worthiness. Being worthy and feeling worthy happen Now—not when, not if, not when you get married, lose five pounds, retire, get that job, have £25,000 in the bank, or get a bigger house.

Although Eckhart Tolle made the Power of Now famous in the 21st Century, the wisdom of now is ancient. The Bible advises us to "Take therefore no thought for the morrow: for the morrow shall take thought for the things of itself." (Matthew 6:34). It also tells us that "Behold, now is the acceptable time; behold, now is the day of salvation." (2 Corinthians 6:2).

3) ASKING FOR GUIDANCE AND POWER

As I've previously mentioned, Step 11 in The 12-Step Programme revolves around prayer and meditation. To reiterate, the concept of prayer initially baffled and repelled me. In retrospect, I'm unsure why I rejected it so vehemently. As a child, I had prayed a few times, knowing the basics – hands together, kneeling on the floor, and reciting the Lord's Prayer. It was all fairly innocuous, and I hadn't experienced any Divine retribution. Nonetheless, for some reason, I simply didn't want to engage in what seemed like a pointless exercise.

However, with the Gift Of Desperation on my side, I began praying daily in the spring of 2019. As with many aspects of the spiritual journey, my perspective on prayer has completely transformed. I now pray every morning, not out of obligation, but because I believe in its efficacy. That's the key to prayer – it works if you believe it works.

The Surprising Prevalence of Prayer

Let's take a step back to explore the world of prayer. Like other pillars of spiritual practice, prayer isn't heavily promoted in our culture of economic growth. Interestingly, though, more people in the UK pray than one might assume. A recent survey conducted for the Church of England revealed that nearly half of all adults (48%) have prayed at some point, with just over a quarter (28%) having prayed in the last month. Surprisingly, younger people are more likely to pray than older individuals; 56% of 18 to 34-year-olds say they have prayed, with a third (32%) reporting having prayed in the last month. In contrast, only 41% of those aged 55+ said they had ever prayed, with 25% having prayed in the last month.

The Rev Dr Stephen Hance, National Lead for Evangelism and Witness for the Church of England, suggests that prayer resonates with people in an age where mindfulness and meditation are increasingly popular. Moreover, with mounting pressures and uncertainty affecting every generation, many individuals of all ages are drawing strength from God through prayer.

Turning to God in Times of Crisis

I find it fascinating that when times are tough, and we don't know where to turn, we instinctively seek God's help. Even those who don't regularly attend church, pray, or strongly believe in God tend to get down on their knees, clasping their hands and looking to the sky when their backs are against the wall. It's almost a reflexive response to crisis: "Dear God, I'm in a mess. I don't know what to do or where to go. Please, God, help me. I need your help."

Even the wisest and noblest among us turn to prayer when feeling lost. The great leader and statesman Abraham Lincoln admitted, "I have been driven upon my knees many times by the overwhelming conviction that I have nowhere to go. My own wisdom...seemed insufficient for that day."

This desperate plea for Divine intervention is a common story among those embarking on The 12-Step Programme, often made by addicts as they approach rock bottom. I, too, made that plea. Overwhelmed by shame and pain, I wanted to stop drinking but lacked the strength. So, I asked a God I barely knew and didn't believe in for help I felt undeserving of. And guess what? I got it. Within weeks, I was in rehab and on the path to recovery.

The Power of Prayer: Coincidence or Divine Intervention?

Naturally, I didn't credit God for this turn of events. In my mind, ending up in rehab was a combination of my wife finding a suitable place (unbeknownst to me), my own submission in accepting the offered help, the support from colleagues at work (despite having tested their patience numerous times before), and unexpected financial assistance from my father. This interconnected series of events led to my recovery - not my kneeling and praying to God for a resolution. Or was it?

Many believe in the direct impact of prayer. Emmett Fox, a prominent spiritual leader, insists that "Miracles in the popular sense of the word can and do happen as the result of prayer. Prayer does change things. Prayer does make things happen quite otherwise than they would have happened had the prayer not been made."

I must admit I'm not as convinced as Emmett that praying alters the material world around us. Perhaps I haven't prayed enough or in the right way, or maybe I simply don't believe prayers are the reason for the changes in my life. When I needed help, I prayed for it and received it. However, it's more rational for me to attribute these changes to the actions of those around me rather than God - but maybe that's just me failing to see the implicit connections.

I've always appreciated the following parable about a man in danger of drowning who prayed for help:

A man, trapped on his rooftop during a flood, prayed to God for salvation. Nothing happened. God didn't appear. After a while, a man in a rowboat came by, offering to save him, but the man on the roof declined, saying, "No, it's okay. I've prayed to God, and He will save me." The rowboat left.

Next, a motorboat arrived, and the man in the boat shouted, "Jump in! I can save you." Again, the man on the roof refused, stating, "No thanks. I've prayed to God, and He will save me. I have faith." The motorboat departed.

Finally, a helicopter appeared, and the pilot lowered a rope, yelling, "Grab this rope, and I will lift you to safety." Once more, the man on the roof replied, "No thanks. I've prayed to God, and He will save me. I have faith." The helicopter flew away.

The water soon rose above the rooftop, and the man drowned. Upon reaching Heaven, he expressed his annoyance to God, saying, "I had faith in you, but you didn't save me. You let me drown. I don't understand why!"

God replied, "I sent you a rowboat, a motorboat, and a helicopter. What more did you expect?"

This story serves as a reminder that the interconnected events of life may not be as random and independent as our logical left hemisphere might lead us to believe. Perhaps all of life's events are connected in some way, with the subtle energies of the universe linking not only entities but also occurrences.

Does that mean it's possible to influence those events by praying?

To answer that question, let's examine what Step 11 says and take it from there. The words in Step 11 state: "Sought through prayer and meditation to improve our conscious contact with God as we understood Him, praying only for knowledge of His will for us and the power to carry that out."

As far as The 12-Step Programme is concerned, there seem to be four important pointers to consider when it comes to prayer:

1. Praying should be done with other spiritual practices, such as meditation.
2. Praying is about improving our conscious contact with God as we understand Him. It's about building a relationship.
3. Praying should only be about asking for knowledge and guidance - understanding what "God's will" is for us.
4. And asking for the power, the strength, to carry out what is being asked of us.

Making Prayer Part of a Daily Routine

The first pointer highlights the need for prayer to be a regular, even daily or hourly activity. Just like meditation, the benefits of prayer grow the more you do it. It should become part of our daily practice. In the book Twelve Steps and Twelve Traditions, Bill Wilson writes:

"There is a direct linkage among self-examination, meditation, and prayer. Taken separately, these practices can bring much relief and benefit. But when they are logically related and interwoven, the result is an unshakable foundation for life." This has been my experience as well. My morning and evening routines, which include a mixture of spiritual practices like prayer, meditation, and self-examination, have become an indispensable foundation for my life. The practices are logically related and interwoven. Indispensable even.

Building a Relationship with Your Higher Power

The second pointer emphasises that prayer isn't just about asking for things or help getting out of sticky situations. It's also about building conscious contact to forge a better relationship with one's Higher Power - however, you conceive of it. This is especially important if you struggle with the concept of God.

As discussed earlier, developing a personally meaningful and believable notion of God is key. When engaging in prayer, you are communicating directly with your conception of that God. Not only are you talking to your God, but you're also asking for help and hoping your God will respond. For that to happen, you have to believe your conception of God is capable of hearing and responding. You must believe that your personal God can positively impact your life.

I grappled with this for a long time, unable to fathom how talking to an imagined heavenly being could result in real change. As I made conscious contact with my God through prayer, meditation and contemplation, I became more familiar with its true nature. I built a relationship with that Higher Power, sensing its presence in moments of stillness.

I saw my God not as a human-like figure but as an ever-present field of intelligent, creative, compassionate energy connecting all of life. Therefore, the way that my God heard my prayers wasn't through sound waves that passed from my mouth to His ears. It was more like the transference of subtle energies from my soul into the God-like ether. The way I heard the response to those prayers was through me sensing subtle energies in my inner spaces via certain types of feelings, thoughts or beliefs. These were the means of communication I learned to use through prayer. Nurturing my attunement to these subtle energies, as discussed in Embodying Wisdom, is how I learned to communicate through prayer.

This is how I came to believe that prayer works. This is the way it works for me. For my understanding of God. And how me and my God communicate. It may not be the way it works for you. You may believe my understanding to be nonsense. And that's fine. That's why you have a God of your understanding, and I have a God of mine. The point here is once you have a vague understanding of your God, you need to become familiar with it. You need to build a relationship with it through conscious contact. You need to start believing that your God can hear and answer your prayers.

In his book The Power of Your Subconscious Mind, Dr Joseph Murphy, Minister-Director of the Church of Divine Science in Los Angeles, emphasises the important role of belief in prayer: "The law of belief is the secret operating principle in all the religions of the world. The Buddhist, the Christian, the Moslem, and the Jew may all get answers to their prayers in spite of the enormous differences among their stated beliefs. How can this be? The answer is that it is not because of the particular creed, religion, affiliation, ritual, ceremony, formula, liturgy, incantation, sacrifices or offerings but solely because of belief or mental acceptance and receptivity about that for which they pray. The law of life is the law of belief. Belief can be summed up briefly as a thought in your mind. As a person thinks, feels and believes, so is the condition of his or her mind, body and circumstances. A technique, a methodology based on an understanding of what you are doing and why you are doing it will help you to bring about a subconscious embodiment of all good things in life. Essentially, answered prayer is the realisation of your heart's desire."

I agree with Dr Murphy's observations about the law of life being the law of belief. I believe that once you start believing that your God can answer your prayers, you can start asking for help and expect to get it. I believe that through prayer and regular practice of other spiritual disciplines, you can start realising your heart's desire. But remember what I said about "heart," meaning "soul." Your heart's desires aren't your ego's, false self desires for pleasure, comfort and security. Your heart's desires are your soul's desires for growth. Your heart's desires may be uncomfortable and inconvenient. Your heart's desire is to feel freedom, wholeness, peace, joy and fulfilment. Your heart's desire is to feel the full rapture of being alive.

Has my God helped me realise my heart's desire? Have my prayers been answered? I would say undeniably yes. As a result of my spiritual adventure, which includes daily prayer and meditation, I believe to the core of my being that a God of my understanding exists in my world. I believe, to the core of my being, that building a relationship with this Higher Power has changed me and my life circumstances for the better. It has stopped my craving for alcohol. It has changed my perception of the world and how to live successfully in it. It has given me a new lease of life. It has opened my eyes to a new purpose and given me the power to go in that direction. It has brought me freedom, wholeness, peace, joy, and fulfilment. And it has generated life situations that I would never have thought possible.

Do I believe all these changes are the direct result of praying? I believe prayer played an important role. It was an integral part of the process. That's because prayer is the part of the process where we ask for help. We bring attention to the specific problems we are struggling with. Just like Abraham Lincoln, we identify the situation where our own wisdom seems insufficient for that day. We ask for help. We get that help in two forms: guidance and power—the subjects of the final two pointers.

Seeking Guidance and Power

The third and fourth pointers highlight that what we should seek from our prayers are not necessarily sudden changes in circumstance. Instead, we should be seeking guidance and power.

It's tempting to pray for specific, tangible outcomes. When we're sick, we want to be cured. When someone else is sick, we pray for their healing. If we're struggling financially, we ask for money. If we're battling addiction, we beg for it to go away. As I learned through The 12-Step Programme, there's nothing wrong with asking God for specific outcomes or wanting the best for ourselves and others. However, we shouldn't expect unfavourable situations to magically resolve themselves simply because that's how we'd like to see them work out. We are not aware of life's full complexity. We take in only the tiniest amount of information available about the reality around us. We're not in a good position to know exactly what is best for us, others, or the world around us in the long run. We have to rely on the inherent intelligence of higher forces to let life unfold as it is meant to unfold.

Sickness, for example, might not make any sense to us at all. We might not like being sick. In the bigger scheme of life, it may serve a purpose that we are totally unaware of. Perhaps we need to build up antibodies. Maybe a certain proportion of the world has to be sick for a cure to be found for future generations. Illness might be part of the journey our soul needs to endure to grow. Or there may be no rational, logical reason for it at all. It might just seem incredibly unfair or cruel. But as we all know, life can appear intolerably cruel at times.

. . .

The Unknowable Reasons Behind Life's Challenges

The point is that we just don't know why things happen the way they do. Why are some people sick and others not? Why do we live in a culture that values money over nature? Why did I become addicted to alcohol when most drinkers don't? Why did my wife have to die so young? I don't know why these things happened. I can speculate. I can hazard a guess. I can research and put forward a relatively coherent rationale. But I don't know for sure. Nobody does. Only the Infinite Creative Intelligence underpinning the web of life knows why these things happen. Even then, it may not be so much about knowing or understanding but more about appreciating that things need to be that way. There's no reason as such—it's all part of life's intricate workings as it unfolds. It's why your family member is sick. It's why you struggle financially. It's why addiction plagues you. These interconnected situations have emerged as we try to live our lives within the story of economic growth, which itself is part of the bigger story of life, the universe, and everything.

Maybe these things can be changed or influenced by you. Maybe they can't. All you can do is try to sense your role in the unfolding nature of the interconnected life we're all part of. You gain that sense by making conscious contact with that Infinite Creative Intelligence and feeling out for guidance and power. You ask the God of your understanding for guidance on what you should do and the power to carry out that action.

Emmott Fox on Prayer and Prosperity

In The Sermon on the Mount, Emmott Fox describes prayer as follows: "We should constantly pray for wisdom and guidance, and for the living action of the Holy Spirit upon us, that the quality of our prayers—our prosperity—may constantly increase." It's interesting how Fox uses the original meaning of prosperity, linking it to the quality of our prayerful lives and, arguably, the realisation of our heart's desire.

What stands out to me is the phrase "the living action of the Holy Spirit upon us." While a very Christian concept, I believe the notion of the Holy Spirit can be likened to the subtle energies we've previously discussed. Using my own conception of God, the living action of the Holy Spirit manifests in me when I take actions and behave in a way that comes directly from the subtle energies I feel attuned to—the subtle energies I'm more aware of when I reach out in prayer and meditation. In fact, this idea of "feeling out" comes directly from Emmott Fox in the same book: "When praying, one should be constantly "feeling out," making himself receptive to Divine Inspiration." That's exactly what I try to do. I try to make myself receptive to Divine Inspiration. It takes time and practice to discern this Divine Inspiration. I've yet to hear the voice of God boom loudly in my ears or be handed stone tablets with detailed instructions. But I have picked up internal hints and nudges in the form of feelings, thoughts, and evolving beliefs—feelings, emotions, and beliefs that stir in the inner spaces, trying to guide me towards actions that will fulfil my heart's true desire.

I also appreciate Emmott Fox's description of what those feelings are like: "Satisfy the sense of lack within yourself with a sense of Divine Love and the missing thing will appear in your life of its own accord." For me, Divine Love comes in the form of sensing freedom, wholeness, joy, peace, and fulfilment. When I focus on nurturing these qualities, I know I'm taking the right actions. When they are lacking, I know I'm on the wrong track. This is the guidance system we get from God— how we navigate life's tricky ups and downs when we feel overwhelmed and our wisdom is insufficient for the day.

But that doesn't mean an easy life, far from it. The Hero's Journey is full of challenges. Our soul is quite the adventurer, not at all content as a backseat tourist. The guidance we get from our Higher Power is seldom the easy option. That's why we also need the power to carry out our guidance instructions. As any addict can testify, getting sober isn't easy. We know our heart's desire is to be free from addiction. We've hit rock bottom. We know exactly what to do. The instructions couldn't be clearer: Do not pick up that first drink. Do not drink. Whatever you do, don't drink. I don't want to drink. I will not drink. Yet, we go right ahead and drink anyway. We feel powerless over alcohol's draw. Our willpower is not enough.

The Weakness of Self-Will and the Power of Prayer

It seems to me that our willpower is linked to our false self and is all too easily swayed by temptation. It craves pleasure, comfort, and security so much that our best intentions can come crashing down even when we don't want to be swayed. You don't need to be a full-blown addict to experience the weakness of self-will and the power of the false self. Think about any New Year's resolutions, any attempt to quit smoking, start a new fitness regime, or be more organised. It may be our heart's desire to do these things, but our willpower doesn't seem strong enough to get the job done. We need a different type of power. To carry out the guidance from our Higher Power, we need access to some of that power to overcome our habitual responses. Our true self's desire needs the help of a higher power to overcome the false self's drives.

Prayer can give us that power. It can provide a resolve we don't normally have access to. It gives us the strength to do the right thing, overcome our self-centred fears, and move in the right direction. Maybe praying gives us access to our subconscious mind, which has power over our false self's habits. Or maybe we get a bolt of divine energy that propels us in the divine direction. Whatever the mechanism, I have found prayer enables me to do things I was previously unable to do.

William James describes the impact of accessing this Higher Power through prayer: "The appearance is that in prayerful communion something ideal, which in one sense is part of ourselves and in another sense is not ourselves, actually exerts an influence, raises our centre of personal energy, and produces regenerative effects unattainable in other ways."

This is pure brilliance, and I love how James describes the impact of prayer:

- In one sense, it is part of ourselves; in another sense, it is not ourselves. It's partly conscious, partly subconscious, partly otherworldly.
- It actually exerts an influence. It works. There is a tangible impact.
- It raises our centre of personal energy. We feel empowered, lifted to do the right thing, imbued with the wherewithal to take action.
- It produces regenerative effects. It brings new life to old things. It revitalises and changes circumstances. It revitalises and changes us.

The practice of prayer, as an integral part of our morning and evening routines, allows us to build a relationship with a God of our understanding. It builds a belief that when our wisdom and strength are not enough, we can ask for guidance and power and expect to receive it. This is yet another method for us to improve our response-ability—our ability to respond to our heart's desire and nurture our true self's soul.

Tips for Effective Prayer

To close this section on asking for guidance and power, I thought I'd share a few tips on how to pray. In The Bible, the disciples said to

Jesus, "Lord, teach us how to pray." He then pointed them in the right direction.

1. Pray in Secret: Jesus suggested not praying to show off, advising, "When you pray, go into your room, close the door and pray to your Father, who is unseen." This alludes to building a close, personal relationship with your God.

2. Learn Prayers by Heart: Jesus gave the disciples the Lord's Prayer as a starting point. The 12-Step Programme also comes with tailored prayers associated with key steps. When I first started praying daily, I learned three of these and the Lord's Prayer, saying them every day.

3. Keep Prayers Meaningful: Jesus warned against babbling like pagans, thinking many words will be heard. Even if you know prayers by heart, try to say them with meaning. Feel the words and the emotion behind them.

4. Develop Your Own Prayers: Pray about the things that matter to you, the areas where you need guidance and power. Talk to your God as honestly, openly, and vulnerably as you can.

4) GROWING THROUGH DISCOMFORT

I'm aware that my take on spirituality features a healthy dose of pain, suffering and discomfort as part of the spiritual adventure. I've talked about the necessary pain of surrender, the excruciation of hitting rock bottom, the death and rebirth required to complete the Hero's Journey and the seemingly never-ending amount of hard work and effort required to even get a sniff of a spiritual awakening. From that point of view, it could be argued that I'm overplaying the downside of the spiritual solution and underplaying the upside of all the peace, joy, and freedom that ensues. I suppose I could be in danger of creating a proposition that is far from compelling.

And now I'm introducing yet another idea that doesn't sound particularly appealing: growing through discomfort. Not only am I warning that further discomfort may be encountered along the way, I'm suggesting it is one of the five core areas to proactively practice. That suffering may be something we might want to invite and welcome into our lives. What type of sadist are you, Farrell? Isn't it possible to get the benefits of the spiritual solution without all this pain, suffering, and discomfort?

I'd like to say, "Of course it is. Here's a lovely five-step process that's nice and easy to do and will only bring you happiness and joy. Rainbows and unicorns, here we come." But I can't say that. Not because it's not true. Maybe it is possible to achieve a spiritual awakening without the discomfort. But because that's not been my experience. Pain, suffering, hard work, effort, demoralisation, ego deflation, dying within, humiliation, confusion, emotional turmoil, and no end of tears have all been part of my spiritual journey. It's just not a very comfortable process. In my opinion, all that discomfort has been absolutely necessary for me to go through in order to get to the other side. Whether the cliché is: "No pain, no gain." "If it's worth having, it's worth working for." Or "You have to kiss many frogs to find your prince." When it comes to spiritual growth, it appears the cliches about effort and reward are true. There may be a lot of pain, but that's because there's a huge amount to gain.

Learning to Embrace Discomfort

So, this next area of spiritual practice is all about learning to deal with that pain and discomfort. Once we've learned to deal with it, maybe we can go as far as welcoming it into our lives because we know it presents an opportunity for growth.

The practice of growing through discomfort is not something we necessarily do as part of our morning or evening routine. We don't have to go out of our way to find new sources of suffering to grapple with. We get plenty of opportunities in the simple act of living our daily lives in this modern world of ours. What we do need to learn is that discomfort and suffering will definitely be part of our journey, and we need to be able to deal with it when it arises.

Growing through discomfort is a particularly important skill for recovering addicts to practice. That's because we've spent a lifetime on a singular quest of not having to grow through discomfort. We found a very effective way of avoiding discomfort at all costs. We numbed it out. We mastered the skill of not having to feel discomfort. Now, without the numbing addictions of our choice available to us, we have to find a way to deal with uncomfortable situations and unpleasant emotions. We need to learn to endure them. Not numb them.

Enduring discomfort is the conscious act of accepting the feelings we're feeling, no matter how unpleasant, and feeling them. Feel those unpleasant feelings. Sit with them. Don't numb them. Know they are only feelings. We discussed the process of "feeling the feelings" in Embodying Knowledge.

By this stage in our spiritual adventure, we've learned about surrender, awareness, and the spiritual disciplines of embodying knowledge, meditation, contemplation and prayer. All these techniques help us endure the discomfort without the numbing. The more we are able to endure, the weaker the grip our addiction has on us. The less likely our actions will be dictated by a strong false self urge. I was told in the early days of my recovery from alcoholism that riding a strong wave of craving made the next craving less intense and shorter. Riding wave after wave of craving heralds the spiritual solution. We endure the discomfort, and through the enduring, we grow. Going through the pain loosens the grip of our addiction, and the feelings of peace, freedom and joy start to filter in.

That's how addicts use this practice as part of their spiritual adventure. But I suspect we're all addicts to some degree or other. We all tend to avoid discomfort by distracting ourselves with some form of numbing or other. That's why everyone can learn how to grow through discomfort by learning to endure our discomfort, using other spiritual practices, and resisting the temptation to succumb to our habitual numbing behaviours. It's not easy. It's downright difficult. Something like 60%-70% of people return to their drug of choice after giving up – and that's people who've benefitted from going into rehab! I suspect a bigger percentage of people return to their usual numbing habit when they decide to give up drinking, smoking, or overeating as part of a New Year resolution. Like all the pillars of spiritual practice, the more we do it, the easier it becomes, and the wider and deeper we feel the benefits across all aspects of our lives.

The Discomfort of Craving and Restlessness

Craving is the first type of discomfort we have the opportunity to grow through. As you get more familiar with meditation and the flow of feelings and emotions passing through your body, you're likely to come across restlessness. Restlessness is a common form of unsatisfactoriness. It is part of our in-built spiritual malady. It is one of the bedevilments. When you sit with the unpleasant feeling of restlessness and endure the associated discomfort, ask yourself, "What am I craving? What am I longing for? What do I want to chase?" If you feel restless in the here and now, it's because you're craving something in the future or running away from something in the past. By looking deeply into the nature of the things we are chasing, the success we are striving for, and the things we think will make us happier, we'll find our hidden addictions and cravings lurking. Becoming aware of these cravings and living through the uncomfortable emotions attached to them allows us to be free of them. We become more comfortable with what we have in the Now. We lessen our ego's immediate need for pleasure, comfort and security. And we nurture our soul's desire to grow. Through the growth, we find freedom, peace, and joy.

Fasting and Temperance: Disciplines of Discomfort

Another form of growing through discomfort is fasting. Typically, we associate fasting with the abstinence of eating over a certain period of time. Fasting is a spiritual practice that has been honoured by many cultures over many years. But it hasn't been widely adopted in modern Western culture until recently. The current health trend of intermittent fasting has been touted as a great weight loss tool and is generally a good thing to do for your health and well-being. But there's also a deeper benefit that helps us grow spiritually. And that benefit is the value of knowing hunger.

The Western world is not good at knowing hunger. We're good at avoiding hunger. We're good at snacking. We like to consume food and drink at every imaginable opportunity. At home. At work. At school. At the hospital. At the gym. On the road. In the air. With people. On our own. Doing something. Doing nothing. There are very few occasions where we believe the moment wouldn't be enhanced by putting something in our mouths. We like the comforting effect of keeping our mouths occupied and our bellies full. And we're given every opportunity to fulfil that need no matter where we are. It's very likely that we're no more than a five-minute walk from food and drink, whether that's the biscuit tin in our kitchen cupboard, a convenience shop on the corner, a café next to work, a supermarket on the way home, or fast-food outlets and vending machines at every other location in between.

We're very good at snacking. We're lousy at being hungry. We've forgotten what it's like to feel hunger. We don't like it. It feels uncomfortable. It feels like suffering. And yet, allowing ourselves to feel physically hungry is a powerful exercise. Not as a way to torture ourselves and deprive ourselves but to allow ourselves to appreciate the physical sensation of hunger. It allows us to appreciate what we have. It allows us to value the feeling of doing without. And not habitually chasing the desire to have more. Befriending hunger is a practice in befriending the moment without adding anything to it.

Fasting needn't just be about abstinence of food. Fasting could be applied to any aspect of life where we feel we're indulging in something that isn't good for the soul. We could abstain from swearing, drinking alcohol, smoking, spending money needlessly, visiting porn websites, gambling or whatever it is we do that we know we shouldn't. Experiencing the hunger and the suffering that comes with abstaining from these things nurtures the soul. It stops us from numbing and allows us to sit more comfortably with the present moment and live with the uncomfortable cravings that ensue.

A better word for fasting in the spiritual context is temperance, moderation, or voluntary self-restraint. In fact, another good word would be frugality. Or even simplicity. All of these words and concepts point to the valuable lesson as taught by Epicurus: the discipline of a simple life leads to the richness of a happy life. Epicurus believed that life is not to be consumed or controlled. Two things that our culture of economic growth is obsessed with and indeed relies on. His view was that the goal in life was to: "Be as happy as Zeus feasting on Mount Olympus when all you have is a glass of water and a barley cake." It sounds like a far cry from the vision of happiness most of us have been brought up on. I believe this vision of a more frugal happiness exists. That's because it's a vision of spiritual happiness. It's this vision of spiritual happiness that we need to work towards if we are to create a sustainable society that truly gets the wisdom of living with "material sufficiency and spiritual abundance."

Suffering and Happiness Intertwined

Growing through discomfort isn't just about dealing with cravings, whether that's dealing with a serious drug comedown, trying to eat fewer biscuits or taming an incessant drive to earn more money.

Discomfort exists everywhere. Suffering is unavoidable. As we discovered earlier, the Buddha proclaimed that the first noble truth is: "All life involves suffering." This is how Thich Nhat Hahn puts it:

> *"The truth is that suffering and happiness inter-are; there cannot be one without the other. It is thanks to overcoming difficult moments in our relationships that we can deepen our love. And the good news is that suffering and happiness are both impermanent. That is why the Buddha continued to practice even after he attained enlightenment. Our suffering is impermanent and that is why we can transform it. And because happiness is impermanent, that is why we have to nourish it."*

Relationships are a great example of the truth that Thich is highlighting, which is that suffering and happiness inter-are. Think of any meaningful relationship you have or have had in your life: partner, spouse, child, parent, sibling, friend, or colleague. Your memories of that relationship are bound to include moments of pure happiness alongside moments that were deeply uncomfortable. I found this to be the case in the days, weeks, months and years following the death of my wife. Through the deep, deep loss and grief I was feeling, profound memories of happiness bubbled up and came to the surface. I would share those memories. With the kids. With my family. With my friends. With strangers. The stories made me laugh, while the loss made me cry. Happiness and suffering are interwoven in my heart and in my soul.

People often say that they don't believe in God because of all the needless and unfair suffering in the world. How is it possible to have faith in an all-powerful, all-loving God who allows innocent people to die? How can God account for the tragedies of war, crime, disease, and poverty? Where is God in all this suffering? I must admit that this is a difficult issue to get my head around, but I like what Richard Rohr says in his book Breathing Under Water. He says that God doesn't stop the suffering but joins us in the suffering. It's part of the Divine process.

Suffering and happiness inter-are. This is how he accounts for God's role in the suffering and discomfort that exists in the world.

> *"If God is somehow IN the suffering, participating as a suffering object too, in*
> *full solidarity with the world He or She created, then I can make some possible*
> *and initial sense of God and this creation. If we are participating in the*
> *suffering together, there is some kind of cosmic meaning.*

That's been my experience of suffering and discomfort. Although much of my discomfort was experienced without conscious contact with my God, I now see that He was there with me in my discomfort. I just didn't know it. I wasn't conscious of his presence at the time. And that makes all the difference. If we can be conscious of the presence of our God, the God of our understanding, whilst we're in the discomfort, whilst we're experiencing the suffering and the pain, we can be aware that it's part of the divine process. It might not mean that the feelings are any less intense or unpleasant, but we can give the intensity meaning. We can see the discomfort as part of the spiritual adventure. We can appreciate the part it's playing in nurturing the soul and allowing it to grow.

The Search for Meaning Amidst Suffering

This process of enduring discomfort with meaning was at the heart of Victor Frankl's breakthrough insight in Man's Search for Meaning. Frankl was an Austrian psychiatrist and Holocaust survivor, and he founded a school of psychotherapy based on his experience and observations as a Jewish prisoner of war in the Nazi death camps. He saw how his fellow inmates dealt with the brutal and inhumane conditions of Auschwitz. Those who could cling on to some meaning and hope amongst the suffering and discomfort survived. Those who couldn't fell into a state of hopelessness that led to their demise. His conclusion was that a search for meaning in life, even in discomfort and suffering, in fact, especially in discomfort and suffering, is the central human motivational force. Frankl's Viennese psychologist contemporaries of the time were Freud and Adler. Freud developed the pleasure principle, believing that man's main motivational force in life was to seek out pleasure, the will to pleasure. Adler believed the main motivational force was to seek out personal power in the form of status or, indeed, money. This was known as the will to power. Frankl believed in the will to meaning.

When I look at the main motivations in my life, I can see how the will to pleasure and the will to power dominated most of my behaviours. I also see how these motivational drives are linked to our egoic, left hemisphere, false selves. They are the personal, individual drives powering our culture of economic growth. The will to meaning is part of our soulful, right hemisphere, true self. It is the unique human motivational drive that nurtures the soul and helps it to grow. Tapping into the meaning behind the discomfort and suffering we are experiencing allows us to participate in the divine process of growth. That's why growth through discomfort is one of our five areas of spiritual practice.

5) LIVING VIRTUOUSLY

The 12-Step Programme is a spiritual solution to any form of addictive behaviour, from drinking and drugs to gambling and overeating. Initially, it didn't make sense to me how one process could effectively tackle such a wide variety of addictions. How could someone with a drug dependency be treated in the same way as someone who can't stop gambling?

The answer is that The 12-Step Programme is a spiritual solution that resolves a spiritual malady. By addressing the root cause of the feelings of unsatisfactoriness that compel us to reach for numbing behaviours, addiction can be resolved. Moreover, the programme encourages us to move away from all forms of soul-sapping destructive behaviours, not just our obviously addictive ones, towards more soul-nurturing constructive behaviours.

Identifying and Overcoming Character Defects

In the language of The 12-Step Programme, these soul-sapping destructive behaviours are called character defects. They include traits such as resentment, fear, self-centredness, and dishonesty. On the other hand, soul-nurturing constructive behaviours are virtues, the opposite of those defects, like contentment, love, generosity, and honesty.

Through Steps 4, 5, 6, 7, and 10 of the 12-Step Process, we identify our core character defects by examining the destructive patterns in our lives - the behaviours we resort to that harm ourselves or others – and begin turning these behaviours around. Some defects are so deeply ingrained that it may take years of meditation, prayer, and guidance from a higher power to overcome them. However, others can be resolved more quickly and easily by consciously choosing to Live Virtuously.

The Path to Virtuous Living

Living Virtuously is a common thread in most religions, from the Ten Commandments in the Old Testament to the Beatitudes in the New Testament and the Noble Eightfold Path in Buddhism. Ancient wisdom has always advised us to do the right thing and stay on the straight and narrow path. Being virtuous is another way to hone our response-ability to the world around us.

Interestingly, it's often easier to identify our character defects when we're not being virtuous than it is to double down on our virtuous attributes. We are more familiar with the seven deadly sins (pride, greed, wrath, envy, lust, gluttony, and sloth) than the seven capital virtues (humility, charity, patience, kindness, chastity, temperance, and diligence). This is because it's easier to see the recurring mistakes and patterns of wrong thinking and behaving that led to the catastrophes in our lives than it is to recognise the good thoughts and deeds that generated positive outcomes.

However, knowing our weaknesses and where we tend to go wrong is a great starting point to being more virtuous. That's because living virtuously is all about changing behaviour by spotting character defects and replacing them with their opposites. If wrath is a common theme in your life, try practising patience. If sloth manifests as laziness or procrastination, try dialling up the diligence. This conscious reversal of behavioural defects gradually changes people from the outside in, as right doing results in right thinking.

When we take virtuous action, we experience new sensations of being selfless, generous, giving, and loving. These open, expansive, warm feelings stand in stark contrast to the closed, contracted, tense feelings that accompany manipulation, dishonesty, or selfishness. Our ability to discern between these two types of feelings becomes our navigation tool and compass for future conduct. By trying, failing, testing, and learning to be virtuous, we feel our way to doing the right thing without having to memorise a list of rules. Living Virtuously is living by qualities rather than regulations - qualities that reveal our true self-nature.

The Pervasiveness of Fear and its Antidote Love

Before embarking on the 12-Step Process, I considered myself a pretty decent human being—a loyal husband, a fun dad, and a fair boss. However, the thorough self-inventory in Step 4 revealed how fear had driven many of my destructive and harmful behaviours. Fear led to dishonesty in the form of secrets and not expressing my true feelings. It led to greed, pride, worry, and anxiety. These character defects prevented me from living with freedom, humility, and generosity and stopped me from living virtuously.

The Step 4 Process highlighted how much of my life had been driven by self-centred fear - fear of not being good enough, failing, not having enough money, and everything ending horribly. This is a character defect I'm still working on. Even now, I can find myself wallowing in self-pity when things don't go my way. In these moments, I have to dig into the five areas of spiritual practice - a walk in nature, an impromptu meditation, a quick prayer, feeling the feelings, and doing something good - to work my way out of self-centredness.

As Marianne Williamson, author of The Return to Love, points out, our thoughts, feelings, and actions come from either a place of fear or a place of love. Fear is not just the opposite of love but also the absence of it. She writes, "Light is to darkness what love is to fear; in the presence of one, the other disappears. All the darkness in my life—the fears, neuroses, dysfunctions, and diseases—are not so much things as the absence of things. They represent not the presence of a problem but rather the absence of the answer. And the answer is love. All fearful manifestations disappear in the presence of love."

When I notice my fear-based character defects arising, I realise there's not enough love in my heart. I'm thinking and acting out of fear instead of love. In those overwhelming moments of fear, I'm reminded of a quote from St. Francis: "All the darkness in the world cannot extinguish the light of a single candle." Even the smallest glimmer of love can break through seemingly all-consuming fear.

These small acts of behaviour change—spotting character defects and choosing to do something differently—are really small acts of love. And they are the foundations of transformation. They are a form of self-sacrifice, a daily practice of systematically destroying the fearful side of us to be born anew—dying every day to the false self so the true self can emerge.

As Thich Nhat Hanh writes, "Loving-kindness, understanding and compassion are there within us. We need only to clear some of the rocks obstructing the way in order to reveal them." Our character defects are the rocks blocking our way, and Living Virtuously allows our true virtues to be revealed.

A Virtuous Sense of Fun

All this talk of being virtuous can come across as being a bit worthy and "do-goody" and I don't want to sell the spiritual adventure as a sterile, lifeless lifestyle devoid of fun and laughter. We are chasing the full rapture of being alive, after all. Not a life of dullness. But the spiritual adventure does mean we're welcoming spiritual happiness and its hallmarks of freedom, wholeness, peace, joy, and fulfilment. By default, it also means we're not chasing pleasure, excitement, indulgence, pride, and sensuality. Remember, these are the hallmarks of conditional happiness and breeding grounds for character defects.

Living Virtuously allows us to do things that fill our hearts and soothe our souls without suffering the comedowns and hangovers. We learn to feel good by doing good, realising that living the high life isn't all it's cracked up to be, and that living the good life isn't as dull as we once imagined.

The biggest challenge in Living Virtuously is our culture of economic growth, which tries to sell us a different story - a thrill-seeking, indulgence-filled, not-good-enough-based, purchase-inducing narrative of more is better. Waking up every morning to a world that wants you to think, feel, and behave in a way that isn't conducive to Living Virtuously is hard. It's a world that doesn't value embodied knowledge, doesn't promote silence or asking for guidance, and doesn't talk openly about growing through discomfort.

To stick with this spiritual path when the world conspires against you, there's no substitute for focused, continuous effort in the form of a daily practice in the spirit of beautiful imperfection. As Emmet Fox puts it, "Sacrifice there has to be, but it is only sacrifice of the things that one is much happier without - never anything that is really worth having." The point is that we only need to sacrifice the things that don't bring us lasting joy. It doesn't sound like such a bad deal when you put it like that. That's the beauty of bringing discipline into your life.

THE IMPORTANCE OF DISCIPLINE IN SPIRITUAL GROWTH

The Habit of Discipline is the character-building trait that builds up our ability to focus and apply ourselves in the consistent manner that a spiritual awakening demands. Half of me wants to shy away from mentioning this aspect of the process. It sounds too strict, too dogmatic, too rule-based, too controlling. It's also the trait that hardens our resolve to the effort, hard work and determination that's required. Half of me wants to shy away from this, too. Who wants to embark on anything if it's going to be hard? It's not a particularly compelling proposition. But I'm not going to shy away from discipline and hard work and the important role they play. Not just yet, anyway.

At the end of many 12-Step meetings, after the group has said the serenity prayer together, people will urge each other to keep on going by saying in unison, "It works if you work it." It's an affirmation to each other, especially those new to The 12-Step Programme who may well be struggling with the spiritual path, that the spiritual solution does work, but you need to put the effort in. "Keep coming back!" is the plea to those early adventurers who are obviously not yet convinced. Put in the effort. Keep trying. The constant effort pays off. These are the messages that newcomers to the programme hear.

This reiteration of constant endeavour and diligence can be overwhelming and demotivating when starting out. It sounds too much like hard work. Too much like a chore. And not like a path to happiness at all. It sounds like you're being told by a teacher to try harder at math when you find numbers simply baffling. It doesn't sound like fun. And that's because, truth be told, it isn't fun to start with. It doesn't feel like fun at all.

Over time, however, the effort starts to melt. The arduous tasks that we sense must be done get easier and easier until they become second nature. Discipline is the tool that turns all this spiritual practice into everyday spiritual living. Our reluctance dissolves, our willingness triumphs, and peace gradually arises. We stop fighting the resistance, and serenity takes its place. This is the beauty and the gift of The Habit of Discipline.

We'll talk more about discipline in the section Cultivating the Habits of Happiness: A Programme of Spiritual Action, but let's continue building our knowledge and understanding of the five spiritual habits as we now delve into the joy-filled world of connection.

SEVEN

THE HABIT OF CONNECTION

FEELING PART OF THE WHOLE

**Desired state of being and inner human need =
A sense of JOY. Not feeling sad or lonely.**

SEVEN

THE HABIT OF CONNECTION

FROM ME TO WE: TAKING THE JOURNEY BEYOND OURSELVES

So far on the spiritual journey, we've explored the realms of surrender, awareness and discipline. These are The Habits of Happiness that are essentially about ourselves. So far, the focus has been an inward one. As we embrace The Habit of Surrender, we admit the problems we have and tentatively start the process of letting go of the old story of "me" and letting in the new story of life, the universe and everything. With The Habit of Awareness, we start re-educating our mind in a relatively logical way in order to build an understanding of reality and what the spiritual solution is all about. By honing The Habit of Discipline, we start the process of re-discovering and nurturing our soulful, true selves. By doing all this work, we are aligning ourselves within ourselves. We are integrating the false self with the true self. And we'll start feeling some of the benefits of spiritual happiness. But we're only halfway there.

Now it's time to take the spiritual journey beyond ourselves. It's time to take our aligned and integrated inner selves out into to the world and align and integrate ourselves relationally. It's time take the inward journey we've travelled so far and turn it outward. It's time to take our true selves out into the world and start the process of co-creating with the flow of life. It's time to nurture the habit of connection.

I like Marianne Williamson's take on how important it is to take the spiritual adventure outwards and not keeping it purely in the internal realm of ourselves. In the following passage, she described the frustration she felt in her predominantly inward spiritual journey until she came across a life-changing spiritual programme called A Course in Miracles. "I felt like I was trying so hard to find the peace of God. I likened it to a flight of stairs that was in front of a gigantic cathedral. Salvation lay behind that big cathedral door. And I walked up those stairs and sometimes my knees were bloody, my elbows were bloody, I wanted so much to open that door. But over and over and over again, I got up the flight of stairs and the door was locked. And I would try so hard, I couldn't unlock the door. Then I read a Course in Miracles and it dawned on me. What I realised was that the door is the person right in front of me. That I couldn't unlock the door until I realised that the door was the person in front of me or the person I was thinking about. So, what I learned from the course is that there is no way to separate your journey to God, your spiritual journey, from your relationship to other people because God is love, and God is love extended. And the purpose of our lives is to learn to love as God loves."

Unless you're a monk or a nun, the spiritual life is not a solitary one. We're an active bunch. We have jobs. We have hobbies. We have families. We have relationships. Most of the things we do and the people we come into contact with don't always align with the spiritual path we're trying to follow. Not at first glance, anyway. However, rather than treating seemingly "non-spiritual" activities and "non-spiritual" people as barriers to growth, they can be treated as opportunities for growth. In fact, they are more than opportunities. They are necessities.

We have to engage with the world around us in order to fully realise our potential. We are not separate from the world. We are inexorably part of it. We cannot grow spiritually in isolation. We need to feel a connection. We cannot grow spiritually by working only for ourselves. We need to be of service. When we work on these final two aspects of the spiritual solution, when we feel connected and work on behalf of those we feel connected to, we start to find our purpose in life. Not only do we find a purpose that makes the most of our unique gifts and talents and allows us to help others in a way that only we can, but we also find the power to act on that purpose. This is where we find the final piece of the spiritual happiness jigsaw: fulfilment.

We've worked on right thinking with our Habit of Awareness. We've worked on right action with our Habit of Discipline. Now it's time to work on right relation with our Habit of Connection. It's time to think less about me and think more about we.

The Energy of Connection and Love

When I first drafted my ideas for this part of the book, I didn't call this section The Habit of Connection. I called it The Habit of Love. But I had a problem with the word love. The main issue I had was one of definition and meaning. Love is one word, but it covers such a broad spectrum of life with so many different connotations. There's romantic love. There's brotherly love. There's love for humanity. There's a love for nature. You can love life. You can love your dog. You can love chocolate biscuits. And you can love Manchester United (even on the days when they're playing badly). There are lots of different types of emotions and feelings for one four-letter word to convey.

Robert Johnson made a very good observation based on this deficiency in the English language:

"Sanskrit has 96 words for love; ancient Persian has 80, Greek three, and English only one. This is indicative of the poverty of awareness or emphasis that we give to that tremendously important realm of feeling. Eskimos have 30 words for snow, because it is a life-and-death matter to them to have exact information about the element they live with so intimately. If we had a vocabulary of 30 words for love … we would immediately be richer and more intelligent in this human element so close to our heart. An Eskimo probably would die of clumsiness if he had only one word for snow; we are close to dying of loneliness because we have only one word for love. Of all the Western languages, English may be the most lacking when it comes to feeling."

If I called this section The Habit of Love, what would people make of it? Which type of love would I mean? Because, if I'm honest, I don't know what the word means to me. I'm ashamed to say that it's a word I'm not used to using all that often. It's a word I've shied away from for much of my life. I'm getting better at demonstrating love. People know I love them because of what I do. I am getting better at dropping the "L" word every now and then. But, as of today, I'm not that comfortable using it as the main heading for a chapter. Progress, not perfection, right?

So, I decided to leave the word "love" to one side (for the time being) and use the word "connection" in the headline instead. That's because I came across a definition of connection that made a lot of sense to me in the context of the spiritual journey. The definition comes from Brené Brown. She wrote about connection in her book The Gifts of Imperfection. For her, connection is at the heart of spirituality. And this is how she defined it:

"Connection is the energy that exists between people when they feel seen, heard and valued: when they can give and receive without judgement: and when they derive sustenance and strength from the relationship."

I love this definition for a number of reasons.

Firstly, she describes connection as an energy. Yes, Brené. Connection is an energy. It's an energy that exists between people. It's an energy that is felt. An energy that is generated and radiated. An energy that is absorbed and sensed. That energy arises when I feel connected to you, and you feel connected to me. We both feel it. The energy is in me. It's also in you. As well as in the space between us. It's tangible. It's palpable. It's beautiful. It's compelling.

So when I talk of connection, I am talking about felt-connection. The experience of sensing connection energy within our bodies.

I particularly like thinking of connection as an energy as it aligns with the idea of the subtle energy forces we talked about earlier. Connection as a subtle form of energy is something we can attune to. We can sense it in our inner spaces. We can use it to inform our response-ability.

Secondly, she suggests that the energy arises under certain conditions. It arises when both parties feel seen, heard and valued. When there's a mutual respect. When there's trust and no sense of threat. It also arises when both parties can give and receive without judgment. Both parties give. Both parties receive. And do so unconditionally. The value is in the connection, not in the giving or receiving. And finally, the energy arises when both parties derive sustenance and strength from the connection. The relationship is nurturing, life-affirming and supports growth. It's vital.

I particularly like the idea of connection energy being generated under certain conditions because it suggests that the more these conditions apply, the stronger the connection will be. The more we focus on creating the right conditions, the more energy we can create. It also widens the scope of connections. It's not just about person-to-person connections. But other connections, too. We can generate connection energy with nature, for example. Or with our Higher Power. Or with ourselves. Or with future generations even. Just think about the connection you have with all of these other different aspects of life. Do they all feel seen, heard and valued by you? And you, by them? Are you giving and receiving unconditionally to all of them? Are you deriving sustenance and strength from them? And them from you?

I'd like to add a third aspect to Brené's definition of connection. That third aspect is meaning. The energy arising from a strong connection is not only a subtle energy that generates strong emotional feelings; it also generates strong emotional meaning. Strong connections mean everything to human beings. We are social animals. We need strong relational bonds to survive. We will do anything for the people we feel strongly connected to. We'll do things that don't make any rational sense to anyone else. Not because it feels nice but because it means the world to us.

As we travel further along the spiritual journey into The Habit of Service, we will be tapping into the indelible meaning strong connections give us as we use them to hone our response-ability and guide us towards our purpose.

As Brené observed, I believe nurturing these connections is an integral part of the spiritual journey, not least because of the life-affirming vitality and meaning that connection energy delivers. I can't see any chance of feeling the full rapture of being alive without strong connection energy. We need that energy to thrive physically, intellectually, emotionally, and of course, spiritually.

Love: The Fundamental Force

With this notion of connection energy in mind, I'd like to re-introduce the word love. Love, as defined as the life-affirming, meaningful connection energy that is generated within ourselves by strengthening our bonds with other people, with nature, with God, and with future generations, is the force that I believe all spiritual traditions latch on to. The English language may be the most lacking when it comes to describing and expressing love in a way that promotes connection energy. But that doesn't make it any the less potent.

It's interesting to note that the three realms McGilchrist suggested could bypass the logical left hemisphere and directly influence the soulful right hemisphere (the body, art and spirituality) have one thing in common. "What ultimately unites the three realms of escape from the left hemisphere's world, which it has attacked over time, is that they are all vehicles of love. For love is the attractive power of the 'other' which the right hemisphere experiences, but which the left hemisphere does not understand."

The experience of loving that is felt in the body, the feeling we get when we are moved by music, or the meaningful connection we sense when we feel part of a universal whole is just too difficult for our logical, language-based left hemispheres to comprehend. All it can do is analyse a four-letter word called "love" as best it can. And it can't do that very well.

But let's not be daunted by the lack in the English language. Let's press on and rejuvenate and regenerate the word love with the life-affirming, meaningful connection energy it was born to express. Let's create a strong connection to the word love. And let's reclaim its potency. Because, as the Beatles claimed, apparently, it's all we need.

The great German philosopher Max Scheler also claimed that love is all we need. He claimed that man is essentially "ens amans," a being that loves. He felt the primary reason for man to do anything was love. In Scheler's paradigm, the attractive power (literally) of love exists as a mysterious and fundamental force field in the emotional and spiritual world, just as the attractive power of gravity exists in the physical world. Both are irresistible and omnipresent force fields that act in a way that bring people, objects, and situations together. It's an interesting analogy to contemplate. A force field of love. A force field of attraction. Let's not forget the all-important aspect of meaning that comes with the energy of connection. Love is a force field of attraction and a force field of meaning.

Viktor Frankl is known as the creator of logotherapy, the theory that man is motivated primarily by finding meaning in life. But he also saw the fundamental role that love played as the source of that meaning. "Love is the ultimate and the highest goal to which man can aspire. Then I grasped the meaning of the greatest secret that human poetry and human thought and belief have to impart: The salvation of man is through love and in love."

There you have it. Love and connection are pretty big deals. I don't think that will come as any great surprise. I doubt there are many of us who would argue with Brown or Scheler or Frankl or The Beatles. I suspect most of us know how vitally important it is to feel the nurturing connection energy of love in our lives. We would all rather live in a world filled with love rather than fear. So, if that's all true, why aren't we doing more of it? Why is our world so lacking when it comes to unconditional love and connection? Why are more and more people feeling disconnected?

THE EPIDEMIC OF DISCONNECTION

In 2022, Gallup and Meta produced a report entitled The Global State of Social Connections, which explored the levels of connectedness experienced by various populations worldwide. The study revealed intriguing differences between countries, with some, like Mongolia, reporting higher levels of connection than others, such as Morocco. It also highlighted a significant disparity between age groups, with younger people (aged 19-29) feeling considerably more lonely than older individuals (65+). However, the most striking finding was that only 35% of the global population felt "very connected," suggesting that the majority (65%) experience some degree of disconnection. This lack of life-affirming, meaningful, and loving connection energy has profound implications for our well-being, as disconnection directly contributes to anxiety, depression, and a general sense of dissatisfaction.

The Roots and Impact of Disconnection

In his book Lost Connections, Johann Hari examines the global rise of anxiety, depression, and unhappiness, asserting that "Every one of the social and psychological causes of depression, anxiety and unhappiness have something in common. They are all forms of disconnection. They are all ways in which we have been cut off from something we innately need but seem to have lost along the way." To understand the pervasiveness of disconnection, it is essential to explore its underlying causes.

Two destructive and mutually supportive forces are at play here. The first is the internal disconnection we feel within ourselves - the disconnection of our thinking from our being. This disconnection stems from granting supremacy to our logical, egoic, self-centred brain while neglecting the value of our intuitive, soulful, holistic brain. This internal split leads to a sense of unsatisfactoriness and a "hole in the soul."

The second force is the external disconnection that arises from our internal disconnection. When we are disconnected from ourselves, we struggle to sense our inherent connection with the world around us. We are undoubtedly part of and connected to the universe. But we simply cannot feel it. Without this felt-connection we create a world of separation and isolation, where success is extrinsic and viewed through the lens of comparison and competition, and where prosperity is financial and operates on a zero-sum game. In short, disconnection creates a sense of scarcity. In turn, this scarcity mindset fosters conditions that are antithetical to generating connection energy.

Connection energy thrives when people feel seen, heard, and valued by each other, but a scarce world rewards manipulation and competition. Connection energy flourishes when people give and receive unconditionally, but a scarce world encourages conditional exchanges based on a zero-sum mindset. Connection energy provides sustenance and strength to all, but a scarce world drains our energy through envy, greed, and selfishness. Connection energy provides us with meaning and purpose, but a scarce world values and rewards material growth over spiritual growth.

The combination of internal and external disconnection has created a world of disconnected, anxious individuals pursuing their own narrow versions of success, often indifferent to the needs of others and the world around them. It is no wonder that such a scarce and disconnected world results in widespread anxiety, depression, and unhappiness. Bruce Alexander, in his book The Globalisation of Addiction: A Study in Poverty of the Spirit, refers to this phenomenon as "dislocation" - a loss of connection to self and others and a sense of meaning and purpose. Just as a dislocated shoulder feels painful and useless, we feel the same way when we are disconnected from our world.

The Power of Felt-Connection

While the picture may seem bleak, there is hope for the 35% of people who feel very connected. These individuals experience a different world, a world fuelled by life-affirming, meaningful, and loving connection energy. They benefit from this connection energy, feeling more aligned within themselves and internally connected, which in turn allows them to build even more external felt-connections that provide sustenance and strength to all they feel connected to.

For this 35%, their ability to connect has the potential to create a world that counteracts the world of scarcity. A connected world can be one of interdependence and support, where success is intrinsic and viewed through the lens of well-being and happiness. It can be a world where prosperity is spiritual and unbounded, where everyone can win and have more. It can be a world of abundance filled with the very conditions that generate even more connection energy.

In an abundant world, everyone can feel seen, heard, and valued. Everyone can give and receive unconditionally. Sustenance and strength are available to all, and meaning and purpose provide the currency for an abundant life.

The Wisdom of Enough

An abundant world creates one vital quality that a scarce world cannot: the quality of enough. In a world full of loving, meaningful connection energy, everyone feels secure, supported, and sufficient. They feel they are enough and have enough.

The wisdom of enough may seem modest, but its presence is profound. Verse 46 of the Tao Te Ching celebrates this wisdom:

> "There is no greater calamity than not knowing what is enough, no greater curse than covetousness, no greater tragedy than discontentment, and the worst of all faults is wanting more – always. Those who know when enough is enough will always have enough."

A disconnected world always wants more, while a connected world knows it has enough. As we navigate the challenges of disconnection and strive to cultivate meaningful connections, we must remember the transformative power of connection energy and the wisdom of recognising when we have enough.

FEELING OUR CONNECTION TO LIFE

Having identified the cause of our anxious, depressed, and unhappy world as disconnection, Johann Hari suggests that reconnection must be the solution. "I started to think of these reconnections as social or psychological antidepressants, in contrast to the chemical antidepressants we have been offered up to now." What a powerful insight. But for me it's not simply about re-connection. We have to help people re-connect and then encourage them to feel that connection. We need to promote felt-connection. Imagine if we had a culture that promoted felt-connection rather than drugs as the first line of defence against mental health issues. Envision a world where we sought support from friends and family, healing each other back to health by generating more life-affirming, loving, and meaningful connection energy.

Unfortunately, we don't have that sort of culture yet. Our current culture prioritises economic growth and chemical solutions as the go-to treatment for mental health issues. This approach supports the $17 billion antidepressant market (Source: The Business Research Company / Global Antidepressant Market) and the profits of big pharmaceutical companies. It's a culture that tolerates a solution where the only clear beneficiaries are the big pharma companies and their shareholders.

It saddens and frustrates me when I consider the societal problem of anxiety and depression and the solution we've settled for. The felt-connection solution, the spiritual solution, seems infinitely better. It doesn't cost anything, requires no prescription or doctor visits, has no negative side effects, and benefits both the healer and the healed by fostering stronger felt-connections. It brings people closer together and is deeply meaningful. It's a win-win-win-win-win solution, even if the big pharma companies might not see it that way. I'm not suggesting we completely abandon chemical antidepressants. But I do believe that promoting felt-connection should at least be considered as an option. What harm could it do? None.

Jesus also believed in the power of felt-connection, which he called "right relation." Richard Rohr, in his book Jesus' Alternative Plan, explains, "Jesus taught that right relationship is the ultimate and daily criterion. If social order allows and encourages good connectedness between people and creation, people and events, people and people, people and God, then we truly have a new world order." It's a

wonderful concept, but Rohr includes a subtle condition: "If social order allows." That's the key. If our culture allows and encourages good felt-connectedness, we will indeed have a new world order.

Changing Our Culture

Waiting for our culture to allow and encourage good felt-connectedness from where we are today seems like a futile thing to do. Jesus spoke about it over 2,000 years ago, and there's little evidence to suggest his idea is taking root. It's important to remember that we are both the product and producer of our culture. We can change it just as it changes us. While attempting to influence an entire culture's behaviour or attitude may seem futile, we can start the process of changing our culture's felt-connectedness now and feel the benefits immediately. We don't need to wait for the majority to join in; we can do it on our own, with friends and family, or within small communities. We can initiate the process, feel the impact, and reap the rewards right away.

How to Feel Connected

"How do we teach people to feel connected?" It may seem like a strange question to ask. It's a bit like asking, "How do we teach people to make friends?" I suspect the answer is the same: you simply encourage people to reach out, make contact with someone, find common ground that benefits both of you and explore that common ground together. Share ideas and concerns, ask questions, listen, grow closer, trust more, give more, receive more, and love more.

If you're still unsure about how to nurture felt-connection, observe a group of five-year-olds in a playground and see what they do. They make felt-connection look easy. As adults, we tend to overthink and overcomplicate the process. I have a small family and a small group of

friends, but we're very close. I invest more time in some connections than others and can feel the difference accordingly. The connections I invest more time in feel stronger and generate the life-affirming, loving, and meaningful connection energy we seek. We need deeper, more meaningful interactions to feel the connection and benefit from it. We need to feel the love to benefit from the love.

Like any spiritual practice, the benefits of felt-connection take time and require a regular investment of time and energy for each specific connection to grow and generate that life-affirming, loving, meaningful connection energy. This may be why the majority of the world's population doesn't feel very connected. We see time as money and tend to prioritise earning money over investing in connection. But that is a prioritisation you can reverse. You don't have to wait for the rest of the world to catch up. You can prioritise spiritual happiness over wealth. You can heed the words of Thich Nhat Hanh and act like time is life and time is love.

True Belonging

We'll talk about belonging and identity shortly in the section Felt-connection to Others, but I'd like to introduce an important aspect of belonging, identity, and felt-connection now. And that is the concept of true belonging. In her book Braving the Wilderness, Brené Brown reveals an important discovery from her research. She notes that people "want to experience real connection with others but not at the cost of their authenticity, freedom, or power." She points out that if we're not careful, our human need for connection and belonging can result in us bowing to peer pressure and changing our true, natural identity in order to fit in and conform with group norms. As soon as we do any of these things, we lose our authenticity, freedom, and power. We lose the feeling of connection. And that's not good for our soul.

Therefore, a key aspect to nurturing the felt-connection to others is to ensure that we have a strong felt-connection to ourselves and to a God of our understanding first. This grounding gives us the courage and power to stand in our own story, believe in ourselves and seek out felt-connections without sacrificing our authenticity. Interestingly, this approach to felt-connection results in the paradox that belonging, and felt-connection can be found not only by being with others but also by being alone.

Brown provides the following definition of true belonging that brings this paradox to life:

"True belonging is the spiritual practice of believing in and belonging to yourself so deeply that you can share your most authentic self with the world and find sacredness in both being part of something and standing alone in the wilderness. True belonging doesn't require you to change who you are; it requires you to be who you are."

Armed with this definition of true belonging and the importance of grounding ourselves in ourselves and our Higher Power first, we're ready to form the habit of connection by nurturing seven specific felt-connections.

SEVEN SOURCES OF FELT-CONNECTION

Once we understand that felt-connection and belonging are not just about forging bonds with other people, we can take the opportunity to generate many different types of life-affirming, loving, and meaningful connection energy with the many forms of felt relationships we find in our lives.

Here are seven suggested felt-connections that not only sustain us personally but also help us build a more abundant and sustainable world:

1. Felt-connection to a God of our understanding
2. Felt-connection to ourselves
3. Felt-connection to others
4. Felt-connection to our communities
5. Felt-connection to nature
6. Felt-connection to our descendants
7. Felt-connection to purpose

What Felt-Connection Is and What It Does for Us

Before delving into the specifics of each felt-connection, let's remind ourselves what felt-connection is and what it does for us:

- Felt-connection is the sensation of the energy that exists and can be generated between us and our God, us and ourselves, us and others, us and our communities, us and nature, us and our descendants, and us and purpose.
- Life-affirming, loving, meaningful connection energy is generated when we feel seen, heard, and valued. It is generated when we can give and receive without judgment and derive sustenance and strength from the relationship. These relationships are important to us, deep, and meaningful.
- All seven forms of felt-connection can generate life-affirming, loving, meaningful connection energy. All seven can be experienced and nurtured to generate even more energy.

Nurturing felt-connection is a simple yet profound process. You reach out, make contact, find common ground that you both benefit from and explore that common ground together. You share ideas, concerns, and questions and listen. You grow closer, trust more, give more, receive more, and love more.

By cultivating The Habit of Connection and investing time and energy into these relationships, we can create a more connected, loving, and meaningful world for ourselves and those around us.

1. FELT-CONNECTION TO A GOD OF OUR UNDERSTANDING

We've already covered a lot of ground when it comes to the felt-connection to a God of our understanding. We covered this ground in the chapter The Habit of Discipline and the sections on Embracing Silence and Asking for Guidance and Power.

The felt-connection we have to a God of our understanding is all about working on conscious contact through those specific areas of spiritual practice. In those sections, we talked about building a relationship with our God and discerning that still, small voice. That's what felt-connection to our Higher Power is all about. It's about us asking questions, listening, growing closer, trusting more, giving more, receiving more, loving more.

All felt-connections are important. All felt-connections are equally important. But maybe this felt-connection is more equally important than the others. If you are struggling to find time to invest in all seven felt-connections, invest in this felt-connection first. Stick with your morning and evening routines (see the section Cultivating the Habits of Happiness: A Spiritual Programme of Action) and get to know, trust and love your God. When you do, you'll find it easier to feel the connection with the others. You'll be more readily able to find the time and invest the time with the other six felt-connections. That's because you'll appreciate that time invested in nurturing felt-connections has a big payback. Your return on investment is the spiritual happiness it yields. In my experience, building a strong felt-connection with a God of your understanding makes it easier to feel the connection with all the others. That's why it's number one on this list!

2. FELT-CONNECTION TO OURSELVES

Again, we've covered a lot of this ground in the chapters on The Habit of Awareness and The Habit of Discipline. Feeling connected to ourselves is really the reconciliation and re-aligning of our split selves.

It's the process of getting that internal felt-connection right, reconnecting our thinking within our being, reconnecting the logical, egoic, left hemisphere, false self within the intuitive, soulful, right hemisphere true self. And making sure each is playing its rightful role. Cultivating a felt-connection with ourselves is the dance between false self and true self and finding peace and wholeness in the process.

However, one point I want to emphasise here when it comes to feeling connected to ourselves is the importance of "take it easy" and "progress, not perfection." Felt-connection does require us to tame the thinking mind and nurture the soul. Both of which require hard work and persistence. But we need to be kind to ourselves as we do so. We need to be more trusting with ourselves. More giving to ourselves. Receiving more for ourselves. And more loving of ourselves.

This may be harder than it first seems. Our thinking, egoic, false self can be an awfully harsh critic. We tend to talk to ourselves in a way that is much crueller than the way we would talk to anyone else. Negative self-talk can be self-destructive if we're not aware of it and are unable to counteract it. That's why it might be useful to remember three tools that can help us reconnect with ourselves in a more loving way as we work on resolving the split self: forgiveness of self, gratitude and self-compassion.

Forgiveness of self

Forgiveness is a spiritual superpower. Some people even call it a technology. We'll cover forgiveness in more detail when we talk about reconnecting with others, but here, I want to talk about forgiveness in the context of reconnecting with ourselves.

When we think about forgiveness, we usually think about forgiving other people for the things they've done to us. Or the things we think they've done to us. However, the spiritual solution also needs to include forgiveness of ourselves. This is a big thing for recovering

addicts. It was a big thing for me. During our active addiction, we did things that harmed ourselves and harmed others. We did things that left us feeling full of guilt and shame. As we'll see later, Step 9 of the 12-Step Process helps us deal with that guilt and shame by asking for forgiveness for the bad things we did and offering to make up for them. In Step 9, we seek forgiveness from others, and we usually get it if we are earnest in our request and willing to make amends. However, we can all too easily forget to forgive ourselves as part of the process. And if we can't forgive ourselves, we can end up with a cold and hardened heart, imprisoned by impenetrable armour. Elizabeth Lesser captures this beautifully, "This armouring around the heart is the accumulation of all the moments we have given ourselves and others so little mercy. We are so hard on ourselves and so hard on each other. Healing begins when we soften our stance toward our own tender selves."

Carl Jung makes the same point, but a bit more emphatically: "What I do unto the least of my brethren, that I do unto Christ. But what if I should discover that the least among them all, the poorest of all the beggars, the most imprudent of all offenders, the very enemy himself – that these are within me, and I myself stand in need of the alms of my own kindness – that I am the enemy who must be loved – what then?"

What then is forgiving ourselves? We see ourselves for who we really are: imperfect beings who are willing to learn, trying to learn, willing to grow, trying to grow, and willing to learn from our mistakes. We acknowledge that we are ever-evolving into the person we are meant to be. The process of "becoming" takes time. We're not perfect. We're not there yet. That doesn't mean we should reject ourselves. We admit our imperfections. We forgive our imperfections. We forgive ourselves for being human. And then we try again, remembering that forgiveness is a superpower and life is forever forgiving.

Gratitude

Gratitude is another spiritual superpower and technology. In fact, it probably deserves its own special section as an area of spiritual practice. The benefits of developing an attitude of gratitude are becoming much more widely accepted these days.

In the US, Time Magazine published an article called The Seven Surprising Benefits of Gratitude:

- Gratitude can make you more patient.
- Gratitude might improve your relationship.
- Gratitude improves self-care.
- Gratitude can help you sleep.
- Gratitude may stop you from overeating.
- Gratitude can help ease depression.
- Gratitude gives you happiness that lasts.

For those in The 12-Step Programme, the benefits won't be all that surprising. We're taught to express gratitude from day 1 of the recovery journey. At 12-Step meetings, it's customary to thank everyone who helped organise the meeting. We thank the people who share their stories at meetings. We finish our own shares by proclaiming, "Grateful to be here. Grateful to be sober." We're also encouraged to write a daily gratitude list.

A gratitude list is a simple but effective way to cultivate thankfulness. Simply contemplate your life. Think about all the good things you have and write them down. I'm grateful that Emma is in my life. I'm grateful for the coffee that Richard bought me yesterday. I'm grateful that I had a good night's sleep. I'm grateful I don't have to go out in the rain today. But I'm also grateful for the rain that's watering my vegetable garden.

Simple. Quick to do. And you can't help but feel good afterwards.

Gratitude definitely lifts the spirits. In his book What Happy People Know, Dan Baker argues that it's impossible to be grateful and fearful or anxious at the same time. Baker writes, "It is a fact of neurology that the brain cannot be in a state of appreciation and a state of fear at the same time. The two states may alternate but are mutually exclusive." I'm not as convinced as Baker that gratitude alone can rid us of fear. But a regular gratitude practice, like a daily gratitude list, certainly encourages us to be positive about all the good things we have rather than bemoan all the things that we don't have

Gratitude is infectious. I'm in a 12-Step Recovery WhatsApp Group with a number of other recovering addicts, and we've re-branded Friday as #GratitudeFriday. It's an opportunity for us all to reflect on the week and share the things we are grateful for with each other. Even if I've had a rotten week and I'm struggling to be grateful for anything, it's really uplifting to see the things other people are thankful for. And that usually reminds me that I'm grateful for those things, too, "Ah, yes. I forgot. I am grateful that the kids made me laugh this week, like Lesley's kids did. And I am grateful that my boss paid me a compliment this week like Alex's boss did."

Writing a gratitude list is a great idea. But I don't believe the full effect of gratitude is realised by simply expressing it in words. Gratitude must be felt. Like connection, I suspect gratitude is an energy. Maybe it's a form of connection energy that is generated by memory. It is generated when we think about the things we appreciate in retrospect. It's an energy cultivated by contemplation. So, for this reason, when undertaking your gratitude practice, rather than just writing something down and moving swiftly on to the next thing, make sure you generate the energy and feel the gratitude. Make sure you feel the connection to the memory. Imagine the moment in all its depth and beauty. Re-live the experience you are grateful for and allow the energy to arise. Feel the gratitude within. And hold on to that feeling. Hold on to it for twenty seconds. Feel the connection energy grow deeper and stronger.

Practicing gratitude in this way allows felt-connections to grow deeper and stronger with everything. The more grateful we are to our God, the deeper and stronger the felt-connection. The more grateful we are to others, the deeper and stronger the felt-connection. The more grateful we are to nature, the deeper and stronger the felt-connection. It's a tool we can use in all seven reconnections. But I chose to put it here, in our journey to feel the connection within ourselves, because gratitude is the energy that nurtures feelings of enough. When we're filled with gratitude, we feel we have enough. When we are filled with gratitude, we feel we are enough.

Self-compassion

It's strange to think that loving ourselves could be difficult. But it does seem that way. For me, anyway. I can often catch myself saying things to "me" that could be classed as abusive if I said them out loud to anyone else. And just as we talked about learning to love our bodies in the section on Embodying Knowledge, there's also a job to be done in learning to love our minds as well as our bodies. And that includes learning to love the false self as well as the true self.

I'm conscious that the term "false self" has negative and critical connotations. It can sound like it's the part of us that is wrong, bad, destructive and maybe even evil. And I apologise to all the false selves out there if my words have come across as judgemental. The false self isn't inherently bad. It's just that it isn't our true self. Our false self is the self-created personality and identity we have built for ourselves in response to the world around us. It has been an invaluable tool in getting us up and running in society. It has helped us succeed in this world based on our culture's definition of success.

Unfortunately, that definition is not based on the truth or reality of life. The false self has tried to look after us as best it can, given the information it has available and access to. It tries to protect us from harm and guide us towards comfort based on what it knows and thinks to be true. But what it knows to be true isn't reality. That's not being bad or evil. That's just being misguided. The false self cannot know what it doesn't know and, indeed, has no way of knowing.

That's why, as part of our spiritual journey, as part of the process of nurturing our true self back to its rightful position, we shouldn't condemn and criticise our false self. We need to be kind and gentle to our false selves, to our whole selves, and know that; sometimes, we will fall short, we will fail, we will feel bad, we will be less than perfect, we will not be embodying all the qualities that the true self 'should' embody.

At these points, when all the character defects of fear, jealousy, self-pity, dejection, hopelessness, resentment and general feelings of lack ("I'm just not good enough or brave enough or disciplined enough or compassionate enough") seem to dominate, and we feel the journey is just too hard, that's when self-compassion is exactly the thing we need. It can help us re-connect to ourselves and love ourselves again. At these moments, we may feel that we're falling short of perfection or our own false self-expectations and ideals, but we can still love ourselves for it. We can know we are on a path and bumps are all part of the journey. We can know that we are doing the best we can. And that our best is more than good enough.

There are two sources of information that I've found useful when it comes to describing and practising self-compassion. The first is from the work of Dr Kristin Neff and the Self-Compassion Research Lab at the University of Texas. According to Neff, self-compassion has three elements as defined below:

Self-kindness: Being warm and understanding toward ourselves when we suffer, fail, or feel inadequate, rather than ignoring our pain or flagellating ourselves with self-criticism. The thing that gets in the way of self-kindness is judgement.

Common humanity: Common humanity recognises that suffering and feelings of personal inadequacy are part of the shared human experience – something we all go through rather than something that happens to me alone. Sharing our failings helps re-connect us back to ourselves and others. The thing that gets in the way of common humanity is isolation.

Mindfulness: Taking a balanced approach to negative emotions so that feelings are felt and not suppressed or exaggerated. We cannot ignore our pain and feel compassion for it at the same time. Mindfulness requires that we not "over-identify" with thoughts and feelings so that we are caught up and swept away by negativity. The thing that gets in the way of mindfulness is over-identification.

Dr Neff has a website and a short test that helps you assess the level of your self-compassion and the things that get in the way. It's available on www.self-compassion.org

The other source of self-compassion information I have found useful comes from Ken Wilber, Terry Patten, Adam Leonard and Marco Morelli in their book Integral Life Practice. As a boy brought up in the tradition of a protestant work ethic, I've always tended to believe that hard work is the pathway to success. If something's not working, the solution is to try harder, work harder, and put more effort in. When I hear that the answer to failing, falling short, or being less than perfect may be to be compassionate with ourselves, red flags start rising in my enculturated, work ethic mind. I can't help but think that being self-compassionate is a fancy way of saying, "I'm giving up." It's an excuse to talk ourselves out of doing the work. It's a "get out of jail card" which makes laziness a virtue. (Does anyone else notice my critical self-talk coming through?)

That's why I liked the way Wilber and crew talked about self-compassion and the connection we have with ourselves. They describe it as follows:

"Sometimes our negative self-talk is based on the very accurate perceptions of our conscience and our discriminative self-awareness. We've blown it! It's not just important to treat yourself compassionately; it's also crucial that you see yourself accurately and take responsibility for living up to your highest values and possibilities."

I like the fact that there's a bit of an edge to self-compassion. Being compassionate to ourselves isn't always about putting our feet up in front the TV and eating chocolate biscuits. We need to be kind. Yes. We also need to be real. We need to be careful that we don't lose our response-ability in a moment of self-justified weakness. This is especially true for addicts who can't afford to slip into old destructive behaviours on the pretence of self-compassion. And that's why the model of self-compassion that is presented in Integral Life Practice is more of a dynamic play of masculine and feminine self-compassion. This is how it is described:

"Masculine self-compassion--the spiritual journey requires clear choices and boundaries. It requires discipline and structure. The river needs the riverbanks to flow to the sea. Without masculine self-compassion, our spiritual practice can drift aimlessly.

Masculine self-compassion has two dimensions to it: discernment, which is the courage to face unpleasant realities, and discipline, which is the willingness to choose and enforce new behaviours and habits in place of older, more destructive ones.

Putting your masculine self-compassion to good use is a tremendous act of self-love. By doing so, you earn more self-respect and empower yourself to show up in your life with authority. This liberates inner energy and an ability to focus – which goes right to your bottom line, enabling you to be the person you want to be in your every day life, at work and in all your most important relationships.

One of the big secrets of transformation is the enormous impact of intentionally interrupting your comfortable habits. To do so consistently is the secret of keeping your spiritual journey alive.

Feminine self-compassion--but applying ourselves in a disciplined and structured way needn't be punishing. Neither discernment nor discipline require harsh judgements or a cruel heart. You don't have to hate yourself to see your patterns and choose new ones. Feminine self-compassion is the softer underbelly of the spiritual journey that actually greases the wheels of discipline because it eases the tendency for parts of the self (the false self) to get locked into unproductive resistance with the other parts (the true self).

The habit of negative self-talk doesn't change easily. Our first best step may be to soften and accept the inner abuser. An interior environment of self-acceptance and forgiveness has to begin somewhere.

Gradually, greeted with compassionate acceptance, the inner judgement and self-hatred will themselves begin to soften. We can't always change the negative self-talk, but we can relax in the midst of it and gently cultivate an inner atmosphere of acceptance and gratitude.

As we begin to treat ourselves with more compassion and appreciation, it becomes natural and authentic to extend that compassion and appreciation to others."

As we begin to feel connected within ourselves and align our false self within our true self in a dance that includes forgiveness of self, gratitude and self-compassion, we become better equipped to feel the connection to others with forgiveness, gratitude and compassion.

3. FELT-CONNECTION TO OTHERS

We are social animals. We have relied on our connectedness to each other to survive and thrive for millennia. Belonging to specific social groups and relying on that social group is part of our evolutionary story. It's how we live our lives. But belonging has its downside. Even if we have a strong internal alignment and a solid felt-connection to a God of our understanding and are grounded in our own authentic selves, embedded in the notion of belonging is the sense of "us" and "them." Those who I view as being part of my group and "safe," and those outside my group who may pose a threat. What's interesting about belonging is that it's contextual and relies on our perceived identity, even our perceived authentic identity, which can change very quickly.

Identity and Belonging

I remember hearing a comedian talk about this point a few years ago. He told the story of a group of five guys sitting in a pub in Leeds, enjoying a few pints in their local, when in walked five guys who drank in a different, rival pub. A stand-off ensued, and it was just about to kick off when a group of Manchester United fans walked in. The ten guys from Leeds looked at each other. These Manchester United fans weren't from around here. They were from a different city —a rival city. So, the Leeds guys ganged together and squared up to the Manchester United fans. Things were about to kick off when a group of Germans walked in. Hold up. We can't have Germans coming in here and giving it the big "I am." They're from a different country— a rival country. So, the Leeds guys and the Manchester United fans ganged together to square up to the Germans. Things were about to get tasty when in walked a group of aliens... You get the picture.

The point is that the criteria we choose to determine our identity directly defines our belonging. If we perceive our identity to be based on the criterion of being from the local pub, which could feel very authentic, then that's where we feel we belong and who we feel we belong to. The same applies if we perceive our authentic identity to be based on being from Leeds, England, or planet Earth. This leads to the conclusion that where and who we perceive we belong to determines how we act, who and what we will fight for, and who and what we'll fight against.

Daniel Siegel, in his book Intraconnected observes that we have the capacity to shift the focus of what criterion we choose to determine our identity and, hence, the capacity to shift the focus of our belonging. He calls this ability to shift our "identity lens." We can adjust from a narrow lens and focus (I belong to the local pub) to a much wider-angle perspective (I belong to the human race).

This ability to widen our identity lens is important as it allows us to generate felt-connection with others in an authentic, honest, compassionate, and loving way. If we identify with other people and feel we belong to them and feel the connection energy with them, we are much more likely to act in a compassionate and loving way towards them. We will naturally take the right action and do the right thing. We will be helpful, useful, and, critically, not selfish. We will work alongside them, not against them.

The Challenge of Genuine Felt-Connection

Ideally, this right action will not involve squaring up to rival gangs, but it will result in considering other people's needs alongside your own. And usually, if you feel very connected to them, you will put their needs ahead of your own.

If you've ever been deeply in love with another person or have felt the connection energy of being a parent, you'll know exactly how automatic right action can sometimes be. You are naturally willing to go out of your way to be loving, giving, and tolerant. It doesn't feel arduous to travel hundreds of miles to be with someone you love. It doesn't feel like a chore to take your kids to their football match. It doesn't feel like hard work to make a big Sunday lunch for the whole family.

But that's only sometimes. Most of the time, we don't consider other people's needs alongside our own. Most of the time, we don't automatically take the right action because, most of the time, we are dealing with people we don't feel particularly connected to. How many people would you say you have a strong felt-connection with? Five, ten, maybe twenty people? It's probably about twenty or so for me, yet I deal with way more people than that on a daily basis. When I do deal with these people I feel less connected to, my natural inclination is to take the action that suits me best, not what suits them best. This results in the selfish behaviour of disconnection, which perpetuates the scarce world we talked about earlier.

Widening Our Identity Lens Through Meditation and Contemplation

That might well be the case, but it does seem a tall order to feel naturally inclined to act in a way that is loving and compassionate to everyone. It also begs the question of whether it's possible to feel genuinely connected to people we don't even know.

It is a tall order, but I believe it is possible and, indeed, arguably necessary if we are to progress further down the spiritual path. One way to nurture felt-connection and strengthen the connection energy we feel to people we don't necessarily know is to widen the lens of our identity and nurture the sense that we belong, not only to the whole human race but to the whole of nature. This might feel like a mammoth task to begin with, but nurturing this wide sense of felt-connection and belonging is essentially what we're doing when we contemplate emptiness, signlessness, and aimlessness—the exercises we discussed in the section Embracing Silence.

By meditating and contemplating these three aspects of being, we are nurturing our felt-connection to life. We are widening the lens of identity to the broadest perspective possible. We are thinking of ourselves not as an isolated, separate being sitting in a coffee shop in Edinburgh but as a coordinated community of 37 trillion cells and a flow of energy that feels the connection to the flowing energy of the universe. We are feeling the connection to our ancestors, descendants, those people we know and are close to, and those that we don't know and are far away. We are feeling the connection to everyone and everything—to the Big Bang, the stars, the ether, and to a God of our understanding.

This type of meditation and contemplation increases the connection energy we feel between ourselves and everyone else. It is a way to widen our lens of identity and move from "me" to "we." Or, to be more accurate, it's a way of moving towards "MWe."

The Concept of MWe

MWe is the term Daniel Siegel coined to describe the conception we might build of ourselves when our lens of identity includes ourselves as being 'intraconnected' with the rest of humanity and nature. This is how he defines it:

"MWe is perhaps a funny and awkward word for some. Yet for others, it is a simple term to remind us of our integrated identity that characterises us as individuals (Me = our individual, authentic inner self, our true self and our false self, our bodies and felt experience) and our wider belonging (We = our relational, interconnected selves, the flow of energy, part of the human race, nature, life, the universe and God of our understanding) and the intraconnected, integrated experience of self in the relational wholeness of MWe."

It may be a hard concept to logically get at first, but if you allow your intuitive, right hemisphere to contemplate your existence as MWe, alongside emptiness, signlessness, and aimlessness, you'll find yourself deepening your felt-connection with life and valuing your unique part within it. A useful analogy Siegel uses is that of a fruit salad, as opposed to a smoothie. A smoothie is blended to create a unified, homogenous whole. We're not that. We are a piece of apple in a fruit salad. On the one hand, we have our own authentic identity as a piece of apple with our own shape, colour, taste, and texture. We can stand on our own ground. But, at the same time, we also have an authentic identity as being part of the whole fruit salad, part of an important and bigger whole, playing our own unique role, benefiting from inclusion and adding value by being there.

I'm not sure how comfortable theologians feel about me likening God to the great universal fruit salad maker, but the analogy works for me.

The Challenge of Maintaining Felt-Connection

As we've said before, tasting the fruits (pun intended) of spiritual practice takes time. Deepening our felt-connections, generating a sense of MWe, and nurturing the natural ability to do the right thing for everyone through meditation and contemplation takes time—years, even decades. I know that it can be done because I've experienced it. I've been able to widen my identity lens to the widest possible perspective and felt a deep connection to life, to all of humanity, and to all of nature as a result. When that happens, I can and want to do the right thing automatically. It feels natural and easy to be generous with my time and my thoughtfulness. I am a compassionate and loving person to everyone. Well, almost everyone. The problem is I can't hold on to that felt-connection. I lose the focus of my meditation and contemplation, and the connection energy dissipates. And it can dissipate quickly.

And that happens even when I am dealing with people I love very much. Sometimes, travelling all those miles does feel arduous. Sometimes, that football match on an early winter morning does feel like a chore. And sometimes, making a big Sunday lunch feels very much like hard work. What's happened? Why does doing the right, loving thing feel harder all of a sudden?

The Danger of Resentment

The difference is the identity lens. All of a sudden, my identity lens has narrowed right back down to one person: me. I've lost the sense of MWe. The heartfelt connection I had with other people has been lost. The connection energy has stopped flowing. The battery has run down. And all those actions are now coming from a place of "What's in it for me?" rather than "What's in it for MWe?" The actions are coming from a place of self-centredness. They are not coming from a place of love.

When this happens, when we find ourselves doing things for others without that connection energy, we come face to face with a whole new set of emotions and feelings—emotions and feelings that are destructive. They disconnect us from others.

We've previously talked about character defects in the section about The Habit of Awareness and the "warts and all review" and how that review can illuminate a raft of destructive traits such as fear, greed, and envy. When it comes to relationships and feeling connected to others, there's one that stands out as more pernicious than the others: resentment.

As 12-Steppers will know, Bill Wilson writes, "The number one offender is resentment. It destroys more alcoholics than anything else." Although Bill was mainly concerned with the welfare and well-being of alcoholics, I'm pretty sure we can apply the observation to be true of all addicts, not just alcoholics. And as I believe we're all addicts to some degree or other, it's not unreasonable to claim that resentment could well be the number one offender for all of us.

So, what is resentment? And why is it so dangerous?

The Poison of Resentment

Resentment is the bitter feeling that we've been wronged by someone or some situation. It's the sense that life is unfair, leaving us with the uneasy sensations of disappointment, disgust, self-pity, and anger. Recall a time when an ex-partner cheated on you, someone stole from you, or your boss treated you unfairly. These situations likely evoke a tight, uncomfortable sensation in your chest and stomach—the unmistakable feeling of resentment.

Resentment has several key characteristics worth examining:

1. It's all about "me." Resentments are a symptom of self-centredness, with "I" at the centre of concern. It's all about how I have been wronged.
2. It involves black-and-white thinking. Resentment thrives on the belief that I am right, and you are wrong, closing us off to other truths and perspectives.
3. It dominates the mind. Resentful thoughts go round and round, obsessing over the unfairness, plotting revenge, or hoping for divine justice. When the mind is in resentment mode, it's not in loving mode.
4. It can last for years. Some resentments, especially those involving parents, teachers, old friends, siblings and first loves, can linger in the psyche for many years, secretly wreaking havoc.

The Futility and Dangers of Resentment

Like worry, resentment serves no purpose other than to harm ourselves. It's such a futile exercise. It's been said that holding a resentment against someone is like swallowing poison and expecting the other person to die. No matter how "justified" the resentment might appear, if we hold on to it, there's only one person who suffers. Us.

It's interesting to reflect on the fact that resentments are pretty commonplace. They seem to be such an accepted part of modern life. That's probably because our culture of economic growth is built on the foundations of comparison and competition. We pit ourselves against each other. If we're playing the zero-sum game of winners and losers in the accumulation of material wealth and status, it's no wonder that resentment features so heavily in everyday life. There's always someone or something to blame for any failure we may experience. There's always a reassuring resentment to hold on to. A resentment that makes it possible to take the blame away from ourselves for any misfortune, failure or problematic situation we find ourselves in.

Because of that, I suspect most people can quickly and easily rattle off any number of resentments that they are aware of and are holding on to. And they are probably holding on to a whole host of other resentments without you even knowing it. Because they are so commonplace, because we all hold on to so many, and because we live in a culture that is quick to blame others, resentments wouldn't appear to be too much of a problem. Not at first glance, anyway. That's why they're dangerous. They're subtle and pernicious. They sit there. Under the surface of our everyday existence, lurking in the background of our memories, waiting to interfere with our peace of mind and connectedness. And that's the key issue.

Resentments allow us to blame everyone else and everything else for our apparent misfortunes. They allow us to point the finger at anyone else but us. They create a barrier of "me being right and everyone else being wrong." And as long as that barrier exists, resentments will always keep us disconnected. They keep us disconnected from ourselves. They keep us disconnected from others. They keep us disconnected from the truth. They keep us disconnected from reality. They keep us disconnected from our response-ability. They keep us disconnected from our God.

Felt-connection is pivotal to spiritual happiness. Therefore, any form of disconnection is a barrier that needs overcoming on our journey towards feeling spiritually well and joyful. Unless we unearth and really examine them, resentments have the ability to hold us back in unhappiness and unsatisfactoriness.

Emmott Fox was unequivocal on this point: *"It is simply not possible to get any experience of God worth talking about, unless and until you have got rid of resentment and condemnation concerning your brotherman. Indignation, resentment, the desire to punish other people or to see them punished, the desire to get even the feeling "it serves him right"– all these things form a quite impenetrable barrier to spiritual power or progress."*

And that's been my experience. The seemingly innocuous ball of resentment that I have held on to for years hasn't just kept me disconnected from those I have a resentment against. The mere act of holding a resentment in the first place disconnects me from the brotherhood of man. It keeps me in "me" and away from "MWe." It is the single biggest cause of connection energy dissipation.

So, if resentments are so dangerous yet so commonplace, what can we do to overcome them? In a word, forgiveness.

The Divine Technology of Forgiveness

I mentioned earlier that forgiveness is a superpower—a Divine technology even. It's at the heart of the Lord's Prayer and arguably the centrepiece of the Christian faith. It's also a big part of The 12-Step Programme. Forgiveness and tolerance of others are how we manage our resentments. They allow us to free ourselves from the negativity created by resentment. They allow us to reconnect.

Sin can be thought of as disconnection, a disconnection and separation from others and a God of our understanding. Forgiveness is the way we reconnect, feel that reconnection and reverse that separation. Forgive us our sins as we forgive those who sin against us.

Emmott Fox describes forgiveness as follows: "If someone injures you do not seek to get your own back, you are to do the very opposite –

you are to forgive him and set him free." The beauty of forgiveness is that as part of the process we don't just set the person who has injured us free. We set ourselves free. Both of us are unbound. If we are unbound by the resentment, we're free to reconnect. We're free to generate loving, meaningful connection energy.

We've talked about feeling the connection energy of MWe and naturally taking the right action. Forgiveness is the superpower we have at our disposal when we're dealing with people who we don't feel strongly connected. Especially when those people appear to be taking the wrong action. And we feel their action has harmed us in some way. Now it's our turn. We can retaliate. We can get our own back. We can take the perceived wrong action and keep the disconnection going. Or we can widen our identity lens to MWe, including them, and take the right action. We can forgive them and choose reconnection. Forgiveness is right re-action. As Emmott Fox puts it: "Right reaction is the supreme art of life. Resist not evil, spiritually understood, is the grand secret of success in life."

Imagine if everyone did this. Imagine the world we would live in if every apparent transgression was met with tolerance and forgiveness rather than resentment, anger and revenge. Imagine how few wars we'd have. Imagine how little violence there would be. Imagine how much peace we'd generate. No wonder it's called a Divine technology. Richard Rohr calls it "the Divine technology for the regeneration of every age and every situation."

The Process of Forgiveness

The process of forgiveness is pretty straightforward. Emmott Fox covers the importance, the process and the mechanics of forgiveness in his book Sermon on the Mount and his essay on the Lord's Prayer. He seems to be a bit of a forgiveness expert to me. This is what he has to say about forgiveness and forgiving:

"The technique of forgiveness is simple enough and not very difficult to manage when you understand how. The only thing that is essential is WILLINGNESS to forgive. Provided you desire to forgive the offender, the greater part of the work is already done. People have always made such a bogey of forgiveness because they have been under the erroneous impression that to forgive a person means that you have to compel yourself to like them. Happily, this is by no means the case – we are not called upon to like anyone whom we do not find ourselves liking spontaneously, and, indeed, it is quite impossible to like people to order. You can no more LIKE to order than you can hold the winds in your fist, and if your endeavour to coerce yourself into doing so, you will finish by disliking or hating the offender more than ever."

The method of forgiving is this: Get by yourself and become quiet. Repeat any prayer or treatment that appeals to you or read a chapter of the Bible. Then quietly say, "I fully and freely forgive X (mention the name of the offender); I lose him and let him go. I completely forgive the whole business in question. As far as I am concerned, it is finished forever... He is free now, and I am free, too. I wish him well in every phase of his life. That incident is finished." And that's it. Just go about your business. No need to do it again. You have granted forgiveness. If the issue crops up again and you sense resentment growing, simply bless the offender, think kind thoughts of them, and let the issue go. Again. You'll find that the issue is all but forgotten, and the resentment has disappeared.

Yet, despite all its power and supremacy, and despite all its simplicity to do, forgiveness remains a rare act. It seems we are more comfortable holding on to the discomfort of resentment and revenge than we are realising the freedom of forgiveness. Why do we find it so hard to forgive and forget?

Forgiveness is a technology of the intuitive, soulful true self, and it makes absolutely no sense to the logical, egoic false self.

When we're wronged, our ego screams for retribution: "That idiot cheated on you and you're just going to let them off scot-free? Are you insane?" "An eye for an eye, remember? You need to get even. They've got it coming!" "If you let them walk all over you now, they'll do it again and again. They win, you lose."

As much as this tit-for-tat mentality appeals to our ego, we must remember that on the spiritual path, our ultimate goal is the peace, joy, freedom and wholeness of spiritual happiness. These arise from fostering connection, not perpetuating animosity. As the Buddha taught, hatred does not cease by hatred but only by love.

Freeing the Sinner from the Sin

One way to wean our logical, egoic, false self off the knee-jerk impulse of instant resentment and revenge is to separate people's hurtful actions from their inherent worth. The 12-Step Programme encourages us to extend love, tolerance, and patience to everyone, even our enemies, by recognising that people who act harmfully do so because they are spiritually sick.

You may think that's just letting people off the hook. But for us addicts, it's a powerful tool and reminder that "there but for the grace of God go I." That's because, as addicts, we usually have a rich history of acting wrongly and causing harm. Having gone through The 12-Step Programme, having found the spiritual solution and experienced a spiritual awakening, we can now see that the wrong we did and the harm we caused were all down to us being unwell. We weren't bad people. But we were doing bad things. We were in the throes of active addiction. We were sick. We were spiritually sick. We realise that now.

As part of Step 9, we seek to make up for those mistakes by making amends and seeking forgiveness. The Step 9 process of making amends is incredibly powerful. This is the part of the process where you come face to face with all the people you have caused harm to; you admit your wrongdoing, ask for forgiveness and offer to make good any harm that you caused. It's an incredibly powerful, humbling, and healing process.

I was halfway through doing my Step 9 amends when I experienced my biggest spiritual shift. It was by applying the superpower of forgiveness that I experienced the power of an awakening. I started feeling the peace, the joy, and the freedom of spiritual happiness.

When we are willing and humble enough to own up to our own misdemeanours and seek forgiveness, we are usually granted forgiveness. Having been granted forgiveness for all the wrong things we did makes us much more likely to forgive those who may wrong us in the future. We were forgiven for the bad things we did because we were sick. We can forgive the bad things others do to us because they are spiritually sick, too. They may be doing bad things. But they are not bad people. They're just like us.

Another way to free the sinner from the sin is through the lens of "situationism." This is a philosophy of life that says that it is the totality of all our external experiences and situations and the way we internalise them that determines our choices, our beliefs and our behaviours. It says, if you had been through what I had been through and were the type of person I am, you would think, say and do exactly as I do.

Thich Nhat Hahn's powerful story of a Thai pirate and a young girl brought situationism to life for me.

"After the Vietnam War, many people wrote to us in Plum Village. We received hundreds of letters each week from the refugee camps in Singapore, Malaysia, Indonesia, Thailand, and the Philippines, hundreds each week. It was very painful to read them, but we had to be in contact. We tried our best to help, but the suffering was enormous, and sometimes we were discouraged. It is said that half the boat people fleeing Vietnam died in the ocean; only half arrived at the shores of Southeast Asia.

There are many young girls, boat people, who were raped by sea pirates. Even though the United Nations and many countries tried to help the government of Thailand prevent that kind of piracy, sea pirates continued to inflict much suffering on the refugees. One day, we received a letter telling us about a young girl on a small boat who was raped by a Thai pirate.

She was only twelve, and she jumped into the ocean and drowned herself.

When you first learn of something like that, you get angry at the pirate. You naturally take the side of the girl. As you look more deeply you will see it differently. If you take the side of the little girl, then it is easy. You only have to take a gun and shoot the pirate. But we can't do that. In my meditation, I saw that if I had been born in the village of the pirate and raised in the same conditions as he was, I would now be the pirate. There is a great likelihood that I would become a pirate. I can't condemn myself so easily. In my meditation, I saw that many babies are born along the Gulf of Siam, hundreds every day, and if we educators, social workers, politicians, and others do not do something about the situation, in twenty-five years a number of them will become sea pirates. That is certain. If you or I were born today in those fishing villages, we might become sea pirates in twenty-five years. If you take a gun and shoot the pirate, you shoot all of us, because all of us are to some extent responsible for this state of affairs.

After a long meditation, I wrote a poem. In it, there are three people: the twelve-year-old girl, the pirate, and me. Can we look at each other and recognize ourselves in each other? The title of the poem is "Please Call Me by My True Names," because I have so many names. When I hear one of these names, I have to say, "Yes."

Unfortunately, our culture of economic growth hasn't been grounded in the philosophy of situationism. We're mired in a philosophy of dispositionism. If you do bad things, it's probably because you're a bad person, and you deserve what's coming your way.

Taking the situationist stance in a dispositionist world and choosing to forgive those who trespass against you isn't always easy. But it's much easier when you experience the forgiveness of your own trespasses. Being accountable, taking responsibility, owning up to mistakes, seeking forgiveness, and making amends. These are the daily practices that demonstrate we are leading by example. The practices that help turn the dial of our culture one notch towards peace and one notch away from revenge. One notch towards love. One notch away from fear and anger.

The practice of forgiveness, of forgiving and being forgiven, is a supreme spiritual superpower. It is the key to regenerating relationships, and that's why it is the key to generating the felt-connection we have with others and practicing the habit of connection.

4. FELT-CONNECTION TO COMMUNITY

In essence, feeling connected to local communities is simply the widening of our identity lens to firmly embed ourselves in the communities we live in and the communities we work in. From that point of view, nurturing the felt-connection we have to community is simply applying the MWe idea to the places you live and work. No big news there.

However, I want to highlight it as a specific form of felt-connection because I believe that strong communities, strong living communities and strong working communities could well be the antidote to our culture of economic growth. Living and working in communities that are bonded by spiritual values rather than junk values is a way that people will not only be able to practice the principles we've discussed in this book, they will be encouraged to do so. These are the communities I dream of.

Re-Imagining the Communities We Live and Work In

There are a small but growing number of such communities in existence that I know of. Findhorn in Scotland is a living community that springs to mind. Patagonia in the US is a working community that I often refer to. Such communities, regenerative communities, are where change happens. They are the islands of sanity that will eventually reverse the culture of economic growth. They are the new wineskins that can hold and nurture new wine.

But they are far too rare at the moment. There are far too few communities that align themselves with the story of life, the universe and everything. Far too few valuing intrinsic spiritual rewards as the key to success. Far too few are able to break free of the destructive junk values we've been acculturated with.

I hope that people reading this book are able to forge more of these strong new communities and celebrate them. Celebrate them in a way that appeals to wider audiences. I can't see myself joining a hippy commune any day soon. But I can see myself working in a business that prioritises well-being over financial reward. I can't see myself renouncing all my possessions. But I can see myself volunteering at an urban farm. I can see myself trying to encourage local residents to use local businesses to support a local economy. I can see myself promoting a sharing economy. I can see myself actively campaigning for everyday spiritual happiness as a new way of living.

I believe these new regenerative communities are emerging all the time. Seek them out and be part of them. And don't be bound by your physical location. As Thomas Moore said, "Community is not a group of people or an organisation. Community is an outlook toward life in which you define yourself in relation to the world around you rather than only in connection with yourself." Finding a community that shares our outlook in life allows us to free ourselves of our self-centredness. It's much easier to stay in the felt-connectedness of MWe.

It's much easier to generate that loving and meaningful connection energy.

Seeking out regenerative communities has another benefit. It allows us to be us. We don't have to try and be what we're not. We can bring our authentic selves and our unique skills and talents to a cause and mission we believe in. We're not in the community to benefit from extrinsic rewards. We're not there to sell anything. We're there to be ourselves, bring what we have to offer and nurture our souls.

Communities require what we have to offer. Communities, whether they are living or working communities, need diversity to grow. They may require a common purpose and a shared set of values. Still, they need a diverse range of skills, knowledge, qualities and abilities to become resilient, sustainable communities that can thrive and survive.

You can express your unique and true self in these communities and be valued for that expression. Finding these communities is vital for us to feel whole and live our purpose, something we'll come back to in the Epilogue, The Pathway to Purpose and Power. We need to find these communities first. And that's not always easy to do. We may even need to start our own. We may have to create our very own island of sanity.

5. FELT-CONNECTION TO NATURE

Humans are, by nature, hunter-gatherers. Anthropologists have discovered evidence dating back as far as two million years that homo sapiens and our distant ancestors lived in hunter-gatherer cultures. Only in the last 12,000 years have we moved away from this way of life. That means for 99.9% of the time we've been on Earth, we've lived off the land, hand-to-mouth with nature, at one with our environment. As hunter-gatherers, our very existence required us to know nature intimately, to observe the fine details of the world around us, and to be responsive to the environment. We had to recognise the subtle changes in the seasons, the shifts in the weather, and the behaviours of animals.

It required us to sense the subtle energies of life around us and act accordingly.

Our Disconnection from Nature

We no longer require this response-ability to feed ourselves. Agricultural technology and economic development have taken care of that. Although we may have lost the need for close contact with nature for our physical sustenance, we haven't lost the need for a felt-connection with nature for our spiritual sustenance. Our soulful, intuitive right hemisphere yearns for this felt-connection - it's in our DNA. We relied on our right hemisphere's ability to respond to our environment and inform our inner knowing to guide us towards a safe and plentiful life. The need for guidance hasn't disappeared. But in our modern world, we've given our egoic, logical left hemisphere and false selves the power to guide us. That's the master right now, and we've lost our felt-connection to nature as a result.

Across most high-income countries – Western Europe, the Americas, Australia, Japan, and the Middle East – more than 80% of the population lives in cities and urban areas. In the UK, that figure is 84%. Based on these statistics, the chances are that you, like me, live and work in a city. That you, like me, breathe in more exhaust fumes than fresh meadow air, hear more cars accelerating than birds singing, and see way more dogs on leads than animals living in the wild. It feels quite depressing to write that down.

And yet, even though this is the place I've chosen to live and the way of life I've chosen to lead, a large part of me longs to be much closer to nature. I know how wonderful I feel by the sea, in a forest, or up a mountain. I feel connected to nature because I am connected to nature. My soulful right hemisphere revels in the felt-connection. It feels nourished, revitalised, and alive. We love being in nature because our true self loves it.

The Benefits of Felt-Connection with Nature

I don't know anyone who doesn't feel better after going for a walk in the country. When I suggest going out for a big yomp to my kids, they usually moan. Playing another game on the Xbox or watching another Friends episode seems so much more enticing to their logical, comfort-seeking left hemispheres. But once we're out, breathing in fresh air and feeling fully connected with nature, we feel fully connected with each other, and we all benefit from it.

I suspect there's no surprise here. Most people know that feeling connected to nature is good for us. Just in case you're in any doubt about how beneficial it is, here's what Mind, the mental health charity, says on their website about our felt-connection to nature:

> "Spending time in green space or bringing nature into your everyday life can benefit both your mental and physical well-being. For example, doing things like growing food or flowers, exercising outdoors, or being around animals can have many positive effects."

It can:

- Improve your mood
- Reduce feelings of stress or anger
- Help you take time out and feel more relaxed
- Improve your physical health
- Improve your confidence and self-esteem
- Help you be more active
- Help you meet and get to know new people
- Connect you to your local community
- Reduce loneliness
- Help you feel more connected to nature
- Provide peer support

Our Unsustainable Consumption of Nature's Resources

While the benefits of feeling more connected to nature may be evident to you, what may be less obvious is that you are, in all likelihood, destroying it. It's a pretty bold accusation to make, but it's true. And I'm not just pointing the finger at you - I'm pointing at me, too. If you are, like me, living and working in a city, own a car, fly occasionally on planes, buy the vast majority of your food from supermarkets, and heat your home and water to keep warm, you are destroying nature. We are destroying nature. There's no two ways about it.

Our modern, Western lifestyle may be comfortable and even luxurious compared to our hunter-gatherer ancestors, but it's coming at a cost - a cost paid by nature. The Living Planet Report 2022, the flagship publication from WWF, reveals an average decline of 69% in species populations since 1970. Some claim that this is the start of the sixth mass extinction the Earth has suffered. The last one was 65 million years ago.

We're losing vital, oxygen-giving trees and forests too. By 2030, there may be only 10% of the world's rainforests left, with agriculture being responsible for approximately 80% of tropical forest loss.

Climate change, fish population collapses, the loss of the Great Barrier Reef, air pollution, water quality issues - the list goes on and on.

The bottom line is that our culture of economic growth and the lifestyle we've become accustomed to is coming at a huge cost to nature. The way we live is literally costing us the Earth. Not only is this depriving us of the opportunity to connect more with nature, but it's also reducing our ability to sustain ourselves in the future. We are depleting, and in fact, we're consuming our biggest asset and the source of life itself - a sustainable and naturally regenerative planet.

The importance of a naturally regenerative planet and how we're slowly losing ours was brought home when I came across the concept of Earth Overshoot Day. You can find out more at https://overshoot.footprintnetwork.org/.

Earth Overshoot Day is calculated by dividing the amount of resources Earth is able to generate in any given year by humanity's demand for those resources in that year and multiplying by 365, the number of days in a year. If we were living within the Earth's means, we would get to the end of December without overshooting. But we're not. We are running out of the resources the Earth can naturally regenerate much earlier in the year. In 2023, we ran out by August 2nd. This is the Earth overshoot day. This is a date that has been getting earlier and earlier in the year since 1971 when we first started consuming more than the Earth can regenerate.

We currently require 1.7 Earths to satisfy our seemingly insatiable demand for more - a demand generated by our culture of economic growth.

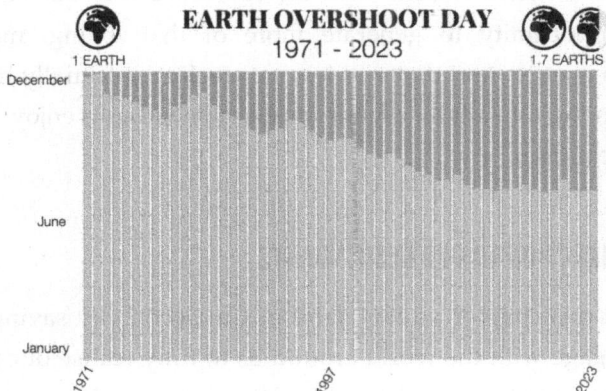

I urge you to take the test for yourself using the tool. https://www.footprintcalculator.org/home/en. It will give you your own personal overshoot day. If you're like me, you'll be surprised by just how much of the world's resources you're using.

Generating a strong felt-connection with nature is not important. It's vital. It's vitality itself. The felt-connection we need is not just about going for a walk in the countryside every so often (although that is a good start). And it's not just about being more environmentally aware and making more sustainable choices (although that's even better). I believe the felt-connection we need, and nature needs from us, must go deeper. I sense that we need to feel connected to our inner hunter-gatherer more. I sense we need to feel the connection to nature and our environment in the way David Suzuki envisions it. He says the environment is not something "out there" to be protected or abused. He says, "We are the environment; through the air we breathe, the water we drink and the soil we grow our food in." The air, the water, and the food are all in us. They are part of us. They give us life. They are integral and inseparable from the 37 trillion cells that create our lives. Nature is part of MWe.

A felt-connection with nature at this deeper level will help us cherish it more. Love it more. Treat it with the reverence it is due. It gives us another opportunity to generate more of that loving, meaningful connection energy. And that will leave us feeling spiritually happier as well as leaving a healthier planet for everyone else to enjoy. Not least our grandchildren.

6. FELT-CONNECTION TO OUR DESCENDANTS

We started this chapter on the Habit of Connection by saying that we have to engage with the world around us to fully realise our potential. We are not separate from the world. We are inexorably part of it. We cannot grow spiritually in isolation. We need to feel connection. And we cannot grow spiritually by working only for ourselves. Felt-connection helps us move out of self-centredness and into concern and usefulness to others.

As a father of four, I feel very connected to my children. Most parents do. It's an easy way to conceive of MWe and act accordingly. And as a result, I feel very connected and concerned about their futures. Most parents are. As I've journeyed on this spiritual path, the connection and concern I feel for my children's future has extended to include the future of other people's children as well. I feel myself being increasingly concerned about the welfare and prospects of future generations in general.

As a day job, I earn money as a Purpose Consultant and advise businesses on being more sustainable. The strap-line I use for my business is "Let's grow the type of business our children will be proud of." It's a sentiment that's very important to me. If we can nurture and grow businesses that have a strong felt-connection to future generations, we'll evolve an economy that isn't growing for growing's sake but growing for the sake of the future. If, indeed, it's growing at all. Now that feels like a much more compelling economic culture to feel part of and contribute to.

The idea of working for the future isn't a new one. In fact, it's an ancient one linked with indigenous cultures and approaches to living, such as seventh generation thinking. Oren Lyons, Native American Chief, puts it like this: "We are looking ahead. as it's one of the first mandates given us as chiefs, to make sure every decision that we make relates to the welfare and well-being of the seventh generation to come, and that is the basis by which we make decisions in council. We consider: will this be to the benefit of the seventh generation."

Imagine that. Imagine if the world's national governments and local councils were making decisions based on the same mandate. Imagine that no policy would be passed if there was a possibility that it negatively impacted people 140 years down the line. We certainly wouldn't be using our world's resources by August 2nd, that's for sure.

Feeling connected to, concerned for and acting on behalf of our descendants is the central theme of the book The Good Ancestor by Roman Krznaric. He identifies a number of ways in which our current culture of economic growth - which is so concerned with short-term thinking on behalf of itself - could expand its horizons to think in longer-term ways on behalf of future generations. He explains his thinking in this way: "Just as our moral imaginations have expanded over the centuries – from concern for our immediate family and tribe to ideals such as universal human rights and animal rights – so too our temporal imaginations have the potential to extend further than the here and now." I love this concept. It's like extending the MWe to include future generations.

Being a good ancestor is a natural by-product of the spiritual solution. I sense it in myself. I sense this felt-connection to future generations growing as I go deeper into my spiritual practises. I especially feel it when contemplating Thich Nhat Hanh's concepts of interbeing and impermanence. There's a felt sense of being one with all humanity and all of life, in the past, in the present and in the future.

Having said that, those moments are fleeting. I have to admit that it's quite a stretch to think that people will suddenly shift to such a radical deferral of gratification. Not only does being a good ancestor mean doing without now for gratification in the future. It means doing without now for a gratification that we won't experience ourselves. Someone else gets the benefit. Our future generations get the gratification. We get the deferring. We just have to be content with doing without.

It might be a stretch, but I think it is possible. I think it's possible because the process of building stronger felt-connections creates living, meaningful connection energy. There's no end to that energy available to us when we realise that we can build stronger felt-connections with ourselves, with our God, with others, with communities, with nature, and with our descendants.

The loving, meaningful, subtle energy generated by The Habit of Connection is expansive. It's an abundant energy. It's an energy that helps reduce our fear of scarcity. It helps us experience a world that is abundant and full. When we feel the world is abundant and full, we feel there is enough. We feel we have enough. We feel we are enough. We feel there's enough to go around. We feel we can be generous with our time. We can be generous with our energy. With our resources. With our concern. With our love. We can be generous to those we know now. And those we don't know yet. Those around us now. And those that are yet to come.

7. FELT-CONNECTION TO PURPOSE

Belonging to the Biggest Family Possible

Values and value-driven behaviour come from what you love. They come from what you feel connected to. If you don't feel the connection to what you're doing and who you're doing it for, the action becomes a chore, or a duty and resentments can grow. The beauty of developing the seven types of felt-connections as discussed above, is that it allows us to find a felt-connection in virtually everything we do. Everything has the opportunity to be meaningful if you have the habit of connection. And the bigger and wider the felt-connection is, the deeper and stronger the connection energy you create.

There's a parable that's often told about three bricklayers that illustrates this point. The story dates back to 1666 when the world's most famous architect, Christopher Wren, was commissioned to rebuild St Paul's Cathedral.

One day, he went to the building site to see how construction was progressing, and he observed three bricklayers on a scaffold: one crouched, labouring under the strain, one half-standing, dutifully getting on with his task, and one standing tall, working proudly and hard.

To the first bricklayer, Wren asked the question, "What are you doing?" To which the bricklayer replied, "I'm a bricklayer. I'm laying bricks, one by one, in order to feed my family." He then asked the second bricklayer the same question to which he replied. "I'm a builder. I'm

focused on building a wall as instructed by my boss and the architect."
When the third bricklayer, the most productive of the three, was asked,
"What are you doing?" he replied with a smile in his heart, "I'm a
cathedral builder. I'm building a great monument to the glory of our
God almighty."

This story is often used in business circles to demonstrate that people
who go about their work with a purpose are more productive. That's
true. The third builder appears to have a greater sense of purpose and
seems more productive because of it. But that's not to say the first
builder hasn't got a purpose. Working for your family is an honourable
endeavour. That's purposeful. This is why I believe this story has a
deeper meaning. That meaning has to do with the felt-connection that
leads to purpose rather than purpose in isolation.

The first builder feels connected to his family. He's connected to the
financial rewards of his work that will support his family. Not a bad
thing. There is a sense of purpose to what he's doing. But the purpose
and the benefactors of that purpose are quite limited.

The second builder arguably feels connected to his family in the same
way as the first builder is. He's likely to feel connected to the financial
rewards, too. But it doesn't stop there. The second builder also feels
connected to the bigger picture of being part of a team creating
something constructive. He wants to be a good team player and he
wants to do a good quality job. He's growing his sense of purpose by
creating broader felt-connections beyond himself and his family to
include his work colleagues, his boss, the architect, and possibly the
people who will admire St Paul's Cathedral once it's complete.

The third builder can take all the felt-connections made by the first and
second builder but add to it by feeling a connection to his God and
arguably the largest family of all; life and all that is in it. No wonder he
is working with so much purpose and a smile in his heart. He is
benefitting from the greatest amount of loving, meaningful connection
energy. It shows in his being, in his work, and those around him.

Some people will feel these wider connections naturally. I didn't. Before I embarked on my own spiritual journey, I was very focused on the financial rewards of my work. I said I was working hard to provide for my family. And that's true. I was. I wanted to give them a comfortable way of living, and therefore, I didn't think I was being greedy or selfish. Everything I did was for them. Actually, that's not entirely true. I also did it for myself. Having a nice house and a big car may benefit the family, but I also benefitted from the status of those things. They made me look good.

I now see how limiting this was. Not feeling connected to anything larger than the comfort of my immediate family is very limiting. It's very myopic and doesn't generate much purpose or connection energy.

I also now see that I couldn't have acted any differently at the time. I wasn't aware that my felt-connections were so limited. Our culture of economic growth doesn't care much for the generation of loving, meaningful connection energy. It doesn't much care for purpose – unless of course it can help you work harder, be more committed and earn more money as a result. This has been one of the harder aspects of working in the field of sustainable business. Being sustainable and purpose-driven are good traits for a business to have. However, the decision to be sustainable and purpose-driven usually hinges on some sort of business case. A business case that purports it only makes sense to do the right thing if it means the business does better as a result. "Do well by doing good" is a sustainable business mantra I often hear. I don't think that should be the mantra. I think it should be "Be well by doing good." But let's not get into that debate just now.

The Power of Purpose and Connection Energy

The key point I want to make here is that there are not that many people who naturally have these deeper felt-connections in place. It's unfortunate but understandable why so few people go to work feeling genuinely purposeful. We're not taught to generate connection energy. We're not taught how to be purposeful. We can learn. The Habit of Connection is a way to make those seven felt-connections stronger.

We can work on widening our lens of identity. We can tap into the five pillars of spiritual practice and the other Habits of Spiritual Happiness to nurture our true selves and the felt relationship we have with life, the universe and everything. We can build our response-ability to the environment and people around us. We can contemplate our interbeing and impermanence. We can work on all seven felt-connections and build our feelings of connectedness well beyond our close-knit nuclear family. When we do that, we start to feel that we belong to the largest, biggest, most loving family of all. We feel we're part of living creation. We feel that connection. We are Me and We at the same time. We feel the fullness and richness of the MWe-ness of life. We feel the full rapture of being alive.

Feeling fully connected to life itself opens up our identity and broadens our belonging. It allows a new sense of self to emerge—a deeper, wider sense of self, a sense of self with greater freedom, wholeness, and meaning. This is our true self coming to the fore and influencing our lived experience. We feel connected to life and its abundance—more life, less fear, and more power to do the right thing.

When we feel connected to the biggest family of all, we are free to be our own true selves and know our contribution is enough and valued. I love the story of Indra's net, which brings this point to life.

Indra's net comes from the Vedic tradition and represents the net of life. The net is made of an infinite number of gems. Each gem represents a human soul. Every one of our true selves is represented. Although each of the jewels is unique, each jewel also reflects on its many polished surfaces the image of all the other jewels. According to the story, it is the sacred duty of every individual human soul to be utterly and completely itself. It is our duty to be THAT jewel, at THAT time, in THAT place, doing THAT thing, in THAT way. By being true to itself and playing its unique role in its unique way, the jewel holds the net together in its own specific corner of space and time. The action of each individual true self holds together the entire net. We all play our role. Our actions are infinitely important as they affect the whole of the net and, consequently, everyone else. Our actions connect us to the soul of the world. Small as they may appear, they have the power to uphold the essential order of the world and of life. How's that for a powerful felt-connection?

A Final Word on Love, Intimacy, Vulnerability and Other Uncomfortable Words

I mentioned earlier that I have a problem with the word love. I really wish I didn't because it seems such a vital component of the spiritual journey—in fact, love probably is the spiritual journey. Marianne Williamson has written a book called A Return to Love, which beautifully captures the essence of the spiritual journey: a return to our true selves and away from our false selves, a return to love and away from fear.

I think Williamson's journey of a return to love is the journey of generating more and more life-affirming, loving, meaningful, connection energy. A return to deeply feeling all seven felt-connections. That's the journey I'm on.

I suspect many people are on a similar journey. Even if the idea of 'a return to love' makes their toes curl. I say that as a fifty-six-year-old man who spent much of his life immersed in the world of commerce where the "L" word doesn't come into the equation for success. It's not talked about. It's not valued. It's not relevant. Tina Turner summed it up well when she said, "What's love got to do with it? It's nothing but a second-hand emotion."

In his book Immortal Diamond, Richard Rohr includes a chapter towards the end called Intimate with Everything. In it, he talks about unconditional love and likens it to energy. It has to flow to do its job. We have to pass on love to receive it. We have to create some sort of internal emptiness that needs filling. And we fill it by loving.

We fill the emptiness by partaking in the act of loving—by loving ourselves, others, our God, our communities, nature, and our descendants. We can love them all. They will love us back—in some way, in some form, at some time. The point is that the flow can start with us. We can start the process of love and create the internal emptiness inside that needs filling.

But that requires intimacy. It requires vulnerability. It requires us to be naked in front of people. Offering up ourselves as we are, warts and all. Being ourselves. Being our true self and proclaiming our love, with no promises that the love will be returned. That's risky. It was for me. It is for me. Hugely risky. I suspect it is for anyone who thinks of themselves as important. Especially people in business. Especially people in power. Especially men like me, who have never been taught how to be vulnerable, how to be naked, offering up unconditional love with no guarantee of it being returned.

I found it hard, and still find it hard, to say the words "I love you." I don't know why. It just doesn't come naturally. Maybe I've been too indoctrinated in a culture of economic growth where men just don't say that type of thing. We don't tell other men that we love them and deeply mean it. Well I don't, anyway. But I am willing to learn. I am also willing to be loving by acting in loving ways.

Whilst I don't necessarily find it easy to say "I love you" to others, I do find it relatively easy to forgive others, easier than telling people I love them. That's a start. It's a way I can express unconditional love. I'm also getting better at asking for forgiveness. I can (mostly) admit my failings, say I was wrong, and offer to make amends for my mistaken behaviours. It's another way of encouraging the flow of unconditional love.

Forgiving and asking for forgiveness are ways of being intimate, vulnerable, and naked. They are risky—for the false self, anyway. But by offering up forgiveness and seeking forgiveness from others, we're giving and receiving love. We are creating an internal emptiness and allowing unconditional love to be passed on. The universe is good— remember. Love hates a vacuum. Give love to receive it and experience the wonderful grace of life, of God, and of others that follow.

When we feel in right relationship to others, we are much more likely to take the right actions and make the right reactions. That brings us to the last of the five spiritual pillars: The Habit of Service. The spiritual habit of helping others and being useful.

EIGHT

THE HABIT OF SERVICE
HELPING OTHERS AND BEING USEFUL

**Desired state of being and inner human need =
A sense of FULFILMENT. Not feeling worthless and helpless.**

EIGHT

THE HABIT OF SERVICE

MAKING SENSE OF SELF-SACRIFICE

At the start of our spiritual journey, we found ourselves in a state of surrender. We yielded to the pain and discontentment that plagued us, becoming humble, honest, open-minded, and willing (H.H.O.W.) enough to explore an unfamiliar yet promising solution to our suffering: a spiritual one. As we progressed, we cultivated a Habit of Awareness. We became aware of our spiritual nature and strived to re-educate and tame the logical, restless false self that had long dominated our lives. Through the Habit of Discipline, we developed spiritual practices that nurtured our true selves, restoring our intuitive, soulful right hemisphere to its rightful position as the master of our destiny. Through the Habit of Connection, we experimented with ways to strengthen our bonds with all aspects of life, generating the vital and meaningful energy called love. Feeling connected allows us to shift our focus from purely fulfilling our selfish needs to being concerned for the well-being of the collective – the well-being of "MWe."

As we've explored these Habits of Spiritual Happiness - Surrender, Awareness, Discipline, and Connection - a recurring theme has been the honing of our response-ability. This is our capacity to sense the reality of the world around us and respond accordingly. In the final part of the book, the Epilogue entitled The Pathway to Purpose and Power, we will see that a significant part of the pathway lies in refining our response-ability and trusting it to guide and power our actions. But first, we must explore the final Habit of Spiritual Happiness: The Habit of Service.

The Interplay of Felt-Connection and Service

If awareness is about filling the internal space of "Me," and discipline is about external actions benefiting "Me," then connection can be conceived as filling the internal spaces of "MWe," and service as the external actions benefiting "MWe." That might sound a bit convoluted, but I hope you can see the pattern that's emerged.

In Richard Rohr's book Immortal Diamond, the chapter Intimacy with Everything begins with a quote from Dostoyevsky that brilliantly captures this interplay of Connection and Service:

> "Love all God's creation, the whole and every grain of sand in it. Love every leaf, every ray of God's light. Love the animals, love the plants, love everything. If you love everything, you will perceive the divine mystery in things. Once you perceive it, you will begin to understand it better every day. And you will come at last to love the whole world with an all-embracing love....Things flow and are directly linked together, and if you push here, something will move at the other end of the world. If you strike here, something somewhere will wince; if you sin here, something somewhere will suffer."

I think this brilliantly captures the idea of loving everything so you can be of service to everything. When we feel connected to the whole, we appreciate the impact our actions have overall. Strike here, and something somewhere will wince. This is the basis of service and of being useful. It's the basis of the golden rule of ethical behaviour, which is present in most major religions. Christians may express it as "Do unto others what you would have them do to you." Hindus might say, "This is the sum of duty: do not do to others what would cause pain if done unto you." Jewish people may claim, "What is hateful to you, do not do unto your neighbour. This is the whole Torah; all the rest is commentary." And, of course, there is the concept of karma that features in a number of Eastern traditions.

The Karmic Principle: Intent and Action

The Karmic Principle states that an individual's intent and actions (the cause) directly influence their future (effect). Good intent and good actions contribute to good karma and happier futures, while bad intent and bad actions contribute to bad karma and less satisfactory futures. One of the things I find interesting in this definition is the fact that it includes both intent and action. It is both a mental and a physical thing. If we think bad things or do bad things, bad things could physically happen to us. However, bad mental states and feelings could also result. Similarly, if we think or do good things, good things could physically happen to us. However, good mental states and feelings could also result. Karma takes effect on both the material and spiritual realms.

At a basic level, the principle of service and being useful is no more complicated than doing unto others as you would have done to yourself. Treat people well. Do the right thing. And above all else, don't be a dick. However, it could be argued that this definition of service makes it a little passive. The teachings of The 12-Step Programme urge us to be more proactive in our efforts to be of service. It urges us to go out of our way to be helpful. It encourages us to seek out opportunities to be useful.

Proactive Service: Going Beyond the Passive

There's a small card often given to addicts at the start of their journey towards sobriety that helps them focus their efforts to get through the next 24 hours without a drink or a drug. It's called the Just for Today card, and it features a list of suggestions to guide the newcomer. These include everything from dressing smartly to having a loose plan for the day to trying not to tackle all our problems at once. One of the suggestions is directly aimed at getting people into the good Habit of Service. It says, "Just for today, I will do something nice for someone and not be found out." I love this idea. I remember reading this card every morning in my first shaky few days without a drink after my last relapse. Most things I could do without too much bother. But it's harder than you think to do something nice for someone without them finding out. Try it.

I resorted to tidying up when my Mum and Dad were out and denying I did it. I'm not sure lying about something is all that spiritual. But it's the best I could do at the time. The point is that going out of our way to be helpful without seeking recognition for doing it helps us build The Habit of Service that embraces the karmic principle: be helpful without seeking to gain anything in return, and you will be rewarded, in some way, in some form, at some point in the future.

The only problem is that we don't know when or how those benefits will return to us. We could get a spiritual boost tomorrow, maybe, if we give our neighbour a helping hand clearing the snow today. We might get a nice bonus from our boss at the end of the year, perhaps, if we help a colleague out with a project this afternoon.

We are told that the Karmic Principle always applies. It's just not always on our terms or time frames. As Bob Proctor says, "We reap what we sow. But there's a season for sowing, and there's a season for reaping. We don't reap and sow in the same season." God takes time for his wonders to perform. And that's a problem for me.

A Cultural Shift Away from Service

Obviously, I'd always try to help out my family and close friends too. Even then, in my "busy life," it's not always easy to think good thoughts and do good things for the people I love most. If I'm too busy, I'm too busy. Sorry, I can't pop over and drop off those plates you want; I have a meeting. Sorry, I can't pick up your prescription for you; I have to see my accountant. Sorry, I can't play Star Wars with you tonight. I have a presentation to finish for an important meeting tomorrow.

In our current culture obsessed with working, these seem like acceptable excuses not to be of service and not to be useful. They do for me. But when I drill down into it, I see how these rationalisations are prioritising me and my needs. I'm making excuses to justify doing things for my benefit, to reap my rewards now, rather than doing things for the benefit of others, which will reap the rewards at some point in the future. When I think about that in some detail, it doesn't feel great. It feels selfish. It feels impatient. It feels petulant. And I don't like that feeling. I guess that's me getting my karmic spiritual payback.

The truth is that I've spent so much of my life doing things that only benefit me, and doing something purely for the benefit of someone else always feels like an inconvenience and a chore. If it's not helping me achieve my main priorities, why bother? Being of service is just not a habit I'm used to. It seems counterintuitive, and I suspect it's countercultural, too.

Not too many years ago, John F Kennedy famously said in his inaugural address, "Ask not what your country can do for you – ask what you can do for your country." It was a call to action that challenged every American to contribute in some way to the public good. It was a call to be useful. A call to service. At the time, it was seen as inspiring and motivational. And it's remembered fondly to this day as a symbol of JFK's visionary leadership style. But roll forward sixty years, and how many political leaders would stand up and tell their voting public to do the same? Not many. I suspect any political leader opening his or her stint at the head of the country with such a call for service would be committing some sort of political suicide. Unfortunately, we have grown to be much more self-serving than we were in the 1960s. We are much more likely to respond to JFKs call to service with the words "But what's in it for me?" rather than "Yes, sir. Happy to oblige."

I'm part of that entitled generation. I've grown up in a culture that is more self-serving and more self-centred than it was in the past. They're not very attractive, helpful or spiritual traits. If we are to embrace the notion of putting ourselves out for the benefit of others, we have to move beyond the notion that service is an inconvenience, a chore and a form of self-sacrifice. Or at least, we have to make sense of the sacrifice.

Sacrificing the False Self

The first way we can make sense of service, especially when it feels like self-sacrifice, is to remember that's exactly what it is. Being of service is putting others' needs first and, in doing so, forgoing our own selfish needs. In that sense, we're breaking the habit and the pattern of acting on the false self's need for security and comfort. We are sacrificing our false self's power over us, slowly killing our small, selfish, old ways of being.

In some traditions, this sort of self-sacrificing is viewed as an act of dying before we die. It sounds pretty unpleasant. And it feels pretty unpleasant to start with. The false self hates doing anything so utterly selfless. Once we've gone through the discomfort of doing something we didn't want to do, we open ourselves up to feel more expansive. We open ourselves to feel the gratitude of others and the subtle loving and meaningful connection energy that selfless action generates. This is part of the Karmic Principle. We do something good in the material realm and receive something good in the spiritual realm. We are giving something up of a lower nature to receive something of a higher nature in return.

Theodore Roosevelt wrote an epitaph to his son, who died in battle six months before he did. It captures the relationship between the rapture of life, the inevitability of death, and the honour of service and sacrifice:

> "Only those are fit to live who do not fear to die. And none are fit to die who have shrunk from the joy of life. Both life and death are parts of the same great adventure. All of us who provide service and stand ready for sacrifice are the torchbearers. We run with the torches until we fall, content if we can pass them into the hands of the other runners."

This sort of selfless service is an integral part of the 12-Step Process. It's one of the three core principles. The three are recovery (getting better by going through the 12-Step Process), unity (being part of a group of people who are committed to supporting each other on their road to recovery), and service (giving back to the group and other individuals what was freely given to you). In the early days of my recovery, service came in the form of making coffee for people or putting out chairs for the meetings. Later, it came as opening up the meeting, sharing my story, and looking after the kitty. Most recently, it involved taking other people through the 12-Step Process, being the secretary of a group, and organising the weekly meetings.

Beyond The 12-Step Programme, my commitment to service comes in many shapes and sizes. Probably the biggest one for me is for the family. Cooking, cleaning, and washing up are daily tasks that, when I'm feeling connected and spiritually well, are things I enjoy doing for the kids. I don't always receive spoken gratitude from them, but I always feel the spiritual rewards when I know my actions are coming from good intent.

I can attest to the fact that the more service we do, the more connection we feel. The more connection we feel, the more service feels self-nurturing rather than self-sacrificing. That's to say, we feel the true self being nurtured more than we feel the false self being sacrificed. A sign that we're on the right spiritual path.

This is all part of the spiritual paradox of giving it away to keep it. The more we experience those moments of self-sacrifice, the more we experience the spiritual rewards in return. We feel the joy, peace, and freedom that come with spiritual happiness. The more we serve, the less we see service as sacrifice at all. Elizabeth Lesser puts it like this:

> "To be in touch with the multiple karmic patterns of life is the way to freedom. It allows you two things: first, it helps you understand that everything that happens to you is part of an interwoven, ever-evolving, enormous, and eternal tapestry. This understanding liberates you from pettiness. It makes it more difficult to assume victim consciousness – self-pity, resentment, anger, or vindictiveness. Secondly, if you train yourself to lead the strands of karma, you begin to choose actions and reactions that spawn happiness and freedom as opposed to more suffering for the whole."

I think that's an amazing attitude to cultivate – a way of being where you are able to perceive events and life not as doing things "to you" but as "you" simply being there, part of the bigger picture as it unfolds. And then also being able to see yourself and your actions as "spawning more happiness and freedom for the whole." How great would it be to encounter that attitude in our everyday lives? Imagine your boss acting in that way. Or your children. Or your neighbour. Or the parking attendant. Or the supermarket cashier. Or you.

Finding Meaning Through Service

The second way we can make sense of service is to think of it in terms of meaning and responsibleness. This is the domain of Viktor

Frankl and a central aspect of his theory of logotherapy. For Frankl, being of service allows people to discover meaning in the world. And discovering meaning is the way to self-actualisation. Service allows us to move beyond our own self-interests by aligning our actions with something or someone that is very meaningful to us.

In his book, Man's Search for Meaning, Frankl claims, "The more one forgets himself – by giving himself to a cause to serve or a person to love – the more human he is and the more he actualises himself." I like the idea of giving ourselves over to a cause or to people to love as part of a process to "actualise." To me, that means these actions of service allow us to become the person we were meant to be. To truly become ourselves. Our true selves.

Frankl continues by saying that this process is one where we become fully aware of our responsibleness. And it's down to us to decide for what, to what, or to whom we understand ourselves to be responsible. But, and here's the neat twist in my view, this isn't necessarily a choice, as such, it's more of a realisation. This process of becoming aware of our responsibleness isn't about us sitting down with a blank sheet of paper and saying, "So, what cause should I support? Or who should I be helping most?" No, it's more about responding to the situation you find yourself in rather than trying to manufacture a situation that you think would give you meaning. Here's how Frankl articulates the point:

> "Ultimately, man should not ask what the meaning of his life is, but rather he must recognize that it is he who is asked. In a word, each man is questioned by life; and he can only answer to life by answering for his own life; to life he can only respond by being responsible. Thus, responsibleness is the very essence of human existence."

That's definitely worth reading again and contemplating. Don't ask what the meaning of life is but recognise that life is asking you how you can create meaning out of this situation. Mmmm. Deep words, indeed.

One slight issue I have with Frankl's words is one word in particular: responsibleness. For me, the word responsibleness conjures up other words like duty. Or obligation. Or chore. Or burden even. That's why I prefer the term response-ability. It has exactly the same sentiment that Frankl talks about but, in my view, links much more directly to his idea of making meaning from life by responding and feeling aligned to it. It's our way of finding meaning, day by day, moment by moment. It's the way we can transcend our false selves, nurture our true selves, and start feeling connected to life as it unfolds around us. It's the method by which we can act our way towards feeling the full rapture of being alive.

Confessions of a Reluctant Servant

It's at this stage that I want to put the brakes on slightly and confess something. It's true that I believe in the benefits of service. I know that applying my response-ability improves my felt-connection and spawns spiritual happiness. I love the whole idea of "spawning happiness and freedom to the whole." I am convinced of the Karmic Principle that you receive as you give. So, from that point of view, I'm all for giving myself to a cause and giving myself to the people I love, as I know I will benefit in some way, at some time, somehow. Sign me up.

However, if I'm being honest, I have a mindset that is inclined to think, "I'm only willing to do that in my spare time. It's something I am prepared to do outside of the day job when I can find the time and spare the inclination after I've earned enough money." In my "business-as-usual" way of thinking, money comes before response-ability. Money comes before spiritual happiness. That's the mindset of our culture of economic growth, which is one I've been educated in from a very early age. And it's a tough mindset to shift. It can be shifted. It just needs practice and faith. Practice and faith. And practice and faith some more.

Initially, my approach to service and response-ability was to help out at the 12-Step groups every other evening for an hour or so. I would look after the household chores once I'd finished my working day. I'd volunteer at the urban farm every other weekend if I got a chance. I suspect it's the same for most people. We do what we feel is the right thing to do, if and when we can fit it around our day jobs.

However, I want to float the idea now that maybe, just maybe, the idea of fully utilising our response-ability is a 24-hour task. It's something we should apply to every aspect of our lives, including our working lives.

Facing Fears and Doubts and the Power to Confront Them

I must admit that this idea fills me with fear. I'm more than willing to apply my response-ability to things like looking after the kids' needs at the weekends or volunteering at the local farm on Saturday afternoons, but am I really all that committed to applying it to my career? Am I willing to risk my steady income to follow my intuition-based response-ability? Am I willing to do what "feels right" rather than what I think will be the most profitable thing to do? Am I trusting enough of the Karmic Principle that it will reward me in some way, in some form, at some point in the future? Am I happy that the reward might be spiritual and not material? I'm not sure I'm 100% there yet. But I am getting closer to the idea that this approach to all aspects of living could be the way to fully experience the "good life." And if that's the case, I'm willing to let go, let God, and give it a go.

Here's why. Firstly, I have to go back to the very beginning and think about where my journey started. It began with me chasing the extrinsic, material goals of wealth and material possessions. I was seeking conditional happiness, thrills, excitement, and achievement. I was looking for things outside me to fill the emptiness I felt inside. None of it worked. The more I chased material success, the worse I felt. It led to me numbing the uncomfortable feelings of misalignment. It led to my addiction. I know this way of living doesn't work for me.

Next, I have to remember what I've learned and how my beliefs have changed over the past few years. Since embracing the spiritual solution, my world has changed. I have changed. The Habits of Spiritual Happiness have brought me to a place where I know that the "good life" is not contingent on financial wealth or comfort. I know it depends on me feeling good about life. That means the life I'm looking to lead has to be filled with feelings of peace, joy, wholeness, freedom, and fulfilment more often during the day than not. It means I have to judge success on how much I feel the full rapture of being alive. My days can be filled by throwing myself wholeheartedly into every moment and losing myself in actions solely guided by my response-ability. It means I'm working towards feeling the aliveness of the world around me and applying my unique skills and abilities in a way that not only brings me joy but also benefits the whole. It means I'm able to show up in the world with my soul and do things that spawn happiness and freedom for everyone, including me.

As I read those words, I feel uplifted and motivated. I feel that that's the life I want to lead. And I feel that 100%. Then doubt pops in. "What if I don't make enough money to pay the mortgage? What if I haven't got enough money to take the kids on holiday this year? What if? What if? What if?"

Doubt is such a killer of ambition and aspiration. It is for me, anyway. The vast majority of my doubts revolve around money and what other people will think of me. I yearn for the good life. I yearn for spiritual happiness. My response-ability is telling me to write a book about spirituality and take it into the business world to help others who have struggled with anxiety and fear as I did. I can see myself losing myself in that work. I can see myself applying my response-ability 24 hours a day in that endeavour. But it seems such an uncertain future. What if nobody likes the idea? What if nobody is willing to pay for what I have to say? What if people laugh at the idea?

When those doubts arise, I yearn for the certainty of a fixed salary and a monthly paycheque. I yearn for the recognition and respect of other people in the business world. I yearn for a 9-to-5 job that will keep me occupied until I'm ready to retire.

It's exactly at that point that I realise my yearning is moving me back to where it all started. That this yearning is for a life that is anything but feeling the full rapture of being alive. I realise that my false self is very much alive, driving me towards a future of comfort and security. I know that my false self isn't bad. It just wants to protect me. But I need to break through that thinking. And here are two ways that help make that breakthrough when doubts occur.

Embracing Uncertainty and Possibility

The first way is to reconceive uncertainty. Doubt, my doubt, is fuelled by uncertainty. It is fuelled by "what ifs" that may or may not occur in the future. I don't like uncertainty. It feels too risky. Too reckless. I can sometimes be overly careful with my life choices, so I'm unlikely to throw myself wholeheartedly into a completely uncertain future. However, there's a different way to think about uncertainty. I picked this tip up from Daniel Siegel's book Intraconnected. He suggested that all our choices are rooted in a plane of infinite possibility. Anything is possible in a universe of connected energy. A universe that, if we go right back to our foundational beginnings, we believe is good. A universe that is on our side.

There may be uncertain outcomes, but if we can stay connected to the plane of possibility, if we can think good thoughts, do good things, and live with the uncertainty, the rewards from a benevolent universe will come to us. This is how Siegel puts it:

"We can learn to drop beneath the illusion of certainty that our constricted identities convey and learn to find comfort and connection in the open plane of possibility, letting uncertainty become a sanctuary, not a feared, unpredictable place with lack of control. We can live the reality of the synonyms for uncertainty: freedom and opportunity."

What a great observation! Without uncertainty, there is no freedom. Only with uncertainty are we free to express ourselves as we want to express ourselves. Only with uncertainty are there opportunities to change, to grow, to do things differently, to be different. Only with uncertainty do we have the freedom and opportunity to do what we're meant to do and be who we're meant to be.

When I let the truth of that statement sink in, I see how important it is to embrace uncertainty. It might be scary, but without uncertainty, there is no freedom or opportunity. And then, all of a sudden, a certain future sounds very, very unappealing.

Cultivating Awe and Wonder

The second way I can break through doubt is to be guided by "awe." This is a concept I picked up from Dacher Kelter. I love the simplicity and profundity of this thought. Kelter suggests that cultivating a sense of "awe" from everyday life allows us to collaborate with others, opens our mind to the possible, and helps us more clearly see the bigger patterns of life. "Awe" puts us more directly in touch with our bigger, true selves. It drops us into the plane of possibility, where anything and everything can happen. According to Kelter, it is the one thing that contributes to happiness more than anything else. I can believe that.

I know that when I'm more able to appreciate, recognise, and be grateful for all the amazing things that surround my everyday life, it helps me break through the doubts I have. Usually, very small, insignificant, petty, self-centred doubts that don't amount to a hill of beans in the grand scheme of things.

Kelter's book is called Awe. I love the simplicity of that title, but I love the sentiment of the subtitle even more: "The transformative power of everyday wonder."

How awesome is that?

FINDING OURSELVES TO LOSE OURSELVES

I want to finish this section on The Habit of Service by exploring the counterpoint to self-sacrifice: self-actualisation. As discussed earlier, Viktor Frankl suggested that we find our true humanity and authentic selves by discovering meaning in life through honing our response-ability.

Initially, being of service can feel like a bit of a chore - something that must be endured as part of our spiritual adventure. It requires conscious effort to help us sacrifice the false self's power over us. Much like meditating or other unfamiliar spiritual practices, it takes effort because we are slowly breaking the habit of prioritising our own comfort and security. We are gradually shifting away from putting our own needs first and beginning to consider the needs of others. This can feel quite foreign to those of us raised amidst a selfish and entitled culture of economic growth.

However, if we push through the uncertainty and embrace the freedom, opportunity, and awe that comes with living life from a state of response-ability, we start experiencing the rapture of being truly alive.

Let Go and Flow

This is where I believe we begin to find "flow" in our lives. Mihaly Csikszentmihalyi, known as the father of positive psychology, coined the term "flow" to describe a state in which people are totally immersed in a specific task, losing track of time and ignoring outside distractions. During this state, people experience effortless attention, and being in flow can be an energising experience.

I believe that this sense of "flow" can extend beyond specific tasks and become a lifestyle. This "flow as a lifestyle" occurs when we feel ourselves to be an authentic whole and are part of an authentic whole. It happens when we are psychologically in harmony with ourselves, living predominantly from our soulful, right hemisphere true selves, and physically in harmony with the world around us, with a wide lens of identity and a strong sense of felt-connection to the MWe around us. When fully integrated internally and externally, we are at one with the world. We sense what our world requires from us and naturally respond, fitting in and feeling a sense of belonging.

I've experienced this sense of "flow as a lifestyle" numerous times throughout my career, sometimes by chance and sometimes by design. When it happens, life feels good and effortless. However, I must admit that I haven't managed to sustain it for much longer than a few months. When circumstances change, challenges arise, financial concerns emerge, or things feel too difficult, I tend to revert to fear. My logical, egoic, selfish left hemisphere takes over, seeking control and certainty. I do the rational, safe, sensible thing that most people raised in a culture of economic growth would do. I lose faith, freedom, opportunity, and connection to everyday awe and wonder.

This raises the question of whether it's possible to sustain "flow as a lifestyle" for prolonged periods. Can we lose ourselves in life permanently rather than in one task at a time? Can we be so absorbed in life that we aren't phased by challenges, burdens, and hardships? Is it possible to forget ourselves so completely?

The Power of Self-Forgetting

I first encountered the term "self-forgetting" in the St. Francis prayer, which speaks of seeking to comfort rather than be comforted, to understand rather than be understood, and to love rather than be loved. It states, "For it is by self-forgetting that one finds. It is by forgiving that one is forgiven. It is by dying that one awakens to Eternal Life."

The act of "self-forgetting" is about putting your own interests aside and being of service. It's about caring more about the needs and wants of others than your own. Interestingly, according to St. Francis, self-forgetting is the secret to spiritual happiness. You can only find what you're looking for by forgetting about yourself.

This is why service is so crucial as part of the spiritual journey. It embodies the final spiritual paradox: you only find happiness for yourself when you "forget" about yourself. You can only achieve "flow as a lifestyle" on a permanent basis when you "forget" about yourself permanently. It's a tall order, but I believe it's possible through practice.

The practice involves losing yourself to find yourself again and again. You lose your false self to find your true self by cultivating the five pillars of habits. Then, you lose your true self in service to fully experience spiritual happiness. When fears and resentments from your false self resurface, you revisit the five habits once more, you surrender to the process once again, you rediscover your true self one more time, and, once again, lose yourself in service. Rinse and repeat.

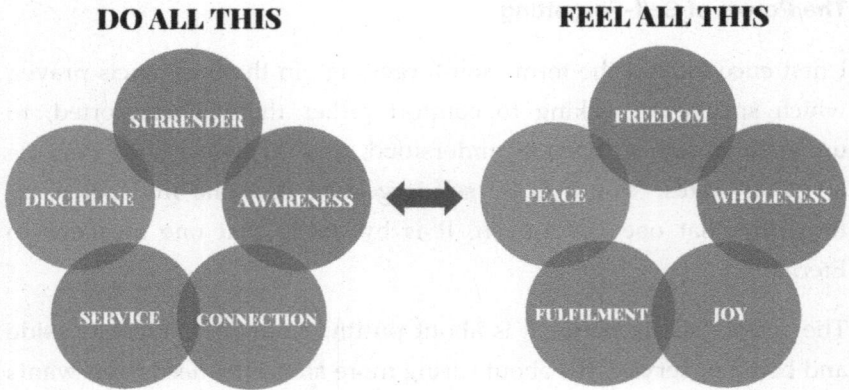

The more we practice losing ourselves to find ourselves through The Habits of Surrender, Awareness, Discipline, Connection, and Service, the more we'll experience freedom, wholeness, peace, joy, and fulfilment. By surrendering more, becoming more aware, deepening our discipline, strengthening our felt-connections, and being of greater service to others, we forget ourselves more completely. Through this process, we'll feel the sensations of spiritual happiness more deeply, strongly, and for longer periods. This is how we can experience "flow as a lifestyle" permanently.

Flow as a Lifestyle: From Service to Surrender and Back Again

I heard a powerful talk by Adyashanti where he beautifully explained how the process of losing ourselves to find ourselves again and again leads to a flow of life on a permanent basis.

He explained that the process of losing ourselves to find ourselves again and again inevitably returns us to a place of surrender, no matter what path we take. Everything we do spiritually guides us to a spontaneous state of letting go of the illusion of the false self and the way we think the world is or should be. This process of surrender involves the relinquishing of our own personal power. It involves us letting go of the steering wheel and giving up the habit that we believe we can figure it out all by ourselves.

In surrendering our illusion of personal will and power, we discover a new guidance mechanism and a new power. A different state of consciousness is born—a resurrection from deep within. We begin to be moved by the completeness and totality of the power of life itself.

The Taoist tradition vividly depicts this movement and expression of The Tao, or truth, through us. When we relinquish the driver's seat, we find that life can drive itself and us through it, flowing in magical ways we never imagined. Decision-making is no longer a matter of right or wrong but more akin to navigating a flow, feeling the natural movement of events. You sense where events are moving you towards. You intuitively know what's the right thing to do. Not right in the sense of right or wrong, but in the sense that a river knows which way to turn around the rock. It has an intuitive, innate sense of knowing.

Underneath the turmoil of thought and emotion and the grasping of personal will, there is a simple yet powerful flow of life. Enlightenment, as defined by Jesuit priest Anthony de Mello, is "absolute cooperation with the inevitable" - not resisting what is inevitable but aligning with the flow of life itself.

As we surrender our wilfulness, meet our fears, and sincerely say yes to life, to uncertainty, to opportunity, to possibility, the flow becomes our new way of navigating existence. It gives us the strength to move forward.

By continually losing ourselves to find ourselves, we can achieve a state of self-actualisation and experience the profound joy of living in harmony with ourselves and the world around us. This is the lifestyle I aspire to and the journey I'm on. It is the journey of the spiritual solution, the hero's journey, and the pathway to purpose and power.

If you're new to the spiritual journey, this will sound like a far cry from the way you live and experience life at the moment. The idea of flow as a way of life and spiritual happiness will seem fantastical, totally unbelievable, totally unrealistic, totally unreachable, and immensely impractical.

I would have thought so, too, a few years ago. But the evidence tells me otherwise. The truth is that you're closer than you think. If you feel the pain of modern life and are humble, honest, open-minded and willing (H.H.O.W.) enough to transform that pain, spiritual happiness is anything but fantastical. It's entirely believable. Entirely realistic. Entirely reachable. And immensely practical. All you need is a solid starting point and a programme of action.

CULTIVATING THE HABITS OF HAPPINESS

A SPIRITUAL PROGRAMME OF ACTION

NINE

BEYOND SPIRITUAL HAPPINESS

The Pathway to Purpose and Power
Hearing Our Calling and Having the Strength to Act

The spiritual solution has many guises and an infinite number of paths that can be followed. I experienced it through the path of The 12-Step Programme of Recovery, which is designed to help people break their addictions and live peaceful, contented lives free from destructive habits. I believe that the spiritual solution, based on the broad principles of The 12-Step Programme, can work for anyone. Although it could be argued that most people suffer from addiction in one form or another, I want to create a spiritual solution and a programme of action that is perceived as relevant to those who don't currently see themselves as addicts. Or at least, aren't quite ready to admit it just yet.

Exploring Spirituality: Motivations and Challenges

There are lots of reasons why people might want to explore spirituality: as means to find spiritual happiness, as a pathway to purpose and power, as route out of anxiety and depression, as an antidote to our culture of economic growth, as a way to reverse junk values, as a means to stop unhealthy habits, as a way to find clarity in the confusion of a midlife crisis, as an opportunity for personal transformation and growth, or as a Hero's Journey to higher levels of consciousness. Regardless of the motivation or the suffering you're trying to resolve, the process that follows is designed to be comprehensive in terms of the ground it covers and the options available. And whilst the programme has been designed to be thorough, I also hope it's relatively simple to follow. By that, I mean there is enough flexibility to create a programme of action for yourself that suits you now and suits your appetite for transformation into the future.

However, simple-to-follow doesn't necessarily mean easy-to-do.

I faced two significant challenges at the beginning of my spiritual journey. The first was intellectual resistance – committing to something that felt inherently mystical, suspiciously religious, and totally non-scientific. That's why I've tried to provide some logical, science-based rationales along the way.

The second challenge was patience. In our world of instant gratification, sitting quietly in meditation for twenty minutes doesn't provide the dopamine rush our thrill-seeking brains crave. That's precisely the point – part of the transformation is training our brains to function differently. Finding peace in our overstimulated world is the path to spiritual happiness. As Blaise Pascal said in the 1600s, "All of humanity's problems stem from man's inability to sit quietly in a room alone."

I was fortunate to have wise guides who knew the spiritual solution worked and pushed me through my own resistance. Against my better judgment, I committed to doing all the things that eventually resulted in a growing presence of peace, joy, wholeness, freedom, and fulfilment in my life. I didn't appreciate that I was going through a process of transformation at the time, that my level of consciousness was shifting upwards. Others could see it in me. I began to see life through a different lens. Life was good. And miraculously, I didn't need alcohol to feel that way. I had a spiritual awakening—that vital spiritual experience. I began to feel spiritually happy.

Since then, I've delved deeply into spirituality – what it means, what it does, and how it works. I've read extensively, talked to many people, and reflected on my own experiences and challenges, especially in the early stages of transformation. All that knowledge has been pulled together in the pages of this book in the hope that it can act as a guide to you and your journey.

Having said that, I fully understand that a book can never replace the immense value of working with someone who has gone through the process themselves on a one-to-one basis. In the fullness of time, I hope to support people on their spiritual journey by recruiting a team of coaches and spiritual guides. Until that happens, here's my best attempt at capturing the core elements that I believe lead to a spiritual awakening.

A Logical Model for the Spiritual Journey

My starting point has been to introduce the concept of spiritual happiness and its five associated core states of being in an attempt to create a logical model of what the spiritual journey entails. This model is designed to make sense to someone like me before my spiritual awakening - someone more comfortable thinking and making decisions with their ego-centred, rational left hemisphere. It's not meant to represent the reality of spiritual happiness after a spiritual awakening. It's meant to act as a logical gateway to get people into action and encourage them to commit to a journey that makes sense now, even if the result is different and better than the picture I paint here in the model.

The model and logic, in a nutshell, goes something like this:

. . .

Step 1 = Re-Imagine Your Identity

Affirm the overall objective of wanting to become spiritually happy by re-imagining your core identity as someone committed to achieving spiritual happiness rather than someone reliant on conditional happiness.

This equates to aligning your life more with the story of life, the universe and everything and less with the story of economic growth and the way work works.

This means coming to terms with the fact that the universe is a friendly place. It means starting to explore what a God of your understanding could be and building a relationship with Him, Her or It.

It means starting to apply yourself to the journey ahead with the qualities of H.H.O.W. (Humility. Honesty. Open-mindedness. Willingness.)

Step 2 = Understand the Process: The States of Being, Goals, and Habits to Achieve Spiritual Happiness

Understand that there are five core human states of being that underpin spiritual happiness. These states arise once our inner human needs are met. In my definition, the five core human states are wholeness, freedom, peace, joy, and fulfilment.

Each core human state of being can be achieved by working towards a specific spiritual goal and pillar of action.

Desired state of being and inner human need = A sense of FREEDOM. Not feeling trapped and confused.
Spiritual goal and pillar of action to achieve freedom = THE HABIT OF SURRENDER: Letting Go and Letting God.

Desired state of being and inner human need = A sense of WHOLENESS
Not feeling out of sync and misaligned.
Spiritual goal and pillar of action to achieve wholeness = THE HABIT OF
AWARENESS: Re-educating and taming the ego

Desired state of being and inner human need = A sense of PEACE. Not
feeling anxious and worried.
Spiritual goal and pillar of action to achieve peace = THE HABIT OF
DISCIPLINE: Rediscovering and nurturing the soul.

Desired state of being and inner human need = A sense of JOY. Not
feeling sad or lonely.
Spiritual goal and pillar of action to achieve joy = THE HABIT OF
CONNECTION: Feeling part of the whole.

Desired state of being and inner human need = A sense of FULFILMENT.
Not feeling worthless and helpless.
Spiritual goal and pillar of action to achieve fulfilment = THE HABIT OF
SERVICE: Helping others and being useful

In purely logical terms, the theory of the model is:

> The Habit of Surrender leads to Freedom
> The Habit of Awareness leads to Wholeness
> The Habit of Discipline leads to Peace
> The Habit of Connection leads to Joy
> The Habit of Service leads to Fulfilment

All five habits practiced concurrently over time lead to spiritual happiness = freedom + wholeness + peace + joy + fulfilment.

Step 3: Build The Habits of Happiness: Continuous, Hard Work and Messy Spirituality

Each pillar of action and habit has two parts: a knowledge part and an experience part.

- Knowledge: Building awareness and understanding of each habit by reading the information in this book and doing further research wherever your interest takes you.
- Experience: Building awareness and understanding of each habit by taking action and adopting the practices suggested throughout the book and summarised in this chapter.

Knowledge and experience lead to a full understanding. And this is best achieved through a process of reducing harmful, distracting habits and nurturing positive, soulful habits under each pillar of action.

It is my belief that the most effective way to reduce the bad habits and nurture the good habits that lead to spiritual happiness is to create and stick with a solid morning and evening routine.

That's it! That's all you need to do.

THE THREE STEPS IN MORE DETAIL

These three steps will help to grow your understanding, establish The Habits of Spiritual Happiness and set you firmly on your way to a spiritual awakening.

My thinking in creating this model is that if we want to build a process that delivers something of value to the ego-centred, rational person, we must start with the end in mind. We must start with the "What's in it for me?" question. And the end I have in mind is a life with less pain and more spiritual happiness, less confusion and more clarity, less entrapment and more freedom, less hopelessness and more power, less dissonance and more wholeness, less anxiety and more peace, less sadness and more joy, less worthlessness and more fulfilment. Does that sound like a life worth working towards? Well, let's go through the three steps in more detail and get into action.

STEP 1: RE-IMAGINE YOUR SPIRITUAL IDENTITY

If you want to benefit from a life blessed with spiritual happiness, the first task you need to do is to think of yourself as a person who leads a life blessed with spiritual happiness. In essence, with this first task, we are saying to ourselves, I am the type of person who no longer wants to let my egoic self run my life according to the story of our culture of economic growth. I want to become the type of person who allows my actions to be influenced by my soulful, true self that is more attuned to the story of life. I am the sort of person who wants to prioritise spiritual happiness as a definition of success.

Re-read the first chapter in Part 2; The Spiritual Solution. Be comfortable with the idea of transformation. Ponder your belief in a friendly universe. Be prepared to get into action. The process is not just about reading and gaining knowledge. Full understanding and change can only happen as a result of action and experiences. It does not come about from gleaning information from a book. Get familiar with the concept of spirituality and what it means to you. Start the process of exploring what a God of your understanding could look and feel like. Try to work through the paradoxes that the spiritual solution throws up. Above all, be ready to embrace the process with a sense of humility, honesty, open-mindedness and willingness (H.H.O.W.)

Once you do this, commit yourself to being the sort of person who takes spiritual happiness seriously.

By re-imagining your identity in this way, you are proclaiming a new start and committing yourself to becoming someone who values, seeks out, and prioritises spiritual happiness over conditional happiness. The sort of person who prioritises spiritual success over the accumulation of material wealth. Someone who is not afraid of giving up the distractions and numbing of uncomfortable feelings. Someone who is willing to work hard. You're not denouncing material wealth or the comforts of life. You are demoting their importance.

In his book Atomic Habits, James Clear suggests this identity-first approach to personal transformation is the surest way to making the lasting changes we need in order to shift how we see ourselves. He basically says it's much more effective to say, "I'm someone who values spiritual happiness over wealth accumulation than it is to set ourselves a goal or an outcome like I want to be happy."

He explains that there are four clear advantages to taking an identity-first approach:

1. Goals are temporary, but identity is enduring: Achieving a goal provides only temporary satisfaction, whereas adopting a new identity leads to long-term change.
2. Habits shape identity: Our repeated actions and habits reinforce our sense of self. By consistently engaging in habits aligned with the identity we wish to adopt, we gradually reshape our self-perception.
3. Small habits lead to significant changes: Clear emphasises the power of atomic habits - small, incremental changes that compound over time. Focusing on tiny improvements in our daily routines, we can make progress towards our desired identity without feeling overwhelmed.
4. Identity-based decisions: When faced with choices, Clear recommends making decisions based on the identity we aspire to embody.

One way to solidify your re-imagined identity is by writing a spiritually guided affirmation card. On a small, blank index card, write down a few sentences that re-affirm, in the present tense, who you want to become and what you value most as you embark on the process of changing your world from the inside out.

My card reads something like this:

> *"I am a creative and contented writer who enjoys the fulfilling work I do. I am committed to my well-being and prioritise activities and habits that bring me spiritual happiness. Although I appreciate that I have financial responsibilities to cover, I won't let aspirations of material wealth dominate my decisions. I am excited to be following my pathway to purpose and know that everything will always work out well in the end, even if things don't seem to be going well just now. I take one day at a time and wake up every morning wanting to feel the full rapture of being alive."*

I don't always feel or act this way, but it truly reflects the person I want to become. The more I see this card, the more I remind myself that this accurately describes who I am deep down inside. Who my authentic, true self is. And the more I believe that to be true, the more likely I am to do the things that will reinforce that identity.

STEP 2: UNDERSTAND THE PROCESS: THE STATES OF BEING, GOALS, AND HABITS TO ACHIEVE SPIRITUAL HAPPINESS

Here's a quick summary of each of the habit chapters and what we're trying to achieve to aide your understanding.

The Habit of Surrender

Desired state of being and inner human need = A sense of FREEDOM. Not feeling trapped and confused.

Spiritual goal and pillar of action to achieve freedom = THE HABIT OF SURRENDER: Letting Go and Letting God

The first desired outcome we're looking to achieve is an increased sense of freedom in our life. A sense that we're no longer trapped or confused. A feeling that there is more clarity in the direction we are taking. This outcome arises by cultivating the habit of surrender and learning to let go. We are going to start practicing surrender by acknowledging necessary pain, accepting what is, releasing the illusion of control and the attachments we hold, letting go of outcomes, surrendering to the present moment and befriending our emotions, especially the uncomfortable ones. The goal is to learn the subtle art of letting go and letting the God of our understanding take more of a lead. The Habit of Surrender helps us cultivate faith in a friendly universe as we drop our inner resistance to what is.

The Habit of Awareness

Desired state of being and inner human need = A sense of WHOLENESS. Not feeling out of sync and misaligned.

Spiritual goal and pillar of action to achieve wholeness = THE HABIT OF AWARENESS: Re-educating and taming the ego

The next desired outcome is one of wholeness. A sense of feeling complete, at one with the world. And not feeling out of sync or misaligned. This outcome is achieved by healing ourselves from the inside out and returning to our true selves. The Habit of Awareness allows us to awaken to what is real and authentic. It allows us to see the mistakes we've made in the past and how our beliefs and actions have caused us suffering. It helps us understand the story of the split self: the ego versus the soul, the left hemisphere versus the right hemisphere, and the false self versus the true self. It is often said that the cause of much of our pain and suffering is that we deny our true nature and live predominantly from an ego-centric, false personality that we create in order to get what we want in our materialistic world. The goal of this part of the spiritual solution is the attempt to heal ourselves from within by appreciating, identifying and aligning these two sides of our human nature. When we do so, we begin to resolve the inner conflict that causes pain and suffering. We do that by learning to recognise both these sides of our being and allowing our true self to shine through in more and more aspects of our daily lives. The Habit of Awareness allows us to heal from the inside and return our true selves to the seat of power. We come to understand the nature of reality by re-educating and taming the ego and we start the process of waking up our mind.

The Habit of Discipline

Desired state of being and inner human need = A sense of PEACE. Not feeling anxious and worried.

Spiritual goal and pillar of action to achieve peace = THE HABIT OF DISCIPLINE: Rediscovering and nurting the soul

The third desired outcome is that of peace. A peaceful mind and a peaceful heart. A sense of equanimity and calm that are the antidote to the feelings of anxiety, worry and fear that dog many people's approach to life in our culture of economic growth. The spiritual goal here is a to find inner peace and a way of living that promotes calm abiding. The purpose of this stage is to embed spiritual practices into our daily lives in order that we can find conscious contact with the god of our understanding. The process of quietening the mind, noticing our racing thoughts, observing our changing emotional states, and feeling out for God is a relatively simple one. There are five areas of spiritual practice that can help us find conscious contact and peace. They are relatively easy things to do in theory. But they are not easy things to do consistently and regularly in everyday life. And that's what's required to achieve the desired outcome. Finding time to invest in these simple practices takes discipline and perseverance. But the benefits are life-changing. Prayer, meditation, contemplation, virtuous living, and other spiritual practices are the bedrock of all major religions and are at the heart of transformation. Finding a place of inner quiet, self-reflection and cultivating a relationship with our

Higher Power is the essence of this stage that brings about peace. The Habit of Discipline allows us to find that peace and calm abiding through consistent effort. We re-discover and nurture our soul by shaping up our behaviours.

The Habit of Connection

Desired state of being and inner human need = A sense of JOY. Not feeling sad or lonely.

Spiritual goal and pillar of action to achieve joy = THE HABIT OF CONNECTION: Feeling part of the whole

The fourth desired outcome is finding a sense of deep joy. A joy of living that comes from a deep sense of love for the simple things of life. A joy that chases away those feelings of sadness, depression and loneliness. The goal here is to learn how to reconnect with the rapture of being alive. It comes by appreciating and being grateful for the beauty and benefits of unconditional love. By experiencing the flow of life as a positive thing despite, and indeed because of, its natural cycles of ups and downs. The focus of this stage is finding our right relationship with everything else. How we relate to the world around us in the right way. How we relate to nature. How we relate to ourselves. To others. To our communities. To God. And future generations. Once we get these relationships in the right order and deepen our connection to the ones that matter most, we find a joyful way of living unfolds. The Habit of Connection allows us to reconnect to a joyful life. We come to experience what it means to feel part of the whole by opening up our hearts.

The Habit of Service

Desired state of being and inner human need = A sense of FULFILMENT, Not feeling worthless and helpless.

Spiritual goal and pillar of action to achieve fulfilment = THE HABIT OF
SERVICE: Helping others and being useful

The final desired outcome is finding a sense of fulfilment in what we do with our lives. This means we feel that our lives are meaningful, and we're not left feeling worthless or helpless about where our life is going. The spiritual goal we're looking to achieve here is learning that selfless service is a path to spiritual happiness. Once we've learned to heal ourselves from the inside, we can't help but want to help others. In doing so, we find deeper levels of meaning. By embarking on the search for more meaning, we find deeper levels of fulfilment help strengthen relationships with those around us and build a resilient way of living in the communities we live and work. This is the blueprint for a much more enjoyable and sustainable way of living. The Habit of Service allows us to find more meaning in life. We come to understand what it means to help others and be useful by showing up with our souls.

These are The Habits of Happiness

The Paradox of a Logical Model

I mentioned the inherent presence of paradox when it comes to spirituality. Remember that "You can't catch a wild ass by chasing it, but if you don't chase it, you will never catch it." Well, that applies here, and it's worth re-iterating. These five desired outcomes, these five aspects of spiritual happiness, can't be pursued. It's not possible to do a series of "peaceful" exercises and suddenly feel peaceful. Or do a series of joy-filled exercises, and lo and behold, you feel joyful. The process is much more nuanced than that. I have found that you need to do a real mixture of exercises, cultivate a variety of good habits, and do them consistently and regularly. Then, one day, unannounced, after an unpredictable period of time "spiritual happiness" ensues. All five aspects arise. All five states of being are experienced as one. They reveal themselves in unison as a result of having had a spiritual awakening, a sign that you've experiencing a shift in consciousness.

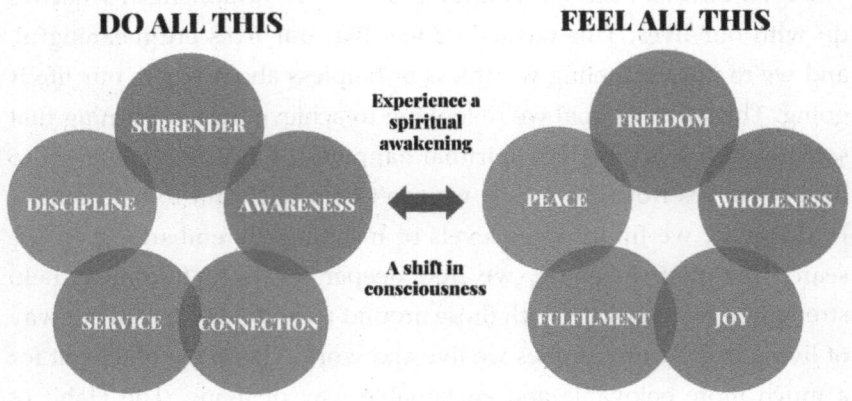

The truth is that there is probably only one inner human need that needs satisfying, not the five that I've alluded to in this model. The one inner human need is to recognise that we are not our false selves. We are not the stories that we have created in our mind to succeed in a material world. We are not the self-made personalities scrambling for attention and manipulating our way up the ladder of economic growth. We are our true selves. We are spiritual in nature. And that nature requires nurturing. Practicing the Five Habits of Spiritual Happiness is the way we nurture our soulful, true selves. It's the way we satisfy our one big inner human need. That's how we fill the hole in the soul. That's how we create an inner sense of freedom, wholeness, peace, joy and fulfilment.

As we've said all along, spirituality is anything but logical. However, I hope this overview gives you a mental model to work with and towards. Its aim is to give you an understanding of the process, even if the result is different and better than I'm able to describe. Once you start feeling the spiritual magic working, you'll discover for yourself the mystical nature of spirituality and the benefits it brings.

My advice is to enjoy the ride and embrace the mystery. It's time to get into real action.

STEP 3: BUILD THE HABITS OF HAPPINESS: CONTINUOUS, HARD WORK, AND MESSY SPIRITUALITY

Faith and works

There's a phrase that is regularly quoted in 12-Step meetings that: "Faith without works is dead." The line is lifted directly from the bible and is at the heart of The 12-Step Programme and the spiritual ethos of doing the work and putting in the effort. I don't know anyone who has recovered from any form of addiction through The 12-Step Programme who didn't think it was hard work. I don't know a single person who relished the prospect of doing the work. And yet, I know countless people who thought it was the best thing they ever did. I am one of those people. I hated "working" the programme. I hated the effort and discomfort it put me through. I hated doing the work. But I had to do the work to experience the transformation. The spiritual awakening doesn't come through faith alone. It comes through faith and work. And it feels like work.

The thing to remember is that we are talking about a spiritual solution to a tangible problem. We are talking about a process of transformation that deals with the problem we have with life (the unsatisfactoriness we're feeling and potentially the addictive numbing that is causing us more pain) and delivers a solution to that problem (we start experiencing spiritual happiness and feeling the full rapture of being alive). That's quite a turnaround. It's a turnaround in thinking, a turnaround in feeling and a turnaround in behaviours. These turnarounds don't come easily. They don't happen overnight. There's a price to pay. And the price is a continuous effort and hard work. The trouble is, we tend not to like hard work.

This is what Emmott Fox had to say on the matter: "Man will seldom try the 'strait' way until he is driven to it, individually, by irresistible pressure. The answer is that, the changing of one's consciousness is really very hard work, calling for constant, unceasing vigilance and a breaking of mental habits which is sure to be troublesome for a time. The natural man is lazy, always tends to take the line of least resistance and so doesn't get down to bedrock principles until he is compelled to." This is why I believe hitting some sort of crisis is important as a kick start to the spiritual adventure. It requires a dedication that can only be found when one is looking to solve a problem that is big enough to warrant the effort required. That's the way it was for me and countless others I see coming into The 12-Step Programme. Hitting rock bottom is the compulsion we need.

Having gone through the process and experienced the life-changing benefits of the spiritual solution, I wish I had the words that did justice to the benefits that would make the effort seem worthwhile. It's so saddening to see the large number of people who are obviously in pain, who want desperately to stop their addiction, who are presented with a solution to their problem, the spiritual solution, and yet choose to stay in pain rather than do the work required to get well. I chose to stay in my pain for a number of years before doing something about it. I wish someone had the words to get me into action sooner. It would have avoided the pain that I and those around me suffered. I was lucky. I did eventually get into action and eventually did the work. Some of those choosing to remain in their pain die because of that decision. And that happens more regularly than you'd think.

Why would making this decision be so difficult? If the benefits are so great, if the spiritual solution is so effective, why are so many people so reluctant to simply get on with it and do the work.

I believe the answer lies in our resistance to changing old habits and the difficulty of creating new ones.

Our Immunity to Change and the Commitment to Break Bad Habits

There's lots of evidence to suggest humans develop and grow through adulthood. Our levels of awareness and consciousness are constantly evolving. History and anthropology show that whole populations and cultures grow and change over time. Even though we can change and grow, even though we do change and grow, and even though we are built to change and grow, we seldom choose to do so. At an individual level, we have a psychological momentum to stay in the business-as-usual modality. We have a resistance to change.

This resistance is captured in the Immunity to Change theory that Robert Keegan and Lisa Lahey have developed. Based on thirty years of adult developmental research, the Immunity to Change model is a way of helping people take a kind of mental X-ray, a picture of their own mindset. Kegan maintains that by allowing individuals to see the ways in which their mental system is making errors or distortions that keep them from letting new ideas come into their head can allow them to accept those new ideas and ultimately change their behaviour.

The Immunity to Change framework can be found in Keegan and Lahey's book of the same name. It's a really interesting exercise to go through to see just what beliefs and mindsets you are holding on to that are keeping you stuck in patterns of behaviour you don't want to hold on to but find you cannot change. Their conclusion is that we need a pivot. A pivotal moment in time when we commit to change. That could be a proactive pivot; we take control of our lives and say, "There's an opportunity for me to grow and develop, and I'm willing to commit. Or it could be a reactive pivot; our lives take control of us through some sort of crisis (addiction, loss of a loved one, loss of a job, breakdown, burnout, or all of the above!), and we are confronted with the reality that 'there is no other option but to change."

Either way, no matter the pivot and how you get to the path, once you're on it, it's down to you. You have to want it. And you have to want it for yourself. There's no point trying to change for your wife, kids, or employer. The spiritual journey requires an effort that can only come with a deep commitment from within. A commitment you can only make to yourself. For yourself.

The commitment and effort you are signing up for is breaking old habits and creating new ones. It sounds deceptively obvious and easy. Especially if you're coming at this from the point of view of addiction. I want to stop drinking, so I break the habit of drinking. I want to stop over-eating, so I stop the habit of over-eating. But the habits I'm talking about also include the less obvious as well as the more obvious ones.

Yes, we have to stop the obviously destructive habits of drinking or overeating. However, the spiritual solution goes one step further. It requires us to break the destructive habit of the wrong thinking that compels us to drink or smoke or whatever it is we do to distract ourselves when we know we don't want to. We need to break our mental obsessions. And that means breaking the habit of the wrong thinking that's keeping us in misery.

It turns out that misery is a habit. So, too, is happiness. Re-training our mind, our heart and our soul through the five spiritual habits we've discussed in this book is a way to break the destructive habit of wrong thinking and replace it with the new habit of right thinking. It's the way to break the destructive habit of choosing misery and create a new habit of choosing happiness.

Stopping drinking is relatively easy. You just don't drink. You simply refuse to put the glass (or the bottle) to your lips. But staying stopped is an altogether different and significantly more difficult challenge. The mental obsession to drink is the reason why every attempt to get sober fails. The alcoholic who has given up drinking and has done so for a few days, or a few weeks, a few months, or a few years, and decides to drink again makes that decision when they are stone-cold sober. They are sober, and they "know" what will happen if they drink. They are sober and "know" it will end disastrously. They are sober but "think" a drink is a good idea. They are sober and "think" it will be different this time. They are sober and "think" they will get away with it. They "think" they'll be able to stop again. This is the habit of wrong thinking that needs changing. This is the habit that requires the re-training of the brain. However, old brain habits and habitual ways of thinking and believing are hard to break, and new brain habits are hard to create. This is why we need to put in the hard work and persevere with it.

Emmott Fox put it like this: "The principle involved is perfectly simple, but unfortunately, doing it is anything but easy. Now, why should this be so? The answer lies in the extraordinary potency of habit; and habits of thinking are at once the most subtle in character and the most difficult to break."

Fortunately, we have a very useful tool available to us in our quest to break the more subtle bad habits and create healthy new ones: daily routines.

The Benefits of Daily Practice through Routines

The bedrock of my recovery and the foundation of my spiritual awakening has been a structured morning and evening routine. I was encouraged to adopt and stick to a strict routine from the very start of my 12-Step adventure. I initially found it difficult as many of the practices were alien to me. But as the days turned into weeks, the weeks turned into months, and the months turned into years, I found that what was once a difficult and arduous morning and evening task turned into second nature. They became the habits that transformed into spiritual happiness.

This is the key point. Spiritual happiness can't be pursued. It is achieved by grounding ourselves and our lives using the foundations of spiritual practice. I believe the quickest and most certain way to embed these practices into your life is to make them habits of your morning and evening routine.

The various practices were just things I did when I got up and things I did before I went to sleep. I just did them. Now, they're part of the way I live.

I'd be lying if I said I do my morning and evening routine every single day of every single year. I don't. I find it especially difficult when I'm ill, away on holiday, or on a business trip. But apart from those three occasions, I'd say I do my daily routines around 80% of the time.

The key to building a routine is to start small and grow. Find out the practices that suit you and work for you. The challenge here is that you need to stick with most of these practices for a few months before you are in a position to feel the benefits, and therefore, you need to give most of these things a few months before you are in a position to reject anything.

Here is a quick summary of the practices and concepts I've mentioned in each of the Five Pillars of Habits. I've put in bold the ones, in my own experience, that make the biggest difference, and I'd recommend you focus on.

The Habit of Surrender

- Embracing necessary pain
- **Breaking the pain-shame-fear cycle of denial**
- Acceptance
- **The Serenity Prayer**
- Surrender to the present moment
- The process of surrender
- Micro-moments of surrender
- **The letting go technique**

The Habit of Awareness

- **Re-reading this book**
- Reading books in the bibliography
- Three wrong views and three concentrations
- **Walking and listening**
- **Mindfulness meditation** (becoming familiar with the workings of the true self and the false self)

The Habit of Discipline

- Embodying Knowledge
- Attuning to intelligence and energy (inside and around our bodies)
- **Feel the feelings**
- Falling in love with your body; **abstinence from bad habits** that affect physical or mental health
- Embracing silence
- **Mindfulness meditation**
- Contemplation
- **Moving into the Now**
- Asking for guidance and power
- Regular prayer (memorised prayers and making up your own)
- Growing through discomfort
- Avoiding numbing (**abstinence from bad habits**)
- Fasting and temperance (**abstinence from bad habits**)
- Happiness and suffering inter-are
- Searching for meaning in suffering
- Living Virtuously
- Reversing character defects
- **A daily evening review** (how well have I lived up to my re-imagined identity)
- Retaining a virtuous sense of fun

The Habit of Connection

- Generating loving, meaningful connection energy
- The wisdom of enough
- Felt-connection to a God of our understanding (**embracing silence and asking for guidance and power**)
- Felt-connection to ourselves; forgiveness of self, **gratitude**, self-compassion
- Felt-connection to others; widening our identity lens to include MWe, **tackling resentment with forgiveness**
- Felt-connection to community; seeking out value-driven communities of work and living
- Felt-connection to nature; **being out in nature**, reducing our ecological footprint
- Felt-connection to future generations; looking after our planet, seventh generation thinking and decision making

The Habit of Service

- The Golden Rule
- Seeking out opportunities for proactive service
- **Being helpful and useful to those around you**
- **Acts of unnoticed kindness**
- Finding meaning through self-sacrifice
- Honing your response-ability

My advice, my guidance and my plea is that you create a morning and an evening routine based on the following framework and stick with it.

1. Agree on the bad habit you want to abstain from (drinking, smoking, sugar, etc. If you suspect the habit you choose is a strong addiction, you may want to consider joining a 12-Step programme).

2. Draw up a shortlist of spiritual habits from each of the five pillars you'd like to experiment with from the lists above.

3. Set an amount of time in the morning and the evening that you can commit to. I would start with no less than 30 minutes in the morning (ideally, try and start with an hour) and no less than 15 minutes in the evening.

4. Draw up your own routine template and allocate the practices you are willing to commit to and make sure you have practices in place for each of the 5 headings. Focus on the ones in bold to start with.

5. Write up your own personalised routine.

6. Stick with it and practice, practice, practice.

Here's an example of a "starter routine." I've suggested 30 minutes in the morning, but if that feels like too much time to commit to, reduce some of the 5-minute activities to 2 minutes—try and protect the 10-minute meditation. It's more important that you get going rather than overwhelm yourself with a long list of things you have no chance of doing. Mediation, prayer, and abstaining from a bad habit are the things to focus on to start with

STARTER ROUTINE	The Surrender Habits	The Awareness Habits	The Discipline Habits	The Connection Habits	The Service Habits
Morning Routine (30mins)	ASKING FOR GUIDANCE & POWER Pray (5 mins)	EMBRACING SILENCE Meditation (10mins) EMBODYING KNOWLEDGE Daily reading (5mins)		GROWING THROUGH DISCOMFORT Bad habit abstinence (5mins)	LIVING VIRTUOUSLY Plan the day - who can you help? (5mins)
Evening Routine (10mins)	ASKING FOR GUIDANCE & POWER Pray (5 mins)		LIVING VIRTUOUSLY Daily review (5mins)		
Kicking the bad habit (abstinence)	USE SURRENDER HABITS TO HELP KICK THE BAD HABIT	USE AWARENESS HABITS TO HELP KICK THE BAD HABIT	USE DISCIPLINE HABITS TO HELP KICK THE BAD HABIT	USE CONNECTION HABITS TO HELP KICK THE BAD HABIT	USE SERVICE HABITS TO HELP KICK THE BAD HABIT

And here's an example of a more ambitious starter routine. Walking and listening is the big practice I would urge you to add into your routine if you can find time.

MEDIUM ROUTINE	The Surrender Habits	The Awareness Habits	The Discipline Habits	The Connection Habits	The Service Habits
Morning Routine (1hr)	ASKING FOR GUIDANCE & POWER Pray (5 mins)	EMBRACING SILENCE Meditation (10mins) EMBODYING KNOWLEDGE Daily reading (5mins) Walking & listening (20mins)	LIVING VIRTUOUSLY Daily spiritual principle (5mins)	LIVING VIRTUOUSLY Gratitude list (5mins) GROWING THROUGH DISCOMFORT Bad habit abstinence (5mins)	LIVING VIRTUOUSLY Plan the day - who can you help? (5mins)
Evening Routine (20mins)	ASKING FOR GUIDANCE & POWER Pray (5 mins)		LIVING VIRTUOUSLY Daily review (5mins)	LIVING VIRTUOUSLY Gratitude list (5mins)	LIVING VIRTUOUSLY Review the day - who did you help? (5mins)
Kicking the bad habit (abstinence)	USE SURRENDER HABITS TO HELP KICK THE BAD HABIT	USE AWARENESS HABITS TO HELP KICK THE BAD HABIT	USE DISCIPLINE HABITS TO HELP KICK THE BAD HABIT	USE CONNECTION HABITS TO HELP KICK THE BAD HABIT	USE SERVICE HABITS TO HELP KICK THE BAD HABIT

Finally, a more advanced routine. This is something like the routine I'm currently practicing most days of the week.

Although, in the spirit of complete honesty, the evening 20-minute meditation is more of a mid-afternoon nap. I'm not perfect!

ADVANCED ROUTINE	The Surrender Habits	The Awareness Habits	The Discipline Habits	The Connection Habits	The Service Habits
Morning Routine (1hr 55mins)	ASKING FOR GUIDANCE & POWER Pray (5 mins)	EMBRACING SILENCE Meditation (20mins) EMBODYING KNOWLEDGE Daily reading (5mins) Walking & listening (30mins)	EMBODYING KNOWLEDGE Physical exercise (30mins) LIVING VIRTUOUSLY Daily spiritual principle (5mins)	LIVING VIRTUOUSLY Gratitude list (5mins) GROWING THROUGH DISCOMFORT Bad habit abstinence (5mins) Daily amends (5mins)	LIVING VIRTUOUSLY Plan the day - who can you help? (5mins)
Evening Routine (40mins)	ASKING FOR GUIDANCE & POWER Pray (5 mins)	EMBRACING SILENCE Meditation (20mins)	LIVING VIRTUOUSLY Daily review (5mins)	LIVING VIRTUOUSLY Gratitude list (5mins)	LIVING VIRTUOUSLY Review the day - who did you help? (5mins)
Kicking the bad habit (abstinence)	USE SURRENDER HABITS TO HELP KICK THE BAD HABIT	USE AWARENESS HABITS TO HELP KICK THE BAD HABIT	USE DISCIPLINE HABITS TO HELP KICK THE BAD HABIT	USE CONNECTION HABITS TO HELP KICK THE BAD HABIT	USE SERVICE HABITS TO HELP KICK THE BAD HABIT

I must admit that this looks like a huge amount of work when it's written down as a list. Who spends nearly two hours doing spiritual things every morning?

Well I do.

But I enjoy doing it. I once heard that an author I like regularly mediates for two hours every morning, and I thought they were insane. But then I thought about the amount of time I can spend watching TV. Or the amount of time I waste scrolling through nonsense on my computer. It all goes back to prioritising spiritual happiness.

And that's the beauty of stacking habits into routines. I've built up to this routine over five years, and so it really doesn't feel that arduous to do—most days. But I really do notice the difference if I don't do at least half of these things every day.

Give yourself time and patience with your routine. You will find that, every now and then, you'll experience what I call a moment of truth.

You will read something. You'll see something. You'll realise something that feels like an "aha" moment. These moments will last a few seconds. You'll feel alive, inspired, fulfilled, and fully connected with the world.

Sticking with it: Finding Moments of Truth through Spiritual Practice

The secret to the spiritual journey is to be patient and savour the moments of truth as they arise. The more moments you experience, the more you will sense the lasting impact of spiritual happiness. You'll be on the path to a spiritual awakening and experiencing greater feelings of freedom, peace, joy, wholeness and fulfilment. Following the spiritual path means following these moments of truth. Because you're feeling the benefits, you'll find that the practices and techniques you read about and apply in your morning and evening routine filter into every part of your day and life.

As your routines become second nature, as the spiritual awakening begins to take root, The Habits of Surrender, Awareness, Discipline,

Connection, and Service will infiltrate all your affairs. The moments of truth and spiritual happiness will become ever more regular and familiar.

Getting Started: Making Time for Spiritual Practice

Don't spend too much time pondering which practises to do first. If you're stuck, just use my starter template. In my experience, it's not necessarily what you choose to practice that matters most. The critical aspect of establishing your routine is finding the time and protecting that time to ensure you follow through. The biggest barrier, or at least the most common excuse for not doing the work, is "I don't have time." In our culture of economic growth, we can always find time to work but often struggle to find time for a nurturing a spiritual routine.

We spend 50% of our waking lives working—a significant investment of time in earning money. Unfortunately, most of us don't even enjoy our jobs, with 87% feeling either disengaged or enraged by our work. This isn't a healthy way to live. As Thich Nhat Hanh reminds us, "Time is not money. Time is life, and time is love."

The more time and energy we devote to chasing material goals (which we know don't lead to lasting happiness), the less time and energy we have available to work towards spiritual goals (which we know do lead to lasting happiness). Therefore, it's crucial that we prioritise our time correctly from the start. I'm not suggesting we spend more time on our daily spiritual practice than we do working, but even dedicating 10-15% of your working time to spiritual practice and your spiritual happiness will make a huge difference.

Interestingly, while our working lives are undoubtedly stressful and full of busyness, data suggests that average working hours have been steadily falling across the world since the Industrial Revolution. Statistics vary from country to country, but in the UK, we are, on average, working fewer hours each day, fewer working days each week, and fewer working weeks in the year (Source: Ourworldinda-ta.org/working-hours). Yet, many people still use the excuse that they "don't have enough time."

Making Time: Rising Early for Spiritual Practice

One way to find time is to get up earlier. As a single parent of four children, the only way I could find and protect time for my morning routine was to get up early. I rise at 4:50 am to allow myself 2 hours for my routine before the kids get up at 7 am. I understand how that might sound like torture to most people. It was for me at first. Now I love this time to myself—the peace, quiet, lack of traffic, and the beauty of the dawn. It's such a nurturing time. I need to go to bed before 10 pm to make sure I get around 6-7 hours of sleep. The cost to me of doing this is missing out on an hour's worth of box set TV binging. It's not a bad trade off, really.

If you're convinced that you can't get to bed earlier in order to get up an hour earlier without feeling tired, I'd argue that you categorically can. You do it every year, without a blink of an eye, when the clocks go forward. Just make the clocks go forward for yourself and your spiritual happiness.

Seeking Support on Your Spiritual Journey

The next piece of advice is to find support as you embark on this journey. The 12-Step Programme comes ready-made with support in the form of a sponsor (who guides you through the process one-on-one), regular meetings (available online and in-person all over the world to reinforce your learning), and fellowship (getting to know others going through the same process). It's truly inspiring to see how much support is not only available via the 12-Step institutions but also how all of that support is free. There is no charge apart from a voluntary, modest contribution — being of service and helping each other out is all part of the process. It's a truly inspiring model.

If you're struggling with an addiction, my first recommendation is to seek support through the most appropriate 12-Step institution. If you don't see yourself as an addict but think you'd benefit from the spiritual solution I've outlined in this book, I recommend finding someone to work with you as you embark on your journey.

At the simplest level, tell someone you know well and trust that you are embarking on this journey. Share your plans and ask them to hold you accountable. Arrange a regular meeting with them, perhaps once a week. Tell them what you plan to achieve and what daily routine and practices you are committing to. Report back to them with H.H.O.W.—especially the honesty. They don't have to be experts on the process; they just need to keep you accountable. If you say you're going to do it, do it. If you didn't do what you said you'd do, explain why, honestly. And go again.

My next suggestion would be to find someone to go on the journey with you—a fellow spiritual adventurer to share your experiences with. If you'd like even more support, I've started guiding people through this process and will continue to do so one-on-one and in groups. In time, I'd like to establish a network of support to guide many more people through the spiritual solution.

You may even seek out a 12-Step sponsor or other spiritual guide to support you. They may not agree with everything I've written, but they will understand the key concepts and practices and are likely to have had a spiritual awakening themselves.

But most importantly, get started and do the work. Put in the effort. Faith without works is dead.

THE PARADOX OF EFFORT: WORKING HARD AND TAKING IT EASY

Throughout the book, I'm aware that I've emphasised the importance of hard work, effort, and persistence—the rather harsh and uncompelling proposition that change is hard, there's no gain without pain, and the answer is to stop complaining and just do it.

However, at this point, I'd like to reintroduce the analogy of catching the wild ass. Remember the saying, "No one catches the wild ass by running after him. Yet only those who run after the wild ass ever catch him." You can apply this paradox to the effort required to stay on the spiritual path. You have to chase after the spiritual solution and do the work. But it's not all about work, effort, and diligence. The paradox of the spiritual solution is that alongside the principle of "faith without works is dead" is the equally relevant principle of "easy does it."

These paradoxes infuriate me and my logical way of thinking. What do you want me to do? Do I work hard and stick with it? Or do I take it easy and be kind to myself? The answer is yes - you do both. You work hard and you take it easy. It's frustrating, isn't it? Well, it is to me.

As an aside, this black-and-white thinking—the type of thinking that says it has to be this or that, it can't be both—is part of the habit of wrong thinking we need to break. This is closely associated with the idea of "stinking thinking" that addicts often talk about. It's the type of thinking that insists: I'm right, you're wrong; it's all or nothing; if something is bad, it can't be good; if I'm sad now, I'll be sad forever. It's because of this wrong or stinking thinking that we have to be H.H.O.W.—especially the open-minded part. If you want to break the habit of black-and-white thinking and create the ability to sit with paradoxes comfortably, I suggest reading the Tao Te Ching and contemplating some of the verses. They really get your brain working!

Progress, Not Perfection: The Key to the Spiritual Journey

Perhaps the easiest way to apply the "work hard" principle alongside the "take it easy" principle is to remember that the spiritual journey is about progress, not perfection. As part of The 12-Step Programme, it's often said that there's only one step you can do perfectly: Step 1, admitting that we have a problem and that we're powerless to solve the problem on our own. We can do that 100%. We need to surrender 100%. All the other steps are done to "the best of our ability"—not anyone else's ability, but your ability, your best ability at this present time. As long as you're doing your best, that's enough.

The truth is that we can be guilty of trying too hard. Philip Shepherd wisely observes, "If you drive yourself and fall short of your goal, you are likely to conclude that you didn't drive yourself hard enough, the world is unfair, or you are a loser. Failure in this mindset won't bring you closer to a state of presence or open your heart to 'what is' (the spiritual solution). Instead, it sets you on a course to feel entitled and/or resentful. Both are dark places as they displace gratitude for what you have with annoyance for what you don't."

The key to the spiritual solution, to embracing and maintaining all the habits of spiritual happiness, is to remember that it is the pursuit of truth that matters, not the possession. I use the terms spiritual adventure, spiritual journey, and spiritual path to conjure up an image of the spiritual solution as an ever-progressing unfoldment rather than a definitive destination. The spiritual solution is not a cure as such. In 12-Step literature, it suggests that alcoholics are never cured of their addiction. "What we really have is a daily reprieve contingent on the maintenance of our spiritual condition." We need to continue to do the work, stay on the path, and continue to progress and grow. If we do, we will keep our addiction and "unsatisfactoriness" at bay. Moreover, the benefits of spiritual happiness and the feelings of freedom, peace, joy, wholeness, and fulfilment will continue to manifest and deepen.

Crafting Your Personal Spiritual Adventure

From this perspective of spirituality as an imperfect progression, as a journey travelled with the best of our individual abilities, I think it's helpful to think of your own personal adventure as something you craft. Think of it as a creative endeavour, an important life project that can be conducted in an artistic way. Create a plan and work with it. See what suits you, what works for you, then tweak it as the spiritual picture starts to emerge. Play with the energy you bring to your spiritual practice. One day, you are determined, persistent, and dogmatic. The next, you are gentle, forgiving, loving. In some ways, this is like applying both the masculine and feminine natures within you. Masculine discipline to achieve one day, feminine discipline to allow the next.

Gabor Maté says, "The spiritual journey, the quest for wholeness, and the tender digging back to our true selves, is not reducible to any one, two, or twenty spiritual practices or approaches. It's a personal journey where 'We are never as close as we hope, and never as far as we fear."

He also makes the brilliant point that "If we remove the hyphen from re-create (the rather arduous process of change and transformation), we are left with the verb form of recreation, as in 'play'. This is an excellent reminder that we do ourselves no favours by taking ourselves, or the process of inquiry, so seriously that we lose a sense of spontaneity and vitality. These steps (the steps towards a spiritual solution) may not be much fun, but they still work best when infused with some lightness. I have seen more than a few people surprise themselves mid-process with a smile."

That's so important to work like you mean it, and smile because you deserve it. This whole process is a process of healing. It's a process away from suffering and towards spiritual happiness and joy. Joy has to make a strong appearance as part of the process. Yes, the spiritual journey requires hard work and can be difficult. Confronting the unhealthy habits of the past and creating new habits of thinking and being is not always easy or pleasant. But you have to come out the other side loving yourself and loving life. You have to come out feeling the full rapture of being alive and it helps to bear that feeling in mind as you're doing the hard work.

Embracing the Messiness of Spirituality

The spiritual solution is a deep process. It's challenging, joyous, full of life and love, and paradoxical. When I think about it, it's an incredibly messy process. It's all over the place—just what our logical, ordered, structured left hemisphere ego hates. We just have to help our ego get over it. Deal with it, ego; life isn't always linear, and neither is healing.

I came across the idea of messy spirituality from a book called Messy Spirituality by Mike Yaconelli. Yaconelli was a writer, theologian, church leader, and youth worker. He was also the pastor of a small church in California, which he lovingly claimed was "the slowest growing church in America." He was the pastor of that church, even though he failed to get ordained at theological school—twice. But he embraced his faults and mistakes and welcomed all sorts of perceived misfits and oddballs to his church, people who weren't necessarily welcomed at other churches but were trying to find their own spiritual path. He mentions alcoholics quite a lot in his book, one of the perceived groups of misfits and oddballs he welcomed. That's how many people in addiction perceive themselves: misfits and oddballs who just don't fit in with the image of perfection that our culture seems to value and even demand.

What I identified with most about Yaconelli's take on spirituality and its messy nature were what he called his four non-principles of spiritual growth. There are no rules to spirituality, so these are non-principles:

1. There is a lifetime of decisions – It's not just one big decision you make to become a spiritual seeker. There are hundreds, if not thousands, of decisions you make daily and weekly. Some decisions will take you closer to spiritual happiness. Some will take you further away. They're all part of the rich adventure that you're on, and you'll learn and grow as a result.

2. Every journey is unique – My journey is my journey. Your journey is yours. I am more than happy to guide and make suggestions, and you are more than welcome to take what works for you and leave the rest. We have to find our own path, and each path is different.

3. Give God 60% – Our culture loves perfection. Our culture loves 100% and is suspicious of anything less. Maybe some days you'll be 100% dedicated to your journey, but some days you'll be a lot less. That's okay. You'll still grow as long as you're averaging out, as Yaconelli suggests, at about 60%. It may not be an A*, but it's a solid pass.

4. Reluctant growth is still growth—Even if you don't feel like doing the work, even if you apply yourself to daily practice with a sense of duty rather than unbridled joy, you'll still be growing in the right direction. This is good news for people like me who really didn't enjoy spiritual practice in the early days.

Reading something like Messy Spirituality really helps me. It helps me realise that it's okay not to be perfect, that a God of my understanding isn't looking for perfection. What the realm of spirit seems to warm and respond to is heartfelt effort. It rewards those who approach spirituality with honesty, humility, open-mindedness, and willingness (H.H.O.W.), as we discussed earlier.

The spiritual solution does require hard work and effort. It does require discipline. But discipline, effort and persistence can come in the form of a loving parent running beside a five-year-old learning to ride a bike. It's there to nudge us in the right direction when we start to wobble. It's there to cheer out loud when we're pedalling on our own for a few yards. And it's there to pick us up and give us a cuddle when we fall off and hurt ourselves.

I've helped all four of my children learn to ride a bike. Not one of them did it without tears or frustration from both parent and child. All four were persistent in their endeavours. I was patient with my support. We got there in the end.

Learning to ride a bike is a messy process.

Building the habits of spiritual happiness is a messy process.

Thank the Lord for messiness.

EPILOGUE

BEYOND SPIRITUAL HAPPINESS

The Pathway to Purpose and Power
Hearing Our Calling and Having the Strength to Act

WHAT IS PURPOSE?

Have you ever thought, "What's my purpose? What exactly am I supposed to be doing with my life?" I did. I couldn't stop thinking those thoughts. I was obsessed with my purpose a few years ago. I guess I still am.

At the end of my drinking, when I was asked to leave the business I co-owned and ran, I felt completely lost. I had no clue what I was supposed to do. I had no sense of what my role in life should be. I had been doing that last job for twelve years. It paid well, and I think I did it reasonably well. But, if truth be told, it never really felt "like me."

A Hard but Bearable Job

When I was initially offered that job, it came to me in the form of an opportunity to buy into a company and take over as Managing Director. It felt like a great business opportunity—a fantastic financial deal. And, at the time, that meant everything to me. But once I got started with the job, the work I was doing didn't make me feel like I had found my purpose.

The job definitely had lots of high points. It wasn't a misery-fest at all. It just happened to be a job that turned out to be much more challenging than I had bargained for. It was not necessarily because it was a hard job but because I found it hard. Hard but bearable. That's how I would describe my experience of that job. The job paid well and came with all the trappings of status and respect that the title of Co-Owner and Managing Director brings—status and control that I had long yearned for. Those seemed like the most important signs of success to me at the time. Being well-paid and well-respected were the rewards. Hard but bearable was the price I had to pay. And I thought that was a pretty good deal.

I didn't realise at the time, but when I joined the business, it wasn't doing as well as I thought it was. It was on a downward financial trajectory to making a loss. That meant the first year or so was all about cutting costs and steadying the ship financially. This was totally outside my skill set. I was a creative brand strategy person, not a turnaround financial guy. But I sucked it up. We made the redundancies, cut the costs, steadied the ship, and got to breakeven. I may have made some shrewd business decisions in those first few months on the job, but I hated every moment of it.

Creative Ideas That Make a Real Difference

Once we were over the worst, we could start thinking about the future. As a creative brand business, I had this idea that our biggest asset to clients was helping them succeed by providing them with creative ideas that made a real difference. That was our strap-line. Not particularly ground-breaking or different, but I believed in it. And so did the rest of the team. But we needed to substantiate our belief.

At the time, the creative industry was awash with award schemes. It struck me that if our promise to our clients was to deliver creative ideas that made a real difference, then we should aim to win awards that proved the point. Luckily, some awards did that. Creative awards celebrated fantastic creative ideas, voted on by respected creative people. Effectiveness awards celebrated campaigns and ideas that made a difference because of their impact on the bottom line—ideas that increased sales, improved market share, or influenced people in some way, voted on by well-renowned marketing people. It became our mission to enter and win as many creative and effectiveness awards as possible, to prove to our clients, potential clients, potential staff, and ourselves that we could indeed deliver creative ideas that made a real difference.

In fact, the aim was more than that. Not content with simply winning these awards, I wanted to put us on the map. I not only wanted to prove we could deliver creative ideas that made a real difference, I wanted us to be the best in the UK at it. And prove it.

There were ranking systems in place that suited our claim perfectly. One ranked UK design agencies based on creativity, while the other ranked them based on effectiveness. The more creative awards you won, the higher up the creative ranking table you went. The more effectiveness awards you won, the higher up the effectiveness table you went. Our aim was to be in the top ten for creativity and in the top ten for effectiveness at the same time. No other agency at the time had achieved that. If we did, we would be the only design agency in the UK that could credibly claim to deliver creative ideas that made a real difference.

The only problem was we didn't feature in the top one hundred of either of those rankings.

A Remarkable Achievement

Our mission began. It took us seven years of hard work, determination, and faith to get there, but we did it. I remember the day we got the news: we were ranked number five in the creative league table and number five in the effectiveness league table. The only design business to achieve the top five in both tables at the same time. What an achievement.

I mention this story for a couple of reasons. Firstly, I believe that it is possible to achieve great things if you put your mind to it. We worked incredibly hard to achieve this outcome. We were so focused and determined. It was a remarkable achievement on many levels, and I was incredibly proud that we did what we set out to do. I also mention it because of what happened after achieving this goal. When I heard we had hit our top five for creativity and top five for effectiveness status, I couldn't believe how flat I felt. I thought I'd be completely over the moon. I wasn't. I was pleased but couldn't help but think, "So what now?" It felt like such a hollow victory in some ways. I remember our staff being surprised I didn't organise a spontaneous party. We did celebrate the achievement later that month at our end-of-month show-and-tell get-together. But I didn't feel the celebration inside.

Looking back, I now believe that the focus and effort were misplaced. We might have said that winning these awards was to prove to our clients that we delivered great ideas that made a real difference. Actually, awards are all about boosting reputation and recognition. They are all about making "us," the agency, and "me," the Managing Director of that agency, look good. Looking back, I can see that the mission I set for the business was completely self-centred and self-serving.

I read a quote from Thomas Merton that highlighted this exact point: "The chief source of my spiritual exhaustion is the selfish anxiety to get the most out of everything, to be a sparkling success in our own eyes and the eyes of other men. We can only get rid of this anxiety by being content to miss something in almost everything we do. We cannot achieve greatness unless we lose all interest in being great. For our own idea of greatness is limited and illusory, and if we pay too much attention to it, we will be lured out of the peace and stability that God gave us."

I see that now. I see that my driving desire was to be a sparkling success in my own eyes and in the eyes of others. I also now see how this driving desire to be a success led to the anxiety that was to follow.

The Pursuit of Profit

Once we achieved the top five and top five goals, my mind turned to money. We had achieved an incredible thing. If we could do that, I thought, we could do anything. My mission then turned to monetising this success. The focus was on growing the business, gaining more clients, and making more profits. We had proved that we were a remarkable design agency. Now, it was time to prove we were a remarkable business. Let's capitalise on our creative and effective success and become rich.

I have to say that this strategy makes complete commercial sense. It did then, and it does now. There was nothing wrong with the strategy. But the impact it had on me personally was crushing. That's because the ensuing few years became soulless and empty for me. My focus on winning awards may have been self-centred, but at least it involved some element of creativity. As my focus moved more and more towards money, I felt the spiritual exhaustion and selfish anxiety that Merton talked about.

The joy of my working life revolved around one single document: the monthly report and accounts. If the figure at the bottom of the top sheet was above a certain amount, I was happy for a few minutes. In fact, I wasn't happy—I was relieved. If it was below that amount, I felt down. Deflated. Depressed. I had reduced the fulfilment of my entire working life to looking at one number. My happiness was dependent on that number. As the years rolled on and that number was consistently lower than I had hoped, I felt ever more deflated and depressed. Drinking was the way I alleviated that selfish anxiety and depression.

After a while, even my ambitions to become rich faded. The ambition to achieve anything faded. At the age of forty-eight, I had the notion that I could just about continue doing the hard and bearable task for the next twelve to seventeen years and then retire. I could just about bear looking at a low number as long as it wasn't a loss. I was relatively happy to slide anonymously into comfortable retirement, having endured a hard but bearable existence. I could retire, having never found my purpose. At least I could drink to make me happy.

Writing that now, I can hardly believe I was willing to settle for that. I now realise that my comfort- and security-seeking false self was happy to settle for that. Unbeknownst to me, my intuitive true self was not at all willing to settle for twelve to seventeen years of grinding it out. It wanted much more out of me. It wanted much more out of life. It wanted to feel the full rapture of being alive. And grinding it out with a hard but bearable job was not feeling the full rapture of being alive.

I believe the conflict I felt inside, the unconscious tension between my false self's rapture-less twelve to seventeen-year plan towards retirement and my true self's hidden desire for rapture were the reasons I drank even more and more. It was easier to numb away the unnamed confusion and complication than to face up to the uncomfortable reality. I wish I had talked to people about this at the time. I wish I had talked to my business partners. I wish I had talked to my wife. My parents. But I didn't. As Managing Director, I had the false belief that it was my job to come up with all the answers. It was my job to solve problems, not come up with them. And now I had two big problems: a confusing life problem and a worsening drinking problem.

A New Beginning and a New Purpose

Ultimately, my drinking made the decision for me. My addiction to alcohol meant I wasn't fit to do the job anymore, and I had to leave. It could be said that my true self won out. It didn't really care how my ego felt about falling into disgrace. It didn't make a difference that I felt like a rejected, alcoholic shell of a man without a job. For my true self, an opportunity presented itself. An opportunity to start afresh, explore my purpose without any attachments, and all the freedom in the world to do whatever I wanted and needed to do. I was presented with an opportunity and freedom to find my purpose. And as the effects of a newfound sobriety started to kick in, I felt compelled to find it.

I had this notion that my purpose would be akin to making a living by doing what I love to do most; almost like being paid to do your hobby. In my case that might have been something to do with music. Maybe I would become that goth band member at long last. As we'll see, I don't think your purpose is necessarily aligned with your hobby. But it certainly isn't aligned with maximising financial gain. When we commit to finding our purpose in life, we have to commit to the fact that it might not be associated with a large financial income. In which case, in our current culture of economic growth, our path to purpose immediately hits the problem of practicality.

For me, the question of practicality revolves around one question: "How will I pay the bills?" I worried (and still worry) about this question. I have four dependent children. That financial responsibility weighs heavy. When I now consider the question, "How will I pay the bills?" Other questions quickly arise: "Is the driving force of my life really about making sure I have enough money to give to the building society? To the energy company? To the supermarket chain? Is that what matters most to me? Is that ever going to allow me to feel the full rapture of being alive?" No. It's not. And my soul knows that. Your soul knows that, too.

Yes, we all have financial responsibilities. Yes, we all need to consider the practicalities of paying the bills. But do not mistake those practicalities as valid reasons to ignore your calling. Don't believe that impracticalities mean your yearning for meaning and purpose isn't real. That yearning is very real. You want to find meaning in your life because you are sensing it. You are picking up those subtle energies that are calling you forward. It isn't imaginary. You are feeling those feelings. You can choose to ignore them like I did. And you can choose to numb them away like I did. But if you're anything like me, those feelings will keep on returning until you do something about it.

This final section of the book is all about making sense of purpose and how you can go about bringing more meaning and purpose into your life, how you can go about hearing your calling more clearly and finding the courage to act on it. It's a spiritual process that follows the path we've started. It's the process of losing yourself to find yourself again and again. It's the process of surrendering more, becoming more aware, deepening your discipline, feeling more connected, and being ever more useful. Over and over and over. The more you do this, the more you restore your intuitive, soulful, true self as the rightful master. The more clearly you hear the small, still voice and sense the subtle energies that are calling you forward. The more you trust your intuition to guide your actions. The more faith you have. The more power you find.

I embarked on the spiritual journey because I wanted to stop drinking. I experienced a spiritual awakening that alleviated the mental obsession to drink. I found peace, serenity and spiritual happiness as a result. As my journey evolved and my practice deepened, it's become evident that the spiritual solution does so much more than stop unhealthy, distracting, numbing habits. I believe the spiritual solution is not only a means to generating spiritual happiness. It is also a means to reveal your purpose to you. And not only revealing it but giving you the tools to go out and put it into action and live it.

I'm not suggesting it's a process that results in God appearing in a flash of lightning and presenting you with your purpose in a tablet of stone. My experience is that it's revealed to you gradually. And it's not so much that your purpose becomes evident, but more that your sense of purpose becomes more highly attuned—a more highly tuned sense of purpose refined by your ever-growing response-ability. I believe you find and live your purpose by acting on your response-ability. By having faith in your response-ability. By having faith in the subtle energies that you are responding to. By having faith in the subtle energies of the universe, of life, of a God of your understanding.

The more you attune yourself through the Habits of Spiritual Happiness, the stronger the connection with your Higher Power. The more you trust your intuitions that emerge from that connection, the more likely you are to act on those intuitions. Your response-ability is heightened. As you flow deeper into this process, your role in life becomes clearer. You get to the point where you have no other option but to live out your purpose fully. You will feel compelled to do so. You will feel the full rapture of being alive because of the work you are drawn to do. The work you were meant to do. And you'll have The Spiritual Habits in place to keep you on purpose as and when times get tough. That's exactly what happened to me. That's exactly why I'm sitting in a coffee shop at this very moment, writing this book. I was compelled to do so. I didn't feel I had an option not to do so. That is my experience of finding my purpose through the spiritual solution.

But let's go back to the beginning and explore the world of purpose and meaning. Let's look at what others make of purpose to get a fuller picture of what's really going on here. As part of my research into purpose, I've come across a number of perspectives. I have my own opinion on what our purpose is and how we discern it and act on it. But I think it's useful to widen the net to bring in other perspectives. It keeps my logical and egoic, left hemisphere, false self happy that I've done a thorough job and covered all the bases.

From my investigations, there appear to be four distinctive but overlapping perspectives to consider:

- Purpose as following our nature
- Purpose as a meaningful goal and statement of intent
- Purpose as applying our unique gifts and talents
- Purpose as a combination of inner purpose and outer purpose

I believe all these perspectives have a role to play and can be brought together in one overarching approach to finding and living our purpose, which I have entitled:

- Purpose as Fulfilling Our Soul's Desire: Hearing Our Calling and Getting into Action

Before we bring them all together, let's look at the first four perspectives one by one.

PURPOSE PERSPECTIVE #1: PURPOSE AS FOLLOWING YOUR NATURE

I'm definitely an over-thinker. I'm not happy until I've fully thought through an issue, researched all possible angles, argued for and against each point, and then, and only then, concluded that the right approach is the most obvious one all along. For some reason, I find it hard to accept that there's such depth in simplicity. As the principle behind Occam's Razor states: "The simplest solution is almost always the best." Taking a leaf out of William of Ockham's book, let's start with the simplest conception of purpose: our purpose in life is simply to be who we are and do what we do. We have no other purpose than to be exactly the person who was born the way we were born and raised the way we were raised. Our purpose is to live out the specific human nature that God gave us. That's it.

Following Our Innate Patterns

C.J. Jung held this philosophy. He said that just as a leaf-cutter ant must cut leaves, the same is true of man. "As a biological being, he has no choice but to act in a specifically human way and fulfil his pattern of behaviour." It's a wonderfully simple point of view. Still, I think a little more depth can be added to this philosophy when you consider the environmental aspect of our "patterns of behaviour."

We fulfil our purpose when we naturally and intuitively act in specific ways in response to our environment. Gill Coombes describes this well in her book Hearing Our Calling. She says, "In any self-regulating whole, there's no redundancy: every constituent part has a function. And if any part ceases to function, the whole adapts by redistributing roles accordingly. In the same way, we humans are all 'FOR' something – we all have a function in maintaining a healthy whole."

The Economy of Purpose

There's certainly great simplicity in this view of purpose. It's almost as if your purpose will find you, presented to you by the needs of the whole to keep the whole healthy. This approach aligns with systems theory from that perspective. It's also how our free economy currently works and allocates jobs. When there's a shortage of barbers, for example, in any given area, up will pop a barber to meet the need. If you can cut hair, hey presto, an opportunity presents itself to you. If a big supermarket needs more cashiers to keep the queues of shoppers steadily flowing, that's what may be presented to you. We find jobs by being attuned to what is demanded of us. By being attuned to what society demands of us. What our economy demands of us.

The problem is, however, that we have confused the allocation of jobs with the allocation of purpose. Our culture of economic growth may allocate tasks and ways to make money, but that doesn't necessarily make us feel good about the tasks presented to us. Our culture presents jobs based on the needs of growing the economy. Big supermarkets will recruit cashiers and reward them financially because those cashiers will make the supermarkets more money. The purpose of the big supermarkets is to grow their profits. Most of them are PLCs and have demanding shareholders, so they must do that. They operate in an economy that measures their success by the amount they can grow those profits. Those are just the facts. That's just the way things are in our current culture. The big supermarkets' purpose isn't to help cashiers find their purpose. They can provide jobs. They can provide a means to make money. But making money and living your purpose are not the same thing. That's something our economy and society have failed to pick up on.

This allocation of tasks also doesn't consider individual skills, talents, and disposition. Barbers may be required to contribute more than just financial growth to the local area. But if I'm not cut out to cut hair, I'm not likely to find meaning in that role. I suppose the good news is that there are lots of different types of jobs that could be presented to us. Our economy is very diverse, and so maybe our purpose will be presented to us if we look hard enough. This presents another challenge.

With all the hundreds of thousands of tasks and jobs available to us today, presented by our complex economy, how do I discern the job that might also be my purpose? How do I know if my purpose is to be a barber, a cashier, a plumber, an accountant, an occupational therapist, a brand strategist, or a goth musician?

Coombes addresses this point, saying, "In pre-modern times we would have known our function and got on with it, but our clever consciousness has overlaid our knowing with so much thinking that it can sometimes take a lifetime of experimenting to uncover something so naked and simple as our purpose."

The Search for What Makes Us Come Alive

A lifetime of experimenting. That's been me. Forty-five years of saying yes to jobs that paid well, that I did reasonably well, but didn't necessarily lift my spirits. I could have shortened the experiment if I had known I was experimenting in the first place and had been clearer about what I was looking for. Psychologist Lawrence LeShan has a great solution to what we should be looking for as a result of this process of job experimentation:

> *"Don't worry about what the world wants from you; worry about what makes you come alive. Because what the world really needs are people who are more alive. Your real job is to increase the colour and the zest of your life."*

Imagine if we conducted our job search on this basis and if businesses recruited staff in the same way. Job interviews and probationary periods would be based on the amount of colour and zest we brought into the world rather than on how well we fit the job description or how many units we made or sold. LeShan is absolutely right. We don't need people to be more efficient, quicker, faster, or better. We need people to be happier, healthier, more alive.

The Tension Between What Is and What Could Be

Here's the problem we face: there's not a strong correlation between what we need as human beings trying to find purpose and meaning in the world, trying to find jobs that make us come alive, and what the world is offering as career opportunities to meet that need. Our culture of economic growth doesn't appear to value bringing colour and zest into the world as a key performance indicator or include it in job description capabilities. Those in charge don't perceive colour and zest as qualities needed to keep our businesses or economy whole and healthy.

We could argue that they should be (and I would be at the front of that queue, but that's a subject for another book). We could argue that they used to be (having recently visited Florence, it's clear that the Renaissance period was a time that really did value colour and zest, which would be a chapter in the other book). So, this leaves us with a tension between how we feel about the work we're doing because it's what's available to us and how we feel about the work we sense we should be doing - the work that we believe will make us come alive.

Viktor Frankl was well aware of this tension when Man's Search for Meaning was published in 1946. He argued that the tension was to be accepted and isn't necessarily a bad thing:

> "Mental health is based on a certain degree of tension, the tension between what one has already achieved and what one still ought to accomplish, or the gap between what one is and what one should become. Such tension is inherent in the human condition and, therefore, is indispensable to mental well-being. I consider it a dangerous misconception of mental hygiene to assume that man needs a tensionless state. What's required is the striving and the struggling for a worthwhile goal, a freely chosen task."

Perhaps the tension between who we currently are and who we are to become is natural. Maybe this tension plays a part in the pain and suffering we feel at work. Part of the stress of modern life may be caused by this disconnection and our internal, possibly subconscious, desire to be more - to be more alive, more ourselves, more determined to add colour and zest. Frankl thought so, and I do too. Here's the point: I don't think we realise that this tension is the cause, or part of the cause, of our discontentment. We call it stress, anxiety, overwhelm, or burnout. But it could be called existential despair - despair of our inability to be the person we yearn to be, to do what we yearn to do. If we misdiagnose the tension, pain, and suffering, we treat it incorrectly.

We tend to treat the tension with antidepressants, alcohol, drugs, overeating, shopping, or binging on social media. We treat our desire to bring zest and colour into the world by numbing it out. Ouch!

This isn't a new phenomenon. Frankl saw it happening over fifty years ago. His solution was to treat people experiencing this existential tension with his own approach to psychotherapy, logotherapy. "The task," he said, "is not to bury the existential despair under a heap of tranquillising drugs but rather to pilot the patient through his existential crisis of growth and development. That's to say, assist the patient to find meaning in his life. The therapeutic process tries to make the patient aware of what he actually longs for in the depth of his being."

This is why searching for purpose is so important. Purpose gives us meaning. With meaning, the tension gives us the drive to move forward. Without meaning, the tension creates a vacuum and existential despair. Purpose helps us come to terms with the tension. It helps us realise it's a natural phenomenon, it's a natural feeling, and it's a sign that growth and development are required. It helps us realise that numbing won't help. It helps us bear the necessary pain. It guides us towards a solution that makes us aware of what's going on in our inner spaces, and that provides meaning rather than distraction. It guides us towards a spiritual solution. A solution that helps meet the inner human need to feel fulfilled.

Perhaps purpose requires a bit more work than simply following our human nature. A more involved process may be required. It seems that, in our complex culture of economic growth, our purpose isn't always neatly delivered to us on a silver platter. We need to spend some time and effort working it out and pondering exactly what has meaning for us. But how do we do this?

PURPOSE PERSPECTIVE #2: PURPOSE AS A MEANINGFUL GOAL AND STATEMENT OF INTENT

When confronted with this realisation, I sought out books and websites that offered processes to help me work this out. As a paid-up member of the Brand Strategist Union, I was on the lookout for a purpose statement - my very own statement of intent, my guiding principle, my North Star, my lighthouse, my strap-line. And the pithier the line, the better. It was at this stage that I came across Simon Sinek's Start With Why. The book was positioned along the lines of "Discover the power of purpose and learn how great leaders and organisations inspire action and create a lasting impact." It's an entertaining, concise book that makes perfect sense. Maybe the fact that Sinek has a background in advertising made it even more appealing to me, given my own brand background.

Finding Our Why

In a nutshell, Sinek tells us that our purpose, our "why," the reason we do what we do, should be at the heart of everything we do. It should be where we start. I loved the simplicity of this idea. It made perfect sense.

As a brand strategist, I knew that basing communications on 'why' a brand does things rather than "what" the brand does makes for better, more compelling messaging. I was sold. And so were millions of others. With over sixty-five million views, Sinek's TEDTalk on the subject is one of the most popular of all time. When he released his follow-up book Find Your Why, promoted as "a practical guide on how to dig deep into your past and find your greater purpose." I bought it straight away.

At the end of the Find Your Why process, you are left with a single line that succinctly defines your why, structured as follows:

TO (*the contribution you make*) _____

SO THAT (*the impact of your contribution on the lives of others*)

_____

Examples of WHY statements could be:

- To use my garden design talents so that my neighbourhood becomes a more beautiful place.
- To use my accountancy skills so that single parents can improve their financial stability.
- To inspire my online community so that they can create their dream home on a budget.

This was an incredibly useful tool for me at the time. It got me thinking about what I do, what I'm good at, who I serve, how my service benefits them, and the impact I have. All fantastic stuff, wrapped up in a pithy line.

My Own Purpose Statement

I sought out other books with similar processes and outputs. I tried them all and even developed my own process. After going through my own thorough two-week process, I arrived at the following purpose statement for myself:

To bring spirituality to a logical world.

I was underwhelmed, to say the least. I went through the workings again and again, re-reading book after book to see if I had missed anything. I hadn't. It seemed that my purpose was to bring spirituality to a logical world, whether I liked it or not. And I didn't like it.

This was back in 2017. I had been sober for a year but hadn't embarked on the 12-Step Process. Whist I was curious about spirituality and had dabbled in meditation for a few months, I hadn't had a spiritual awakening. I'd only read a handful of books on the topic and hadn't experienced the joy, peace, freedom, and wholeness that comes with the habits of spiritual happiness. So, this purpose statement wasn't just underwhelming; it was nonsensical.

My head was still reeling from the previous year, having been in and out of rehab and losing my job. I had some money in the bank but no steady income. I needed to support my family and establish myself, showing everyone that I wasn't a washed-up alcoholic. I needed to re-establish myself and thought the best way of doing that was by becoming a financial success. I couldn't see how my purpose of bringing spirituality to a logical world would further that aim. It just didn't make sense to me. I didn't know what to do with it.

So, I ignored it.

I left it in the notebook as a purpose statement and did nothing with it. Seven years on, I now see how profoundly spot-on this statement was - uncannily so. I also see that I wasn't ready to implement my purpose back then. I wasn't ready to act on it and live it. I didn't have the power to bring it to life. It's only when you act on your purpose that you reap the spiritual rewards, and I still had work to do before I was in a position to realise that.

Spiritual Happiness Through Action

This idea of applying ourselves to our purpose to reap the rewards is at the heart of Stephen Cope's book The Great Work of Our Lives: A Guide for the Journey of Your True Calling, which draws on the Hindu concept of dharma and the teachings of the Bhagavad Gita. Cope describes dharma as a potent Sanskrit word packed with meaning, referring to "path, teaching, law, vocation, sacred duty, and above all, truth." Yogis believe that our greatest responsibility in life is to this inner possibility - our dharma - and that every human being's duty is to utterly, fully, and completely embody their own idiosyncratic dharma.

Cope emphasises that people feel happiest and most fulfilled when meeting the challenge of their dharma in the world, bringing highly concentrated effort to a compelling activity for which they have a true calling. Fulfilment happens not in retreat from the world but in profound engagement with it. Spiritual happiness comes from doing, serving, and contributing to life through actions uniquely aligned with our own specific dharma.

However, whilst our dharma is unique to us, it is not chosen by us. It is mysteriously within us at birth. To live a fulfilling life, we must dedicate ourselves to finding out who we are and then act accordingly. When I initially unearthed my purpose statement in 2017, I couldn't act on it because I didn't know who my true self was.

Cope's book spells out the path of dharma as outlined in the Bhagavad Gita, bringing it to life through examples of people who found their true calling. The most profound teaching for me was about doubt - the central problem I've wrestled with throughout my purpose journey. Even sensing that "bringing spirituality to a logical world" was my true calling, I was paralysed with doubt when it came to making decisions to follow that path. What if I didn't make enough money? What if the logical world didn't want to listen? What if I wasn't any good at it?

This is the sort of doubt faced by Arjuna, the central character in the Bhagavad Gita. At a crossroads in his life, not knowing what to do or how to choose, Arjuna is guided by the Hindu God Krishna, who says, "You don't know what to do because you don't know who you are." These words sent chills down my spine when I first read them, and I have found them to be undeniably true.

My doubt, informed by concerns coming from my false self, had always held me back. Only by getting to know my true self could I act on my purpose. This realisation led me on a five-year journey of learning about myself through the 12-Step Process and the spiritual habits of surrender, awareness, discipline, connection, and service. It was through this process that I started to rid myself of doubt and learn about my true and false selves. Seven years after writing my initial purpose statement, I was finally ready - or rather, compelled - to act out my purpose. I finally found the power to act.

The Path to True Self

Finding and acting on one's purpose isn't always a quick and simple process, especially if you don't know what you're doing. Thankfully, I think I do now. My journey has taught me that finding a sense of purpose is related to working towards a meaningful goal. It's related to being of service and acting in the world. I also know that it is possible to figure out our uniquely meaningful purpose and write it down in a statement. However, to successfully act on it, we need to dedicate ourselves to fully understanding who we truly are first. In this way, we could say that the path to purpose and power isn't just a pathway of finding direction; it's also the pathway to finding our authentic, true selves. A pathway we're committed to as we apply ourselves to The Habits of Spiritual Happiness.

PERSPECTIVE #3: PURPOSE AS APPLYING YOUR UNIQUE GIFTS AND TALENTS

I've mentioned Brené Brown a number of times in this book. I like the way Brené speaks spiritual truth in a very down-to-earth and practical way. She tells it how it is from her own perspective. How it is for her as an ordinary person (albeit a very talented and articulate ordinary person.) And I like the fact that she's a researcher. She bases all her findings on data and the thousands of interviews she's done. In her book The Gifts of Imperfection she has a chapter dedicated to Cultivating Meaningful Work. It's a chapter about purpose and what she discovered through her research.

Unsurprisingly, her research told her that finding meaningful work results in people living wholeheartedly. They feel the full rapture of being alive. But it wasn't quite as simple as "go out and find meaningful work and all will be well." It was a bit more complex than that. As she went deeper into her research notes, she came up with a "pesky list" of complications when it comes to finding our purpose and living it. That list included gifts and talents, spirituality, making a living, commitment, supposed to, and self-doubt. Yep – I recognise those complications. So, in true researcher style, she did more research to better understand what finding meaning and purpose is. Here's what she came up with:

- We all have gifts and talents; when we share our unique talents with the world, we create meaning and purpose.
- Squandering our gifts brings distress; we feel disconnected from ourselves, empty, frustrated, resentful, shame, disappointment, fear and even grief.
- Spiritual connection isn't just by looking skyward in stillness. It comes from action. Sharing our gifts to help others is the most powerful way to connect your true self with God.
- Using our gifts and talents to create meaningful work takes tremendous commitment, but it's often not what pays the bills. Maybe a "slash" approach is a practical way to bring meaningful work into your life. Define yourself by all your jobs, not your main wage earner, e.g. "I'm an accountant/DJ" or "I'm a driving instructor/writer" or "I'm a taxi driver/farm volunteer."
- Meaning is unique to each person. No one can define it for us, and it may change over time.

Not a bad set of guidelines. It certainly makes sense and rings true. And I like the way Brené's list builds on the ideas from the Bhagavad Gita. We don't know what to do as we don't know who we are. And that includes what our gifts and talents are.

How many of us have got a got a strong sense of what our real gifts and talents are? I knew that I was a relatively creative person. And I wasn't bad at writing. But I didn't realise I could write 3,000 words a day until I tried writing this book. I didn't know how much I would relish the process. I didn't realise how meaningful I would find it until I actually did it. As Brené says, spiritual connection can come from action.

Being true to our nature, working towards a meaningful goal, knowing ourselves and applying our gifts and talents seem to be the key themes so far. But there's one final insight into purpose that I believe underpins all the insights discussed so far. And that's why it's such an important one.

PURPOSE PERSPECTIVE #4: PURPOSE AS A COMBINATION OF INNER AND OUTER PURPOSE

As part of my exploration into purpose and the quest to find my own, another key insight arose when I read Eckhart Tolle's The Power of Now. As with The Great Work of Your Life and also Thich Nhat Hahn's The Art of Living, this book landed so many "aha" moments of truth. The largest of them all was when Tolle described what he called our inner purpose and our outer purpose.

Having a meaningful goal and statement of intent certainly gives us a clue of where our purpose may lie. I had a purpose statement of "Bringing spirituality to a logical world." And from that perspective, Tolle would say I had an outer purpose. He explains that it's certainly helpful to know where you're going but he also suggests that most people "completely miss the inner purpose which has nothing to do with where you are going or what you are doing but everything to do with how. The outer purpose belongs to the horizontal dimension of space and time; the inner purpose concerns a deepening of your being on the vertical dimension of the timeless Now. Your outer journey may contain a million steps; your inner journey only has one: the step you are taking right now."

I love the picture Tolle paints with the horizontal line of outer purpose and the journey of "doing" comprised of a thousand consecutive steps, intersected by the vertical line of inner purpose and the journey of "being" comprised of the single step we're taking now. Stunning insight.

Tolle goes on to say that it's important to be conscious of both your outer and inner purpose, but always to remember the primacy of the inner purpose of being. "True change" he says, "happens within, not without."

A sentiment that is echoed by Thich Nhat Hahn is, "We have a tendency to think in terms of doing and not in terms of being. Our time is, first of all, for us to be. To be what? To be alive, to be peaceful, to be joyful, to be loving. And this is what the world needs the most. We all need to train ourselves in our way of being, and that is the ground for all action."

Yet more stunning insight. Yet more clues on how to find and live our purpose. This brings me to my summary of all this learning; purpose as fulfilling our soul's desire. This comes in two specific parts. The first part is hearing our calling and recognising it as such. The second part is acting on it by having the power, faith and commitment to do so.

BRINGING ALL PURPOSE PERSPECTIVES TOGETHER:

Purpose as Fulfilling Our Soul's Desire: Hearing Our Calling and Getting into Action

As part of my spiritual journey, I've often wrestled with the nature of desire. On one hand, desire can be destructive; yearning stirs up unpleasant feelings like greed, jealousy, resentment, and selfishness. The Buddha taught that craving is the root of all suffering. From this view, desire seems inherently problematic.

Yet, try as I might, I can't stop myself from desiring things. Some desires, like craving junk food, are clearly unhealthy. But other desires feel worthwhile, even noble. Wanting to provide a comfortable home for my children so they don't live in poverty - is that wrong? Or my strong compulsion to write this very book - is that misguided? What about the desire to walk a spiritual path? How do we make sense of desire if our deeper purpose often manifests as a yearning of the soul?

Aimlessness: Removing the Goal

Buddhists advise contemplating aimlessness to answer these questions. Aimlessness means removing the object of pursuit. It means letting go of fixed goals. If you want to realise nirvana, don't run after it, know that nirvana is already there in this moment, in yourself and in everything. If you want to realise Buddhahood, don't chase the Buddha; be aware that the Buddha is already in you. Now. The point is not to focus on the fixed goal that you want to achieve in the future. It's okay to have a goal and an aspirational direction. Don't focus on achieving the specifics. Instead, focus on the present moment and act as guided by your own true self.

As Thich Nhat Hanh so eloquently puts it: "To practice aimlessness doesn't mean we don't have dreams or aspirations...it means staying in touch with the ultimate dimension in the present moment, so we can realise our dreams with joy, ease and freedom. Each of us has a deep desire to accomplish something meaningful in our lifetime. This isn't just a fleeting wish but a profound intention that may have taken root in our hearts from a young age. This is our dearest dream, our ultimate concern. When we identify and nurture our deepest desire, it becomes a wellspring of happiness, energy and motivation - providing us with drive and direction to carry us through life's challenges."

Discerning Your Soul's Calling

This perspective perfectly captures what finding and living our purpose looks and feels like. It's about recognising the dream or aspiration residing deep in your soul. You may not be fully aware of it yet, but chances are it's been lying dormant within you since youth. This is your calling.

Once you recognise your calling as your soul's truest desire, you must put it into action - but action anchored in the present, not fixated on future outcomes. Release attachment to the end goal and pour yourself fully into the work at hand. Now is when we experience a sense of purpose and a sense of flow. Now is when we feel that profound fulfilment. Now enables us to invest 100% in today's endeavours without the anxiety of results.

This is how we access the wellspring of happiness, energy and motivation Thich Nhat Hanh describes. It's how we find flow as an ongoing way of being. This is the power of purpose lived in the Eternal Now. Arriving at this state of flow takes time, diligence, patience, and courage. We must learn to discern our soul's pure desires from the cravings of the ego. We must distinguish our true self's deepest longings from the false self's selfish wants. We must understand the difference between the will of the Divine and the misguided whims of the small self. And I believe this discernment develops as we progress further along our spiritual path using the habits of spiritual happiness.

The more we surrender, cultivate awareness, commit to disciplined spiritual practice, feel a sense of connection, and are of service – the more readily we can distinguish between soulful desire and selfish desire. This enables us to hear our authentic calling with increasing clarity. The spiritual journey supports us in the first phase of finding and embodying our purpose. Then, once we recognise our true calling, we need the power to carry it out. This power comes from faith, courage, commitment, and strength. This power allows us to translate the still, small voice into committed action. These are all qualities we develop as we delve deeper spiritually.

The Spiritual Pathway to Purpose and Power

This is why the spiritual journey is at the heart of the purpose process. First, it helps us discern the soul's deepest desire. Second, it fortifies us with the inner resources to fulfil that desire. Recognising and enacting our soul's purpose is thus a two-stage spiritual process - one that unfolds gradually as we progress along the path of spiritual awakening. The more we surrender, the more aware we are, the more disciplined our spiritual practices are, the more connected we feel and the more service we do, the more able we are to hear our calling and find the wherewithal to carry it out.

Through this ongoing journey of growth and self-discovery, we come to know, trust and boldly live out the unique purpose we're each destined to fulfil. But first, we need to be able to discern our soul's desire from our selfish desires.

PURPOSE: HEARING OUR CALLING

Finding and living our purpose is a spiritual process and a spiritual practice. Finding meaning is a task of the soul, residing in the realm of spirit and our true self. We've likened the spiritual journey to the archetypal Hero's Journey as described by Joseph Campbell. Finding and living our purpose is a continuation of that journey, the next part of the adventure.

Like any adventure, there will be trials and tribulations, difficulties, disappointments, and no doubt some tears. But ever-deepening levels of fulfilment, freedom, wholeness, peace and joy await those adventurers who stay on course. As we travel further along this road, we start to hear our calling - the recognition that our soul is asking us to fulfil its hidden desire. Discerning a soul-centred yearning from an egotistical craving to be a sparkling success is the task of a lifetime. Having had a spiritual awakening, we are better positioned to distinguish God's will from our own.

Attuning to the Still, Small Voice

By adhering to The Habits of Surrender, Discipline, Awareness, Connection, and Service, we become more attuned to the still, small voice that calls us forward and more aware of the distracting and destructive clamours of our false self's need for comfort and security.

Hearing that calling is an art form. It requires being in touch with our intuitive, soulful, right-hand hemisphere and how it connects and communicates with the world around us. Writing down a meaningful goal and statement of intent, like "bringing spirituality to a logical world," can help give direction. But that's a very logical, left-hemisphere thing to do. It keeps our rational, false self happy as an articulation of our calling, but it's not the calling itself.

I experience the calling as a sensation, an experienced, emergent quality felt in the moment. It's the sense of purpose we feel when taking action that has meaning for us. Our calling will emerge as we experiment with service and being helpful to those we are connected to. But it's still a subtle intuition we're looking for. So, how will we recognise it when we sense it?

Rumi suggests you recognise your calling as a subtle form of desire and love: "Let yourself be silently drawn by the stronger pull of what you really love."

Philip Shepherd says you recognise your calling: "When the wild peace of the presence nourishes your being, you will feel yourself held by it even as it calls you to action. You need not ask, 'What do I need? What should I do? What would make me feel better?' Standing in the presence of that sensitive, mindful whole – the Thou of the presence – you whisper, 'What do you ask of me?' And with that question, the hero's quest is ignited. In service to the wild peace of the whole, helping it to newly harmonise."

Using Suffering and Gifts as Guides

Shepherd's suggestion guides us towards service and "harmonising the whole" as clues to recognising our calling. When we attune ourselves to the world around us and hone our response-ability, we can sense when things aren't working well, when the "whole" is not in harmony, and we feel the suffering it causes. As we do so, we sense a particular type of suffering. A suffering that we're familiar with because we've experienced it ourselves. As Stephen Cope puts it, "Those of us who have been in bondage and have made the journey to freedom are particularly touched by the suffering of others who are still in shackles."

That's one of the reasons why I am writing this book. I am particularly touched when I see others who are affected by the suffering I endured. A specific type of suffering that I suspect is caused directly by us being blindly shackled to our culture of economic growth. Especially when our soul is calling us in another direction. I am touched by those who suffer as they valiantly try to succeed but are unaware of the toxic nature of success based on junk values. I am touched by those who drive themselves into further pain by numbing away the discomfort. I am touched by those tortured by the pain of addiction.

Having made the journey towards freedom, I hear this shackled suffering calling me. I believe I have a solution to that suffering. I believe the spiritual journey is that solution. Or one of the solutions. And I feel compelled to share it with others.

The Intersection of Gift, Wound, and Times

Our calling may pull on the heartstrings of our own suffering, but it will also appeal to our gifts and talents. As Cope identified: "Dharma (our calling) is born mysteriously between The Gift (the talents we have to offer the world) and (being of service to) The Times. Dharma is a response to the urgent – though often hidden – need of the moment. Each of us feels some aspect of the world's suffering acutely. It tears at our heart. Others don't see it or don't care. But we feel it. And we must pay attention. We must act. This little corner of the world is ours to transform. This little corner of the world is ours to save."

I love Cope's insight into recognising our calling as the intersection of our gift (the talents and skills we have to give the world), the wound (the suffering we've felt and found some form of freedom from), and the times (the call of our times and what our suffering world needs now). When I find myself acting at the intersection of these three things, I know I find meaning. I come alive. This is when service doesn't feel like a chore. Your purpose won't call you to do something you can't do. It won't call you to a hard but bearable job. It will call you to become yourself, and you will come alive when you find the power to act upon it.

Giving What We Have: The Path to Freedom

There is a caution to acting on this calling: we can't give what we don't have. You may find the perfect intersection of the wound, the gift, and the times, but if you haven't experienced the full path to freedom, you may not be able to help. We can only give what we have.

I'm acutely conscious of this fact. Perhaps the reason I didn't act on my purpose to "bring spirituality to a logical world" back in 2017 was that I didn't have access to the full path to freedom, just part of it. And maybe I'm not aware of the full path even now. But I sense that I now have enough experience of freedom and purpose to encourage those who are suffering towards the same path. I can encourage them to join me on the journey. And maybe together we can discover the full path to freedom.

Another important part of the calling is that as we heal others of the suffering we experienced, we heal ourselves. We receive as we give it away. The more we give, the more we receive. The healing spurs us on to do more and be more. William James said it like this: "I suddenly heard as it were these words: 'You will be healed and do a great work you never dreamed of.'"

We recognise our calling when we see a need that others might not notice. We notice it because we're acutely aware of the suffering we see in the faces of those around us. It's a specific type of suffering that we recognise in an instant, and we instantly know we can help. James continued his experience: "We have drunk too deeply of the cup of bitterness to ever forget its taste. We have realised a good which broke the effective edge of the shadow. We could and did find something welling up in the inner reaches of our consciousness by which extreme sadness can be overcome." We know the bitter taste. We know the antidote. The "something" welling up inside which can overcome great sadness is the "something" we want to share. It's the "something" we have, and have to have, in order to give it away.

Small As Large

Cope also advises us to "think of the small as large" when recognising our calling. Our calling may draw us towards seemingly small acts of kindness that may feel insignificant. Our purpose may not reveal itself as a movement to change the world or revolutionise the human race. It may reveal itself as a continuous string of small moments of healing. Each moment counts. It's important to acknowledge your part as important, no matter how trivial it might seem to you. It might not feel trivial to those you've helped. I remember a friend telling me how some advice I gave him changed his life. He even mentioned it on a podcast. I never would have thought it would have had the impact it did, but I'm glad I told him. And who knows where your small acts of healing will lead? Who knows what one small healing offered in the here and now will lead to in the fullness of time?

The Barriers to Hearing Our Calling

Despite all the advice and guidance available, hearing that still small voice of our calling remains a tricky task. In her book Hearing Our Calling, Gill Coombs identifies sixteen barriers that prevent us from recognising our true purpose. She asserts, "Every single person has a purpose. It doesn't have to be grand or mystical: we are parts of a greater whole, and we all have our unique role to play in maintaining our whole's health and well-being. But maybe we don't hear because..." and she goes on to identify various obstacles that can hinder our ability to hear and respond to our calling.

- **Passivity**: Waiting for things to come to us rather than creating them.
- **Sensible advice:** Well-meaning advice pointing our careers in a certain direction.
- **Childhood humiliation:** The things we're told at an early age "we're no good at."

- **Lack of compassion:** If we do not care about others and the world around us, we will not respond.
- **Inappropriate education:** Our current education system is geared more towards feeding the culture of economic growth than it is supporting us in finding our true vocation.
- **Isolation:** We tend to struggle with our search for meaning on our own. Maybe we're too scared to admit that we are unfulfilled with the job we have and our role in life. Engaging with our community opens up opportunities to serve.
- **Context:** Hearing our calling becomes all the harder if our friends, family, culture, or place don't support us. If our current context is a barrier, maybe it's time to find "our tribe" as part of the purpose process.
- **Conformity:** Fear of following an unconventional path can hamper many of our attempts to hear and follow our calling, despite our current culture of economic growth and the way we work being a relatively modern norm.
- **Fairness versus reciprocity:** Sometimes, we withhold our urge to serve others because we feel "we've done enough" or "it's somebody else's turn." This happens because we don't see much reciprocity in our current culture, which can be selfishly entitled. "It's not fair that I do all the work" is a mindset I'm guilty of holding on to, but one that steers us only towards work that is directly rewarded for our efforts if we're not mindful.
- **Status anxiety:** We miss our true calling because we're too attached to the status we've earned in earlier life. We're too proud to do something that might be good for the soul but bad for the image. This is another barrier I've had to grapple with.
- **Excessive modesty:** Conversely, don't let your calling pass you by because you worry that you're not good enough. Don't let the gremlins of "people will think I'm doing something beyond my capabilities" or "who am I to put myself forward for this?"

- **Depression:** When we're depressed, our natural energy is low, we withdraw from life and lose our capacity to care for others. We lose our response-ability. Ironically, depression can be a symptom of not having a sense of purpose. And it may inhibit you from finding one.
- **Unfitness:** When we're physically unfit, we tend to languish in survival mode rather than being alert and energised by the possibilities life presents to us.
- **Unseen illness:** With so many toxins in our food, water, and air, as well as the pollution in and around our homes, we're probably carrying unknown health issues that are keeping us from 100% peak condition and from hearing our subtle calling.

I list these fourteen as they may well show up in your life, and it's useful to know what may be blocking your path to purpose and power. They all feel like pertinent and credible barriers. I recognise many of them, and I feel the truth in all of them. However, I want to highlight the final two barriers and give them special attention. These are the two barriers that stopped me from hearing my calling for so many years: fear and distraction.

Fear and Distraction: The Two Big Barriers

Fear, in all its guises, has been a dominant force in my life. It has stopped me countless times from following my soul's desire, driving me back to the path of conventional thinking and junk values. Coombes captures this fear eloquently: "Fear lies just below the surface of many of the preceding factors. In a society where norms of economic growth, competition, and conformity are so explicit, the emergence of values-based, intuitive ideas is repressed through (often unconscious) fear: fear of control, ridicule, or being excluded. Fear also keeps us from relinquishing our tight grasp on the familiar; whispers to us of all that could go wrong if we dare to follow our calling. Fear tries to keep us safe, although our perception of danger may be out of date."

Distraction, which Coombes describes as "busy-ness," is another significant barrier. She explains it as "losing our capacity for reverie" through disconnection, which "leaves a feeling of emptiness without stimulation: displacement activities such as television, consumption, social media, or being busy at work – even if the work is unfulfilling." This echoes the concept of the "hole in the soul" that emerges as we focus our efforts on gaining conditional happiness and accumulating material wealth. Coombes emphasises the importance of reverie, stating, "Reverie is essential for big ideas to emerge, connections to be made, spirituality to be experienced. What ideas and aspirations might emerge if we allowed ourselves to indulge in reverie every day?"

Breaking Through Fear and Distraction

For me, The 12-Step Programme of Recovery was the way I was able to break through the fear and distractions that kept me from spiritual experiences and my purpose. As these barriers subsided, thanks to the habits of spiritual happiness, I am now able to hear my calling much more clearly. I am more attuned to it. The spiritual solution helps me overcome these fears and distractions on a daily basis, a process that continues to deepen and become clearer with each passing day.

I sense my purpose is evolving to help others break through their fears and distractions, enabling them to hear their own calling more clearly using the spiritual process and habits I've outlined in this book. I also sense that I should focus my efforts in places where "reverie" and "spirituality" may feel marginalised, such as workplaces entrenched in a culture of economic growth.

The Role of Subjectivity in Purpose: Driven Workplaces

In these workplaces, I know that another barrier will be the mindset that "objectivity" is king. Businesses tend to be run as impersonal and objective entities. That means they tend to use impartial, distant, factually verifiable data. This type of information is valued because it is believed to be true.

"Subjectivity," on the other hand, tends to be avoided. That's because we currently associate subjective views with idiosyncrasy and bias. There is doubt inherent with a subjective point of view because there are no verifiable facts. And facts don't lie.

Businesses believe they need to base decisions on robust facts, not hunches or hobbyhorses. I understand why this mentality prevails, but I would like to put forward a counterargument.

If we are to promote purpose in the workplace and highlight all the many benefits businesses can realise as a result of building a workforce driven by meaning rather than money, we have to recognise that meaning is personal, felt and idiosyncratic by nature. It is known only from the inside. It cannot be verified from the outside. Therefore, businesses that want to be more purpose-driven have to become more comfortable with the fact that one of its primary performance indicators, how purposeful its workforce feels, is a purely subjective one.

While there may be attempts to quantify purpose and track it, we risk missing the point if we do so. Trying to turn the purely subjective into something tangible and objective is a temptation because businesses are more comfortable in that mode. However, purpose and meaning aren't there to be measured; they are there to be experienced, relished, and developed, just like our spiritual happiness and our experience of life.

As Gary Vaynerchuk once asked, "What's the Return on Investment (ROI) of your mother?" It's not a metric you want to measure, and I believe the same applies to purpose and meaning in the workplace. They are inherent in the work that's done, the culture that evolves, and the well-being of everyone involved. They are not separate "things" that can be measured in isolation. However, businesses need to be comfortable with promoting a policy that may not be easily quantified.

Coombes concludes her section on the barriers to hearing our calling with this powerful statement: "Given all the factors working against us, our quest to find our calling isn't simple as we make our way through a sometimes bewildering world, taking turnings that lead to dead ends or disappointment. But when we do hear our calling and are able to respond, it's good for us, good for those around us, and good for the entire community of our planet home." This beautifully illustrates the win-win-win nature of purpose working in the workplace. And spirituality in action in the world.

The Emergent Nature of Purpose

As we come to the end of this section about hearing our calling, I want to leave you with two passages that I believe both point to the dynamic nature of purpose and how it emerges for us. I experienced that emergence as a result of following The Habits of Spiritual Happiness, surrendering more, becoming more aware, being more disciplined, connecting more, being of service and being more useful.

The two passages, written by Shepherd and Coombes, allude to similar journeys but do so in slightly different ways. I don't believe there is only one way to hear your calling. By reading these two passages, I hope you sense that embracing the Hero's Journey is a path you don't necessarily have to choose, as it's a path you're already on.

Gill Coombes summarised the purpose process as follows: "In the perpetual moment between past and future, with its subtle sense of infinite possibilities, we are constantly becoming ourselves through a complex mix of emergence, intention and flow. It's possible that as we develop greater consciousness, we come to comprehend purpose rather than construct it. Will or intention, combined with the path of least resistance already laid down by our innate qualities and our acquired values, together show a harmonious, dynamic flow. This means we don't sit and wait, and the universe will eventually drop your life's work beautifully and neatly on your lap. But it also means you don't go out and force things to happen that aren't the right things. It means you actively and gently experiment, testing different directions and being sensitive to circumstances until you find a way that yields like honey. That's when you'll find yourself gaining momentum. You'll find yourself in flow, and you will know you are on the right path. There's not one right path. Just as there isn't one Mr or Mrs Right. And rightness can and does change over time. Perceive your path and actions rather than judge them."

Philip Shepherd describes the process this way: "There is a gravity that is calling to your heart, and that loves you in all your brokenness. It is gently inviting you into a dance of surrender to your wholeness – a surrender to its freedom, passions, and luminous truths and its provisions for unconditional service. That dance of surrender does not end, and it isn't without risk – but it is a dance that could not be more deeply grounded in the security of being. And when you take a chance on that dance and venture even one step into its wild peace, you will be helping us all."

Both of these passages inspire me to keep on journeying through the dynamic process of hearing my calling. I feel my past pushing me towards my purpose. And I sense my future, drawing me closer to it. I willingly take those risky steps into "wild peace" and surrender to the dance of life.

It's an exhilarating process. But there's no escaping from the fact that our culture puts up many barriers to finding and acting on our purpose. It is a tricky thing to do. And it does feel very risky sometimes. Hearing our calling and responding to it, is the journey of a hero. A journey that requires faith. Faith that the universe is on our side. Faith that a God of our understanding can help. Faith in spiritual habits that we don't yet understand or like. Faith in our ability to discern our soul's desires from our ego's wants. Faith that if we begin this journey by surrendering to it, all will be well.

At some point, I believe we all have to come face to face with faith. We may choose not to act on faith. We may choose to let fear and distractions keep our purpose and spiritual experience at a distance. For many, there will come a point where fear and distractions can no longer contain the pain we are feeling from keeping our calling at bay. We will come to a point where we ask ourselves, "How much fulfilment am I willing to forgo? How much disappointment and suffering am I willing to bear in order not to keep my purpose buried deep inside?" When the lack of fulfilment and suffering is enough, we will finally be ready to surrender and take action.

When I reached that point, one quote struck me and spurred me into action. It was a quote from Jesus in the Gnostic Gospel of Thomas: "If you bring forth what is within you, what you bring forth will save you. If you do not bring forth what is within you, what you do not bring forth will destroy you."

As I contemplated the calling, I sensed I had to write this book. I felt it was a path calling me towards freedom and peace. A path that would save me from confusion and fear. More than being saved, though, I sensed that not acting on this calling would cause no end of harm and pain. I felt that "dying with the music inside me" could destroy me. That was the conviction I needed to put faith into action and heed to call to adventure.

POWER: GETTING INTO ACTION

The Dance of Purpose: Being and Doing

I sense that moving towards a more purposeful life is indeed a dance, as Shepherd describes above. In my mind, it's a two-step dance. The first step is hearing our calling. This is all about being and sensing—being our true selves and sensing the world around us. The second step is getting into action. This is all about finding the power and doing what we're meant to do.

In a world obsessed with doing, you'd think that the second step would suit us down to the ground. But unfortunately, not quite. We are used to acting, but usually, we act more from our false selves than our true selves. We're used to acting when it suits us - when there's something in it for us. When we can see the direct benefit to us and demand something in return. This is the sort of action that is readily supported by our society, the sort of action that shows the world we're doing well because we've got a good job, are gainfully employed and are paying the bills. It shows we are responsible adults. Only we're not. We're adults conforming to the norms of our culture of economic growth.

Now, there's nothing inherently wrong with that. I did it for many, many years and benefited from the material gains that came with it. But it did come at a price - a price of discontentment, restlessness and anxiety that, after a while, became unbearable.

As we start to hear the calling of our true selves, we will hear the call towards a life of purpose, meaning, and fulfilment. If you're anything like me, you will be terrified to follow that path. You will be filled with fear, filled with two particular types of fear: fear of poverty and fear of criticism.

Napoleon Hill highlighted both these types of fear in his book Think and Grow Rich. Despite the book's obsession with success based predominantly on financial gain (which is understandable as it was written just after the Great Depression, when financial anxiety gripped virtually everyone in the US), it is quite a spiritual book. That's why I believe there is some merit in Hill's analysis of the fear that stops us from doing what we know to be true to our soul's desire.

The Paralysing Fears: Poverty and Criticism

Hill describes the fear of poverty as one of life's most destructive fears. It can lead to a negative state of mind, significantly affecting our ability to get on and do what we feel is the right thing to do. He suggests that this fear manifests itself in a variety of symptoms, such as indifference, indecision, doubt, worry, over-caution, and procrastination. The root cause of this fear is financial insecurity, and it's this insecurity that can lead us to compromise our values and stop us from travelling further down the pathway to purpose.

On the other hand, the fear of criticism is rooted in our desire for social acceptance and our aversion to being judged negatively by others. Hill contends that this fear can severely limit our willingness to take risks or pursue unconventional ideas, leading to a lack of innovation and progress. Symptoms of this fear include self-consciousness, lack of poise, an inferiority complex, extravagance, and lack of initiative.

I recognise both these forms of fear intimately. They have stopped me from doing so many things in life that would have brought me joy and freedom - things that I now believe would have moved me closer to my purpose earlier in life. But instead, my fears kept me from doing those things and kept me firmly rooted in the culture of economic growth.

Looking at these fears and addressing them has been a big part of my spiritual journey and is at the heart of The 12-Step Programme. In my first stint of sobriety, I was told about The 12-Step Programme and some of the benefits it can deliver. These benefits are often called "the promises," The full list of promises makes a compelling argument for why you might want to embark on the programme. They include knowing a new freedom and a new happiness, comprehending the word serenity, the disappearance of feelings of uselessness and self-pity, as well as a change in our whole attitude and outlook on life. These are enticing promises to anyone, let alone those desperately suffering in active addiction.

One promise, however, rose above the rest for me. It reads: "Fear of people and economic insecurity will leave us." That's what had been hampering me all those years - fear of people criticising me and fear of not having enough money. I could hardly believe what I was reading. My mind was in a spin. I was so excited. "So, what you're telling me is that if I do these 12 Steps, people will stop criticising me, and I'll have enough money for me and my family to live on?" That's a promise and a half. Sign me up. That's what I thought would happen. No more criticism. And plenty of income. That's what I wanted to happen. But that's not what the promise is.

The promise made is not about people stopping their criticism or about me gaining financial security. The promise is about not being afraid of those things. It is the fear inside us that will leave; it is not circumstances outside us that will necessarily change. Although it's fair to say that external relationships and circumstances are bound to improve once we stop drinking ourselves into the ground.

Finding the Power to be Fearless on the Journey

This, for me, is one of the life-changing benefits of the habits of spiritual happiness as we embark on our purposeful journey to follow our calling. There are no promises of financial riches or immunity from criticism when we start following our soul's desire. But what we do have, and can constantly nurture, is a fearless attitude - a fearlessness that is powered by faith in the spiritual path and allows us to overcome those barriers to action and step boldly onto the path of purpose.

This is the dance of purpose and power - the dynamic interplay between being our true selves, sensing our calling in the world, and courageously stepping into aligned action, even in the face of fear, by tapping into our Higher Power. It is a dance that requires both stillness and movement, introspection and expression, faith and works, love and strength, peace and fortitude. It is a dance that, with practice and perseverance, can lead us to a life of profound meaning, joy, and service.

The Risky Nature of Following Your Calling

We have said it before, but it bears repeating: "Faith without works is dead." The quickest way to know your truth is to live your truth. You may have sensed your calling through intuition, conscious contact with your Higher Power, or a God-given path. No matter how your calling comes to you, you must play an active role in God's plan. You have to take action. You can't expect fate, your Higher Power, or your God to do for you what He, She or It can only do through you or with you. You must break through any inner resistance and put in the work.

I realise it's easy to say those words but much harder to put them into action. When I've gone through this purpose process with others, the sticking point invariably comes when the fears of financial insecurity and the prospect of criticism loom large and stop them from doing what their heart is telling them. They may have a clear idea of their calling, but the reality of mortgages, bills, and family obligations become too onerous. Money becomes the barrier to taking action.

I don't want to encourage reckless decisions that may jeopardise livelihoods and put families' well-being at risk. I don't want everyone to give up their well-paid job to pursue a life as a yoga instructor. Or do I? Would that really be so bad?

In our late teens and twenties, we tend to seek work that allows us to achieve independence. The drivers are often financial, to afford independent living, and status-related, to achieve self-worth. This is what Stephen Cope calls our "identity project"- a project driven by our logical, egoic, false self. The issue of purpose and calling tends to arise when we reach adulthood, with unsettling murmurings often beginning in our late thirties and growing stronger as we hit the midlife years of forty-five through fifty-five. At this point, we start turning our thoughts towards our true self's desires and what this may mean for how we spend the last decades of our lives. Wayne Dyer alludes to this change in midlife perspective in his book The Shift.

The big problem is, however, that as we age and our midlife responsibilities to both younger and older generations seem never-ending, it becomes increasingly difficult to act on our authentic calling. It feels like a risky reinvention, with the stakes higher due to those responsibilities. Taking a leap into an uncertain calling can seem like too much upheaval for those around us. We may feel that such leaps are better left to younger people who have less to lose. Younger people don't sense the calling as strongly as we do in midlife. Midlife is when we are most likely to hear the call to action - to fully use our gifts in service of our times, despite the responsibilities and fears.

Stephen Cope speaks of the fear of taking the leap and compares it to the story of Arjuna and Krishna in the Bhagavad Gita. Krishna tells Arjuna that he cannot hold onto his life and asks, "Why not use yourself up giving everything you've got to the world?" There's no escaping the risky nature of following your calling. It always involves jumping off a cliff at some point, with no guarantees. We need to have faith in God, in ourselves, and in the leap itself.

One could argue that it is perfectly possible to muddle through this midlife calling without taking a leap. We could cling to our old life and job while trying out the calling in our spare time. We don't have to give up being an operations director at a big tech company to try being a yoga instructor on weekends. We could try out the "slash" career for a while.   Be an operations director/yoga instructor, a marketing director/urban gardener, a brand strategist/writer. The "slash" career idea allows us to experiment without risking everything, acknowledging that every small act of purpose matters on the journey from one chapter to the next. It recognises that we're always in transition, taking one step at a time.

There's another sound reason why muddling through without taking the big leap might be wise: when it comes to purpose, we should treat the small as big. Our calling could start by simply helping a friend in need. That small act is being of service, coming from a place of love. It may be a big deal to the person you've helped, and you don't know where that act may lead.

Building Faith and Building Power

Whilst I want to say that this softly, easy approach to getting into action works, a big part of me is screaming, "Is that truly getting into purposeful action?" I can't help but think this playing-it-safe approach is simply pandering to the fears of financial insecurity and criticism. I sense the hesitation in the compromise. I feel the lack of surrender and the lack of faith.

There's something supremely powerful in surrendering to faith and belief. I can't explain it, but I know it plays a huge part in the spiritual journey, specifically in taking the leap into purpose. Without faith, progress may be limited. With faith, it's limitless. Faith is the source of power.

In The 12-Step Programme, the foundational Steps 2 and 3 are about belief and faith. Belief that a God of our understanding can return us to sanity, and enough faith in that God to hand over our lives and will. They are massive leaps, especially if you're coming to the steps with no conception of or connection to a Higher Power. But without taking these leaps, the results can be limited.

Those with belief and faith seem to have much less trouble making the leap. They have every faith that God will do for them what they can't do for themselves. I love Emmet Fox's confidence when he talks about getting into action and following your calling:

"If only you will find out the thing God intends you to do and do it, you will find that all doors will open to you; all obstacles in your path will melt away; you will be acclaimed a brilliant success; you will be most liberally rewarded monetarily; you will be gloriously happy. There is a true place in life for each one of us, upon the attainment of which we shall be completely happy and perfectly secure."

How wonderful it would be to have Emmet's confidence and faith. There's no equivocation in his words: Do as God intends, follow your calling, and you'll be financially rewarded, happy, and secure. I'm all in!

However, I can't help but think, "That's all well and good for you, Emmet, but you don't have the responsibilities and worries I have." And therein lies the problem. I have gremlins of doubt - self-doubt and doubt about God's ability to melt away all obstacles in my specific path. Gremlins that lack belief and faith. These are the gremlins that will undermine the process of me finding the power to fulfil my soul's desire. As Henry Ford said, "There are two types of people. Those who believe they can do something and those who believe they can't. They are both right."

The key is that we can't let fear undermine our faith. Faith is built up and nurtured through The Habits of Surrender, Awareness, Discipline, Connection, and Service. This process nurtures our soul and restores our true self as our rightful master. It takes time and patience. This is where our newfound power lies. We find the power to put our purpose into action by nurturing more and more faith in the intuitive way our true self guides us. We feel the benefits of this newfound power. It gives us the security we need in an uncertain future that all will be well. It allows us to surrender to The Habits of Spiritual Happiness and deeper into our calling. It allows us to surrender to our inner and outer purposes. The more we surrender, the more our sense of freedom, peace, wholeness, joy, and fulfilment deepen and grow.

This ongoing process should spur us on to further action when we hear that still, small voice guiding us, beckoning us further down the road. But fear will always be there, in the form of other people's opinions and definitions of success as defined by our culture of economic growth—a culture that wants to pull us back to its junk values. This creates a tension between where our soul's desire wants to take us and what our culture thinks about us going there.

This is the cross we have to bear as people wanting to experience the full rapture of being alive. We have to bear the tension of holding these two worlds together. If we revert to the false idols of financial success, status, and security or distract ourselves from the discomfort, we turn the tension into suffering. We're also adding to the unhealthy, co-dependent nature of our addictive culture. A culture that requires us to yearn for material gain and status for it to succeed. A culture within which we feel the need to chase material gain and status for us to succeed. Reverting to false idols makes us the product of our old culture.

But we can resist the temptation to revert to the old junk values to relieve the tension. We can reaffirm our commitment to spiritual happiness not conditional happiness. We can draw on the spiritual tools of meditation, prayer, and contemplation to strengthen our resolve. We can tap into our newfound source of power to move us ever forward and deeper into purposeful action. In doing so, we co-create the seeds of a new culture. Following our calling makes us the producer of a new culture.

So, when you feel the tension of faith versus fear arising, don't be co-dependent. Don't let the fear win out. Be co-creative. Tap into your newfound Higher Power and let your faith lead the way.

For those who have discerned their calling and are on the verge of moving into action, there are bound to be doubts. There are bound to be uncertainties about the viability of the new path and what it will deliver. There are bound to be thoughts of success and failure. This is where faith comes in. Faith that is built up over time by taking action. Faith that accumulates the more you do. Hear the calling, take the leap, take the action, sense the benefits of spiritual happiness, and have faith in your calling to take more action. Have faith to go deeper into your purpose.

Obviously, not all actions will lead to success. There is a chance of failure. But be mindful of how that failure is defined and who has defined it. Be mindful that failure in a culture of economic growth may be a success for those seeking spiritual happiness. Even if it feels like a failure, don't be disheartened. Feel the tension. Feel the feelings. Pick up the tools and spiritual habits, convert those feelings of failure into co-creative energy, and go again. Be persistent. Be still. Don't let fear win out. Reconnect to your Higher Power. Recommit to your soul's desire. Renew your faith in your calling.

The path of faith and power is a path of surrender and letting go. It's a path of turning over the results of our work and actions to the care of our Higher Power. It's a matter of walking by faith. Doing by faith and not getting too hung up on the results. Our job is to focus on the task at hand. The universe will dictate what the results will be. We can't control as much as our logical, egoic, false selves would love to think we can. The more we walk by faith, the more we learn to surrender our will and our lives over to the care of the universe, and the more we'll feel the power to act on purpose. The more we will empower our response-ability. This is how we learn to let go and let God. To let go and let life flow.

This is how we make our purpose a viable option. We keep going. We follow our "guidance system." We tap into our Higher Power. We take action and wait for further guidance. We build our faith through action. We build faith in our guidance system. Faith and action reinforce each other. Together, they are "fire and gasoline," as Stephen Cope describes it. Discerning our calling and putting it into action strengthens our faith. They beautifully re-enforce each other.

I have to admit that the path to purpose and power via action and faith does sound a little daunting. And a bit scary. It certainly felt like that for me when I decided to give up paid work for six months to write this book. It felt like I needed all the faith I could muster to overcome the fear of financial insecurity and criticism. I've found the process of writing to be so fulfilling. It really has lifted my spirits. It's delivered lots of spiritual happiness. And it is starting to open up the next stage of my calling. I sense I'm being guided to investigate ways to make this book into a course or take it into businesses. I'm not at that stage yet. Just for today, my purpose is to write this page for this book. And I thank God that I've been given the power to put my purpose into action.

THE THRILL OF ENTHUSIASTIC ACTION

One thing is for sure, as and when the next phase of my calling starts to become clearer, I know I'll feel less daunted by the next leap. In fact, I'll probably be excited by the prospect. I think this is due to the process of building my faith having taken the first big leap to write this book in the first place. It's also due to the positive mindset that I believe my stronger faith has revealed.

I can best describe this more positive mindset using an observation by Daniel Seigel about how enthusiastically adolescents take on life.

Seigel explains that as adolescents, we tend to live with a fearless vigour and optimistic attitude that could serve us well in later life, too. Imagine how different we might feel as an empty nester if we looked at the leap of faith required to live our purpose as a teenager might feel as they leave home for the first time. Imagine all those feelings of excitement and something new to embrace. Imagine if we acted on our calling as a mid-lifer the same way a rebellious adolescent wants to challenge the status quo of authority. And imagine taking that leap as a sixty-year-old with all the confidence of a twenty-year-old to get out there and "just f****** do it". How different might the task of following our calling feel with these attitudes?

Attitudes that embraced the passion to fully feel a wide range of emotions. The connection to join and collaborate interpersonally. The courage to take risks and leave the safe and certain behind. And the imagination to envision and innovate in new ways

The passion, the connection, the courage, the imagination—that sounds a lot more exciting and enticing, doesn't it? It adds a real energy to the process that I find invigorating and inspiring. Embarking on a life of purpose with these attitudes of adolescence is not only exciting but also, according to Seigel's research, the best predictor of well-being. This is proof that purpose enhances our quality of life and delivers spiritual happiness.

I also believe it's a powerful call to arms for all sorts of people working to change the status quo of our current culture of economic growth. It's a mindset and attitude that helps us move beyond the purely resilient mindset of being able to cope with change (having to deal with pandemics such as COVID, the financial crisis, climate change, etc.) to having a much more proactive and regenerative mindset by encouraging change (wellbeing economy, purpose-driven business, Inner Development Goals).

With purpose in our souls and enthusiasm in our hearts, we are well placed to take the leap to act on purpose and go out and give it our all. And revel in it.

Go All Out

When it comes to purpose and following our calling, there's one quote that I've come across a number of times. It's from the English explorer W.A. Murray and relates to one expedition to Mount Everest he was about to embark on. He said, "Until one has committed, there is hesitancy, the chance to draw back, always ineffectiveness. Concerning all acts of initiative and creation, there is one elementary truth, the ignorance of which kills countless ideas and splendid plans. That the moment one definitely commits oneself then providence moves too. All sorts of things occur to help one that would never otherwise have occurred. A whole stream of events issues from the decision, raising in one's favour all manner of unseen incidents and meetings and material assistance, which no man could have dreamt would come his way. I have learned a deep respect for one of Goethe's concepts: Whatever you can do or dream, you can do. Begin it. Boldness has genius, power and magic in it."

I love those words. They inspire me into action. Boldness has genius, power and magic in it. How uplifting. And I believe it to be true.

As I've said before, I'm a relatively conservative person, and I wouldn't want to promote recklessness. But I do know what it feels like to make a bold move. I backpacked around the world when I was twenty-one. I moved to Taunton for my first job, a town I didn't know and hadn't even visited. I started my own club night in Manchester in my mid-twenties as I fancied myself as a DJ. I moved to Scotland, bought into a business, and moved the family to a city neither my wife nor I knew well. We just did it. And unbeknown to me, there was faith and power underpinning all these bold moves. When I made those moves, provenance moved too. I appreciate that now. At the time, I think the boldness was underpinned by egotistic and naive ambition. It wasn't my soul's desire that was driving me onwards. Or maybe it was. Maybe all of these bold moves were necessary for me to arrive where I am today.

The point is that overcoming doubt and making the decision to act brings a certainty that generates an energy to keep going. Stephen Cope talks about it in this way: "The vacillating mind is the split mind. That mind at war with itself. 'The ignorant, indecisive and lacking in faith waste their lives. They can never be happy in this world or any other,' says Krishna to Arjuna in the Bhagavad Gita. Acting in unity with your purpose itself creates unification. Actions that consciously support dharma have the power to begin to gather our energy. These outward actions, step-by-step, shape us inwardly. Find your dharma and do it. And in the process of doing it, energy begins to gather itself into a laser beam of effectiveness."

This is how we find "flow as a lifestyle". And how we can sustain flow beyond the fleeting moments of a task or a short period of time. When we find our purpose and go all out, we derive the greatest fulfilment because all our spiritual, emotional, mental and physical capabilities are drawn together in service of our response-ability. In this state of absorption, we experience extraordinary satisfaction and joy. We experience oneness. We feel the full rapture of being alive.

Human beings are naturally attracted to this feeling. It's the feeling of self-actualisation and self-transcendence. It's the feeling of self-forgetting. We are born to be useful. We are made to be response-able. It's in our nature to find our purpose, hear our calling and get into action. All we need to do is find out who we are. Ask for the guidance and power to be who we are. And do it all out.

ALWAYS BEING READY TO RESPOND TO THE CALL OF OUR TIMES

There are many reasons why I wanted to write this book. I sought to make sense of my own spiritual journey over the past few years, to capture the learnings I had gleaned from the many books I've read, and to create a guide to help others find spiritual happiness as I had. I also had a grander idea. I thought possibly that a collective commitment to spiritual happiness could maybe, just maybe, be an antidote to our culture of economic growth.

I've been fairly critical of our current culture and the junk values we've become accustomed to because I can see the harm they cause. I witness the stress they create for us as individuals, for our communities, and for our planet - stress that is slowly killing us. I see how we are encouraged to numb that stress with unhealthy, addictive distractions. I see how we have been shepherded and possibly brainwashed into a world enthralled by conditional happiness.

I want to feel the full rapture of being alive and I want everyone to have the chance to experience that same rapture. But I just don't think that's possible if we're constantly being pulled back by a culture that promotes the exact opposite. Actually, that's not true. It is entirely possible to feel the full rapture of being alive in this culture. It's just more difficult. It takes more guts. And it might even take a lot more suffering for more people to get there.

The Call of Our Times

I urge people to look at our current culture of economic growth as the call of our times. Examine the problems our collective obsession with material accumulation is causing: the impact on nature, our communities, social cohesion, the ever-widening gap of wealth inequality, and the ever-rising levels of anxiety, depression, and suicide. Look at the sugary food we eat, the alcohol we drink, the social media we waste time on, and the drugs we take to numb ourselves from the stress and confusion. And look at how prominently these numbing, life-sapping distractions are promoted to us and our children. Notice what your heart tells you when you look at these signs. Does your soul desire a different future? Do you hear your calling from the suffering you see around you?

In his book The Good Ancestor, Roman Krznaric identifies six strategies that can help us become good ancestors and do our bit to leave this beautiful and precious planet of ours in reasonable shape for future generations. The most fundamental strategy he suggests is: "Identifying a transcendent goal for humankind and striving to achieve it." This is fantastic news. This is hearing our collective calling and finding our collective power to get into action. Not only is this exactly what we need to do to find our own purpose, but we'll be helping future generations, too.

Although Krznaric doesn't necessarily come at the problem from a spiritual perspective, he knows only too well how important purpose is for our human nature. He says, "One of the greatest discoveries in philosophical thought over the past 2000 years is that human beings thrive on striving for meaningful future goals that give life, purpose and direction." He then goes on to site Aristotle's "some object for the good life to animate" and Nietzsche's "he who has a why can endure any how" and Frank's "concrete assignment" and Sagan's "sacred project" as expressions of purpose in action.

To my mind, this is where spirituality and activism intersect. This is where we can develop and grow personally and do good in the world. This is where we can aim for self-forgetfulness by not neglecting the impact we're having on future generations. And this is exactly how regeneration works.

THE REGENERATIVE SPIRIT

I initially considered calling this book The Regenerative Spirit to make the point that we regenerate our suffering souls by helping others regenerate theirs. The Regenerative Spirit heals us as we heal the world around us. We give away what was given to us - it's the spiritual gift that keeps on giving. And it seems to me that the world is in desperate need of much more of this regenerative spirit. There is plenty of suffering that needs healing now. And there may well be much more to come.

Our culture of economic growth cannot keep on growing and growing without causing ever more damage. The more we keep on doing exactly what we're doing and growing exactly as we're growing, causing all the damage and suffering we're causing, there will inevitably be some sort of environmental crisis (possibly more acutely felt than climate change) or a financial crisis (more lasting than the financial crash of 2007) or a health crisis (more damaging than COVID) that will bring us to our knees. We will suffer as individuals, and we will suffer as a society.

It is bound to happen unless we can create a new regenerative economy that helps us live and work within the naturally regenerative planetary boundaries that are non-negotiable. We cannot keep eating into nature's future storehouse without repercussions. We need a regenerative economic revolution to make that happen.

While there are seeds of economic revolution in the air, it's a slow, disjointed, and fragmented rebellion against growth. As a professional working to encourage businesses to be more purpose-driven, I see how challenging it is for well-intentioned business leaders to act in a regenerative way when the dominant market model forces them to compete against businesses that are anything but regenerative.

That's why I believe we also need to encourage a regenerative cultural revolution. We need more individuals to experience the benefits of the regenerative spirit, to let consumers at the heart of our consumer economy truly feel how amazing life could be if we were able to live by the maxim of "material sufficiency and spiritual abundance." If more people were able to feel the full rapture of being alive, there would be much less grasping after material accumulation, much less stress at work and home, much less need for numbing and addictive distractions, and much less harm and suffering for people, communities, and the planet.

One Step at a Time, One Day at a Time

It's a big idea, I know. Maybe it's a pipe-dream, a naive idea of how the world might evolve. But boldness has genius, power and magic in it, right? Despite its potential idealistic and possibly impractical nature, this vision of a regenerative cultural revolution keeps me motivated. I sense it's part of my calling and draws me into action. The action is to promote and support spiritual happiness in a world obsessed with material growth. I realise that I can only do what is right in front of me. I can only deal with today. So that's where I'll start. That's where we all have to start. I will focus on my own quest and commitment to spiritual happiness. And you can focus on yours. By doing this, we acknowledge that if we want to see change on a global scale, we need to take it one step at a time, one day at a time. We can only go up the ladder of personal and collective evolution rung by rung. We can't miss any rungs out. One step at a time, one day at a time, one person at a time.

We also need to acknowledge that once we take the personal leap towards spiritual happiness and away from junk values, once we commit to finding out who we really are and embark on our purpose, we will be in the minority. It's not always easy being in the minority. We will stand out from the crowd, and we'll feel awkward.

But if we're true to our calling and feel the sign of our times drawing us into action, we will have no choice but to take the leap to be a good ancestor and join the minority. We'll feel compelled to join the revolution. We will know that we have a part in building a new story and a new culture. And we will find the power to play our part. As Krznaric points out, "A good ancestor recognises a dying system when they see one, and rather than trying to pass on their own dysfunctional civilisation to the next generation, they take part in the historic act of seeding a new civilisation that can grow in its place and maintain the conditions conducive to life into the long future."

The journey out of the old story of economic growth and into the new regenerative story of life, the universe and everything can feel very lonely. It can feel like you're standing out from the crowd as a crazy person. A misfit with a mad idea. But that's how all revolutions start. That's where all change begins. I loved Steve Jobs' advert for Apple in the late 1990s, which celebrated people like Gandhi, Einstein, and Martin Luther King Jr. The ad said, "Here's to the crazy ones, the misfits, the rebels, the troublemakers, the round pegs in the square holes... the ones who see things differently — they're not fond of rules... You can quote them, disagree with them, glorify or vilify them, but the only thing you can't do is ignore them because they change things... they push the human race forward, and while some may see them as the crazy ones, we see genius, because the ones who are crazy enough to think that they can change the world, are the ones who do."

I'm not quite crazy enough to think I can change the world. But I do feel some of the alienation and "squarepegness" that Jobs alludes to. And that's why I think it's important to find support. To find like-minded people who can celebrate our craziness. People who appreciate our new spiritual perspectives and can nurture our drive for purposeful action. Without that support, our everyday interactions with a culture of economic growth can pull us back to its way of thinking. It can pull us back into its conventional junk values. It can derail our efforts.

Observing the signs of our times and listening out for that still, small voice to hear our calling requires us to be awake. It requires us to be aware. Anthony de Mello, the Indian Jesuit priest, psychotherapist and spiritual teacher, says spirituality is all about awareness. It's all about sitting in silence to let the truth filter in and allowing the paradoxes of life sink deep. Learning to listen to the messages born of stillness and silence is the big skill we need to learn. It allows us to be aware. It allows us to be awake. It allows us to be ready.

As we start to have faith in the messages and start acting on them, we're bound to experience failures. That's when we can return to our Hero's Journey for guidance and power, always seeking to evolve our habits of spiritual happiness. We need to surrender to the mistakes we might make. We need the discipline to continue our practices. We need to connect more to ourselves, to the people around us, to nature, and to God. To feel the union with all of them. To sense the MWe-ness of life. And we need to be of service to those connections. We need to be aware of the suffering of our times and act on our calling.

This is the cycle of Surrender, Awareness, Discipline, Connection, and Service that becomes our spiritual grounding and compass. It keeps us centred in the being of our inner purpose and primed to act on our outer purpose. Always being alert and connected to the world around us builds our response-ability to suit up, step up, and show up when the need arises. This is what it means to find and live our calling, to follow our dharma. This is The Pathway to Purpose and Power.

I used to think purpose was all about finding direction. I now believe that The Pathway to Purpose and Power is more about an alertness to what is required than defining a definitive direction to take. Purpose is a pathway we discern one step at a time, one day at a time. And we receive just enough power to take that path one step at a time, one day at a time. The pathway may be inspired by a long-term transcendent goal, but we must let go of that future aspiration and focus on what we can do on a daily basis. That daily discernment and daily power means sticking close to the spiritual habits and listening for that small still voice at all times.

It also means enduring the challenges when things get tough. All spiritual traditions talk of the mystery of suffering, the necessity of pain, and learning to deal with the rise and fall of life. Like nature, our Pathway to Purpose and Power will have a rhythm. It will have cycles. It will require part of us to die so something new can be born. It will require us to change direction and try again if something is not working.

All we can do is be alert to those rhythms, cycles, and challenges and be ready for what comes next. All we can do is be as prepared as we can for the Hero's Journey that lies ahead. But how do you prepare to be a hero?

Getting Ready for the Hero's Journey

Richard Rohr asks this very question. How do you prepare to be a hero? He responds by saying, "Do you go to hero school? Do you decide to do risky and dramatic things? No, that will just get you into ego. All you can do is be ready, and time and God will create your heroism, which won't even feel heroic to you. Just ask the Lord to ready your heart. Don't try to build your own door or heroically create your own project. Don't even search for the door through which you're supposed to enter. Just ask that when the door shows itself, you'll have the eyes to recognise it and the courage to walk through it." Wise words, Richard.

And that, in a nutshell, is what I believe The Habits of Happiness give us on our journey. They give us the eyes to see the door of our calling and the courage to walk through it. They give us the guidance to discern our purpose and the power to carry it out.

I was introduced to the spiritual solution and The Habits of Happiness as a means to stop the pain my addiction to alcohol was causing me and my family. It did help me put down the drink. It did help alleviate the mental obsession I had to numb myself from the pain of everyday life. And it did bring me peace and serenity, freedom and joy. It's also given me so much more than that. More than I could have possibly dreamed of.

As I sit in this coffee shop contemplating the journey that I've been on, I can't help but marvel at the miracles that have unfolded on my path. I can't believe the transformation in my thoughts, feelings and perspectives. I can't believe the change in my behaviours and habits. I can't believe that I'm sitting in a coffee shop at 8:46 am, writing the closing words to a book I have written. Not so many years ago, I'd have been sitting in a pub at the same time, finishing off my second pint of cider in an attempt to summon the courage to face the day in a hard but bearable job.

Life really is a miracle, and it's right there in front of our very noses, ready to be cherished and savoured. Feeling the full rapture of being alive is available to everyone who is ready.

You'll know you're ready when the busyness of modern life no longer makes sense to you, when the daily grind leaves you feeling lost and disconnected.

You'll know you're ready when the thought of spiritual happiness appeals to you and when the thought of earning more money to spend on indulgences feels more and more meaningless. And more and more wasteful.

You'll know you're ready when you sense your soul is calling you towards the mystery of uncertainty, when the pathway to purpose and power feels invigorating and exciting.

That pathway lies behind a door. Ask for that door to present itself to you. And when it does, I pray you have the eyes to recognise it. And if you do, I pray you have the courage to walk through it.

The Habits of Happiness helped me find my door. I hope they help you find yours.

ACKNOWLEDGMENTS

This is the first book I've attempted to write, and I thank everyone who has inspired me, supported me, questioned me, pushed me, and loved me along the way.

All the words of wisdom contained in these pages have undoubtedly come from those I have learned from. And any words of confusion have undoubtedly come from my own misunderstanding. I am in awe of all the people who wrote the books listed in the bibliography. You inspired me to write this one, and I thank you.

The story I'm attempting to tell in The Habits of Happiness reflects the story of my life and the ups and downs I've experienced along the way. There are so many people who have helped and guided and I'm thankful to each and every one of you.

I'm especially grateful to Gillian, James, Lorna, Amy and Daniel. To my Mum, Dad and Justine. To Fiona and Monica. To Graham N, Alex R. and Chris M. To Emma. To Nicky Boy. To Jefed. To Richard and Malcolm. To Sean, Karen, and Neve. You have all played a significant role in my life and this book. I thank you. I love you.

BIBLIOGRAPHY

A New Earth, Eckhart Tolle

A Path through the Jungle, Prof Steve Peters

A Return to Love, Marianne Williamson

A Swim in a Pond in the Rain, George Saunders

Abounding Grace: An Anthology of Wisdom, M. Scott Peck M.D.

Alcoholics Anonymous, Bill Wilson

An Everyone Culture, Robert Kegan, Lisa Laskow Lahey, Matthew L. Miller, Andy Fleming, Deborah Helsing

Anything You Want, Derek Sivers

As a Man Thinketh, James Allen

Atomic Habits, James Clear

Autobiography of a Yogi, Paramahansa Yogananda

Awareness, Anthony de Mello

Becoming Nobody, Ram Dass

Being Nobody Going Nowhere, Ayya Khema

Belong, Radha Agrawal

Beyond Entrepreneurship 2.0, Jim Collins

Bird by Bird, Anne Lamott

Brave New World, Aldous Huxley

Braving the Wilderness, Brené Brown

Breaking the Habit of Being Yourself, Joe Dispenza

Breathing Under Water: Spirituality and the Twelve Steps, Richard Rohr

Change the Story, Change the Future, David C. Korten

Change Your Paradigm, Change Your Life, Bob Proctor

Change Your Thoughts Change Your Life, Dr. Wayne W. Dyer

Confronting Our Freedom, Peter Block, Peter Koestenbaum

Conscious Leadership, John Mackey, Steve Mcintosh, Carter Phipps

Cutting Through Spiritual Materialism, Marvin Casper Chögyam Trungpa

Discipline Is Destiny, Ryan Holiday

Doughnut Economics, Kate Raworth

Driven, Paul R. Lawrence, Nitin Nohria

Earth for All, Sandrine Dixson-Decleve, Owen Gaffney, Jayati Ghosh, Jorgen Randers

Elegant Simplicity, Satish Kumar

Essays by Ralph Waldo Emerson, Ralph Waldo Emerson

Essential Spirituality, Roger Walsh M.D. Ph.D.

Every Good Endeavour, Timothy Keller

Everybody Matters, Bob Chapman, Raj Sisodia

Falling Upward, Richard Rohr

Finding Your Purpose, Christine Whelan

Fluke, Dr Brian Klaas

Follow Your Joy, Robert Holden Ph.D.

Fulfilled, Anna Yusim, Eben Alexander - foreword

Go Big, Ed Miliband

Greatest Thing in the World, Henry Drummond

Grow the Pie, Alex Edmans

Higher Purpose, Robert Holden Ph.D.

How to Hear God, Pete Greig

How to Practice Dharma, Lama Zopa Rinpoche, Gordon McDougall - editor

How to Pray, Pete Greig

How We Believe, Michael Shermer

I May Be Wrong, Bjorn Natthiko Lindeblad

Immortal Diamond, Richard Rohr

IntraConnected, Daniel J. Siegel MD

Jesus' Alternative Plan, Richard Rohr OFM

Krishnamurti: Reflections on the Self, Jiddu Krishnamurti

LEAD . . . For God's Sake!, Todd G. Gongwer

Leading from the Emerging Future, Otto Scharmer, Katrin Kaeufer

Less Is More, Jason Hickel

Letting Go, David R. Hawkins M.D. Ph.D

Lost Connections, Johann Hari

Loyalty to Your Soul, H. Ronald Hulnick PhD, Mary R. Hulnick PhD

Making Sense of God, Timothy Keller

Man's Search for Meaning, Viktor E. Frankl

Memories, Dreams, Reflections, Carl Jung

Messy Spirituality, Mike Yaconelli

Midlife and the Great Unknown, David Whyte

Mindfulness, Bliss, and Beyond, Ajahn Brahm

Miracles, C. S. Lewis

Mission Economy, Mariana Mazzucato

Net Positive, Paul Polman, Andrew Winston

Notes on Complexity, Neil Theise

On the Path to Enlightenment, Matthieu Ricard

Open Mind, Open Heart, Thomas Keating

Peace Is Every Step, Thich Nhat Hanh

Perennial Philosophy, Arthur Versluis

Phantastes, George MacDonald

Radical Wholeness, Philip Shepherd, Jeff Brown, Grover Gardner

Range, David Epstein

Ravenous, Henry Dimbleby, Jemima Lewis

Real Magic, Dr. Wayne W. Dyer

Rebel Ideas, Matthew Syed

Recovery, Russell Brand

Reflections on the Psalms, C. S. Lewis

Religion for Atheists, Alain de Botton
Revelation, Russell Brand
Rules for Radicals, Saul D. Alinsky
Sacred Economics, Charles Eisenstein
Sermon on the Mount, Richard Rohr
Shine, Carley Hauck
Small Is Beautiful, E. F. Schumacher
Spiritual Intelligence in Seven Steps, Mark Vernon
Start Finishing, Charlie Gilkey
Stewardship, Peter Block
Surprised by Joy, C. S. Lewis
The Alchemist, Paulo Coelho
The Art of Being, Erich Fromm
The Art of Happiness, Howard C. Cutler, His Holiness the Dalai Lama
The Art of Living, Thich Nhat Hanh
The Artist's Way, Julia Cameron
The Bhagavad Gita, Jack Hawley
The Biology of Belief, Bruce H. Lipton PhD
The Buddha and the Badass, Vishen Lakhiani
The Craving Mind, Judson Brewer, Jon Kabat-Zinn - foreward
The Day the World Stops Shopping, J. B. MacKinnon
The Divine Matrix, Gregg Braden
The Easy Way to Control Alcohol, Allen Carr
The End of Your World, Adyashanti
The Everlasting Man, G. K. Chesterton
The Fifth Discipline, Peter M. Senge
The Four Agreements, Miguel Ruiz
The Gifts of Imperfection, Brené Brown
The Good Ancestor, Roman Krznaric
The Great Work of Your Life, Stephen Cope
The Heart Is Noble, The Karmapa, Ogyen Trinley Dorje
The Hero with a Thousand Faces, Joseph Campbell
The Holy Science, Swami Sri Yukteswar
The Human Condition (Second Edition), Hannah Arendt
The Impersonal Life, Joseph S. Benner
The Laws of Human Nature, Robert Greene
The Master and His Emissary, Iain McGilchrist
The Mental Equivalent, Emmet Fox
The Moneyless Man, Mark Boyle
The Hero with a Thousand Faces, Joseph Campbell
The Holy Science, Swami Sri Yukteswar

True Self, False Self, Richard Rohr O.F.M.
Twelve Steps and Twelve Traditions, Bill Wilson
Uncluttered, Courtney Ellis
Until the End of Time, Brian Greene
Value(s), Mark Carney
Waking Up, Sam Harris
Walden, Henry David Thoreau
What Christians Believe, C. S. Lewis
When Things Fall Apart, Pema Chodron
Who Do We Choose to Be?, Margaret J. Wheatley
Why Buddhism Is True, Robert Wright
Yes to Life in Spite of Everything, Viktor Frankl, Joelle Young, Daniel Goleman
Yoga and the Quest for the True Self, Stephen Cope
You Are the Guru, Gabrielle Bernstein
You Were Born Rich, Bob Proctor

THE 12 STEPS

Step 1. Accept reality: Admit we are powerless over alcchol, that our lives have become unmanageable.

Step 2. Find hope: Start to believe that a power greater than ourselves can restore us to sanity.

Step 3. Surrender: Decide to turn our will and our lives over to the care of a God of our own understanding.

Step 4. Reflect on our behaviours: Make a searching and fearless moral inventory of ourselves.

Step 5. Share our findings: Admit to God, to ourselves, and to another human beingthe exact nature of all our wrongs.

Step 6. Be prepared to change: Are entirely ready to have all our defects of Character removed.

Step 7. Show humility: Humbly ask the God of our understanding to remove our shortcomings.

Step 8. Be willing to make amends : Make a list of all those we have harmed and be willing to make amends to all of them.

Step 9. Make amends: Make direct amends to all the people on the list wherever possible, except when to do so would injure them or others.

Step 10. Continue to improve: Take regular personal inventory, and when we are wrong, promptly admit it and make amends.

Step 11. Pray, meditate and contemplate your purpose : Improve our conscious contact with a God of our own understanding, asking only to know His will for us and the power to carry that out.

Step 12. Help others and be useful : Having had a spiritual awakening as the result of these steps, we carry this message to other alcoholics and practice these spiritual principles in everything we do.

www.ingramcontent.com/pod-product-compliance
Ingram Content Group UK Ltd.
Pitfield, Milton Keynes, MK11 3LW, UK
UKHW020652170325
456356UK00010B/87

9 781738 421886